Second CIPS-SIGHAN Joint Conference on Chinese Language Processing

(CLP 2012)

Tianjin, China
20-21 December 2012

ISBN: 978-1-62748-363-6

Printed from e-media with permission by:

Curran Associates, Inc.
57 Morehouse Lane
Red Hook, NY 12571

Some format issues inherent in the e-media version may also appear in this print version.

Printed by Curran Associates, Inc. (2013)

For permission requests, please contact the Association for Computational Linguistics
at the address below.

Association for Computational Linguistics
209 N. Eighth Street
Stroudsburg, Pennsylvania 18360

Phone: 1-570-476-8006
Fax: 1-570-476-0860

acl@aclweb.org

Additional copies of this publication are available from:

Curran Associates, Inc.
57 Morehouse Lane
Red Hook, NY 12571 USA
Phone: 845-758-0400
Fax: 845-758-2634
Email: curran@proceedings.com
Web: www.proceedings.com

Preface

In the big data age, Chinese language data online is expanding rapidly, and the application of natural language processing technology is drawing growing interest from the research community across the globe to harness Chinese language content. The rise of China as a global power with increasing influence on the world stage is only fanning this interest. The Chinese language also has a number of characteristics that make Chinese language processing particularly challenging and intellectually rewarding.

To meet the challenge, the CIPS-SIGHAN Joint Conference on Chinese Language Processing(CLP) is organized under the auspices of CIPS (Chinese Information Processing Society of China) and SIGHAN, a Special Interest Group of the ACL. CLP-2012 is the second conference jointly organized by the Chinese Language Processing Society of China (CIPS) and the ACL Special Interest Group on Chinese Language Processing (SIGHAN). The first conference, CLP-2010, was held on Aug 28-29, 2010 in Beijing, China, in conjunction with COLING 2010.

The goal of CLP2012 is to provide a platform for researchers around the world to present their research, share ideas, explore new research directions, and advance the state-of-the-art in Chinese language processing. The conference will also feature an international bakeoff on four tracks: word segmentation on Chinese Mirco-blog data, Chinese personal name disambiguation, simplified Chinese parsing, and traditional Chinese parsing.

The four bakeoff tasks have attracted 31 groups to submit their results.The proceedings also includes 4 overview papers that introduce the bakeoff tasks as well as the 32 bakeoff papers.

We would like to thank CIPS and SIGHAN for their continuing support of the conference, as well as the Asian Information Retrieval Society for allowing us to be a co-event of their Eighth Asian Information Retrieval Societies Conference (AIRS-2012). Especially we would like to thank professors, Zhifang Sui, Houfeng Wang, Qiang Zhou, Liang-Chih Yu, and Yuexian Hou, for initiating and proposing to hold this conference, and we are deeply indebted to all the reviewers for their tireless and generous work. Besides, we really appreciate Prof. Chunliang Zhang and Doctor Huizhen Wang for their dedication with all the publicity and publication issues. Most of all, we are grateful that the two keynote speakers, Prof. Xiaoyan Zhu and Prof. Guodong Zhou, share their inspiration in NLP research. Finally, we would like to thank all the authors for submitting their papers and reports to the conference.

We wish you all an enjoyable and thought-provoking conference.

Le Sun, Hsin-His Chen	*CLP2012 General Co-Chairs*
Jingbo Zhu, Fei Xia, Houfeng Wang	*CLP2012 Program Co-Chairs*

Organizers

General Chairs:

Le Sun,*Chinese Information Processing Society of China*
Hsin-His Chen, SIGHAN & National Taiwan University

Program Chairs:

Jingbo Zhu, *Northeastern University*
Fei Xia, University of Washington
Houfeng Wang, *Peking University*

Bakeoff Chairs:

**Chinese Micro blog Word Segmentation:*

Huiming Duan, Peking University
Zhifang Sui, *Peking University*

**Simplified Chinese Parsing:*

Qiang Zhou, Tsinghua University

*Traditional Chinese Parsing:
Yuen-Hsien Tseng, *National Taiwan Normal University*

**Chinese Personal Name disambiguation:*
Houfeng Wang, Peking University
Sujian Li, *Peking University*

Publications Chair:

Huizhen Wang, Northeastern University

Publicity Chair:

Chunliang Zhang, *Northeastern University*

Local Arrangements Chair:

Yuexian Hou, Tianjin University

Reviewers:

Wanxiang Che	Jiajun Chen	Jinying Chen
Keh-Jiann Chen	Huiming Duan	Xuanjing Huang
Donghong Ji	Heng Ji	Olivia Kwong
Juanzi Li	Mu Li	Sujian Li
Chin-Yew Lin	Hongfei Lin	Yang Liu
Qin Lu	Yajuan Lv	Shaoping Ma
Jianyun Nie	Xiaodong Shi	Keh-Yih Su
Zhifang Sui	Maosong Sun	Yuen-Hsien Tseng
Xiaojun Wan	Bin Wang	Houfeng Wang
Xiaojie Wang	Kam-Fai Wong	Hua Wu
Yunfang Wu	Yunqing Xia	Deyi Xiong
Jinan Xu	Nianwen Xue	Muyun Yang
Kun Yu	Weidong Zhan	Jiajun Zhang
Min Zhang	Hai Zhao	Jun Zhao
Guodong Zhou	Ming Zhou	Qiang Zhou

Table of Contents

Keynote Speaks:

Research Papers:

Task 1: Micro-blog word segmentation

Task 2: Chinese personal name disambiguation

Task 3: Simplified Chinese parsing

Task 4: Traditional Chinese parsing

Conference Program

Thursday, December 20, 2012

8:30–8:50 Opening

8:50–9:50 Keynote Speech: Xiaoyan Zhu, *QA: from Turing Test to Intelligent Information Service*

9:50–10:10 Coffee Break

Session 1: Overview of All tasks

10:10–10:25 *The CIPS-SIGHAN CLP 2012 ChineseWord Segmentation onMicroBlog Corpora Bakeoff*
Huiming Duan, Zhifang Sui, Ye Tian and Wenjie Li

10:25–10:40 *The Task 2 of CIPS-SIGHAN 2012 Named Entity Recognition and Disambiguation in Chinese Bakeoff*
Zhengyan He, Houfeng Wang and Sujian Li

10:40–10:55 *Evaluation Reportof the third Chinese Parsing Evaluation: CIPS-SIGHAN-ParsEval-2012*
Qiang Zhou

10:55–11:10 *Traditional Chinese Parsing Evaluation at SIGHAN Bake-offs 2012*
Yuen-Hsien Tseng, Lung-Hao Lee and Liang-Chih Yu

Session 2: Research Paper

11:10–11:25 *A Language Modeling Approach to Identifying Code-Switched Sentences and Words*
Liang-Chih Yu, Wei-Cheng He and Wei-Nan Chien

11:25–11:40 *Semi-automatic Annotation of Chinese Word Structure*
Jianqiang Ma, Chunyu Kit and Dale Gerdemann

11:40–11:55 *Building a Chinese Lexical Taxonomy*
Xiaopeng Bai and Nianwen Xue

11:55–12:10 *Extending and Scaling up the Chinese Treebank Annotation*
Xiuhong Zhang and Nianwen Xue

Thursday, December 20, 2012 (continued)

12:10–13:30 Lunch

Session 3: Bakeoff 1 Micro-blog word segmentation

13:30–13:45 *Word Segmentation on Chinese Mirco-Blog Data with a Linear-Time Incremental Model*
Kaixu Zhang, Maosong Sun and Changle Zhou

13:45–14:00 *Soochow University Word Segmenter for SIGHAN 2012 Bakeoff*
Yan Fang, Zhongqing Wang, Shoushan Li, Zhongguo Li, Richen Xu and Leixin Cai

14:00–14:15 *CRFs-Based Chinese Word Segmentation for Micro-Blog with Small-Scale Data*
Longyue Wang, Derek F. Wong, Lidia S. Chao and Junwen Xing

14:15–14:30 *A Cascaded Approach for CIPS-SIGHAN Micro-Blog Word Segmentation Bakeoff 2012*
Bei Shi, Xianpei Han and Le Sun

14:30–15:00 Coffee Break

Session 4: Bakeoff 2 Chinese personal name disambiguation

15:00–15:15 *SIR-NERD: A Chinese Named Entity Recognition and Disambiguation System using a Two-StageMethod*
Zehuan Peng, Le Sun and Xianpei Han

15:15–15:30 *A Template Based Hybrid Model for Chinese Personal Name Disambiguation*
Hao Zong, Derek F. Wong and Lidia S. Chao

15:30–15:45 *Attribute based Chinese Named Entity Recognition and Disambiguation*
Han Wei, Liu Guang, Mao Yuzhao and Huang Zhenni

15:45–16:00 *Chinese Name Disambiguation Based on Adaptive Clustering with the Attribute Features*
Wei Tian, Xiao Pan, Zhengtao Yu, yantuan Xian and xiuzhen Yang

Thursday, December 20, 2012 (continued)

Session 5: Bakeoff 4 Traditional Chinese parsing

16:00–16:15 *NEU Systems in SIGHAN Bakeoff 2012*
Ji Ma, LongFei Bai, Zhuo Liu, Ao Zhang and Jingbo Zhu

16:15–16:30 *Adapting Multilingual Parsing Models to Sinica Treebank*
Liangye He, Derek F. Wong and Lidia S. Chao

16:30–16:45 *Improving PCFG Chinese Parsing with Context-Dependent Probability Re-estimation*
Yu-Ming Hsieh, Ming-Hong Bai, Jason S. Chang and Keh-Jiann Chen

16:45–17:00 *Sentence Parsing with Double Sequential Labeling in Traditional Chinese Parsing Task*
Shih-Hung Wu, Hsien-You Hsieh and Liang-Pu Chen

Friday, December 21, 2012

8:30–9:30 Keynote Speech: Guodong Zhou, *Linguistic foundation for NLP*

9:30–9:50 Coffee Break

Session 1: Bakeoff 3 Simplified Chinese parsing

9:50–10:05 *Multiple TreeBanks Integration for Chinese Phrase Structure Grammar Parsing Using Bagging*
Meishan Zhang, Wanxiang Che and Ting Liu

10:05–10:20 *Parsing TCT with Split Conjunction Categories*
Dongchen Li and Xihong Wu

10:20–10:35 *Parsing Simplified Chinese and Traditional Chinese with Sentence Structure Grammar*
Xiangli Wang

Friday, December 21, 2012 (continued)

Session 2: Bakeoff Posters

10:35–11:35 Bakeoff Posters

11:35–11:45 Closing

Bakeoff Poster List

1. Adapting Conventional Chinese Word Segmenter for Segmenting Micro-blog Text: Combining Rule-based and Statistic-based Approaches
Ning Xi, Bin Li, Guangchao Tang, Shujian Huang, Yinggong Zhao, Hao Zhou, Xinyu Dai and Jiajun Chen

2. Cascaded Chinese Weibo Segmentation Based on CRFs
keli Zhong, xue Zhou, hangyu Li and caixia Yuan

3. Rules-based Chinese Word Segmentation on MicroBlog for CIPS-SIGHAN on CLP2012
Jing Zhang, Degen Huang, Xia Han and Wei Wang

4. Semi-supervised Chinese Word Segmentation for CLP2012
Saike HE, Nan HE, Songxiang CEN and Jun LU

5. Micro blogs Oriented Word Segmentation System
Liu Yijia, Zhang Meishan, Che Wanxiang, Liu Ting and Deng Yihe

6. Rules Design in Word Segmentation of Chinese Micro-Blog
Hao Zong, Derek F. Wong and Lidia S. Chao

7. A Comparison of Chinese Word Segmentation on News and Microblog Corpora with a Lexicon Based Method
Yuxiang Jia, Hongying Zan, Ming Fan and Zhimin Wang

8. A MMSM-based Hybrid Method for Chinese MicroBlog Word Segmentation
Xiao Sun, Chengcheng Li, Chenyi Tang and Jiaqi Ye

9. Chinese Tweets Segmentation based on Morphemes
Chaoyue Wang and Guohong Fu

10. Explore Chinese Encyclopedic Knowledge to Disambiguate Person Names
Jie Liu, Ruifeng Xu, Qin Lu and Jian Xu

11. A Joint Chinese Named Entity Recognition and Disambiguation System
Longyue Wang, Shuo Li, Derek F. Wong and Lidia S. Chao

12. Chinese Personal Name Disambiguation Based on Vector Space Model
Qing-hu FAN, Hong-ying ZAN, Yu-mei CHAI, Yu-xiang JIA and Gui-ling NIU

13. A Simplified Chinese Parser with Factored Model
Qiuping Huang, Liangye He, Derek F. Wong and Lidia S. Chao

14. Parsing TCT with a Coarse-to-fine Approach
Dongchen Li and Xihong Wu

15. A Conditional Random Field-based Traditional Chinese Base Phrase Parser for SIGHAN Bake-off 2012 Evaluation
Yih-Ru Wang and Yuan-Fu Liao

16. Hierarchical Maximum Pattern Matching with Rule Induction Approach for Sentence Parsing
Yi-Syun Tan, Yuan-Cheng Chu and Jui-Feng Yeh

QA: from Turing Test to Intelligent Information Service

Xiaoyan Zhu
Tsinghua University
Beijing, China.
zxy-dcs@tsinghua.edu.cn

Abstract

In the history of Artificial Intelligence (AI), Turing Test, a question answering imitation game was proposed to determine whether the computer system has intelligence. It becomes the ultimate goal to answer all the natural language questions for generations of AI researchers. In the past century, AI changed tremendously from its theories to its applications, while with this goal unchanged. Especially in the past 20 years, along with the development of the Internet, computers have the ability to acquire, store and process huge volumes of data, which makes the AI-related techniques deeply involve themselves in the domain of intelligent information processing. On one hand, Question Answering develops in theories, models and methods with the combination of the large scale data processing. On the other hand, the next-generation information service engines are expected to integrate Question Answering as an important part to retrieve and display information, where knowledge is important for information accumulation, understanding and serving. This presentation will present the history and development of the Question Answering, its related key technologies and applications in the background of big data and AI.

QA: 从图灵测试到智能信息服务

图灵实验（Turing Test）可知,回答自然问题的能力有史以来就是衡量计算机系统是否具有智能的基本标准。半个世纪以来，人工智能从理念到内容发生了巨大的变化，尤其是近 20 年来随着互联网产业的发展，大规模数据获取和计算能力的提高使得人工智能的相关技术在智能信息处理领域中得到了充分体现。 一方面，人工智能和大规模数据处理的结合，对于问答系统在理论、模型和方法上都有了质的飞跃和发展，另一方面，在下一代信息服务引擎的发展理念中，问答系统也成为信息获取与展现的重要手段，知识也成为网络信息积累与服务的重要支撑。本报告将介绍问答系统的发展历史与现状，以及相关的关键技术与应用。

About the Speaker

Xiaoyan Zhu, professor, she got bachelor degree at University of Science and Technology Beijing in 1982, master degree at Kobe University in 1987, and Ph. D. degree at Nagoya Institute of Technology, Japan in 1990. She is teaching at Tsinghua University since 1993. She is director of state key lab of intelligent technology and systems, director of Tsinghua-HP Joint research center and the director of Tsinghua-Waterloo Joint research center, Tsinghua University. She is International Research Chair holder of IDRC, Canada, from 2009. She was deputy head of Department of Computer Science and Technology, Tsinghua University from 2004-2007. Her research interests include intelligent information processing, machine learning, natural language processing, query and answering system and bioinformatics. She has authored more than 100 peer-reviewed articles in leading international conferences including SIGKDD, IJCAI, AAAI, ACL, ICDM, CIKM, COLING, and journals including Int. J. Medical Informatics, Bioinformatics, BMC Bioinformatics, Genome Biology and IEEE Trans. on SMC.

自然语言处理之语言学基础

Guodong Zhu
Natural Language Processing Lab
School of Computer Science and Technology
Soochow University
Suzhou, China.
gdzhou@suda.edu.cn

Abstract

目前自然语言处理从业者广泛缺乏语言学基础，严重影响着基础研究的深入展开。本讲座将简要介绍与自然语言处理相关的一些语言学基础知识，特别是结构主义语言学、形式语言学和功能语言学的一些语言学观点，希望能对相关从业者有所启发。

About the Speaker

周国栋, 1997 年 12 月毕业于新加坡国立大学获得博士学位；1998 年 1 月至 1999 年 3 月在新加坡国立大学从事博士后研究；1999 年 4 月-2006 年 8 月在新加坡资讯通信研究院担任副研究员、研究员博导和副主任研究员博导；2006 年 8 月底加入苏州大学担任教授博导和计算机学科带头人。研究方向：自然语言理解、信息抽取、机器学习等。

近 5 年来发表国际著名 SCI 期刊论文 10 多篇和国际顶级会议 AAAI/IJCAI/SIGIR/CIKM/ACL/EMNLP/COLING 论文 40 多篇，主持 NSFC 项目 4 个，获得教育部科技进步二等奖 1 项。目前担任国际顶级 SCI 期刊 Computational Linguistics 编委、ACM 杂志 TALIP 副主编、《软件学报》责任编委、CCF 中文信息技术专委会副主任委员和 NSFC 信息学部会评专家。

A Language Modeling Approach to Identifying Code-Switched Sentences and Words

Liang-Chih Yu[1], Wei-Cheng He[1] and Wei-Nan Chien[1,2]
[1]Department of Information Management, Yuan Ze University, Taiwan, R.O.C.
[2]Information Technology Center, National Taiwan Normal University, Taiwan, R.O.C.
Contact: lcyu@saturn.yzu.edu.tw

Abstract

Globalization and multilingualism contribute to code-switching – the phenomenon in which speakers produce utterances containing words or expressions from a second language. Processing code-switched sentences is a significant challenge for multilingual intelligent systems. This study proposes a language modeling approach to the problem of code-switching language processing, dividing the problem into two subtasks: the detection of code-switched sentences and the identification of code-switched words in sentences. A code-switched sentence is detected on the basis of whether it contains words or phrases from another language. Once the code-switched sentences are identified, the positions of the code-switched words in the sentences are then identified. Experimental results on Mandarin-Taiwanese code-switching sentences show that the language modeling approach achieved a 79.52% F-measure and an accuracy of 80.23% for detecting code-switched sentences, and a 51.20% F-measure for the identification of code-switched words.

1 Introduction

Increasing globalism and multilingualism has significantly increased demand for multilingual services in current intelligent systems (Fung and Schultz, 2008). For example, an intelligent traveling system which supports multiple language inputs and outputs can assist travelers in booking hotels, ordering in restaurants, and navigating attractions. Multinational corporations would benefit from developing automatic multilingual call centers to address customer problems worldwide. In such multilingual environments, an input sentence may contain constituents from two or more languages, a phenomenon known as code-switching or language mixing (Hoffmann, 1991; Myers-Scotton, 1993; Ayeomoni, 2006; Liu, 2008). A code-switched sentence consists of a primary language and a secondary language, and the secondary language is usually manifested in the form of short expressions such as words and phrases. This phenomenon is increasingly common, with multilingual speakers often freely moving from their native dialect to subsidiary dialects to entirely foreign languages, and patterns of code-switching vary dynamically with different audiences in different situations. When dealing with code-switched input, intelligent systems such as dialog systems must be capable of identifying the various languages and recognize the speaker's intention embedded in the input (Ipsic, et al., 1999; Holzapfel, 2005). However, it is a significant challenge for intelligent systems to deal with multiple languages and unknown words from various languages.

In Taiwan, while Mandarin is the official language, Taiwanese and Hakka are used as a primary language by more than 75% and 10% populations, respectively (Lyu, et al., 2008). Moreover, English is the most popular foreign language and compulsory English instruction begins in elementary school. The constant mix of these languages result in various kinds of code-switching, such as Mandarin sentences mixed with words and phrases from Taiwanese, Hakka, and English. Such code-switching is not limited to everyday conversation, but can frequently be heard on television dramas and even current events commentary programs. This paper takes a linguistic view towards the problem of code-switching language processing, focusing on code-switching between Mandarin and Taiwanese. We propose a language modeling approach which divides the problem into two subtasks: the detection of code-switched sentences followed by identification of code-switched words within the sentences. The first step detects whether or not a given Mandarin sentence contains Taiwanese words. Once a code-switched sentence is identified, the positions of the code-switched words are then identified within the sentence. These code-switched words can be used for lexicon augmentation to improve understanding of code-switched sentences.

The rest of this work is organized as follows. Section 2 presents related work. Section 3 describes the language modeling approach to the identification of code-switched sentences and words in the sentences. Section 4 summarizes the experimental results. Conclusions are finally drawn in Section 5, along with recommendations for future research.

2 Related Work

Research on code-switching speech processing mainly focuses on speech recognition and synthesis (Lyu, et al., 2008; Wu, et al., 2006; Hong, et al., 2009; Chan, et al., 2006; Qian, et al.,2009). Lyu et al. (2008) proposed a three-step data-driven phone clustering method to train an acoustic model for Mandarin, Taiwanese, and Hakka. They also discussed the issue of training with unbalanced data. Wu et al. (2006) proposed an approach to segmenting and identifying mixed-language speech utterances. They first segmented the input speech utterance into a sequence of language-dependent segments using acoustic features. The language-specific features were then integrated in the identification process. Hong et al. (2009) developed a Mandarin-English mixed-language speech recognition system in resource-constrained environments, which can be realized in embedded systems such as personal digital assistants (PDAs). Chan et al. (2006) developed a Cantonese-English mixed-language speech recognition system, including acoustic modeling, language modeling, and language identification algorithms. For speech synthesis, Qian et al. (2009) developed a text-to-speech system that can generate Mandarin-English mixed-language utterances.

Research on code-switching and multilingual language processing included applications of unknown word extraction (Wu, et al., 2011), text mining (Yang, et al., 2011; Zhang, et al., 2011), and information retrieval (Tsai, et al., 2011). Wu et al. (2011) proposed the use of mutual information and entropy to extract unknown words from code-switched sentences. Yang et al. (2011) used self-organizing maps for multilingual document mining and navigation. Zhang et al. (2011) addressed the problem of multilingual sentence categorization and novelty mining on English, Malay, and Chinese sentences. Tsai et al. (2011) used the FRank ranking algorithm to build a merge model for multilingual information retrieval.

3 Language Modeling Approach

Language modeling approaches have been successfully used in many applications such as grammar error correction (Wu, et al., 2010) and lexical substitution (Yu, et al., 2010; 2011). For our task, a code-switched sentence generally has a higher probability of being found in a code-switching language model than in a non-code-switching one. Thus we built code-switching and non-code-switching language models to compare their respective probabilities of identifying code-switched sentences and code-switched words within the sentences. Fig. 1 shows the system framework. First, a corpus of code-switched and non-code-switched sentences are collected to build the respective code-switching and non-code-switching language models. To identify code-switched sentences, we compare the probability of each test sentence output by the code-switching language model against the output of the non-code-switching one to determine whether or not the test sentence is code-switched. To identify code-switched words within the sentences, we select the *n*-gram with the highest probability output by the code-switching language model, and then compare it against the output of the non-code-switching one to verify whether the n-*th* word in the given sentence is a code-switched word.

3.1 Corpus collection

A non-code-switching corpus refers to a set of sentences containing just one language. Because Mandarin is the primary language in this study, we used the Sinica corpus released by the Association

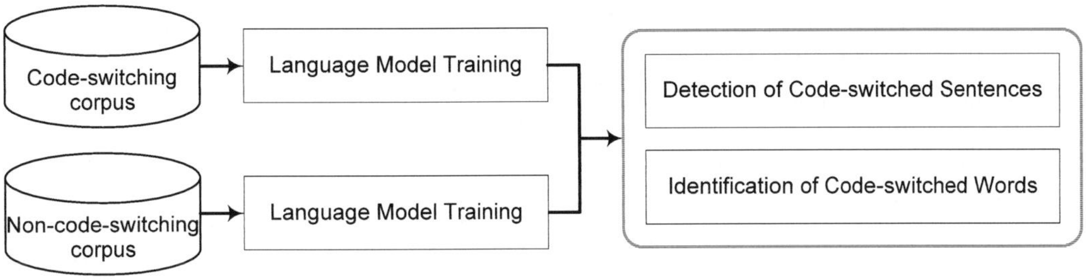

Figure 1. Framework of identification of code-switched sentences and words in the sentences.

for Computational Linguistics and Chinese Language Processing (ACLCLP) as the non-code-switching corpus. A code-switching corpus refers to a set of Mandarin sentences featuring Taiwanese words. However, it can be difficult to collect a large number of such sentences, and training a language model on insufficient data may incur the data sparseness problem. Therefore, we used more common Mandarin-English sentences as the code-switching corpus, based on the assumption that the code-switching phenomenon in Mandarin-English sentences has a certain degree of similarity to Mandarin-Taiwanese sentences because, in Taiwan, both English and Taiwanese are secondary languages with respect to Mandarin. The Mandarin-English sentences were collected from a large corpus of web-based news articles which were then segmented using the CKIP segmentation system developed by the Academia Sinica, Taiwan (http://ckipsvr.iis.sinica.edu.tw) (Ma and Chen, 2003). The sentences containing words with the part-of-speech (POS) tag "FW" (i.e., foreign word) were selected as code-switched sentences.

3.2 Detection of code-switched sentences

Generally, an n-gram language model is used to predict the n-*th* word based on the previous n-1 words using a probability function $P(w_n|w_1...w_{n-1})$. Given a sentence $S=w_1...w_k$, the non-code-switching n-gram language model is defined as

$$\begin{aligned} P_{\overline{CS}}(S) &= P(w_1)P(w_2 \mid w_1)\cdots P(w_k \mid w_1...w_{k-1}) \\ &= \prod_{i=1}^{k} P(w_i \mid w_1...w_{i-1}) \\ &\approx \prod_{i=1}^{k} P(w_i \mid w_{i-1}...w_{i-n+1}) \end{aligned} \quad (1)$$

where $P(w_i|w_{i-1}...w_{i-n+1})$ is estimated by

$$P(w_i|w_{i-1}...w_{i-n+1}) = \frac{C(w_i...w_{i-n+1})}{C(w_{i-1}...w_{i-n+1})}, \quad (2)$$

where $C(\bullet)$ denotes the frequency counts of the n-grams retrieved from the non-code-switching corpus (i.e., Sinica corpus). Instead of estimating the surface form of the next word, the code-switching n-gram language model estimates the probability that the next word is a code-switched word, i.e., $P(cs_n|w_1...w_{n-1})$, defined as

$$\begin{aligned} P_{cs}(S) &= P(w_1)P(cs_2 \mid w_1)\cdots P(cs_k \mid w_1...w_{k-1}) \\ &= \prod_{i=1}^{k} P(cs_i \mid w_1...w_{i-1}) \\ &\approx \prod_{i=1}^{k} P(cs_i \mid w_{i-1}...w_{i-n+1}) \end{aligned} \quad (3)$$

where $P(w_i|w_{i-1}...w_{i-n+1})$ is estimated by

$$P(cs_i|w_{i-1}...w_{i-n+1}) = \frac{C(cs_i...w_{i-n+1})}{C(cs_{i-1}...w_{i-n+1})}, \quad (4)$$

To estimate $P(cs_n \mid w_1...w_{n-1})$, the code-switching corpus is processed by replacing the code-switched words (i.e., the words with the POS tag "FW") in the Mandarin-English sentences with a special character *cs*. The frequency counts of $C(cs_i...w_{i-n+1})$ can then be retrieved from the code-switching corpus. This processing may also reduce the effect of the data sparseness problem in language model training.

Once the two language models are built, they can be compared to detect whether a given sentence contains code-switching. That is,

$$c = \frac{P_{CS}(S)}{P_{\overline{CS}}(S)}. \quad (5)$$

The sentence S is predicted to be a code-switched sentence if the probability of the sentence output by the code-switching language model is greater than that output by the non- code-switching one (i.e., $c \geq 1$).

3.3 Identification of code-switched words

This step identifies the positions of the code-switched words within the sentences. To this end, the code-switching n-gram language model (Eq. (3)) is applied to each test sentence and the probability of being a code-switched word is assigned to every next word (position) in the sentence. Among all the n-grams in the sentence, the one with the highest probability indicates the most likely position of a code-switched word. That is,

$$cs^* = \arg\max_i P(cs_i | w_{i-1}...w_{i-n+1}), \quad (6)$$

where cs^* denotes the best hypothesis of the code-switched word in the sentence. However, not all n-grams with the highest probability suggest correct positions. Therefore, we further propose a verification mechanism to determine whether to accept the best hypothesis. That is,

$$cs = \begin{cases} cs^* & P^*(cs_i | w_{i-1}...w_{i-n+1}) \geq P(w_i | w_{i-1}...w_{i-n+1}) \\ \phi & P^*(cs_i | w_{i-1}...w_{i-n+1}) < P(w_i | w_{i-1}...w_{i-n+1}) \end{cases} \quad (7)$$

where $P^*(cs_i | w_{i-1}...w_{i-n+1})$ represents the probability of the best hypothesis in the code-switching corpus, and $P(w_i | w_{i-1}...w_{i-n+1})$ represents its probability in the non-code-switching corpus. The best hypothesis cs^* is accepted if its probability in the code-switching corpus is greater than that in the non-code-switching corpus.

4 Experimental Results

This section first explains the experimental setup, including experiment data, implementation of language modeling, and evaluation metrics. We then present experimental results for the identification of code-switched sentences and words within the sentences.

4.1 Experimental setup

The test set included 86 sentences where 43 sentences were Mandarin only (i.e., non-code-switched) and another 43 Mandarin sentences containing Taiwanese words (i.e., code-switched). N-gram models for both code-switching and non-code-switching were trained using the SRILM toolkit (Stolcke, 2002) with n=2 (i.e., bigram). The evaluations metrics included recall, precision, F-measure, and accuracy. The recall was defined as the number of code-switched sentences correctly identified by the method divided by the total number of code-switched sentences in the test set. The precision was defined as the number of code-switched sentences correctly identified by the method divided by the number of code-switched sentences identified by the method. The F-measure was defined by defined as $\frac{2 \times recall \times precision}{recall + precision}$. The accuracy was defined as the number of sentences correctly identified by the method divided by the total number of sentences in the test set.

4.2 Results

To identify code-switched sentences, the code-switching and non-code-switching bigram models were used to determine whether or not each test sentence features code-switching (Eq. (5)), with results presented in Table 1. The language modeling approach correctly identified 33 code-switched sentences and 36 non-code-switched sentences, thus yielding 76.74% (33/43) recall, 82.50% (33/40) precision, 79.52% F-measure, and 80.23% (69/86) accuracy.

To identify code-switched words in the sentences, all word bi-grams in each test sentence were first ranked according to their probabilities. The top N word bi-grams were then selected as candidates for further verification using Eq. (7). To examine the effect of the data sparseness problem, we built an additional POS bi-gram model from the code-switching corpus. Table 2 shows the results for the identification of code-switched words using the word and POS bi-gram models. With more candidates included for verification (i.e., Top 1 to Top 3), more code-switched words were correctly identified, thus dramatically increasing the recall of both word and POS bi-gram models, while slightly decreasing the precision of both models.

	Recall	Precision	F-measure	Accuracy
Bi-gram	76.74%	82.50%	79.52%	80.23%

Table 1. Results of the identification of code-switched sentence.

Word Bi-gram	Recall	Precision	F-measure
Top1	39.53%	42.50%	40.96%
Top2	62.79%	32.93%	43.20%
Top3	88.37%	33.33%	48.41%
POS Bi-gram	Recall	Precision	F-measure
Top1	41.86%	42.86%	42.35%
Top2	74.42%	39.02%	51.20%
Top3	93.02%	34.78%	50.63%

Table 2. Results of the identification of code-switched words.

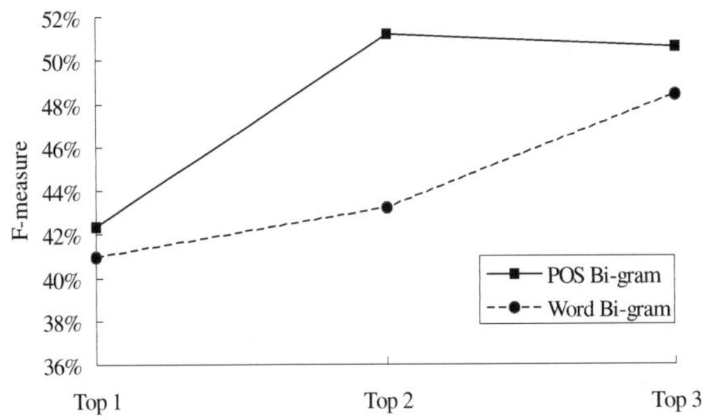

Figure 2. Comparative results of word and POS bi-gram language models.

Overall, the F-measure of both models increased as the number of candidates included increased. Figure 2 compares the word and POS bi-gram models, showing that the POS bi-gram model outperformed the word bi-gram model in terms of F-measure, as well as for recall and precision (see Table 2). This finding indicates that training with the POS tags can reduce the impact of the data sparseness problem, thus improving the identification performance.

5 Conclusions

This work presents a language modeling method for identifying sentences featuring code-switching, and for identifying the code-switched words within those sentences. Experimental results show that the language modeling approach achieved a 79.52% F-measure and 80.23% accuracy for the detection of code-switched sentences. For the identification of code-switched words within sentences, the POS bi-gram model outperformed the word bi-gram model, mainly because of the reduced impact of the data sparseness problem. The highest F-measure for this task was 51.20%. Future work will focus on improving system performance by incorporating other effective machine learning algorithms and features such as sentence structure analysis. The proposed method could also be integrated into practical applications such as a multilingual dialog system to improve effectiveness in dealing with the code-switching problem.

Acknowledgement

This work was supported by National Science Council, Taiwan, R.O.C (NSC99-2221-E-155-036-MY3), and Aim for the Top University Plan, Ministry of Education, Taiwan, R.O.C. The authors would like to thank the anonymous reviewers and the area chairs for their constructive comments.

References

Ayeomoni, M. O. 2006. Code-Switching and Code-Mixing: Style of Language Use in Childhood in Yoruba Speech Community. Nordic Journal of African Studies, 15(1): 90–99.

Chan, J. Y. C., Ching, P. C., Lee T. and Cao, H. 2006. Automatic Speech Recognition of Cantonese-English Code-mixing Utterance. In Proc. of Interspeech, pages 113-116.

Fung, P., and Schultz, T. 2008. Multilingual Spoken Language Processing. IEEE Signal Processing Magazine, 25(3): 89-97.

Hoffmann, C. 1991. An Introduction to Bilingualism. London. New York: Longman.

Holzapfel, H. 2005. Building Multilingual Spoken Dialogue Systems. Archives of Control Sciences, 15(4): 555-566.

Hong, W. T., Chen, H. C., Liao, I. B. and Wang W. J. 2009. Mandarin/English Mixed-Lingual Speech Recognition System on Resource-Constrained Platforms. In Proc. of the 21st Conference on Computational Linguistics and Speech Processing (ROCLING-09), pages 237-250.

Ipsic, I., Pavesic, N., Mihelic, F. and Noth, E. 1999. Multilingual Spoken Dialog System. In Proc. of the IEEE International Symposium on Industrial Electronics, pages 183-187.

Liu, Y. 2008. Evaluation of the Matrix Language Hypothesis: Evidence from Chinese-English Code-switching Phenomena in Blogs. Journal of Chinese Language and Computing, 18(2): 75-92.

Lyu, D. C., Hsu, C. N., Chiang, Y. C. and Lyu R. Y. 2008. Acoustic Model Optimization for Multilingual Speech Recognition. International Journal of Computational Linguistics and Chinese Language Processing, 13(3): 363-386.

Ma, W. Y. and K. Chen J. 2003. A Bottom-up Merging Algorithm for Chinese Unknown Word Extraction. In Proc. of the ACL Workshop on Chinese Language Processing, pages 31-38.

Myers-Scotton, C. 1993. Social Motivations for Code Switching: Evidence from Africa. Oxford University Press, New York.

Qian, Y., Liang, H. and Soong F. 2009. A Cross-Language State Sharing and Mapping Approach to Bilingual (Mandarin–English) TTS. IEEE Trans. on Audio, Speech, and Language Processing, 17(6): 1231-1239.

Stolcke, A. 2002. SRILM — An Extensible Language Modeling Toolkit. In Proc. of the 7th International Conference on Spoken Language Processing (ICSLP-02), pages 901-904.

Tsai, M. F., Chen, H. H. and Wang Y. T. 2011. Learning a Merge Model for Multilingual Information Retrieval. Information Processing and Management, 47(5): 635-646.

Wu, C. H., Chiu, Y. H., Shia, C. J. and Lin C. Y. 2006. Automatic Segmentation and Identification of Mixed-language Speech using Delta-BIC and LSA-based GMMs. IEEE Trans. Audio, Speech, and Language Processing, 14(1): 266-276.

Wu, Y. L., Hsieh, C. W., Lin, W. H., Liu, C. Y. and Yu L. C. 2011. Unknown Word Extraction from Multilingual Code-Switching Sentences In Proc. of the 23rd Conference on Computational Linguistics and Speech Processing (ROCLING-11), pages 349-360.

Wu, C. H., Liu, C. H., Matthew, H. and Yu L. C. 2010. Sentence Correction Incorporating Relative Position and Parse Template Language Models. IEEE Trans. on Audio, Speech, and Language Processing, 18(6): 1170-1181.

Yang, H. C., Hsiao, H. W., and Lee, C. H. 2011. Multilingual Document Mining and Navigation Using Self-organizing Maps. Information Processing and Management, 47(5): 647-666.

Yu, L. C., Wu, C. H., Chang, R. Y., Liu, C. H. and Hovy, E. H. 2010. Annotation and Verification of Sense Pools in OntoNotes. Information Processing and Management, 46(4): 436-447.

Yu, L. C., Chien, W. N. and Chen, S. T. 2011. A Baseline System for Chinese Near-Synonym Choice. In Proc. of the 5th International Joint Conference on Natural Language Processing (IJCNLP-11), pages 1366-1370.

Zhang, Y., Tsai, F. S. and Kwee A. T. 2011. Multilingual Sentence Categorization and Novelty Mining. Information Processing and Management, 47(5): 667-675.

Semi-automatic Annotation of Chinese Word Structure

Jianqiang Ma† **Chunyu Kit‡** **Dale Gerdemann†**

† Department of Linguistics
University of Tübingen
Tübingen, Germany

‡Department of Chinese, Translation and Linguistics
City University of HK, HKSAR, China

{jma,dg}@sfs.uni-tuebingen.de ctckit@cityu.edu.hk

Abstract

Chinese word structure annotation is potentially useful for many NLP tasks, especially for Chinese word segmentation. Li and Zhou (2012) have presented an annotation for word structures in the Penn Chinese Treebank. But they only consider words that have productive affixes, which covers 35% of word types in that corpus. In this paper, we propose a linguistically inspired annotation that covers various morphological derivations of Chinese in a more general way, such that almost all multiple-character words can be structurally analyzed. As manual annotation is expensive, we propose a semi-supervised approach to automatic annotation, which combines the maximum entropy learning and the EM iteration for the Gaussian mixture model. The proposed method has achieved an accuracy of 90% on the testing set.

1 Introduction

In contrast to the pervasive success in creation and use of various language resources for corpus linguistics and natural language processing (NLP), *Chinese word structure annotation* has rarely been studied, although it is likely to be particularly useful to many NLP tasks, especially to Chinese word segmentation (CWS). In this paper, we propose a semi-supervised approach to automatic annotation of Chinese word structures.

Li (2011) shows many problems in CWS, including wordhood, granularity of lexical units for different applications, as well as several other linguistic phenomena, such as the so-called separable words, and points out that they can only be solved with adequate knowledge of word structure.

Our motivation for creating such an annotation is to test the usefulness of morphological information for the Out-Of-Vocabulary word (OOV) detection, a major challenge in CWS (Huang and Zhao, 2007). All state-of-the-art word segmenters (Zhao and Liu, 2010) based on classification (Berger et al., 1992; Xue, 2003) and sequence labeling (Lafferty et al, 2001; Peng et al., 2004) have to rely on using character n-grams as features. Despite recent advances in model combination (Wang et al., 2010; Sun, 2010), joint learning (Jiang et al., 2008; Zhang and Clark, 2008; Sun, 2011) and integration of supervised and unsupervised methods (Zhao and Kit, 2008; Sun and Xu, 2011), etc., an inherent problem with OOV words is that they are novel character combinations seldom occurring in a training corpus, giving machine learning methods little evidence for prediction. Like other linguistic elements, the distribution of character n-grams also obeys Zipf's (1949) law, indicating that *exponentially* more tokens have to occur before more distinct types are encountered. In other words, we need an exponential growth of annotated corpora to offset the *data sparseness problem* (Zhao et al., 2010), which is certainly expensive and impractical.

Morphology, on the other hand, offers a principled way to capture internal word structure and model the dynamic and productive *word formation process* for all words, including OOV ones. In this work, we will adhere to the conventional linguistic analysis of Chinese morphology (Packard, 2000; Xue, 2001). Chinese words are known to be poor in inflections and rich in derivations, including compounding, affixation and abbreviation, among many others. Li and Zhou (2012) introduce an affixation annotation on the Penn Chinese Treebank version 6.0 (CTB, Xue et al., 2005), which covers 35% word types.

The annotation to be addressed in this paper goes beyond affixation and explores for a general approach to accommodating more predominant processes including *compounding*. Our linguistically inspired annotation scheme (Section 3) is based on part-of-speech (POS) like tags for both characters and words, together with syntactic and morphological rules to derive these tags. In principle, our annotation covers most multiple-character words, except multi-char morphemes or binomes, such as 葡萄 'grape'.

Manual annotation is expensive and inefficient. To get around this problem, we propose a semi-supervised learning approach to automatic annotation of Chinese word structures, with a focus on two-character words. This method combines the maximum entropy learning and the EM iteration for Gaussian mixture models (Section 5). Our experiments show that it works significantly better than (1) two classic semi-supervised learning algorithms, self-training and co-training (Section 6), and (2) the supervised learning baseline (Section 4). The accuracy of the 1-best assignment of char tags by our approach is 90%. It is expected that the probabilistic nature of this approach can lead to an even lower error rate in real applications. To the best of our knowledge, this is the first attempt on wide-coverage semi-supervised automatic annotation of Chinese word structures.

2 Related Work

The morphology of Chinese has been studied in early works such as (Zhao, 1968; Lü, 1979) and more recently in the framework of generative linguistics, such as (Huang, 1984; Dai, 1992; Duanmu, 1997; Packard, 2000; Xue, 2001). Packard (2000) treats the morphology as an extension of syntax at the word (X0) level. Having a lexicalism flavor, it considers both morphemes and complex words with their "precompiled" morphological structures in the lexicon, except for complex words containing grammatical affixes.

In contrast, Xue (2001) has proposed a system that derives virtually *all* the complex words *with syntactic rules* or with the morphology module after syntactic analysis. The boundary of syntax and morphology further blurs and the operation scope of syntax rules expands most part of the morphology. Both Packard (2000) and Xue (2001) adopt form class descriptions, which assign words and their components (characters) POS-like tags called *form classes*. Also, rules in both systems are more or less syntactic.

Computational linguists have also started rethinking the limitations of feature-based machine learning approaches to CWS and have called for morphology-based analysis of OOV words (Dong et al., 2010). There are a few pivotal works in this direction, such as Zhao (2009), Li (2011) and Li & Zhou (2012). Zhao (2009) has proposed a character-based dependency parsing model, based on the annotation of unlabeled in-word character dependencies. While this is a valuable investigation, the deadlock of OOV word detection suggests that pure character-wise dependencies may be inadequate to model the morphological process.

Li (2011) and Li & Zhou (2012) have proposed models of joint morphological and syntactical analysis, for constituent and dependency parsing, respectively. Both are based on the same annotation of word structures for CTB. Influenced by Packard (2000), they only annotated words that contain productive affixes, which are only a *small subset* of words formed by morphological derivations. With a low coverage of the word formation phenomena, their models do not improve OOV word detection. The morphological model is expected to be effective in improving the performance of OOV word recognition, once syntax-like rules can be used to analyze most of, rather than a small portion of complex words, as illustrated in Xue (2001).

Our annotation differs from Li & Zhou's (2012) in that our annotation goes beyond affixation and aims at a thorough description of the derivational morphology in Chinese. Its ultimate goal is to construct a linguistic resource for training wide coverage word formation analyzers for Chinese.

3 Manual Annotation

3.1 Form-class description

Following Packard (2000) and Xue (2001), we adopt the *form class description* to describe the word formation analysis, as opposed to other possible descriptions of word structures, such as relational description, modification structure descriptions[1]. Character form classes refer to POS-like class identities for component morphemes of a word. For example, the word 吃饭 'to dine' can be analyzed as a verb $[\ \ ]_V$ made of a verbal and a nominal element $[V\ N]_V$ 吃 'to eat' and 饭

[1] See Packard (2000) for a detailed discussion

'rice', where character form classes are denoted by the symbols inside the bracket while the word classes/POS tags are denoted by the subscript symbol of the bracket. Another example is the analysis of the adjective 先进 'advanced' as [A V]$_{\mathrm{J}}$. In addition to form class identities, longer words have hierarchies in their elements as well.

The existence of monosyllabic words, with or without ambiguous POS tags, provides the initial link between character and word form classes (Packard, 2000). The form classes of bounded morphemes are more difficult to determine and requires extra clues such as morpho/lexical semantics.

3.2 Words to be annotated

Our annotation is carried out on CTB 5.0. Since longer words can be recursively analyzed similarly to single- and two-character words, we have chosen to focus on two-character words, which are shortest words that have inner structures. Note that the annotation of single-character words is trivial. Another reason for giving this priority to two-character words is mono- and bisyllabic words together account for 64% and 92% word types and tokens in CTB 5.0, respectively. Our annotation has covered all 21151 open-class two-character words in CTB 5.0.

3.3 The annotation scheme

With form class description, annotating a two-character word equals to specifying its POS tags, form class co-occurrences of component characters and the association of the two. We have written programs to (1) extract the possible word and character form classes from CTB 5.0 and online resources[2], and (2) generate all the possible structures for a two-character word by calculating the Cartesian product of the sets of possible form classes of its left and right character, respectively.

The task of a human annotator is to choose the best structure for a <Word, POS> entry from computer generated candidates, if there are multiple ones. An annotator needs to figure out the optimal structure analysis, considering various information and constraints, including:

- *Semantic compatibility*. For example, word 发展 'to develop; development' [V V]$_{\mathrm{V}}$ [V V]$_{\mathrm{N}}$ can be interpreted as [N V]$_{?}$, if the nominal form of 发 'hair' is assumed. But this is incompatible with the overall word meaning, compared with the verbal form of 发 'open; send; get started'
- *Syntactic patterns*. Certain patterns such as N+N, V+V and J+J compounding are more likely than others, e.g. V+ C (verb + classifier) combination.
- *Word POS influence*. In many cases, the form class identity of a word may largely determine the form class identity of one or both of its constituents.

It is often necessary to refer to classic Chinese to properly use semantics clues. And note that most entries with the same word form but distinct POS tags can be captured by zero derivations and thus share the same structures as well. For example, word 发展 'to develop; development' has a base form with POS of verb [V V]$_{\mathrm{V}}$, which zero-derives the noun form [V V]$_{\mathrm{N}}$. As for the actual manual annotation, we have manually analyzed the 600 most frequent words in CTB 5.0. The whole annotation took about 30 annotator hours.

4 Supervised Annotation with ME

The number of manually annotated two-character words is less than 3% of the those in CTB 5.0. Given the limited resource, we have opted for training machine learning models from manual annotation to *automatically* annotate the rest 20551 two-character words. As described in Section 3.3, the annotation can be viewed as a tagging task that assigns each word entry a tag from a finite tag set of possible words structures, such as [V N] [V V]. In our annotation, the majority of the words turn out to be tagged as one of 14 most popular structures.

Tagging is a typical NLP problem that can be well solved by supervised classification. We have chosen the maximum entropy model (ME, Berger et al., 1992) to do the task, for its ability of accommodating overlapping features to achieve the state-of-the-art empirical performance.[3]

4.1 Features

For ME modeling, the choice of features strongly affects the result. As semantic features are more difficult to obtain and encode, we have mostly utilized *word POS tags* and *character syntactic patterns* as features, as shown in Table 1. In Table 1, $i(y)$ denotes the indicator function, which

[2] Mostly from http://www.zdic.net/

[3] We used Le Zhang's implementation in our experiments, available at: https://github.com/lzhang10/ME

Feature Type	Feature Group	Representative Feature
Word POS tag	Individual POS tags	$i(NN)$, $i(VV)$, $i(JJ)$, $i(AD)$, $i(VA)$, most_frequent_tag
	POS tag co-occurrence	$i(NN \& VV)$, $i(NN \& JJ)$, $i(JJ \& AD)$, $i(JJ \& VA)$
	Set of POS tags	set_of_all_possible_tags, $i(VV\ or\ NN\ or\ NR\ or\ NT)$
Left character form class	Individual form class	$i(N)$, $i(V)$, $i(J)$, $i(A)$, most_frequent_form_class
	Form class co-occurrence	$i(N\&V)$, $i(N \& J)$, $i(J \& A)$
	Set of form classes	set_of_all_possible_form_classes
Right character form class	*Similar to left character form class features*	
Possible structure	*Possible word structures both character classes of which are in the set of open-class*	

Table 1 Features of the ME based automatic annotator

represents whether the current feature matches pattern y. For example, $i(NN)$ in the first row says that "*NN* is a possible tag of the current word". We have systematically explored various feature configurations within these categories, among which the current feature set has achieved a better result.

4.2 Evaluation

We assume that (1) the word structures are independent and identically distributed variables and (2) automatic annotator's performance on samples of the complete set of two-character words, e.g. the manually annotated ones may reflect the performance on the complete set. We randomly split the manual annotation into a training set and a testing set, of 500 and 100 words, respectively. The performance of the model trained on the training set is measured by its *accuracy* on the testing set, which is calculated as follows:

$$Accuracy = \frac{number\ of\ correctly\ annotated\ words}{number\ of\ total\ words} \quad (1)$$

The average accuracy with 6-fold cross validation is *81%*. Note that the popular pair of metrics, *precision* and *recall* for binary classification does not apply for the evaluation of the collective result of multiple tags, as the original difference in denominators of the two metric formula no longer exists.

4.3 Discussion of ME results

In the incorrectly tagged cases, a few are impossible to learn, due to unseen classification tags. The majority are, however, related to *inherent ambiguities* of word structures, such as 完全 'complete(ly)' [J J] [A A], 实行 'to implement' [A V] [V V], and 影响 'to influence; impact' [N N] [V V]. Although one structure may be more plausible than the other for a word, the distinction is somehow inconclusive. This suggests that it is probably NOT the best to assign a single structure analysis for every case.

From a machine learning perspective, the model is characterized by *high variance* or over-fitting, indicated by the big performance gap between the training (97%~92%) and testing (81%) accuracy. Besides the optimized regulation factors and the feature set, the only next thing that can improve the accuracy is probably to significantly increase the size of the annotated training set. In fact, the accuracy of 81% is a *reasonably good* result that can be obtained by ME with a relatively small set of available annotated examples.

5 Semi-supervised Annotation with Gaussian Mixture Model

5.1 Soft assignment of structures

Section 4.3 shows that many words are inherently ambiguous in structure. A better way of structure tagging may be soft assignment, i.e. allowing assignment of multiple structures to a word and using probabilities to indicate the likelihood of each assignment. For example, a soft assignment for 实行 'to implement' may look like:

[V V] : 0.8, [A V] : 0.15, [A N] : 0.01 ...

5.2 POS fingerprint features

POS features used in the ME model are discrete tag co-occurrence indicators. A drawback is that the distribution of POS tags is ignored. A better feature set is the distribution of the probabilities of seeing a certain POS tag T, given that the word is W, which can be estimated by normalized empirical counts with maximum likelihood estimation as follows:

$$P(T|W) = \frac{C(T,W)}{\sum_{T'} C(T',W)} \quad (2)$$

In practice, we only consider 10 open-class POS tags: *AD, CD, JJ, M, NN, NR, NT, OD, VA* and *VV*. The POS fingerprint, is a 10-dimensional vector that represents a word, each element of which is the conditional probability of the corresponding POS. With the model described in section 4, using original word POS features alone achieves an accuracy of 70%, while using POS fingerprint features alone achieves 74%.[4]

5.3 The generative model

Word POS tags strongly correlate with word structures (Packard, 2000). Human annotators use the single base POS tag to help annotate a word and utilize zero-derivation to generate ambiguous POS tags. But a computational model may need to keep POS ambiguities and use the distributions as features, as both base POS finding and zero-derivation probability estimation can be tricky. Even if a model can find the correct base POS for a word, the word structure may still be ambiguous in many cases, such as $[V\ V]_V$, $[V\ N]_V$ and $[N\ V]_V$. In short, it is an m-to-n non-deterministic mapping between an observable POS tag T and the latent structure S. A generative model that captures the joint distribution, $P(S,T)$ can generate all words represented by their POS fingerprints in repeated two steps:

1. Randomly choose a structure according to the structure distribution $P(S)$.
2. Draw a POS fingerprint data point according to the POS fingerprint distribution $P(T|S)$ given the chosen structure.

Each structure S determines a POS fingerprint distribution, which should somehow differ from the distributions of other structures, yet might considerable *overlaps* with that of others. This trait formalizes the observation that POS distribution has a significant correlation with structures, although words of different structures may show up with the same POS.

$P(T|S)$ should be a continuous distribution, as the data points, i.e. POS fingerprints, are continuous values. We choose the *Gaussian distribution,* following the central limit theorem stating that the average of a sufficiently large number of independent random variables can be approximated by the Gaussian. The prior distribution of structures $P(S)$ is a multinomial distribution, which neatly describes the random choice of discrete categories. An advantage of the generative model, as opposed to zero derivation, is that all possible POS tags of a word are treated in a similar way, which avoids the problems of base POS selection and derivation probability estimation.

5.4 Gaussian mixture model

The unsupervised version of the generative model can be formally described as a Gaussian mixture model (GMM, Bishop, 2006). The training data is a set of POS fingerprints $\{t^{(1)},..., t^{(m)}\}$ representing the word forms. The structures of these words, $\{s^{(1)},..., s^{(k)}\}$, are unknown, i.e. there is no structure annotation for any word. The data is specified by a joint distribution:

$$p\left(t^{(i)}, s^{(i)}\right) = p(s^{(i)})p(t^{(i)}|s^{(i)}) \tag{3}$$

$$s^{(i)} \sim Multinominal\ (\emptyset)$$

$$t^{(i)} \mid \left(s^{(i)} = j\right) \sim Gaussian\ (\mu_j, \Sigma_j)$$

where the parameter of the multinomial distribution $\emptyset_j = p(s^{(i)} = j) \geq 0, \sum_{j=1}^{k} \emptyset_j$. And μ and Σ are the vector of mean and variance of the Gaussian distribution, respectively.

The EM algorithm (Dempster et al., 1977) is the standard technique to estimate the parameters that maximize the likelihood of the data distribution with latent variables $s^{(i)}$. The algorithm runs the E-step and M-step iteratively until coverage:

1. **E-step:**

For each i and j, set:

$$w_j^{(i)} = p\left(s^{(i)} = j \mid t^{(i)};\ \emptyset, \mu, \Sigma\right) =$$

$$= \frac{p\left(s^{(i)} = j;\ \emptyset\right)p\left(t^{(i)} \middle| s^{(i)} = j; \mu, \Sigma\right)}{\sum_{l=1}^{k} p\left(s^{(i)} = l;\ \emptyset\right)p\left(t^{(i)} \middle| s^{(i)} = l; \mu, \Sigma\right)} \tag{4}$$

2. M-step:

$$\emptyset_j = \frac{1}{m}\sum_{i=1}^{m} w_j^{(i)} \tag{5}$$

$$\mu_j = \frac{\sum_{i=1}^{m} w_j^{(i)} t^{(i)}}{\sum_{i=1}^{m} w_j^{(i)}} \tag{6}$$

$$\Sigma_j = \frac{\sum_{i=1}^{m} w_j^{(i)}\left(t^{(i)} - \mu_j\right)\left(t^{(i)} - \mu_j\right)^T}{\sum_{i=1}^{m} w_j^{(i)}} \tag{7}$$

The quantity that we calculate in the E-step, the posterior probability of the structure $s^{(i)}$, given $t^{(i)}$, the POS fingerprint that represents the word is exactly the soft assignment of structures

[4] Note that simple substituting original POS features with POS fingerprints leads to little performance improvement in our supervised annotation experiment.

that we need. The $P(S|T)$ values obtained in the last iteration make the final annotation.

5.5 Semi-supervised GMM

A problem with EM is that there is no guarantee of finding the global optima, i.e. it often suffers from local optima. So EM is usually sensitive to the initialization and the default random initialization often leads to poor results, which has also been observed in NLP tasks (Lamar et al., 2010; Peng and Schuurmans, 2001). To solve this problem, we propose a semi-supervised version of GMM that uses the probabilistic output of the ME model for the EM initialization.

We train the ME model for automatic annotation in the same way as in section 4 with 500 training words. Then we apply the model to predict the structures of the all the 21151 words in this study except the 100 testing words. Instead of using the single best prediction, here we utilize the *probabilistic output* of the ME model, which gives all possible structures of the words together with their marginal probabilities.

We use this output as $p(s^{(i)}|t^{(i)})$ to initialize the E-step of the EM algorithm. Since the EM algorithm runs on GMM, from now on, POS fingerprint features represent the words instead. The following points may explain why it can improve the performance: (1) Even though the best testing accuracy with "hard assignment" given by the ME model is only 81%, the "true" structure analyses may still exist as the top-k candidate with relatively large probabilities, while irrelevant ones may have only small probability mass. (2) In general the assignments that EM induce do not necessarily correspond to the desired classification tags, but the ME outputs can give the EM a better starting point to move towards the right one among all possible local optima, given the data likelihood and the classification accuracy are well correlated. (3) From the perspective of the original ME model, the connections and similarities between data points from a much bigger sample (21151 vs. 500) may help fix the high variance problem discussed in section 4.3.

The final soft assignments for the 100 testing words are obtained by applying the E-step for them with the parameter estimated in previous iterations. To get the hard assignment, we simply select the assignment with the highest probability for each word. The evaluation for the hard assignments is still based on testing accuracy, which stays at *90%* in multiple runs that we have tried.

6 Comparison Experiments

We have tried other approaches to automatic annotation to compare with the proposed method. Since our semi-supervised approach is a combination of supervised ME model and unsupervised GMM, two natural baselines would be the performance that could be achieved by applying two models independently, the former is **81%** as shown in section 4.

6.1 Unsupervised GMM

We have run the traditional unsupervised GMM, which is characterized by the random initialization of the EM algorithm. As there is no prior mapping between assignment IDs and word structures, their optimal one-to-one mapping is found via our implementation of the Hungarian algorithm (Kuhn, 1955). With 1-to-1 mapping, the testing accuracy is *54%* for several trial of random initialization.

6.2 Self-training

Self-training is a classic semi-supervised learning approach widely used in NLP. We have implemented and experimented with the Yarowsky (1995) version. It is a meta- algorithm based on a basic learning model, for which we use the ME model with the same features, training set and testing set as described in section 4. The unlabeled data U are the rest of the two-character words. We evaluate intermediate and final models with their performance on the testing set, the best of which is kept as the result.

Other setups: (1) *Loop stopping criterion.* We choose the performance on the testing data, conditioned on the current accuracy ≥ (the previous accuracy- tolerance). The tolerance avoids stopping too early. (2) *Selection criteria.* We use the standard one, namely, the classifier's confidence on its best prediction of each instance, which is highest marginal probability for ME. The selection relies on a parameter k, which defines the minimum confidence score needed for an instance to get selected. In our experiment, we have tried scores from 0.95 to 0.5 with an interval of 0.05.

We have tested with different configurations of k, splitting of U, and regularization parameters. The result of self-learning giving an *accuracy of 82%* is not too good- one percentage point beyond that of the baseline ME model.

6.3 Co-training

Co-training (Blum and Mitchell, 1998) is another classic semi-supervised algorithm. Two classifiers trained with independent views (feature set) are expected to teach one another in the iteration. Two views that we have adopted are: 1) left char and right char derived features and 2) POS fingerprint features.

With a standard setup of the co-training experiments, we have tried different selection criteria and regularization parameters. There is also only *slightly (1%) improvement* brought by co-training. It looks like that neither feature set of the two views provides the other with much additional information for classification, as the initial classifiers trained with these two views have already reached an accuracy of 68% and 74%, respectively.

To summarize, neither self-training nor co-training is capable of enhancing their performance to a level comparable to our proposed approach, which improves the accuracy from 81% to 90%. An overview of the performance of all tested methods in our research is given in Table 2.

Methods	Test Accuracy
ME	81%
Self-training	82%
Co-training	82%
Unsupervised GMM	54%
Semi-supervised GMM	*90%*

Table 2 Performance of the tested methods

7 Discussion

The performance of the proposed semi-supervised approach suggests that the distribution of the data has good characteristics that tightly link to the underlying structures. In other words, the form class descriptions of word structures provide much information for inducing the structural *regularities* of Chinese words.

To the best of our knowledge, this is the first work on automatic annotation of Chinese word structures based on semi-supervised learning. We are unable to find any existing work to directly compare with it. However, there are previous works on semi-supervised learning for other NLP tasks, such as document classification (Nigam et al., 2006). They used naïve Bayes for both the supervised learning and unsupervised learning, whereas our supervised and unsupervised models are ME and GMM, respectively. In our design, we use ME as our initial model, because it can incorporate overlapping features to get better baseline. We could not simply keep using ME as the model for EM iterations, because it does not take probabilistic (soft) assignment for training. We use Gaussian mixture for EM iteration out of two main reasons: (1) we observe a strong correlation between POS distribution and word structures, and (2) Gaussian can deal with continuous features and suffers not too much from the data sparseness, for it has only a few parameters to estimate.

A message from Nigam et al. (2006) is that in their experiments, the performance gap between the supervised model and the semi-supervised model that utilize extra unlabeled instances decreases from initially 20%~10% to complete diminishing when there are abundant labeled data to such a degree that unlabeled data do not provide any extra information. Despite the differences in modeling and application, we assume that these semi-supervised learning algorithms follow similar tack of performance improvement over the baselines.

In this sense, the performance improvement from 81% to 90% of our semi-supervised method is *very good*, especially in view of the high baseline and the relative error reduction (52%) it has achieved. Besides, we can directly use the probabilistic annotation to train models for real applications, which is probably a more sensible way than training on the hard-assignment (top-1) of structure analyses, due to the inherent ambiguities of word structures themselves. In this probabilistic/soft mode, the error rate for applications is expected to be further decreased, as the training of probabilistic grammar can be similar to EM: Even if the top-1 candidate is incorrect in a strict sense, the correct analysis may still exist in the top-k best with considerable amount of probability mass, in contrast with truly irrelevant ones. The accumulations of a large number of instances will push the probability distribution towards the right direction.

Of course, the ultimate purpose of this automatic annotation approach is to facilitate tasks such as grammar learning, Chinese word segmentation, and joint segmentation and parsing. As for the question of how good this accuracy of 90% can be to these applications, its answer has to be explored through further experiments. The success of existing works in this direction certainly points to a promising prospect.

8 Conclusion

We have developed a semi-supervised approach to annotating Chinese word structures, based on Chinese morphology and applied it to automatic annotation of two-character Chinese words with the aid of a Gaussian mixture model, which utilizes the output of the ME model for its initialization for EM iterations. The proposed method can achieve an accuracy of 90% on a test set of 100 words, using 500 manually annotated words as training examples. This method works significantly better than pure supervised model and two other typical semi-supervised learning techniques, namely self-training and co-training.

Since this work focuses only on structure annotation of two-character words in Chinese, our plan for future work will be to semi-automatically annotate longer words. This needs to incorporate annotation techniques in Li & Zhou (2012) and develop necessary models to describe the recursive nature of word derivation in Chinese. With a complete word structure annotation of all words in CTB, we expect to have more experiments with novel word structure-driven models for Chinese word segmentation and even a joint modeling of word segmentation and parsing, with a focus on the typical problems of OOV word recognition.

Acknowledgments

The research described in this paper has received funding from the European Commission's 7th Framework Program under grant agreement n° 238405 (project CLARA, a Marie Curie ITN), and is partially supported by Research Grants Council (RGC) of Hong Kong SAR, China through the GRF Grant 9041597 (CityU 144410).

References

Adam Berger, Stephen Della Pietra, and Vincent Della Pietra. 1996. A maximum entropy approach to natural language processing. *Computational Linguistics*, 22(1): 39-71.

Christopher Bishop. 2006. *Pattern Recognition and Machine Learning*. New York: Springer.

Avrim Blum and Tom Mitchell. 1998. Combining labeled and unlabeled data with co-training. In *Proceedings* of *COLT*, pp. 92-100. Madison, USA.

Xiang-Ling Dai. 1992. *Chinese Morphology and its Interface with the Syntax*. PhD Dissertation, Ohio State University.

A.P. Dempster, N. M. Laird, D.B. Rubin. 1977. Maximum likelihood from incomplete data via the EM algorithm. *Journal of the Royal Statistical Society. Series B (Methodological)* 39 (1): 1–38.

Zhendong Dong, Qiang Dong and Changling Hao. 2010. Word segmentation needs change - from a linguist's view. In *Proceedings of CIPS-SIGHAN Joint Conference on Chinese Language Processing*, pp. 1-7. Beijing, China.

San Duanmu. 1997. "Wordhood in Chinese", in Jerome J. Packard ed. *New Approaches to Chinese Word Formation*, pp. 135-196. Mouton de Gruyter, New York, USA.

Changning Huang and Hai Zhao. 2007. Chinese word segmentation: A-decade Review. *Journal of Chinese Information Processing*, 21(3): 8-20

James C. T. Huang. 1984. Phrase structure, lexical integrity, and Chinese compounds. *Journal of the Chinese Language Teachers Association*, 19(2): 53-78.

Wenbin Jiang, Liang Huang, Qun Liu, Yajuan Lu. 2008. A cascaded linear model for joint Chinese word segmentation and part-of-speech tagging. In *Proceedings of ACL: HLT*, pp.897-904. Columbus, USA.

Harold Kuhn. 1955. The Hungarian Method for the assignment problem. *Naval Research Logistics Quarterly*, 2:83–97.

John Lafferty, Andrew McCallum, and Fernando Pereira. 2001. Conditional random fields: probabilistic models for segmenting and labeling sequence data. In *Proceedings of ICML*, pp. 282-289. Williamstown, MA, USA

Michael Lamar, Yariv Maron, Mark Johnson, Elie Bienenstock. 2010. SVD and clustering for unsupervised POS tagging. In *Proceedings of* ACL (Short Papers), pp. 215-219. Uppsala, Sweden.

Zhongguo Li. 2011. Parsing the internal structure of words: A new paradigm for Chinese word segmentation. In *Proceedings of ACL: HLT*, pp. 1405-1414. Portland, Oregon, USA.

Zhongguo Li and Guodong Zhou. 2012. Unified dependency parsing of Chinese morphological and syntactic structures. In *Proceedings of* EMNLP-CoNLL, pp. 1445-1454. Jeji, Korea.

Shuxiang Lü. 1979. *Hanyu Yufa Fenxi Wenti "Problems in Syntactical Analysis of Chinese"*. Shangwu Yinshuguan, Beijing, China.

Kamal Nigam, Andrew McCallum and Tom Mitchell. 2006. Semi-supervised Text Classification Using EM. In Chapelle, O., Zien, A., and Scholkopf, B. (Eds.) *Semi-Supervised Learning*, 33-56. MIT Press: Boston.

Jerome Packard. 2000. *The Morphology of Chinese: A Linguistic and Cognitive Approach*. Cambridge University Press, Cambridge, UK.

Fuchun Peng, Fangfang Feng, and Andrew McCallum. 2004. Chinese segmentation and new word detection using conditional random fields. In *Proceedings of COLING*, pp. 562-568. Geneva, Switzerland.

Fuchun Peng and Dale Schuurmans. 2001. Self-supervised Chinese word segmentation. In *Proceedings of the Fourth International Symposium on Intelligent Data Analysis,* pp. 238-247. *Cascais, Portugal*

Weiwei Sun. 2010. Word-based and character-based word segmentation models: Comparison and combination. In *Proceedings COLING*. pp. 1211-1219. Beijing, China.

Weiwei Sun. 2011. A stacked sub-word model for joint Chinese word segmentation and part-of-speech tagging. *In Proceedings ACL:HLT*, pp. 1385-1394. Portland, USA.

Weiwei Sun and Jia Xu. 2011. Enhancing Chinese word segmentation using unlabeled data. In *Proceedings EMNLP*, pp. 970-979. Edinburgh, UK.

Kun Wang, Chengqing Zong and Keh-Yih Su. 2010. A character-based joint model for Chinese word segmentation. In *Proceedings of COLING*, pp. 1173-1181. Beijing, China.

Nianwen Xue. 2001. *Defining and Automatically Identifying words in Chinese*. Phd Thesis, University of Delaware.

Nianwen Xue. 2003. Chinese Word Segmentation as Characater Tagging. *Computational Linguistics and Chinese Language Processing*, 8(1): 29-48.

Nianwen Xue, Fei Xia, Fu-Dong Chiou, and Martha Palmer. 2005. The Penn Chinese Tree bank: Phrase structure annotation of a large corpus. *Natural Language Engineering*, 11(2) 207-238.

Davide Yarowsky. 1995. Unsupervised word sense disambiguation rivaling supervised methods. In *Proceedings of ACL*, pp. 189-196. Cambridge, USA.

Yue Zhang and Stephen Clark. 2008. Joint word segmentation and POS tagging using a single perceptron. In *Proceedings of ACL: HLT*, pp. 888-896. Columbus, USA.

Hai Zhao. 2009. Character-level dependencies in Chinese: usefulness and learning, pp. 879-887. In *Proceedings of EACL*, pp. 879-887. Athens, Greece.

Hai Zhao and Chunyu Kit. 2008. Unsupervised segmentation helps supervised learning of word segmentation and named entity recognition. In *Proceedings of the Sixth SIGHAN Workshop on Chinese Language Processing*, pp. 106-111. Hyderabad, India.

Hai Zhao, Yan Song and Chunyu Kit. 2010. How large a corpus do we need: Statistical method vs. rule-based Method. In *Proceedings of LREC*, pp. 1672-1677. Malta.

Hongmei Zhao and Qun Liu. 2010. The CIPS-SIGHAN CLP 2010 Chinese Word Segmentation Bakeoff. In *Proceedings of the First CPS-SIGHAN Joint Conference on Chinese Language Processing*, pp. 199-209. Beijing, China.

Yuen-Ren Zhao. 1968. *Grammar of Spoken Chinese*. University of California Press.

George Zipf. 1949. *Human Behavior and the Principle of Least Effort: An Introduction to Human Ecology*. Addison-Wisley. Oxford, UK.

Building a Chinese Lexical Taxonomy

Xiaopeng Bai, Nianwen Xue
Department of Computer Science, Brandeis University, Waltham, MA, USA 02453
{xpbai, xuen}@brandeis.edu

Abstract

In this paper, we present a Chinese lexical taxonomy, a hierarchically organization of Chinese lexical classes of nouns, verbs and adjectives. We first describe the structure of this taxonomy and then present the methods we used to build it. The distinctive characteristics of this lexical taxonomy are: 1) we use *definition frame* to describe each lexical class, as well as its members, 2) the lexical classes for nouns, verbs and adjectives are inter-connected. We also compare this taxonomy with the Chinese Proposition Bank, to look for possible ways to link these two independently developed language resources.

1 Introduction

A lexical semantic taxonomy is a hierarchical organization of lexical semantic classes. Such a taxonomy is a useful resource for Natural Language Processing, because it groups word senses into lexical semantic classes by their shared lexical meaning, and produces a finite set of lexical semantic classes. Since the lexical classes capture the shared meaning of individual senses, they can be used as a tagset to annotate words in a natural language corpus, which can then be used to train automatic lexical semantic classifiers. Compared with words sense disambiguation, where senses have to be defined for each word, classifying words based on their lexical classes is a more general task. The advantage is that there is no need to train classifiers for each individual word, as is typically the case for word sense disambiguation systems.

Building lexical semantic resources and systems has attracted much interest in the NLP and lexical semantics communities. (Picca et al., 2007, Ciaramita & Johnson, 2003) described a corpus annotated with the upper level synsets of WordNet (Fellbaum, 1998). (Gao et al, 2005) used lexical classes from Tongyici Cilin (Mei et al., 1983) for Chinese document retrieval, and (Tian et al, 2010) used the same resource to compute Chinese word similarity. One main drawback of these two lexical classification systems is that because the criteria for the lexical classification is not explicitly spelled out, when there is an out-of-vocabulary (OOV) sense, it is hard to determine its appropriate membership without going back to their original developers. Without explicit criteria, it is hard to ensure consistency when a new lexical taxonomy is established or an old one is extended. One desideratum in lexical taxonomy creation is consistency. Ideally, when a new word sense is put in taxonomy, different lexicographers/annotators should come up with the same class. This is also the biggest challenge in taxonomy/ontology development, and the key is to address this is to come up with concrete and explicit criteria that different lexicographers/annotators can follow so that there is no need to go back to the original creators every time a new word sense needs to be added to the taxonomy.

The rest of the article is organized as follows. In Section 2, we provide a brief review of related work. In Section 3, we present the structure and size of the current CLT as well as the corpus that is annotated with the lexical classes of the CLT. In Section 4, we show syntactic performances, semantic roles and selectional constraints are used to create the definition frame of each class. Comparison of CLT and Chinese Propbank (CPB) is performed in Section 5, and possible ways to link CLT to CPB are discussed in section 6.

2 Related Work

There have been several past efforts to produce (Chinese) lexical taxonomies aimed to provide lexical knowledge for NLP tasks (Chen, 1998; Chen, 2001; Wang etc., 2003). (Wang et al, 2003) used lexical classes to describe word sense in SKCC (Semantic Knowledge Base of Contemporary Chinese), along with syntactic and argument structure features.

WordNet (Fellbaum, 1998). Gather senses with similar lexical meaning according to one or more dictionaries, and the lexical classes (synset in WN) are generated based on the judgment of word sense similarity. The judgment of similarity between word senses is depend on either the sense definition in dictionary or the intuition of developer. Such method is easy to use, but could be suffered with inconsistency among sense definitions (from different dictionaries) and different developers/annotators. It doesn't cost much at the initial stage of building taxonomy, but causes significant high cost to maintaining and expanding.

HowNet (Dong & Dong, 2006). HowNet uses "meaning primitives" (sememe in HN) as tagset to describe word senses, the computing of sense similarity and the generating of lexical classes can be automatically done. There is inconsistency problem encountered when adapting this method in such aspect: creating "meaning primitives" and expanding them in the future; selecting proper "meaning primitives" for defining word senses in consistent way.

As we argued in Section 1, a concrete definition for each class in a lexical taxonomy is required to ensure consistency. However, current Chinese lexical taxonomies generally do not provide such definitions. People have to create and extend their taxonomies by using dictionaries or the taxonomy made by other researchers, or by relying on their own intuition. Our work differs from others in that we use concrete linguistic features to define lexical classes. These class definitions can be used to extend the taxonomy by other researchers when new word senses need to be added to the taxonomy.

3 Status of CLT

In this section, we describe the structure and scale of the CLT taxonomy, as well as the corpus annotated with the lexical classes of this taxonomy.

3.1 Structure of CLT

CLT is a hierarchical structure formed by lexical classes, and each lexical class is a set of word senses that have shared lexical meaning and linguistic features. Currently we have three sub-taxonomies for nouns, verbs and adjectives respectively. Each sub-taxonomy has one root class, which dominates any number of terminal and non-terminal lexical classes. A given class can have one parent, one or more sisters and one or more children. Terminal classes do not have children. Table 1 shows part of the verb taxonomy in CLT.

1 自主变化 (self changing)
1.1 过程 (process)
——1.1.1 存现 (exist): 出土, 出现
——1.1.2 位移 (move): 流入, 上升
——1.1.3 变化 (transform): 消融, 变化
1.2 状态 (status)
——1.2.1 境遇 (situation)
———1.2.1.1 情绪 (emotion): 费心, 感恩
———1.2.1.2 生理状态 (physical situation): 打鼾, 咳
———1.2.1.3 其他 (other): 见鬼, 失礼
——1.2.2 自然现象 (natural phenomenon): 结冰, 降温
——1.2.3 一般状态 (circumstance): 无力, 作罢
——1.2.4 运动 (motion): 摆动, 翻卷
1.3 经历 (experience)
——1.3.1 经历 (experience): 处身, 拘泥
——1.3.2 感知意向 (attitude): 向往, 对得起
——1.3.3 所有 (possess): 装有, 有着
——1.3.4 影响 (influence): 震撼, 照耀
——1.3.5 产生 (generate): 组成, 泛起

Table 1: part of verb taxonomy

In table 1, node "1 自主变化 (self changing)" is a non-terminal class that has three children: "1.1 过程 (process)", "1.2 状态 (status)" and "1.3 经历 (experience)". These three classes are also non-terminal classes. They are sisters that inherit all the features of their parent "1 自主变化 (self changing)", and they also have some unique features of their own that distinguish themselves from one another. Classes "1.1.1 存现 (exist)", "1.1.2 位移 (move)" and "1.1.3 变化 (transform)" are terminal classes, because they have no child, and they are sisters. "1.2.2 自然现象 (natural phenomenon)" is a terminal class, while its brother, "1.2.1 境遇 (situation)" is a non-terminal class, since it has three children. The depth of taxonomy is not even, and among sister classes, some classes might be terminal nodes while others might be non-terminal classes. Only terminal node classes contain word senses, while non-terminal classes have only the definition of the class, which we will discuss in detail in Section 4.

3.2 Scale of CLT

The members of each terminal class are word senses. The sense entries from Xiandai Hanyu Cidian (XH, 5th edition, Commercial Press, China) are our starting point. Different word senses of a polysemous word may be grouped together into the same lexical class or put into different lexical classes. For example, verb 落 has two senses in the XH Dictionary. One is the action of things dropping as a result of gravity, as in 树叶落下 ("The leaves dropped on the ground"). Another denotes the action of descending, as in 飞机落地 ("The aircraft landed"). These two senses are grouped into the same lexical class "1.1.2 位移 (move)". 1357 word types in corpus are polysemous and have more than one sense and are classified into different lexical classes.

There are 33480 word types and 46934 sense entries in the CLT that belong to 153 terminal classes.

Noun taxonomy. 25801 noun senses are grouped into 97 terminal classes. The maximum depth of the noun taxonomy is 5. Table 2 is part of noun taxonomy.

1 具体物 (concrete)
——1.1 生物 (living creature)
———1.1.1 人 (human)
————1.1.1.1 身份 (identification): 学生, 冠军
————1.1.1.2 关系 (relative): 司令, 科长
————1.1.1.3 超人 (superman): 观音, 上帝
————1.1.1.4 其他 (other): 汉人, 小伙子
———1.1.2 动物 (animal)
————1.1.2.1 兽 (beast): 狗, 老虎
————1.1.2.2 鸟 (bird): 麻雀, 大雁
————1.1.2.3 鱼 (fish): 鲤鱼, 青蛙
————1.1.2.4 虫 (insect): 蜈蚣, 苍蝇
————1.1.2.5 微生物 (micro living): 结核菌, 酵母
———1.1.3 植物 (botany)
————1.1.3.1 草木 (plant): 常青藤, 报春花
————1.1.3.2 果实 (fruit): 银杏果, 鸭梨
———1.1.4 群体 (group)
————1.1.4.1 机构 (institute): 总统府, 医学院
————1.1.4.2 团体 (organization): 训练团, 媒体
————1.1.4.3 其他 (other): 猪群, 人类
———1.1.5 生物部分 part
————1.1.5.1 肢体 (body): 触手, 右腿
————1.1.5.2 器官 (organ): 小肠, 五脏
————1.1.5.3 其他 (other): 落叶, 鹅毛
——1.2 非生物 (non-living creature)

Table 2: part of noun taxonomy

Verb taxonomy. 15920 verb senses are grouped into 37 terminal classes. The maximum depth is 4. Table 1 shows part of verb taxonomy.

Adjective taxonomy. The adjective senses taxonomy is the smallest. There are 5213 adjective senses in 19 terminal classes. Table 3 is part of adjective taxonomy.

1 生物属性值 (attribute value of living creature)
——1.1 生理 (physiological): 年轻, 疲劳
——1.2 心理 (mental): 困, 反感
——1.3 品性 (ethic): 酸, 清高
——1.4 状况 (situation): 背运, 没出息
2 其他属性值 (other attribute value)
——2.1 物理 (physical)
———2.1.1 可度量值 (measurable): 深, 粗
———2.1.2 不可度量值 (unmeasurable): 黏, 松
——2.2 内容值 (content): 深, 粗犷
——2.3 状态值 (situation): 顺, 袅袅
——2.4 其他 (other): 毒, 经济
3 方式事件值 (attribute of behavior and event): 正面, 自动
4 时空值 (attribute of spatio-temporal)
——4.1 时间值 (temporal): 原先, 悠久
——4.2 空间值 (spatio): 浩渺, 闹哄哄

Table 3: part of adjective taxonomy

3.3 Corpus Annotation

We also used the CLT to annotate a Chinese text corpus. The corpus we annotated is called the Chinese Sense Corpus, which consists of texts of Chinese textbooks. The corpus has 2,008 texts, 51,343 word types, 1,475,913 word tokens, and 2,186,853 character instances. The corpus is developed by National University of Singapore (Singapore), Commercial Press (China) and Peking University (China). We also used this corpus to extract the linguistic features to help create the sense classes.

4 Definition Frame for CLT

According to (B. Levin, 1993), the syntactic behaviors of word are determined by the meaning of the word. Therefore, we assume that senses with similar syntactic behaviors or other linguistics features (e.g. argument structure), can be considered as in one lexical class. Table 4 shows the definition frame of verb lexical classes "1.1.1 存现 (exist)" and "1.1.2 位移 (move)" and table 5 is the definition frame of noun class "2.1.3 生理属性值 (physiological attribute)".

1.1.1 存现 (exist) (v.) Syntactic performance: + subject, + object Argument structure: subject: Theme, Location; object: Theme, Location Selectional restriction: N.A 1.1.2 位移 (move) (v.) Syntactic performance: + subject, + object Argument structure: subject: Theme; object: Location Selectional restriction: N.A

Table 4: verb classes "1.1.1 存现 (exist)" and "1.1.2 位移 (move)"

2.1.3 生理属性值 (physiological attribute) (n.) Syntactic performance: *modifier Semantic role: subject: Theme; object: Content, Experiencer Selectional restriction: in modifier-head structure, the modifier can only be nouns of Living Creature

Table 5: definition frame of noun class "2.1.3 生理属性值 (physiological attribute)"

4.1 Linguistic Features in Definition Frame

There are three components in the definition frame, and each one presents a type of linguistic features of word sense:

Syntactic performance. Each sense is eligible to occupy certain syntactic positions in sentence. Senses in the same lexical classes have similar syntactic performances. We have syntactic frames to test the syntactic performances of word senses. For example, "verb (object)" frame is used to test whether a verb sense takes object. "verb (head)" is used to test whether a verb sense occupies adverbial position. "noun (head)" tests whether a noun sense occupies modifier position. "(head) adjective" tests whether a adjective occupies complement position. In table 4, operator "+" means "takes", both "1.1.1 存现 (exist)" and "1.1.2 位移 (move)" take subject and object. Operator "*" means "cannot occupy", senses of "2.1.3 生理属性值 (physiological attribute)" class cannot occupy the modifier position in "noun (head)" frame.

Argument structure/ semantic role. For verb senses, those in the same lexical class may share same argument structure: same number of arguments and same semantic roles. For noun senses, it concerns what specific semantic roles a noun sense acts. We have a scheme to identify the number of arguments that verb sense governs, and a semantic roles list noun acts.

The identification of arguments of a word sense is based on its syntactic frame. If a particular noun sense can be in the subject or object position, we identify the semantic roles of the noun sense in the positions. Notice that it is possible for a syntactic position to have more than one type of arguments. In table 4, since both "1.1.1 存现 (exist)" and "1.1.2 位移 (move)" take a subject and an object, the semantic roles of their arguments are identified in these positions. That is why we specify the syntactic positions before the semantic role labels. These two verb classes have similar syntactic behaviors and selectional restrictions, but they are distinguished from each other by their argument structure.

We have 10 semantic roles for arguments: Agent, Theme, Patient, Experiencer, Participant, Result, Content, Instrument, Time, and Location.

Selectional restrictions. Also known as semantic preferences, selectional restriction denotes semantic constrains between word senses within a syntactic constructions.

The definition frame is set of linguistic features for creating lexical classes and identifying which class a particular word sense should be assigned to. There are three components in each definition frame, and they are used sequentially. If the syntactic features can be used to create sub-classes, or assign a particular word sense to a proper lexical class, we will not use argument structure and selectional restriction features. In other words, syntactic structures are given precedence over the other two types of features.

Some of the selectional restriction features are lexical classes in the CLT. For the "2.1.3 生理属性值 (physiological attribute)" class, it takes noun class "1.1 生物 (living creature)" as a selectional restriction. From a particular lexical class, we can trace other lexical classes via the lexical class tags in definition frame of that class. This makes the lexical classes inter-connected, a point we will discuss in greater detail in Section 4.3.

4.2 How Definition Frame Works

In this subsection we present three examples to show how a definition frame works. Example 1 shows how to use definition frames to distinguish different senses. Example 2 shows how the senses of a polysemous word are determined to belong to one lexical class. Sample 3 shows how senses of a polysemous word are determined to belong to different lexical classes.

Example 1: distinguishing word senses. Sample members from verb class "1.1.1 存现 (exist)" and "1.1.2 位移 (move)" to show how senses belong together, and how they are separated to different classes. Table 6 gives some member senses of these two classes:

1.1.1 存现 (exist) (v.)
出土 (to be excavated), 充满 (fulfill), 出现 (appear), 发生(happen)
1.1.2 位移 (move) (v.)
通过(1, pass), 上升(1, raise), 后退 (fall back), 落入 (fall into)

Table 6: sample senses (the number inside the parentheses indicates the sense number from XH)

For these 8 verb senses, they all take both subject and object:

1) [这件 文物]/subject 出土 [于 龙门石窟]/object
   the antique excavate Yu Longmen Shiku.
   The antique is excavated in Longmen Shiku.
2) [难闻的味道]/subject 充满 了 [房间]/object
   smelly De scent fulfill Le room
   The room is fulfilled with smelly scent.
3) [太阳]/subject 出现 [在 东方]/object
   sun appear at east
   The sun appeared from the east.
4) [事故]/subject 发生 [在 南京路]/object
   accident happen at Nanjing Road
   The accident is happened at Nanjing Road.
5) [火车]/subject 通过 [隧道]/object
   train pass tunnel
   The train passed the tunnel.
6) [飞机]/subject 上升 [到 高空]/object
   aircraft raise to high altitude
   The aircraft has raised to high altitude.
7) [洪水]/subject 后退 [到 警戒线 以外]/object
   flood fall back to alarm line behind
   The flood has fallen back behind the alarm line.
8) [树叶]/subject 落入 [水中]/object
   leaf fall into water inside
   The leaf is falling into the water.

In examples 1) to 8), the semantic role of the argument in the subject position is Theme, and the semantic role of the argument in the object position is Location. That's why the 8 senses are in verb class "1.1 过程 (process)". For 1) to 4), the semantic role of the argument in the subject position can be Location, and Theme for the argument in the object position (see example 1a) to 4a)), while this is illegal for 5) to 8) (see 5a) to 8a)):

1a) [龙门石窟]/subject 出土 了 [这件 文物]/object
   Longmen Shiku excavate Le the antique
   The antique is excavated in Longmen Shiku
2a) [房间]/subject 充满 了 [难闻 的 味道]/object
   room fulfill Le smelly De scent
   The room is fulfilled with smelly scent.
3a) [东方]/subject 出现 了 [太阳]/object
   east appear Le sun
   The sun appeared from the east.
4a) [南京路]/subject 发生 了 [事故]/object
   Nanjing Road happen Le accident
   The accident is happened at Nanjing Road.
5a) *[隧道]/subject 通过 [火车]/object
   tunnel pass train
6a) *[高空]/subject 升上 [飞机]/aircraft
   high altitude raise to aircraft
7a) *[警戒线]/subject 以外 后退 [洪水]/object
   alarm line behind fall back flood
8a) *[水中]/subject 落入 [树叶]/object
   water fall into leaf

Since the position of arguments of 通过, 上升, 后退 and 落入 cannot exchange (as which is legal to 出土, 充满, 出现 and 发生), they are put in class "1.1.2 位移 (move)", while 出土, 充满, 出现 and 发生 are classified into "1.1.1 存现 (exist)".

Example 2: senses of a polysemous word go to one lexical class. Chinese noun 阿姨 has three senses according to XH:

阿姨 (n.)
1. 母亲的姐妹 (sisters of mother, aunt)
2. 和母亲年龄差不多大的女性 (ladies at mother's age)
3. 保姆 (babysitter or maid)

Table 7: sense definitions of 阿姨 from XH

The three senses of 阿姨 denote human being, so they go to noun class "1.1.1 人 (human)", and we should choose each sense a lexical class from the children of "1.1.1 人 (human)". The candidates are "1.1.1.1 身份 (identification)", "1.1.1.2 关系 (relative)", "1.1.1.3 超人 (superman)" and "1.1.1.4 其他 (other)". We first exclude "1.1.1.3 超人 (superman)", which denotes fictional human, like 上帝 (God), 菩萨 (Buddha). If the senses cannot fit definition frame of either "1.1.1.1 身份 (identification)" or "1.1.1.2 关系 (relative)", then they will be put into "1.1.1.4 其他 (other)". Therefore, we need to test the senses only in the definition frames of "1.1.1.1 身份 (identification)" and "1.1.1.2 关系 (relative)". Table 8 and 9 are definition frames of "1.1.1.1 身份 (identification)", "1.1.1.2 关系 (relative)":

1.1.1.1 身份 (identification) (n.)
Syntactic performance: subject, object, modifier, head
Semantic roles: Agent, Theme, Experiencer, Patient, Participant
Selectional restrictions: if occupy head position of "modifier-head" structure, the modifier can be nouns of country, city, organization.

Table 8: definition frame of "1.1.1.1 身份 (identification)"

1.1.1.2 关系 (relative) (n.)
Syntactic performance: subject, object, modifier, head, parenthesis
Semantic roles: Agent, Theme, Experiencer, Patient, Participant
Selectional restrictions: if occupy head position of "modifier-head" structure, the modifier can be people's name

Table 9: definition frame of "1.1.1.2 关系 (relative)"

The three senses of 阿姨 can be used as "title for people" in a sentence, for people to call other people. And if they occur in the head position of a "modifier-head" structure, the modifier can be people's names, but not names of countries, cities or organizations:

9) 张 阿姨
zhang aunt/lady/maid
Mrs. Zhang/ Aunt Zhang

9a) *中国 阿姨 / 北京 阿姨 / 大学 阿姨
China aunt/ Beijing aunt/ university aunt

According to definition frame of "1.1.1.2 关系 (relative)", three senses of 阿姨 should be put into this class.

Example 3: senses of a polysemous word go to different lexical classes. In XH, Chinese verb 爆发 has two senses:

爆发 (v.)
1. 火山的岩浆冲破地壳，向四外迸出 (volcanic eruption)
2. 突然发生 (suddenly happen)

Table 10: sense definitions of 爆发

For the argument of the subject of either of the senses, the semantic roles are Theme, thus both of them are fallen into class "1 自主变化 (self changing)". Syntactically, sense 1 of 爆发 is intransitive, i.e. it cannot take object:

10) 火山 爆发 了
volcano erupt LE
The volcano is erupting.

10a) *爆发 [火山]/object 了
erupt volcano LE

While sense 2 is transitive:

11) [多个 城市]/subject 爆发 [抗议 活动]/object
several city suddenly happened protest event
Protests are suddenly happened in several cities.

According to the definition frame of sub-classes of "1 自主变化 (self changing)", "1.2 状态 (status)" is for intransitive verb senses, "1.1 过程 (process)" and "1.3 经历 (experience)" are for transitive senses. Therefore, sense 1 of 爆发 falls into either "1.1 过程 (process)" or "1.3 经历 (experience)", and sense 2 falls into "1.2 状态 (status)".

The subject of sense 2 is specific to volcano, which is a kind of geographic entity. According to the selectional restrictions of sub-classes of "1.2 状态 (status)", only "1.2.2 自然现象 (natural phenomenon)" requires geographic entity for the subject, so the lexical class for sense 2 of 爆发 is "1.2.2 自然现象 (natural phenomenon)".

For sense 1, the semantic roles of arguments of subject and object are Theme and Location, and it barely takes other roles. Semantic roles required by "1.3 经历 (experience)" are Theme, Patient, Content, Result and Experiencer, thus sense 1 of 爆发 is not belong to "1.3 经历 (experience)". Additionally, the positions of the arguments of sense 1 are exchangeable, which matches the definition frame of "1.1.1 存现 (exist)", so sense 1 of 爆发 is grouped into class "1.1.1 存现 (exist)".

4.3 Inter-Connectivity of Classes

The classes in sub-taxonomies are inter-connected, via the selectional restriction part of the definition frame of lexical classes. For example, the selectional restriction part of definition frame of "1.1.1 人 (human)":

1.1.1 人 (human) (n.) Syntactic performance: …… Semantic roles: …… Selectional restrictions: When occupying subject position in "subject-predicate" structure, requires predicates denoting: verb senses of social act, intended mental act; When occupying head position in "modifier-head" structure, requires modifiers denoting: noun senses of institute or organization, or adjective senses of human physiological, mental or social features.

Table 11: the selectional restriction part of definition frame of "1.1.1 人 (human)"

According to the selectional restrictions, senses of "1.1.1 人 (human)" collocate with verb senses of social act or intended mental act, noun senses of institute or organization, adjective senses of human physiological, mental or social features. Most of these senses can match classes in the taxonomy. There are verb classes "3.1.2 社会行为 (social behavior)", "3.3 社会活动 (social act)" denoting the meaning of social act, "3.4 心理活动 (mental act)" denoting intended meaning of intended mental act. We have noun classes with institution and organization meanings: "1.1.4.1 机构 (institute)" and "1.1.4.2 团体 (organization)". And there are adjective classes "1.2 心理 (mental)" denoting human mental features, and "1.3 品性 (ethic)" denoting human social features. So, noun class "1.1.1 人 (human)" is connected with verb classes "3.1.2 社会行为 (social behavior)", "3.3 社会活动 (social act)" and "3.4 心理活动 (mental act)", and with adjective classes "1.2 心理 (mental)" and "1.3 品性 (ethic)".

4.4 Complications

The motivation we use definition frame in building lexical taxonomy is to ensure the consistency for identifying lexical classes for word senses. The definition frame is a schema we follow when trying to assign a particular word sense to a proper lexical class and we want it to play an essential role in building and extending lexical taxonomy, but there are complications as a result of the morphological processes in Chinese.

The morphology structure of a word can mirror the syntactic structure of a phrase at the syntactic level, and this creates difficulties when classifying the words. For example, according to the definition frame of noun class "2.1 属性 (attribute)", senses belonging to this class denote a kind of attribute of entities and cannot be the subject by itself in a "subject-predicate" structure. For example, 颜色 (color) belongs to this class, the sentence 颜色 很好看 (color is beautiful) cannot be understood unless we add "host word" to form "modifier-head" structure to specify "whose/what thing's color is beautiful". So, 衣服 的 颜色 很 好看 (color of the cloth is beautiful) is interpretable, because the "host word" 衣服 is added forming "modifier-head" structure 衣服 的 颜色 (color of the cloth). In some cases, such the "host word" is a morpheme of a word. For example, in 月色 ("color of the moon"), the morpheme 月("moon") is the "host word" of 色 ("color"), so for the sense 月色, it breaks the syntactic performance rule in definition frame, therefore we cannot treat 月色 as member of "2.1 属性 (attribute)". But lexical semantically, 月色 denotes a particular attribute of moon, it doesn't make any sense if we do not put 月色 in "2.1 属性 (attribute)". Such cases also happen for verb senses, and some verb senses have an object morpheme, like 拜师 (to become a student to a mentor), 播音 (broadcast).

5 Linkability of CLT and CPB

Propbank is a corpus that annotates predicates with argument labels. It is based on Treebank, where the syntactic trees present the syntactic relations between a predicate and its arguments. Verb senses in Propbank are called "framesets", which are defined based on the argument structure of a predicate. Annotation of the arguments of a verb sense follows the framesets of the sense. Chinese Propbank (CPB) (Xue and Palmer, 2009) is based on the Chinese Treebank (Xue et al, 2005).

As one type of features for formally describing the lexical semantic meaning of a word sense, argument structure plays essential role in the CLT as well. CLT uses semantic roles of arguments globally, which is a major difference between CLT and CPB. Table 12 presents a sample of frameset of the verb "爱".

```
<id>爱</id>
<frameset cdef="" edef="" id="f1">
  <role argnum="0" argrole="love giver"/>
  <role argnum="1" argrole="thing, person loved"/>
  <frame>
      <mapping>
      <V/>
      <mapitem src="sbj" trg="arg0"/>
      <mapitem src="npobj" trg="arg1"/>
    <comment/>
</mapping>
```

Table 12: sample of frameset of "爱"

The "argrole" field is the semantic role of argument, which in CPB is individually for each frameset. There is not a global list of semantic roles for the CPB, as shown in table 12. Verb sense is described by selectional restrictions that are similar to noun lexical classes in the CLT. For "爱" in Table 12 , ARG0 is "love giver", which can be nouns denoting people; ARG1 is "thing/person loved", which can be entities or person. The lacking of global semantic role list makes the verb senses in CPB are isolated from each other and are not connected.

Although CLT and CPB are independently developed language resources, lexical meanings of verb in both are represented by argument structure. Therefore, we believe CLT and CPB are linkable by replacing CPB's semantic roles with CLT's.

6 Conclusion and Future Work

In this paper, we presented the Chinese Lexical Taxonomy, and the Chinese Sense Corpus annotated with the lexical classes in the taxonomy. Each lexical class in CLT is described via a definition frame, which is collection of linguistic features. We show the definition frame reduces the possible inconsistency that may happen in taxonomy creation. Compared to WordNet and HowNet style, CLT is being unique on the way we create it. The methodology creating CLT enables its predictivity for the possible lexical classes of an OOV word sense. It also maintains the inter-consistency among different annotators. The definition frame is the key to our goal, which is constituted of steps can be followed both in making corpus annotation and taxonomy expanding.

We also compare the CLT with the CPB. The absence of a global semantic role list in the CPB makes verb senses disconnected from each other. Since there is not a global list of semantic roles in the CPB, we will use the semantic roles of the CLT to annotate arguments in CPB. We will also add new semantic roles if the current semantic roles are insufficient for the CPB. We will also acquire a list of syntactic frames and alternations to create a more fine-grained definition frames for the CLT.

Acknowledgement:
This work is supported partial by DARPA via Contract HR0011-11-C-0145. All views expressed in this paper are those of the authors and do not necessarily represent the view of DARPA.

References

Bai, Xiaopeng. 2012. Building Word Sense Taxonomy and Automatic Annotation for Mandarin Chinese. PhD Thesis, National University of Singapore.

Bai, Xiaopeng. 2008. The Word Sense Category based on Semantic Features of Argument. *Proceeding of Chinese Lexical Semantics Workshop*, Singapore.

Chen, Qunxiu. 2001. Expanding of Machine Tractable Dictionary of Contemporary Chinese Predicate Verbs and Research on Relations of Slots Centering on Noun of Contemporary Chinese. *Applied Linguistics (Yuyan Wenzi Yingyong)*, No. 4, P98-04.

Chen Xiaohe. 1998. A Lexical Classification System for Language Engineering. *Applied Linguistics (Yuyan Wenzi Yingyong)*, No. 2, P71-76.

Ciaramita, Massimiliano & Johnson, Mark. 2003. Supersense tagging of unknown nouns in WordNet. *Proceedings of the 2003 conference on Empirical methods in natural language processing*, Stroudsburg, PA, USA.

Dong, Zhendong & Dong, Qiang. 2006. Hownet And the Computation of Meaning. World Scientific Publishing Company, Singapore.

Fellbaum, Christiane. 1998. WordNet: An Electronic Lexical Database. MIT Press, USA.

Gao, Liqi et al. 2005. Thesaurus-Based Semantic Smoothing in Language Modeling for Chinese Document Retrieval. *International Conference on Mutilingual Information Processing.*

Picca, David et al. 2007. Semantic Domains and Supersense Tagging for Domain-Specific Ontology Learning. *Conference RIAO2007*, Pittsburgh, PA, USA.

Levin, Beth. 1993. English Verb Classes and Alternations: A Preliminary Investigation. The University of Chicago Press, Chicago, US.

TIAN, Jiu-le et al. 2010. Words Similarity Algorithm Based on Tongyici Cilin in Semantic Web Adaptive Learning System. *Journal of Jilin University (Information Science Edition)*, 2010-06.

Wang, Hui et al. 2003. The Specification of The Semantic Knowledge Base of Contemporary Chinese. *Journal of Chinese Language and Computing*, 13(2).

Xue, Nianwen, et al. 2005. The Penn Chinese Treebank: Phrase Structure Annotation of a Large Corpus. *Natural Language Engineering*, 11(2):207-238.

Xue, Nianwen. 2008. Labeling Chinese Predicates with Semantic Roles. *Computational Linguistics*, 34 (2): 225-255.

Xue, Nianewn and Palmer, Martha. 2009. Adding semantic roles to the Chinese Treebank. *Natural Language Engineering*, 15(1):143-172.

Extending and Scaling up the Chinese Treebank Annotation

Xiuhong Zhang, Nianwen Xue
Brandeis University
Waltham, MA 02453, USA
{xhzhang,xuen}@brandeis.edu

Abstract

We discuss on-going efforts to scale up the Chinese Treebank annotation and extending Chinese treebanking to informal genres like conversational speech, news groups and weblogs, as well as discussion forums. The original Chinese Treebank annotation scheme was designed for formal genres such as newswire and magazine articles, where the language is very formal and each document is carefully edited. When moving to informal genres, we can no longer assume that the data is error-free and we have to extend the annotation scheme to account for disfluencies. We show that the disfluencies can be characterized into a finite set of categories, consistent with what has been reported in theoretical linguistic literature. Treebanking is also a time-consuming process that requires extensive linguistic training from annotators, and the limited pool of qualified treebankers is a major obstacle for large-scale treebanking efforts. To address bottleneck, we implemented a procedure that decomposes the treebanking process into five self-contained steps. In so doing, we reduced the cognitive load on the annotators at each step and thus enlarged the annotator pool, and we show that we are able to increase the throughput by 30%.

1. Introduction

Large-scale treebanks [13,16] have proved to be instrumental in advancing the state of the art in syntactic parsing, a fundamental technology in Natural Language Processing. Early treebanking efforts started with the annotation of carefully edited textual data such as Wall Street Journal articles (Penn Treebank) and Xinhua newswire articles (Chinese Treebank) where the data can be assumed to be error-free. There is a growing need, however, for annotated data in informal genres, which include conversational speech, news groups, web blogs, and online discussion forums. Annotation of such informal genres requires substantial extension to the original annotation guidelines to cover new linguistic (and sometimes non-linguistic) phenomena. We show that while these new linguistic phenomena are diverse, they have clear patterns that can be characterized and classified, a pre-requisite to successful annotation.

Treebanking is a time-consuming process and scaling up treebanking efforts while maintaining annotation quality is always a challenge. This is because it takes a long time to train new treebankers and they have to have significant prior formal linguistic training to be able to understand the grammatical formalisms and make the necessary linguistic distinctions between different types of linguistic structures. These requirements severely limit the pool of qualified treebankers, making it difficult to scale up an annotation effort simply by hiring more qualified annotators, even if cost is not a factor. In reality, cost is another factor that has to be considered.

We address this challenge by decomposing the treebanking process into smaller, self-contained tasks, which reduces the cognitive load on the annotators so that more annotators can participate without having to understand all aspects of the treebanking annotation efforts. This is in keeping with the trend of using crowd-sourcing to quickly collect large amount of annotated data using platforms such as Mechanic Turk, although we did not go as far, as there has been no evidence thus far for successful treebanking effort by using a large number of minimally trained annotators, to the best of our knowledge. What we sought is a middle ground between crowd sourcing and the traditional treebanking practice of using highly trained annotators. The rest of the paper is organized as follows. In Section 2, we give a brief overview of the Chinese Treebank annotation scheme. Section 3 describes characteristics of informal genres and how the new phenomena are treated in our revised annotation scheme. In Section 4 we present our new workflow that decomposes our annotation task into smaller, self-contained tasks. We also discuss advantages of such an approach and problems that still exist. Section 5 presents some relevant statistics and Section 6 discusses related work. Section 7 concludes our paper.

2 An overview of the existing Chinese Treebank annotation framework

The Chinese Treebank (CTB) is a fully segmented, part-of-speech (POS) tagged, and syntactically bracketed Chinese corpus annotated in a phrase structure framework [16]. The CTB adopts the same architectural and representation framework used by the Penn Treebank [13], as is natural given the success of the Penn Treebank annotation style and the affinity of the research groups. Just like the Penn Treebank, the CTB has three layers of annotation: word segmentation / tokenization, part-of-speech (POS) tagging, and syntactic bracketing. There are three sets of guidelines [17,18,19], one for each layer, and the syntactic bracketing guidelines are by far the most complex among the three. At the part-of-speech tagging layer, each word token in the corpus is assigned one of the 34 tags in the CTB POS tagset. At the syntactic bracketing level, the CTB annotation framework uses three types of formal devices to represent the syntactic structure of a sentence. They include labeled brackets for representing constituents (See Appendix 1 for a list of phrase labels), function categories for representing the grammatical functions in the form of dash tags attached to the phrase label, and empty categories and traces that represent phonological null elements and long-distance dependencies. An example taken from the Penn Chinese Treebank is presented below, and this example has all three elements.

(1)

```
(IP-HLN (NP-SBJ (NN 经济/economics)
                (NN 专家/expert))
        (VP (VV 提出/propose)
            (NP-OBJ (CP-APP (IP (NP-SBJ (-NONE- pro))
                                (VP (ADVP (AD 进一步/further))
                                    (VP (VV 扩大/expand)
                                        (NP-OBJ (NP-PN (NR 海南/Hainan))
                                                (PP (P 对/toward)
                                                    (NP (NN 外/outside)))
                                                (NP (NN 开放/open))))))
                            (DEC 的/DE))
                    (NP (NN 系列/series)
                        (NN 建议/recommendation)))))
```

"Economic experts proposed a series of recommendations to further expand the opening of Hainan to the outside."

The original CTB was annotated in two stages. The first stage is the word segmentation/POS tagging stage where Chinese sentences are segmented into words and each word token is assigned a POS tag. The second stage is the syntactic bracketing stages, where each constituent is grouped together and assigned a phrase label. Where appropriate, one or more functional tag is appended to the phrase label and empty categories are added.

3 Extending the Chinese Treebank annotation to informal genres

The original CTB annotation scheme [2] was designed for genres such as newswire and magazines, where the language is very formal and each document is carefully edited. As we move to informal genres such as forum discussions, web blogs, online instant chatting, telephone phone conversations and so on, we encounter many new phenomena that have to be accounted for. These include typographic errors, incomplete sentences, non-speech elements such as background noises that are recorded in transcriptions of speech, disfluent (and yet understandable) utterances. These new phenomena fall into two broad categories: non-linguistic phenomena such as typographical errors that are introduced due to haste and carelessness, and linguistic phenomena such as disfluencies in conversational speech where a speaker has to repair the utterance s/he produced under the time pressure. We discuss these broad categories and how they are treated in our annotation framework in the next two subsections. As of this writing, we have annotated over 400,000 words in the informal genre based on the extended annotation guidelines.

3.1 Typographical errors and non-speech elements

Typographical errors do not have a linguistic explanation, and they are produced due to carelessness, fatigue, or haste on the part of the authors or transcribers. Because we adhere to the practice of "not altering the source data and only adding annotation" in the annotation process, we add tags at both the part-of-speech tagging and syntactic bracketing levels to mark up these errors where appropriate.

The first type of typographic error is mis-spelled Chinese characters. Since words with this type of typographic error usually can still be interpreted, we segment and POS-tag them as if we were annotating their correct counterpart. For example, we annotate 幸口开河 as if it were 信口开河. We treat it as one word and label it as VV at the POS level. We do NOT change the original characters in the text, as a matter of principle.

(2) 幸(信)口开河/VV
talk irresponsibly "talk irresponsibly"

The second type of typographic error is characters written in the wrong order. It is different from the first type in that the word boundaries are messed up and cannot be segmented and POS-tagged as if it were correct. In this case we add a new POS tag NOI ("Noise") to tag the messed up parts and group the entire string as TYPO, a phrase label:

(3) (TYPO 事/NOI 类/NOI 各/NOI 故/NOI)

	?	type	each ?
Correct:	各/DT	类/M	事故/NN
	every	type	accident

"all sorts of accidents"

The mechanical errors are random and cannot be fully anticipated, so broad encompassing categories such as NOI (POS tag), TYPO (phrase label) are used to label them.

We also added a phrase label SKIP to mark up sequences of non-speech elements, indicating that this portion can be ignored when the text is interpreted. Non-speech elements include background noises recorded in speech transcripts, boundary markers and so on.

3.2 New linguistic phenomena in informal genres

There are also a large number of new linguistic phenomena that cannot be accommodated by the original annotation framework, and these include incomplete sentences, embedded speech, fillers and other types of disfluencies. These are linguistic issues whose cognitive processes and pragmatic effects have been widely discussed in the literature [3] [4] [5] [6] [7]. Based on the studies of these issues in the literature, we added 4 phrase labels and 2 functional tags to account for them.

Incomplete utterances (INC)

In informal genres, especially in conversational speech, there are often incomplete utterances. To label such utterances, we added the phase label INC to the original annotation scheme. INC is a label for root nodes only, similar to FRAG, IP, CP in the original guidelines. It is different from FRAG in that the latter is semantically complete even though it does not have the typical structure of a sentence. Utterances marked INC are incomplete both in its syntactic structure and in its semantic interpretation. (4) is an example.

(4)

```
(INC (CP-CND (ADVP (CS 如果/if))
                    (IP (NP-SBJ (PN 他们/they))
                        (VP (VV 来/come))))
     (PU ，)
     (ADVP (AD 那/then)
     (NP-SBJ (PN 我/I)
     (VP-UNF (ADVP (AD 就/then))))))
```

"If they come, then I will …"

Fillers (FLR)

In conversational speech, the speaker often needs to think about what s/he wants to say and use fillers to buy her/him some time. The linguistic devices s/he uses for this purpose are called fillers. Fillers do not have a significant role to play in the syntactic structure of a sentence and they do not add to the semantic content of a sentence either. Fillers form a close set because there are only a finite number of them, but there is little restriction on where they can occur in the sentence. Fillers in

Chinese include “嗯/um, uh-huh” , “呃/Ugh”, “唔/oh”, “啊/Ah”, “这个/Eh”, “那个/Eh”, etc.

(5)
(IP (NP-SBJ (PN 你/you))
 (VP (ADVP (AD 多/more))
 (FLR (INF 那个/that one))
 (VP (VV 长/grow)
 (NP-OBJ (QP (CLP (M 个/CL)))
 (NP (NN 心眼儿/mind))))))
“You should be more mindful.”

Disfluency (DFL)

In conversational speech, a speaker often has to repeat what s/he has just said, or abandon what s/he just said and restart with revised content. This is a phenomenon called *repair* in speech literature. There is extensive literature on speech repairs [8][9][13]. Typically, a speech repair instance can be characterized as a template that consists of a *reparandum* and an *alteration* [13]. The reparandum is the speech sequence that is erroneous or inappropriate, while the alteration represents the correction of the problematic sequence. The alteration can delete from, add to, substitute for, or repeat the problematic sequence. Or it can be a fresh restart that has little resemblance to the problematic sequence. The alteration is essential to the completeness of the syntactic structure of a sentence, while the reparandum, like fillers, can be considered to be “extra” material. We label such extra material with the phrase label DFL. The idea is that when such extra material is stripped, the remaining structure is a syntactically well-formed sentence.

(6a) Repetition
(IP (PP-TMP (P 到/up to)
 (NP (NT 现在/now)))
 (FLR (SP 啊/Ah))
 (PU ，)
 (NP-SBJ (-NONE- **pro**))
 (VP (DFL (VP (ADVP (AD 已经/already))
 (VP (VE 有/have))))
 (PU ，)
 (ADVP (AD 已经/already))
 (VP (VE 有/have)
 (IP-OBJ (NP-SBJ (DNP (DNP (QP (CD 七百多万/more than 7 million)) (DEG 的))
 (DNP (NP (NN 个人/individual travelling 游))
 (DEG 的))
 (NP (NN 旅客/visitors))))
 (VP (VV 来/come)
 (NP-PN-OBJ (NR 香港/Hongkong)))))))
“Up to now, there have been, have been more than 7 million individual visitors visiting Hongkong.”

(6b) Substitution
((NP-Q (SPK [Speaker_A1])
 (DFL (NT 昨天/yesterday))
 (FLR (IJ 哎/ah))
 (PU ,)
 (NP (NT 今天/today))
 (SP 啊/Ah)
 (PU ?)))

“Yesterday, (you mean) today?”

(6c) Restart
((CP-Q (SPK [Speaker_A])
 (INTJ (NN 咯/um))
 (PU ,)
 (DFL (ADVP (INF 那/then))
 (NP-SBJ (PN 它/it))
 (VP-UNF (ADVP (AD 怎么/how come))))
 (PU ,)
 (IP (NP-SBJ (-NONE- **pro**))
 (VP (ADVP (AD 不/not))
 (VP (VV 知道/know)
 (NP-OBJ (DP (DT 怎么/how))
 (QP (CLP (M 回/Classifer)))
 (NP (NN 事儿/matter))))))
 (SP 啊/Ah)
 (PU .)))

“Uh, then how come it, I don’t know what the matter is.”

Embedded utterances (MBD)

Embedded utterances are cases where the utterance of one speaker is embedded in the utterance of another speaker. This happens when one speaker interrupts when another speaker has not finished his/her sentence. The embedded utterances are usually short comments that indicate consent, etc.

(7)
(SPK [Speaker_A])
(CP (IP (CP-ADV (IP (NP-SBJ (-NONE- **pro**))
 (VP (ADVP (CS 一/at first))
 (VP (VV 开始/begin))))
 (SP 吧/ba))
 (PU ,)
 (MBD (INTJ (SPK [Speaker_B])
 (IJ 啊/Ah)
 (PU ,)))
 (SPK [Speaker_A])
 (CP (IP (NP-SBJ (PN 他/he))
 (VP (VV 要/want)
 (VP (VP (VV 做/do)
 (NP-OBJ (NN 科学/science)
 (NN 研究/research)))
 (VP (VV 用/use)))))
 (SP 的/DE))
 (PU ,)
 (DFL (IP (NP-SBJ (-NONE- **pro**))
 (VP-UNF (VC 是/BE)
 (PP (P 用/by means of)
 (NP (PN 我/I)))))
 (DEG 的/DE))
 (PU ,)
 (CP (IP (NP-SBJ (-NONE- **pro**))
 (VP (VC 是/BE)
 (IP-PRD (NP-SBJ (PN 我/I))

(VP (MSP 去/go)
(VP (VV 申请/apply))))))
(SP 的/DE))))

"Speaker A: 'At first'
Speaker B: 'Ah'
Speaker A: 'He wanted to use it for scientific research. He used mine, it's me who applied for it.'"

In addition to the new phrase labels above, we have also added two new functional tags (-DIS,-UNF). –DIS represents discourse markers and – UNF denotes incomplete phrases in a syntactic parse. –UNF is different from INC in that INC is a root node label (label for the entire sentence) while –UNF is functional tag indicating a non-root node label is incomplete. In general, functional tags can be attached to any phrase label to provide additional information. A constituent bearing the -UNF tag can be a NP, VP, etc.. A constituent bearing the –DIS tag is usually an adverbial phrase (ADVP), although it can be other types of phrases.

-DIS: functional tag indicating discourse marker

In spoken discourse, some lexical items demonstrate the discourse function of linking two stretches of discourse, with their original semantic meanings weakened or 'bleached' [10] [11]. They serve to indicate that an adverbial phrase functions as a discourse marker rather than an indicator of time, location, manner, reason and so on. The following is an example of discourse markers:
"*就是说/that is to say*" （sometimes for further clarification, but often indicates that the speaker has got something to say)

(8)
(CP (IP (CP-CND (IP (ADVP (AD 所以/so))
(NP-SBJ (PN 你/you))
(VP (ADVP (AD 要是/if))
(VP (VV 回来/return))))
(SP 的话/if))
(NP-SBJ (PN 你/you))
(VP (ADVP (AD 就/then))
(VP (VV 可以/can)
(VP (VV 知道/know)
(PU ,)
(IP-OBJ (ADVP-DIS (AD 就是说/that' s to say))
(PU ,)
(FLR (INF 这/this))
(NP-SBJ (DP (PN 那些/those))
(NP (NN 东西/stuff)))
(FLR (SP 啊/Ah))
(PU ,)
(VP (PP-ADV (P 跟/with)
(NP (PN 他/him)))
(VP (VV 对路/fit))))))))
(SP 啦/la)
(PU .))

"So if you come back, then you know, that's to say, those stuff fit him.'"

-UNF: Functional tag indicating unfinished constituent

(9)
(INC (CP-CND (ADVP (CS 如果))
(IP (NP-SBJ (PN 他们))
(VP (VV 来))))
(PU ，)
(ADVP (AD 那)
(NP-SBJ (PN 我)
(VP-UNF (ADVP (AD 就))))))
"If they come, then I will …"

For the sake of completeness, the revised tagsets (phrase labels and functional tags) for the Chinese Treebank are presented in Tables 1 and 2 respectively, with new tags marked by *.

Label	Description	Label	Description
ADJP	Adjective phrase	LCP	Localizer phrase
ADVP	Adverb phrase	LST	List marker
CLP	Classifier phrase	*MBD	Embedded utterance
CP	Clause headed by a complementi Zer	IP	Simple clause
*DFL	Disfluency	NP	Noun phrase
DNP	Phrase formed by "XP+DEG"	PP	Prepositiona l phrase
DP	Determiner Phrase	PRN	Parenthetica l
DVP	Phrase formed by "XP+DEV"	QP	Quantifier phrase
*FLR	Filler	*SKIP	Skip
FRAG	Fragment	*TYPO	Typographic error
*INC	Incomplete	UCP	Unlike coordination
IP	Simple sentence	VP	verbphrase
LCP	Localizer Phrase		

Table 1: revised phrase labels. * indicates new labels

Function tags			
Tag	**Description**	**Tag**	**Description**
ADV	Adverbial	MNR	Manner
APP	Appositive	OBJ	Direct object
BNF	Beneficiary	PN	Proper noun phrase
CND	Condition	PRD	Predicate
DIR	Direction	PRP	Purpose or reason
*DIS	Discourse connective	Q	Question
EXT	Extent	SBJ	Subject
FOC	Focus	TMP	Temporal
HLN	Headline	TPC	Topic
IJ	Interjective	TTL	Title
IMP	Imperative	*UNF	Incomplete phrase
IO	Indirect Object	VOC	Vocative
LGS	Logical subject	WH	Wh-phrase
LOC	Locative		

Table 2: Revised functional tags. * indicates new tags

4 Scaling up the CTB annotation by broadening the annotator pool

The original Chinese Treebank was annotated in two stages: the word segmentation/POS tagging stage and the syntactic bracketing stage. In the word segmentation/POS-tagging stage, an annotator adds word boundaries and POS tags to words in a corpus. In the bracketing stage, an annotator groups the constituents and organizes them into a hierarchical structure, adding functional categories and empty categories to the syntactic structure of a sentence, following a set of treebanking guidelines that are close to 200 pages [20].

Moving to informal genres and scaling up the annotation effort magnify two challenges in Chinese Treebanking. The first one is that in informal genres, the rules for using punctuation marks are very loose, and in conversational speech, punctuations are of course not used at all and they are added later on by transcribers. These lead to unreliable sentence boundaries if we follow the standard practice of using periods, question marks and exclamation marks as markers of sentence boundary. Another challenge is that as we increase the volume of annotation, we need more trained treebankers. Training a treebanker takes a long time and treebankers have to come with extensive formal linguistic training to begin with.

To meet these challenges, we implemented a new workflow that consists of five stages, illustrated graphically in Figure 1. The new workflow decomposes the treebanking process into five self-contained steps, namely, sentence boundary detection, word segmentation/POS tagging, constituent grouping, functional category and empty category annotation, and post-processing and validation. Compared with the original Chinese Treebank workflow, we added a sentence boundary detection stage where we perform sentence segmentation. More importantly, we decomposed the bracketing stage, the most difficult aspect of treebanking, into two steps. The first step is to group the constituents of a sentence into a hierarchical structure. This step produces a bare-bone syntactic parse for a sentence. In the second step, we add functional tags and empty categories to the bare-bone structure to produce a full parse.

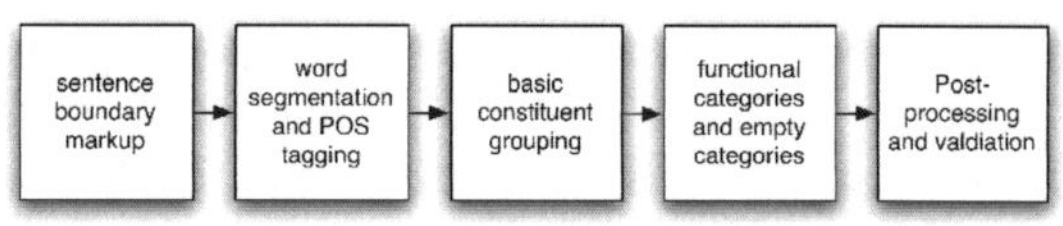

Figure 1: Annotation work flow

The purpose of the new workflow is to reduce the cognitive load of the annotators and thus increase the pool of qualified annotators. Treebankers now do not all have to understand all aspects of treebanking. Some treebankers can concentrate on grouping the constituents correctly and others can focus on the functional tags and empty categories. This is in keeping with the spirit of crowdsourcing [12], the essence of which is to design annotation tasks in a way that increases the annotator pool so that minimally trained annotators can work on them. Our new workflow can be viewed as a small step in that direction. As a result of this new workflow, four treebankers rather than two can work on this project. We did an internal performance evaluation about the amount of data we are able to annotate per week, and compared to our work rate prior to the introduction of the new work flow, our speed accelerated by 30% with more consistency and accuracy.
The new workflow also allow cross-checking between different layers of annotation. Treebankers working on the bare-bone structure can check er-

rors in word segmentation and POS tagging, and treebankers working on functional tags and empty categories can check the bare-bone structures. The new workflow also opens up more opportunities for automation. Automatic pre-processing was performed at each step. Sentence-segmented data is automatically word segmented and POS-tagged using a word segmenter/POS-tagged we developed in-house [14] before they are manually corrected. Word segmented and POS-tagged data is then automatically parsed using the Berkeley parser retrained on available Chinese Treebank data. Finally, we developed a simple rule-based tool that automatically adds functional tags and empty categories to the bare-bone parses before they are corrected.

5 Some relevant statistics

Our raw texts include newswire, magazine articles, broadcast news, broadcast conversations, and weblogs. As of this writing, we have annotated over 400,000 words in the informal genre based on the extended annotation guidelines. Here is some statistics based on an analysis of 461 files with 396,874 words:

label	occurrences
DFL tags	2819
FLR tags	1854
INC tags	637
TYPO tags	13
SKIP tags	281
MBD tags	167
-DIS tags	150
-UNF tags	924

6 Related work

The success of the Penn Treebank [15] has spurred the development of a large number of treebanks in many different languages, but most of the early treebanking efforts are directed at the formal genres. Specific to Chinese, there are number of significant treebanking efforts (Sinica Treebank and Tsinghua Treebank), but the Chinese Treebank is one of the early ones. There are relatively few efforts directed at annotating informal genres. The Switchboard Corpus is one notable exception [17]. It is a speech corpus annotated following guidelines that extend the Penn Treebank annotation guidelines. To the best of our knowledge, there is no similar annotation in Chinese.

7 Conclusion

We presented our effort to extend the Chinese Treebank annotation to informal genres, and in the process, we extended the Chinese Treebank annotation guidelines to account for new linguistic phenomena, which include typographic errors and disfluent speech. We also presented a new workflow aimed at scaling up the current treebanking effort. The new workflow decomposes the complex treebanking into more manageable subtasks. In doing so, it reduces the cognitive load on treebankers and thus increases the annotator pool.

Acknowledgements
We gratefully acknowledge the effort of our annotators. This work is funded by the DAPRA via contract HR0011-11-C-0145 entitled "Linguistic Resources for Multilingual Processing". All opinions expressed here are those of the authors and do not necessarily reflect the views of DARPA.

References

[1] Nancy Ide, Laurent Romary, International standard for a linguistic annotation framework, SEALTS '03 Proceedings of the HLT-NAACL 2003 workshop of Software engineering and architecture of language technology systems – Volume 8 Pages 25-30

[2] Nianwen Xue, Fei Xia, Fu-Dong Chiou and Martha Palmer. 2005. The Penn Chinese Treebank: Phrase Structure Annotation of a Large Corpus. Natural Language Engineering, Volume 11 / Issue 02 / June 2005 , pp 207-238

-

[3] Yan Wang, 2011. A Discourse-Pragmatic Functional Study of the Discourse Markers Japanese *Ano* and Chinese *Nage*. Intercultural Communication Studies XX: 2 (2011)

[4] Arnold, J. E., and M. K. Tanenhaus. in press. Disfluency effects in comprehension: How new information can become accessible. The processing and acquisition of reference, ed. by E.Gibson and N. Perlmutter. MIT Press

[5] Blackmer, E. R., and J. L. Mitton. 1991. Theories of monitoring and the timing of repairs in spontaneous speech. Cognition 39.173-194.

[6] Bortfeld, H., S. D. Leon, J. E. Bloom, M. F. Schober, and S. E. Brennan. 2001. Disfluency rates in spontaneous speech: Effects of age, relationship, topic, role, and gender. Language and Speech 44.123-147.

[7] Shriberg, E. 1996. Disfluencies in Switchboard. Proceedings, International Conference on Spoken Language Processing, Addendum, 11-14. Philedephia

[8] Lin, Che-kuang, et al., 2005 Important and New Features with Analysis for Disfluency Interruption Point (IP) Detection in Spontaneous Mandarin Speech. Proceedings of DiSS'05, Disfluency in Spontaneous Speech Workshop

[9] Georgila, Kallirroi, et al., 2010 Cross-Domain Speech Disfluency Detection. ACL

[10] Biq, Yung-O. 2001. The Grammaticalization of Jiushi and Jiushishuo in Mandarin Chinese. Concentric: Studies in English Literature and Linguistics 27. 53-74.

[11] Su, Lily I-wen. 1998. Conversational coherence: The use of ranhou in Chinese spoken discourse. In Shuanfan Huang (ed.), Selected papers from the second international symposium on languages in Taiwan, 167-181. Taipei: Crane

[12] Crowdsourcing Translation: Professional Quality from Non-Professionals. Omar Zaidan and Chris Callison-Burch, 2011. In Proceedings ACL-2011.

[13] Tseng, S.-C. 2006. Repairs in Mandarin conversation. *Journal of Chinese Linguistics* 34(1): 80-120.

[14] Nianwen Xue. 2003. Chinese Word Segmentation as Character Tagging. International Journal of Computational Linguistics and Chinese Language Processing, 8(1):29-48.

[15] Mitchell P. Marcus, Mary Ann Marcinkiewicz, and Beatrice Santorini. 1993. Building a large annotated corpus of English: the penn treebank. *Comput. Linguist.* 19, 2 (June 1993), 313-330.

[16] Nianwen Xue, Fu-Dong Chiou and Martha Palmer, 2002, Building a Large-Scale Annotated Chinese Corpus. In Proceedings of the 19th. International Conference on Computational Linguistics (COLING 2002), Taipei, Taiwan, 2002.

[17] Godfrey, J. J., Holliman, E. C., and McDaniel, J., "SWITCHBOARD: Telephone speech corpus for research and development," Proc. IEEE Int. Conf. Acoust. Speech Sig. Proc., pp. 517-520, 1992.

[18] Xia, Fei. 2000a. The Segmentation Guidelines for the Penn Chinese Treebank 3.0. _University of Pennsylvania Technical Report, IRCS00-06

[19] Xia, Fei. 2000b. The POS Tagging Guidelines for the Penn Chinese Treebank 3.0. University of Pennsylvania Technical Report, IRCS00-07

[20] Xue, Nianwen and Fei Xia. 2000. The Syntactic Bracketing Guidelines for the Penn Chinese Treebank 3.0. University of Pennsylvania Technical Report, IRCS00-08

The CIPS-SIGHAN CLP 2012 Chinese Word Segmentation on MicroBlog Corpora Bakeoff

Huiming Duan **Zhifang Sui** **Ye Tian** **Wenjie Li**
Key Laboratory of Computational Linguistics (Peking University)
Ministry of Education, CHINA
{duenhm, szf, ytian, lwj}@pku.edu.cn

Abstract

The CIPS-SIGHAN CLP 2012 Chinese Word Segmentation on MicroBlog Corpora Bakeoff was held in the autumn of 2012. This bake-off task of Chinese word segmentation is focused on the performance of Chinese word segmentation algorithms on MicroBlog corpora. 17 groups submitted 20 results, among which the best system has all the P, R and F values near 95%, and the average values of the 17 systems are 0.8931, 0.8981 and 0.8953, respectively.

1 Preface

After years of intensive researches, Chinese word segmentation has achieved a quite high precision. Five prior word segmentation bakeoffs, have been successfully conducted in 2003 (Sproat and Emerson, 2003), 2005 (Emerson, 2005), 2006 (Levow, 2006), 2007 (Jin and Chen, 2007) and 2012 (Zhao and Liu, 2010). These evaluations have established benchmarks for word segmentation with which researchers could evaluate their segmentation system.

However, the performance of segmentation is not so satisfying for the MicroBlog corpora. The corpus of a specific domain may have its characteristics in vocabulary, sentence pattern and style. MicroBlog makes no exception. The MicroBlog texts are much similar to oral expression, with a casual style and less deliberation in writing, resulting in a simple and comfortable style: the MicroBlog style. Like other domains, the vocabulary used in MicroBlog texts includes special "terms" and symbols, with which the authors may attract the reader's attention using simple and witty expressions. The MicroBlog style also indicates usage of words inconsistent with normative language, including homophonic word, character variants, word consisting of letters and misusage of punctuation.

In consideration of the characteristics described above, a successful word segmentation system on the MicroBlog corpora should take into consideration the special linguistic phenomena of the MicroBlog corpora and develop corresponding strategies, in addition to the techniques used for general-purpose word segmentation. This CIPS-SIGHAN-2012 bake-off task of Chinese word segmentation will focus on the performance of Chinese word segmentation algorithms on MicroBlog corpora.

2 Task Descriptions

This evaluation involves the following task: opened evaluation on simplified Chinese word segmentation task. This task provides no training set, and participants are free to use data learned or model trained from any resources.

Only a tiny amount of segmented data is given as a format reference of the segmentation systems, which consists of original data and segmented data. The standard of segmentation is in accord with the *Specification for Corpus Processing at Peking University*[1].

Most of the corpus used in this evaluation is selected from the randomly-collected large-scale MicroBlog corpora. Moreover, we manually added the MicroBlog corpus after new events to the corpora, in order to carry out new experiments of evaluation methods. The final corpora consist of 5000 sentences (or articles, strictly. For simplicity, we refer to the individual article as a sentence, since most of the MicroBlog articles consist of only one sentence.)

For evaluation, we adopt the evaluation method used in previous bake-off tasks, and use precision, recall and F-measure to measure the over-

[1] http://www.icl.pku.edu.cn/icl_groups/corpus/coprus-annotation.htm

all performance of a system. Metrics used in this bake-off task are:

$$\text{Precision} = \frac{\text{Number of words correctly segmented}}{\text{Number of words segemented}} \times 100\%$$

$$\text{Recall} = \frac{\text{Number of words correctly segmented}}{\text{Number of words in the reference}} \times 100\%$$

$$\text{F measure} = \frac{2 \cdot \text{Precision} \cdot \text{Recall}}{\text{Precision} + \text{Recall}}$$

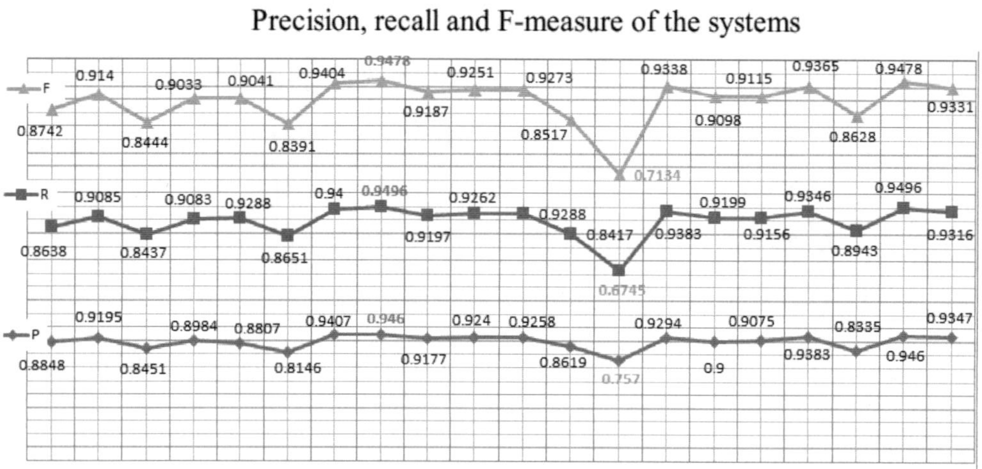

Figure 1 Precision, recall and F measure of the systems

3 Performance of the Contestants

Table 1 lists all the 17 groups of the bake-off task.

Site name	Contact
NLP group at the University of Macau	Longyue Wang (2 systems submitted)
Beijing Institute of Technology	Haizhao Lei
Beijing Information Science & Technology University	Chuan Xu
Beijing University of Posts and Telecommunications	Caixia Yuan
Dalian University of Technology	Jing Zhang
Fudan University	Xipeng Qiu
Individual	Kaixu Zhang
Harbin Institute of Technology	Yijia Liu
Harbin Institute of Technology at Weihai	Xiao Yang
Hefei University of Technology	Xiao Sun
Heilongjiang University	Heyu
Nanjing University	Bin Li (3 systems submitted)
Soochow University	Richen Xu
Zhengzhou University	Hongying Zan
Institute of Software, Chinese Academy of Sciences	Le Sun
Shenzhen Institute of Advanced Technology, Chinese Academy of Sciences	Dan Tian
Institute of Automation, Chinese Academy of Sciences	Saike He

Table 1 List of contestants.

The maximal, minimal and average performances are listed as follows.

	Precision	Recall	F-measure	Number of correct sentences	Percentage of correct sentences
Max	0.946	0.9496	0.9478	2244	44.88%
Min	0.757	0.6745	0.7134	186	3.72%
Ave	0.8931	0.8981	0.8953	1370	27.396%

Table 2 Overall performance of the systems.

4 Results and Analysis

In addition to the traditional evaluation measures (precision, recall and F-measure), we added additional analyses and tests to gain a comprehensive view of the systems.

4.1 Performance of sentence segmentation

As indicated in Figure 2, the performances of sentence-level segmentation (the percentage of the correctly-segmented sentence) are uniformly lower than 50%, despite the fact that the precision, recall and F-measure of word-level segmentation of the systems reach 0.95. (Note: the arrangement of Figure 2 is different with figures above.)

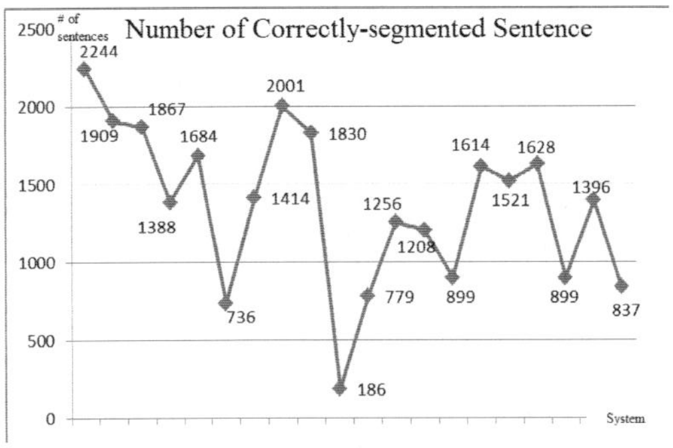

Figure 2 Number of correctly-segmented sentences of the systems.

Automatic word segmentation is known as the first step towards Chinese natural language processing. However, satisfactory results have not been yielded as far as the performance of sentence-level segmentation is concerned. Through investigating a series of test points, we can make further analysis and evaluation of the systems.

4.2 Test point evaluations

Test points are set to measure the relative strengths and weaknesses of the systems and to provide reference for further evaluation and improvement of segmentation systems, even if the test point evaluations are not fully convincing.

4.2.1 Settings

We chose 10 test points for this bake-off task: general term, MicroBlog term, symbols and emoticons, new word (unregistered word), location name, person name, proper name, combination ambiguity, overlapping ambiguity and rule-based combination of words.

test point 0	general term	坐班、做梦、不幸
test point 1	MicroBlog term	肿摸办、咋米、肿么、娘的、介个、下五
test point 2	symbols and emoticons	>_<、~~~~(>_<)~~~~
test point 3	new word	足管、住总、刑辩[abbrev]、叽里咕噜、官二代
test point 4	location name	迦错拉、渣滓洞、南市区
test point 5	person name	菅直人、仲井真弘多、郎咸平
test point 6	proper name	正大、粤来粤好、亮牌
test point 7	combination ambiguity	在外、再见、接下来
test point 8	overlapping ambiguity	真经典、在职场上、在手机上面
test point 9	rule-based combination of words	一串串、迷迷糊糊[duplication]、可信度[prefix]、暧昧感、装饰品[suffix]、昨儿[Erhua]

Table 3 Settings of test points

It remains dubious whether such classification is comprehensive, and various opinions exist towards the specific classification of each individual word. We leave such issues to further discussion.

4.2.2 Distribution of the test points

Some of the sentences in our evaluation corpus are easier, containing no test points. This evaluation contains 2147 test points in total, which are distributed in 1639 sentences, composing 32.78% of the sentences. Several sentences contain multiple test points.

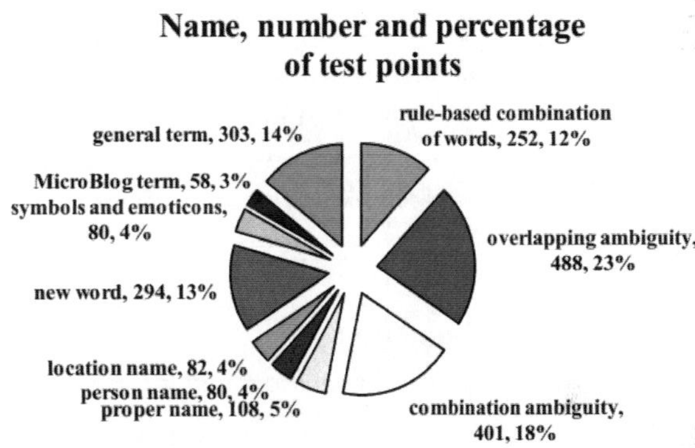

Figure 3 Distribution of test points

In a further merge, we combine combination ambiguity and overlapping ambiguity as ambiguity, combine location name, person name and other proper names as proper names, and combine MicroBlog term, symbols and emoticons as MicroBlog. The distribution of merged test points is illustrated in Figure 4.

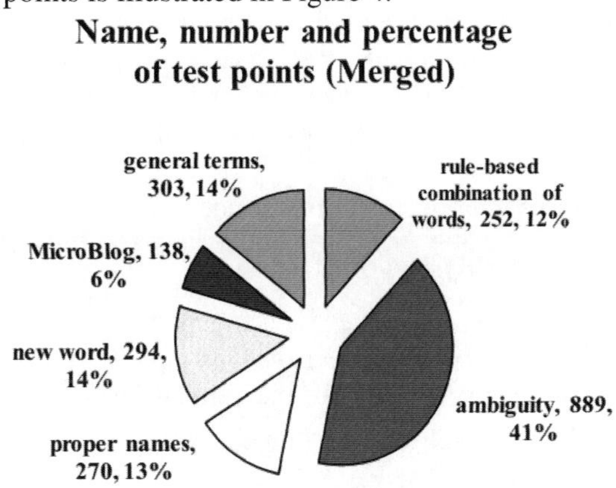

Figure 4 Distribution of merged test points

4.2.3 Evaluation results of test points

Figure 5 demonstrates the respective total number of the 10 test points and the comparison of the maximal segmentation performance of the system in these test points.

Figure 6 shows the percentage of correctly-segmented sentence and percentage of correct test points for each system.

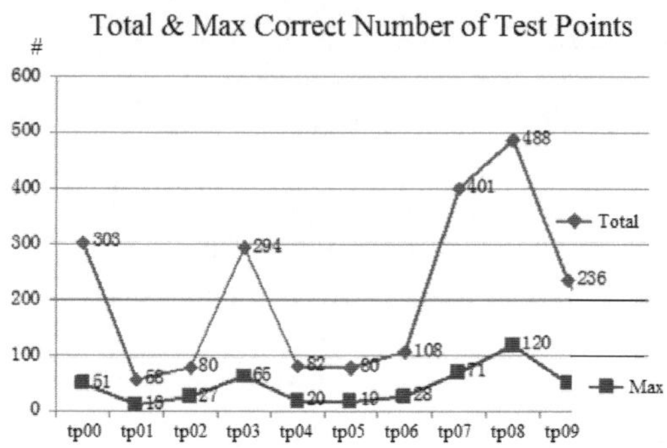

Figure 5 Comparison of the performance of the 10 test points

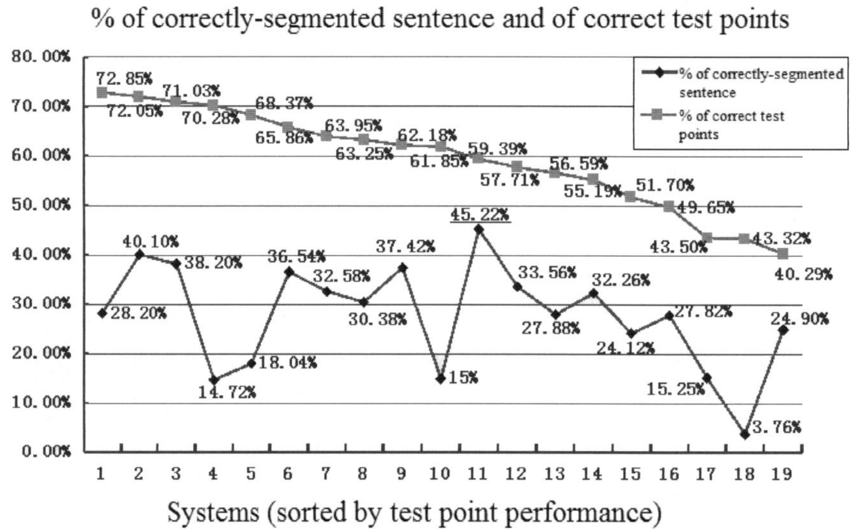

Figure 6 Number of correctly-segmented sentence and correct test points

It is shown in Figure 6 that the best system reaches a 73% precision in the test points, which proves that the bottleneck is almost broken through with more deliberation. We could also make further analysis and find out the weakness of each system. Figure 6 also shows that for systems that have a better performance in test points, they generally yield a low sentence-level performance. By making further development for the sentence-level tasks, such systems may further improve their overall performance.

4.2.4 Analysis

The final results of the systems generally outperform our expectations. However, space of improvement still exists in the critical issues, including ambiguity and proper names (refer to Figure 5).

For the sentences which contain neither ambiguity nor special terms, an optimal system may likely yield a satisfying result, but Figure 6 indicates that some systems perform quite well in sentence-level segmentation, but fail to handle with the test points well. Several possible explanations are as follows:

- Such systems may not deal with ambiguity, proper names and unregistered words well.
- Some systems tend to combine single characters to form complement structures or objective structures using its inbuilt "word formation" strategy.
- Contestants fail to combine some cases (e.g. year-month-date and family name-given name) due to misinterpretation of the task specification.

For the systems that perform well in test points, such issues have been paid more attention and are dealt with well.

Some issues are still under debate, including the definition of word, rules of word formation, towards which there exists no uniform standard. It is not necessary to demand a uniform standard, but without which the evaluations are impossible to realize.

5 Suggestions

5.1 Further considerations in segmentation evaluation

Word segmentation, though a seemingly simple task, has been making no substantial progress despite the continuous research in recent years. As far as ambiguity is concerned, it involves lexical semantics, word formation and the size of vocabulary. Researchers have made enough efforts in expanding the scale of vocabularies, but the inner structure of words still requires further consideration in scale and depth. Words of ambiguity are prevailing and ubiquitous rather than a closed set. For example:

"总会" is a noun when treated as one word, but "adverb + auxiliary verb" when treated as two words.

Example: 游戏里每个人总会分到一些钱

Translation: Every one of the game always gets some money.

"看中" is a verb and is pronounced *kan4 zhong4* when treated as one word, but "verb + localizer" and *kan4 zhong1* when treated separately.

Example: 拿到书了，慢慢看中……

Translation: I have got the book and have been reading slowly…love creatures, love life.

Example: 我看中一只包就问服务员多少

Translation: I fancied a bag and asked the salesman how much it was.

"着手" is a verb and is pronounced *zhuo2 shou3* when treated as one word, but "particle + noun" and *zhe5 shou3* when treated separately.

Example: 从小处着手，大处着眼

Translation: Start small, and see the big picture.

Example: 看着手都抽筋啊

Translation: Even looking at it makes my hand cramp.

Example: 所有的同学都拿着手机在埋头苦忙 (overlapping ambiguity)

Translation: All the students are holding their cell phones and burying themselves, busied.

Furthermore, after a close investigation of the segmentation results, we found that for the systems trained by statistical data, rule-based post-processing is basically employed to increase recall and avert errors. Each of the systems has further space for improvement, which is easy to achieve as long as the researchers refine their systems.

5.2 Suggestions for future evaluations

Due to various factors and complication of the evaluations, we could only ensure relative fairness for each of the evaluation results. We expected the participants to conform to the segmentation standard proposed by Peking University, but we observed from the final results that some systems failed to take it into consideration, which resulted in unnecessary errors.

Is there any fairer method to evaluate the segmentation systems?

Is it possible to adopt a standardized core vocabulary?

From the technical specifications returned by the participants, we could we that the scale of vocabularies and the scope of domains vary from system to system, which influenced the evaluation results and may yield to difficulties in further analysis.

To make the evaluation results comparable, we should use a uniform standard to make evaluation (though standard of segmentation is specified for this bake-off task, it is possible that systems are not adjusted accordingly due to time limitations or just ignorance of the standard).

Above are our preliminary views towards this evaluation task. We wish to listen to the participants for their viewpoints and make the evaluation task play its due role.

Acknowledgements

This work is supported by NSFC Project 61075067 and National Key Technology R&D Program (No: 2011BAH10B04-03).

Reference

1. Richard Sproat and Thomas Emerson. 2003.The first international Chinese word segmentation bakeoff.In *The Second SIGHAN Workshop on Chinese Language Processing,* pages 133–143, Sapporo, Japan.
2. Thomas Emerson. 2005. The second international Chinese word segmentation bakeoff.In*Proceedings of the Fourth SIGHAN Workshop on Chinese Language Processing*, pages 123–133, Jeju Island, Korea.
3. Gina-Anne Levow. 2006. The third international Chinese language processing bakeoff: Word segmentation and named entity recognition.In*Proceedings of the Fifth SIGHAN Work-*

shop on Chinese Language Processing, pages 108–117, Sydney, Australia, July. Association for Computational Linguistics.

4. Guangjin Jin and Xiao Chen. 2007. The Fourth International Chinese Language Processing Bakeoff: Chinese Word Segmentation,Named Entity Recognition and Chinese POS Tagging.In*The Sixth SIGHAN Workshop on Chinese Language Processing*, pages 69-81, Hyderabad,
5. Hongmei ZhaoandQun Liu, The CIPS-SIGHAN CLP 2010 Chinese Word Segmentation Bakeoff, *The first CIPS-SIGHAN Joint Conference on Chinese Language Processing (CLP2010)*, August 28-29, Beijing, China

Word Segmentation on Chinese Mirco-Blog Data with a Linear-Time Incremental Model

Kaixu Zhang † **Maosong Sun** ‡ **Changle Zhou** †
†Xiamen University, Fujian Province 361005, China
‡State Key Laboratory on Intelligent Technology and Systems
Tsinghua National Laboratory for Information Science and Technology
Department of Computer Science and Technology
Tsinghua University, Beijing 100084, China
kareyzhang@gmail.com sunmaosong@gmail.com dozero@xmu.edu.cn

Abstract

This paper describes the model we designed for the word segmentation bake-off on Chinese micro-blog data in the 2nd CIPS-SIGHAN joint conference on Chinese language processing. We presented a linear-time incremental model for word segmentation where rich features including character-based features, word-based features as well as other possible features can be easily employed. We report the performances of our model on four datasets in the SIGHAN bake-off 2005. After adding more features designed for the micro-blog data, the performance of our model is further improved. The F-score of our model for this bake-off is 0.9478 and 44.88% of the sentences are segmented correctly.

1 Introduction

Chinese word segmentation is an important and fundamental task for Chinese language processing. General-purpose word segmentation is widely studied. Micro-blog-related topic emergences and becomes a new research topic in recent years. Therefore researchers pay more and more attention to the word segmentation model for Chinese micro-blog data.

Motivated by the linear-time incremental parser proposed by Huang and Sagae (2010) and the word-based word segmentation model proposed by Zhang and Clark (2011), first we presented a linear-time incremental word segmentation model. Various features including character-based features and word-based features can be employed while exponentially many segmented results can be tested in linear-time. We report the performances of our model on four datasets in the SIGHAN bake-off 2005.

One of the difficulties of training word segmentation model on micro-blog data is the lack of annotated micro-blog data (only 500 sentences of micro-blog data are provided and used by us). Following the annotation adaptation method proposed by Jiang et al. (2009), we train a general-purpose joint word segmentation and part-of-speech tagging model using People's Daily corpus. Then, the decoding results of such a model are used as features in the final word segmentation model for micro-blog data.

Moreover, various lexicon features such as dictionaries and word list of idioms are employed to segment micro-blog data. Preprocessing is also conducted to deal with URLs and special characters.

Finally, The F-score of our model for the bake-off is 0.9478 and 44.88% of the sentences are segmented correctly. The performance of our method is still far from perfect. The lack of segmented micro-blog data is one of the bottlenecks of our model. If more training data is provided, our model can reach better performance.

2 The Linear-Time Incremental Word Segmentation Model

2.1 Word Segmentation Definition

First, we give a formal general definition of word segmentation.

A raw sentence X is a Chinese sentence where no spaces are presented to separate words, while a segmented sentence Y is a sentence in which words are separated by spaces. For example, "材料利用率高" is a raw sentence, and "材料 利用 率 高" is one of the possible segmented sentences corresponding to the raw sentence.

Given a raw sentence X, a word segmentation model needs to find a segmented sentence $\hat{Y}$ among all possible segmented sentences $\mathrm{GEN}(X)$ corresponding to the raw sentence. This can be seen as an optimization problem:

$$\hat{Y} = \arg\max_{Y \in \text{GEN}(x)} f(Y, \Lambda) \quad (1)$$

where the objective function $f(Y, \Lambda)$ is used to evaluate segmented sentences and Λ is the parameter.

In the following subsections, we will describe the detail of this function and how to learn the parameter.

2.2 Word Segmentation as Action Sequence Generation

In this paper, word segmentation is treated as action sequence generation. Each action is corresponding to a character interval of the input sentence. For an input sentence of $|X|$ characters, the corresponding action sequence $A = (a_0, \ldots, a_{|X|})$ has a length of $|X| + 1$ (including the "intervals" at very beginning and very end of the sentence). There are two kinds of actions ($a_i \in \{\mathbf{s}, \mathbf{c}\}$), namely separate (denoted as **s**) and combine (denoted as **c**). The action $a_i = \mathbf{s}$ means that the i-th character and the $i+1$-th character in the input sentence are belong to two separated words; while $a_i = \mathbf{c}$ means that they are belong to the same word.

Given A, the corresponding segmented sentence Y is determined and denoted as Y_A. For example, for the input sentence "材料利用率高", the action sequence $(\mathbf{s}, \mathbf{c}, \mathbf{s}, \mathbf{c}, \mathbf{s}, \mathbf{s}, \mathbf{s})$ could generate a segmented sentence Y_A as "材料 利用 率 高".

The problem of finding a best segmented sentence is now equivalent to the problem of generating a best action sequence.

We introduce $S = (s_0, \ldots, s_{|X|})$ determined by A as a sequence of statuses to generate feature vectors for the action sequence and then evaluate any segmented sentence Y_A as

$$f(Y_A, \Lambda) = \sum_{i=0}^{|X|+1} \Phi(s_i, X) \cdot \Lambda_{a_i}^T \quad (2)$$

where $\Phi(s_i, X)$ is a feature vector generated by the input and status s_i corresponding to action a_i. And $\Lambda_{\mathbf{s}}$ and $\Lambda_{\mathbf{c}}$ are two weight vectors for two kinds of actions.

The status sequence S can be defined in different ways. In this paper, we define it as follows.

A status s_i in S is defined as a tuple $\langle i, u_i, v_i \rangle$, where u_i is the index of the last **s** action, and v_i is the index of the second last **s** action. Thus given A, s_i can be formally recursively calculated as

$$s_i = \begin{cases} \langle i, -1, -1 \rangle & \text{if } i = 0 \\ \langle i, i-1, u_{i-1} \rangle & \text{if } a_{i-1} = \mathbf{s} \\ \langle i, u_{i-1}, v_{i-1} \rangle & \text{if } a_{i-1} = \mathbf{c} \end{cases} \quad (3)$$

Following Huang and Sagae (2010), the generation of the action sequence can also be formalized as a deductive system described in Figure 2.2.

The next subsection will describe the feature vector $\Phi(s_i, X)$ in detail.

$$\begin{array}{ll} \text{input} & X \\ \text{axiom} & \langle 0, -1, -1 \rangle : 0 \\ \mathbf{s} & \dfrac{\langle i, u, \_ \rangle : c}{\langle i+1, i, u \rangle : c + \sigma} \\ \mathbf{c} & \dfrac{\langle i, u, v \rangle : c}{\langle i+1, u, v \rangle : c + \gamma} \\ \text{goal} & \langle |X|+1, \_, \_ \rangle : c \end{array}$$

Figure 1: The deductive system used to describe our model. In this system, i is the step, c is the cost, $\sigma = \Phi(s_i, X) \cdot \Lambda_{\mathbf{s}}^T$ is the **s** cost and $\gamma = \Phi(s_i, X) \cdot \Lambda_{\mathbf{c}}^T$ is the **c** cost. The best derivation is the derivation of the goal with the highest cost.

Atom features	Description
x_j	characters in X
a_{i-1}, a_{i-2}	last two actions
$\mathbf{w}_0$	current (partial) word
$\mathbf{w}_{-1}$	last determined word

Table 2: Atom features for the i-th action a_i

2.3 Feature Templates

We define feature vectors by using feature templates. First, atom features are generated based on s_i and X. All the feature templates can then be generated by using atom features.

Atom features are shown in Table 2. The last two actions a_{i-1} and a_{i-2} can be determined by the status s_i. The (partial) word $\mathbf{w}_0$ is the string between the index of last **s** action u_i and the current position i.

Feature templates are defined as tuples and shown in Table 1. $|\mathbf{w}|$ is the length of the word $\mathbf{w}$. $\mathbf{w}[0]$ and $\mathbf{w}[-1]$ are the first and last character

action-based	$\langle \textbf{a-1}, a_{i-2}, a_{i-1} \rangle$
character-based	$\langle \textbf{c-1}, x_{i-2}, a_{i-1} \rangle$, $\langle \textbf{c-2}, x_{i-1}, a_{i-1} \rangle$, $\langle \textbf{c-3}, x_i, a_{i-1} \rangle$
	$\langle \textbf{c-4}, x_{i-3}, x_{i-2}, a_{i-1} \rangle$, $\langle \textbf{c-5}, x_{i-2}, x_{i-1}, a_{i-1} \rangle$,
	$\langle \textbf{c-6}, x_{i-1}, x_i, a_{i-1} \rangle$, $\langle \textbf{c-7}, x_i, x_{i+1}, a_{i-1} \rangle$
word-based	$\langle \textbf{w-1}, \mathbf{w}_0 \rangle$, $\langle \textbf{w-2}, \lvert\mathbf{w}_0\rvert \rangle$
	$\langle \textbf{w-3}, \lvert\mathbf{w}_0\rvert, \mathbf{w}_0[0] \rangle$, $\langle \textbf{w-4}, \lvert\mathbf{w}_0\rvert, \mathbf{w}_0[-1] \rangle$, $\langle \textbf{w-5}, \mathbf{w}_0[0], \mathbf{w}_0[-1] \rangle$
	$\langle \textbf{w-6}, \mathbf{w}_{-1}[-1], \mathbf{w}_0[-1] \rangle$, $\langle \textbf{w-7}, \lvert\mathbf{w}_{-1}\rvert, \mathbf{w}_0 \rangle$, $\langle \textbf{w-8}, \mathbf{w}_{-1}, \lvert\mathbf{w}_0\rvert \rangle$
	$\langle \textbf{w-9}, \mathbf{w}_0[0], x_i \rangle$, $\langle \textbf{w-10}, \mathbf{w}_0[-1], x_i \rangle$

Table 1: Feature templates

of word **w**, respectively. Each tuple is corresponding to one dimension of the feature vector and the value of that dimension will be set to 1 if this corresponding feature was generated.

There are action-based, character-based and word-based templates. Note that when only action-based and character-based templates are used, these feature templates are equivalent to the templates used by conventional word segmentation models based on character tagging (Zhang et al., 2011). And the word-based features are mainly based on the work by Zhang and Clark (2011).

2.4 Decoding and Learning Algorithms

We apply the decoding algorithm used by Huang and Sagae (2010).

Beam search is used in the decoding algorithm, while different hypotheses with the same status at a certain step will be merged in a dynamic programming manner. This decoding algorithm can efficiently search exponentially many hypotheses in linear-time ($O(nb)$ where b is the width of the beam). Comparatively, the time complexity of the decoding algorithm using fully dynamic programming is $O(n^3)$ (or $O(nL^2)$ if the max length of words L is specified).

The parameter Λ is trained using an average perceptron algorithm (Collins, 2002). We also tried early update (Collins and Roark, 2004) in the learning algorithm. Although it is reported that early update helps the learning of parsers, we do not observe that early update helps the learning of word segmentation models. So we do not implement early update in our experiments.

3 Word Segmentation for Micro-Blog Data

In order to segment the micro-blog data better, we modified the word segmentation model described in the last section by adding a preprocessing and more features.

We just perform feature engineering manually for the development to decide which feature is useful for segmenting micro-blog data [1].

3.1 Preprocessing

A rule-based preprocessing is conducted before the statistical model. This preprocessing is mainly used to reduce the search space of the statistical model by assigning the action a_i of certain position before the decoding algorithm. Thus the decoding algorithm will only search either hypotheses that $a_i = \mathbf{s}$ or hypotheses that $a_i = \mathbf{c}$.

URLs and other micro-blog-specified characters (such as "@" means "at somebody" and "#" means to annotate a tag) are first recognized. The boundaries of these components are assigned to **s**, while the inner character intervals of the URLs are assigned to **c**.

Likewise, the punctuations (such as Chinese full stop "。" and comma "，") are recognized and the boundaries of these are assigned to **s**. The intervals between two Arabic numbers or two Latin letters are assigned to **c**.

White spaces can also be found in the raw micro-blog data between two English words or at the end of a micro-blog user's name after the '@' character. The preprocessing will remove these white spaces and assigned **s** for the left character intervals.

3.2 Character-Type-Based Features

Since there are more non-standard uses of non-Chinese characters in micro-blog data than in news data and adding character-type-based features can improve the performance of general-

[1] Word-based feature templates in Table 1 are also modified slightly for the word segmentation model for micro-blog data.

Method	Dataset			
	AS	CityU	MSR	PKU
Best05	0.952 (Asahara et al., 2005)	0.943	0.964 (Tseng et al., 2005)	0.950 (Chen et al., 2005)
(Wang et al., 2010)	0.956	0.956	0.972	0.957
(Zhang and Clark, 2011)	0.954	0.951	0.973	0.944
(Sun et al., 2012)	NA	0.948	0.974	0.954
Our model	0.953	0.948	0.973	0.952

Table 3: F-scores of our model and models in related work on SIGHAN 05 bake-off data

purpose word segmentation model (Zhao et al., 2006), we employ character-type-based features.

We define a function $\text{type}(x_i)$ that returns the type of the characters

$$\text{type}(x_i) = \begin{cases} \textbf{C} & \text{if } x_i \text{ is a Chinese character} \\ \textbf{L} & \text{if } x_i \text{ is a Latin letter} \\ \textbf{A} & \text{if } x_i \text{ is a Arabic numeric character} \\ x_i & \text{otherwise} \end{cases} \quad (4)$$

The additional feature templates that we use are $\langle \textbf{ct-1}, \text{type}(x_i) \rangle$, $\langle \textbf{ct-2}, \text{type}(x_{i-1}) \rangle$, $\langle \textbf{ct-3}, \text{type}(x_{i+1}) \rangle$, $\langle \textbf{ct-4}, \text{type}(x_{i-1}), \text{type}(x_i) \rangle$ and $\langle \textbf{ct-5}, \text{type}(x_i), \text{type}(x_{i+1}) \rangle$.

3.3 Lexical Features

Lexical features are used as additional word-based features for word segmentation for micro-blog data. Each lexical feature template $\langle \textbf{lex-}k, \text{lex}_k(\mathbf{w}_0) \rangle$ is based on a function whose variable is a word.

Since we have various lexical resources, we can define several functions lex_k to create different lexical feature templates. If the lexical resource is just a word list, the $\text{lex}_k(\mathbf{w}_0)$ could just return a binary value to indicate whether this word $\mathbf{w}_0$ is in the word list or not. If the lexical resource is about the frequencies of words, $\text{lex}_k(\mathbf{w}_0)$ could return $\log_2(\text{freq}(\mathbf{w}_0) + 1)$ where $\text{freq}(\mathbf{w}_0)$ is the frequency of word $\mathbf{w}_0$.

We use several word lists to add lexical feature templates, including a word list of idioms from Sun (2011), word lists based on People's Daily corpus, Yuwei Corpus and Tsinghua Treebank. We also use words with frequencies counted from the three mentioned segmented corpora.

Additionally, we add another lexical feature template based on whether these four characters x_{u_i}, x_{u_i+1}, x_{u_i+2} and x_{u_i+3} form an idiom.

3.4 Tagger-Based Features

The annotated micro-blog data contains only 500 micro-blogs. So more annotated data are required. We train a character-based joint word segmentation and part-of-speech tagging model using the People's Daily corpus (Zhang, 2012)[2], and then use the decoding results of this model as features for the word segmentation model for the micro-blog data.

Three templates $\langle \textbf{tb-1}, a'_i \rangle$, $\langle \textbf{tb-2}, a'_i, \text{POS}_{i-1} \rangle$ and $\langle \textbf{tb-3}, a'_i, \text{POS}_i \rangle$ are added. a'_i is the action based on the results of the tagger, and POS_i is the part-of-speech tag of the word that x_i belongs to.

4 Experiments

We report the performances of our model on four SIGHAN05 datasets (Emerson, 2005). Then we report the performance our model on the micro-blog data. We use 5-fold cross validation for the development and use the whole dataset to train the final model for the test.

The F-score is used to evaluate the performance, which is the harmonic mean of precision (percentage of words that are correctly segmented in the results) and recall (percentage of words that are correctly segmented in the gold standard).

The results of our model and related work on the SIGHAN05 datasets are listed in Table 3.

The results of the micro-blog data are listed in Table 4. The first row is the final performance on the test data, while the following rows show the performances with different feature sets for the cross validation using 500 micro-blog sentences. We can see that the additional features of the micro-blog data improve the performance.

[2]The code we use is a part of the tool THULAC (Tsinghua University - Lexical Analyzer for Chinese) `http://nlp.csai.tsinghua.edu.cn/thulac/`.

	F-score
All features for test	0.9478
All features for cross validation	0.9413
w/o character-type-based features	0.9383
w/o lexical features	0.9201
w/o tagger-based features	0.9310

Table 4: Experiment results of our model on the micro-blog data

For the annotated micro-blog data for the training is quite limited, the lexical features and tagger-based features are important for the performance. Note that the F-score for the test is better than the F-score for the cross validation. This may caused by that the training set for the former model is one-quarter larger. It may imply that the performance of our model is limited by the size of the training data and the performance of our model will be improved when larger training data was provided.

5 Discussion and Conclusion

In this paper, we describe the model we designed for the word segmentation bake-off on Chinese micro-blog data in the 2nd CIPS-SIGHAN joint conference on Chinese language processing. We presented a linear-time incremental word segmentation model in which various features can be easily employed. After employing more features of the micro-blog data, the performance of our model is further improved. The final F-score of our model on the test set is 0.9478 and 44.88% of the micro-blogs are segmented correctly.

The performance of our model is still far from perfect. Word segmentation for micro-blog data is not as good as word segmentation for news data (see Table 3 and Table 4). More manually annotated data or employing semi-supervised method can be used to improve the performance. We also notice that outputting inconsistence words is a problem for statistical word segmentation models. Therefore a post-processing could be used to adjust the output for better performance. We spend much time comparing the performances of combinations of different feature templates. A more sophisticated method is needed for the selection of feature templates.

Acknowledgments

The authors want to thank ZHANG Junsong from the cognitive lab and SHI Xiaodong, CHEN Yidong and SU Jinsong from the NLP lab of Xiamen University for the support of experiments.

The authors are supported by NSFC under Grant No. 61133012 and 61273338.

References

M. Asahara, K. Fukuoka, A. Azuma, C. L. Goh, Y. Watanabe, Y. Matsumoto, and T. Tsuzuki. 2005. Combination of machine learning methods for optimum chinese word segmentation. In *Proc. Fourth SIGHAN Workshop on Chinese Language Processing*, pages 134–137.

A. Chen, Y. Zhou, A. Zhang, and G. Sun. 2005. Unigram language model for chinese word segmentation. In *Proceedings of the 4th SIGHAN Workshop on Chinese Language Processing*, pages 138–141.

Michael Collins and Brian Roark. 2004. Incremental parsing with the perceptron algorithm. In *Proceedings of the 42nd Meeting of the Association for Computational Linguistics (ACL'04), Main Volume*, pages 111–118, Barcelona, Spain, July.

Michael Collins. 2002. Discriminative training methods for hidden markov models: theory and experiments with perceptron algorithms. pages 1–8.

Thomas Emerson. 2005. The second international chinese word segmentation bakeoff. In *Proceedings of the Fourth SIGHAN Workshop on Chinese Language Processing*, pages 123–133. Jeju Island, Korea.

Liang Huang and Kenji Sagae. 2010. Dynamic programming for linear-time incremental parsing. In *Proceedings of the 48th Annual Meeting of the Association for Computational Linguistics*, pages 1077–1086, Uppsala, Sweden, July. Association for Computational Linguistics.

Wenbin Jiang, Liang Huang, and Qun Liu. 2009. Automatic adaptation of annotation standards: Chinese word segmentation and POS tagging - a case study. In *Proceedings of the 47th ACL*, pages 522–530, Suntec, Singapore, August. Association for Computational Linguistics.

Xu Sun, Houfeng Wang, and Wenjie Li. 2012. Fast online training with frequency-adaptive learning rates for chinese word segmentation and new word detection. In *Proceedings of the 50th Annual Meeting of the Association for Computational Linguistics (Volume 1: Long Papers)*, pages 253–262, Jeju Island, Korea, July. Association for Computational Linguistics.

Weiwei Sun. 2011. A stacked sub-word model for joint chinese word segmentation and part-of-speech tagging. In *Proceedings of the 49th Annual Meeting of the Association for Computational Linguistics: Human Language Technologies*, pages 1385–1394, Portland, Oregon, USA, June. Association for Computational Linguistics.

H. Tseng, P. Chang, G. Andrew, D. Jurafsky, and C. Manning. 2005. A conditional random field word segmenter for sighan bakeoff 2005. In *Proceedings of the Fourth SIGHAN Workshop on Chinese Language Processing*, pages 168–171. Jeju Island, Korea.

Kun Wang, Chengqing Zong, and Keh-Yih Su. 2010. A character-based joint model for chinese word segmentation. In *Proceedings of the 23rd International Conference on Computational Linguistics (Coling 2010)*, pages 1173–1181, Beijing, China, August. Coling 2010 Organizing Committee.

Y. Zhang and S. Clark. 2011. Syntactic processing using the generalized perceptron and beam search. *Computational Linguistics*, (Early Access):1–47.

Kaixu Zhang, Ruining Wang, Ping Xue, and Maosong Sun. 2011. Extract chinese unknown words from a large-scale corpus using morphological and distributional evidences. In *Proceedings of 5th International Joint Conference on Natural Language Processing*, pages 837–845, Chiang Mai, Thailand, November. Asian Federation of Natural Language Processing.

Kaixu Zhang. 2012. *Study on Chinese Word Segmentation and Part-of-Speech Tagging with Compact Representations*. Ph.D. thesis, Tsinghua University.

H. Zhao, C. N. Huang, and M. Li. 2006. An improved chinese word segmentation system with conditional random field. In *Proceedings of the Fifth SIGHAN Workshop on Chinese Language Processing*, pages 162–165. Sydney: July.

Soochow University Word Segmenter for SIGHAN 2012 Bakeoff

Yan Fang Zhongqing Wang Shoushan Li Zhongguo Li Richen Xu Leixin Cai
Natural Language Processing Lab
Soochow University, Suzhou, China, 215006
{fangyan0108, wangzq.antony, shoushan.li, eemath}@gmail.com,
xurichen@yeah.net, leixincai@gmail.com

Abstract

This paper presents a Chinese Word Segmentation system on MicroBlog corpora for the CIPS-SIGHAN Word Segmentation Bakeoff 2012. Our system employs Conditional Random Fields (CRF) as the segmentation model. To make our model more adaptive to MicroBlog, we manually analyze and annotate many MicroBlog messages. After manually checking and analyzing the MicroBlog text, we propose several pre-processing and post-processing rules to improve the performance. As a result, our system obtains a competitive F-score in comparison with other participating systems.

1 Introduction

Because Chinese context is written without natural delimiters, word segmentation becomes an essential initial step in many tasks on Chinese language processing. Though recognizing words seems easy for human beings, automatic Chinese Word Segmentation by computers is not a trivial problem (Xue, 2003; Li et al., 2012). The state-of-the-art Chinese Word Segmentation systems have achieved a quite high precision on traditional media text. However, the performance of segmentation is not so satisfying for MicroBlog corpora. MicroBlog messages are often short, and they make heavy use of colloquial language. Furthermore, they require situational context for interpretation. Thus, we first analyze and annotate some MicroBlog messages, and then propose a novel pre-processing and post-processing approach on the CRF-based segmentation system for the MicroBlog corpora. The experimental results show that our system performs well on MicroBlog corpora and could yield comparable segmentation results with other participants.

2 Our System

2.1 Overview

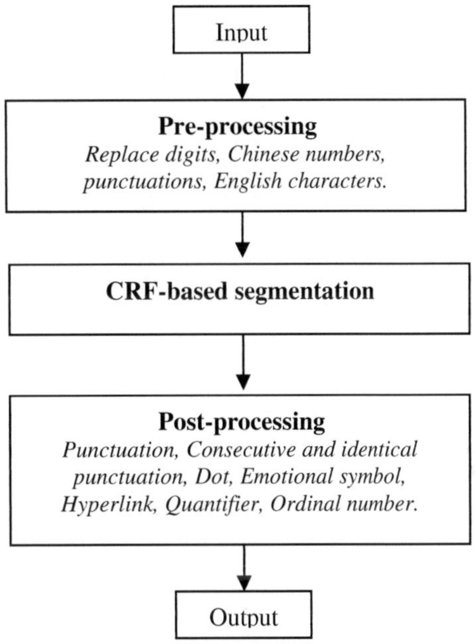

Figure 1: The architecture of our Chinese word segmentation system

Figure 1 illustrates the framework of our Chinese word segmentation system. The whole system contains three main components: preprocessing, CRF-based segmentation, and post-processing. We will introduce them in the following subsections in detail.

2.2 Resources

Note that the 2012 SIGHAN bakeoff task of Chinese Word Segmentation on MicroBlog corpora provides no training data. To make our system more adaptive to the new domain, we get the training data by ourselves. The training data we used consists of two parts. The first one is the Peking University Corpora (PKU) from January to June. Secondly, we collect a certain amount of raw sentences from Sina MicroBlog (The size is 90M) for further manual annotation. Due to the big size of the data, we conduct an active learning approach to actively select the informative boundaries for manual annotating and the size of the selected data is reduced to about 3% annotation size (Li et al., 2012).

2.3 Segmentation Method

The approach of character-based tagging is popular for Chinese word segmentation (Xue, 2003; Xue and Shen, 2003). The backbone of our system is a character-based segmenter with the application of CRF (Zhao and Kit, 2008; Li and Huang, 2009) that provides a framework to use a large number of linguistic features. It can avoid the so-called 'label-bias' problem in some degree and is originally introduced into the language processing tasks in Lafferty et al. (2001).

The probability assigned to a label sequence for a particular sequence of characters by a CRF is given by the following equation:

$$P_\lambda(Y \mid X) = \frac{1}{Z(x)} \exp(\sum_{c \in C} \sum_{k} \lambda_k f_k(Y_c, X, c))$$

Y is the label sequence for the sentence; X is the sequence of unsegmented characters; $Z(X)$ is a normalization term; f_k is a feature function, and c indexes into characters in the sequence being labeled.

The character based tagging model for Chinese word segmentation is usually based on either maximum entropy or CRF which regards a segmentation procedure as a tagging process. For detailed information, please refer Adwait (1996). The probability model and corresponding feature function is defined over the set $H \times T$, where H represents the set of possible contexts and T represents the set of possible tags. Generally, a feature function can be found as follows,

$$f(h,t) = \begin{cases} 1, \text{if } h{=}h_i \text{ is satisfied and } t{=}t_j \\ 0, \text{otherwise}, \end{cases}$$

where $h_i \in H$ and $t_i \in T$

The features used in our experiments are straightforward and include the following types:

$$c_0, c_1, c_{-1}c_0, c_0c_1, c_1c_2$$

Where c stands for character (Zhao et al., 2006). The subscripts are position indicators. 0 means the current word; -1,-2, the first or second word to the left; 1, 2, the first or second word to the right.

A forward-backward algorithm is used in training and the Viterbi algorithm is used in decoding.

As for tag set, we apply a four-tag tagging scheme. That is, each Chinese character can be assigned to one of the tags in {B, M, E, S}. The tag B, M, E represent the character being the beginning, middle, and end of a multiple-character word respectively while the tag S represents the character being a single-character word.

3 The Preprocessing and Post-processing Rules

3.1 Preprocessing

Before applying the training data to train CRF, we use some preprocessing rules on training data.

Because English characters and digits are frequently out-of-vocabulary words, we replace all the English character and digits to special characters before segmentation processing, and we will restore all these special characters to the original character after segmentation processing. The following table shows the character type we choose in the pre-processing step.

Type	Example
English characters	Today is Friday
Chinese digital	一百五十九
Digital	2012
Punctuations	“，”，“。”，“！”

Table1 Explaining of preprocessing

3.2 Post-processing

In the segmentation result from the CRF segmenter, we find that some errors could be corrected by some heuristic rules. For this purpose, we propose seven rules as follows.

- **Punctuation**: punctuation tends to be a single-character word. If a punctuation's previous character and next character are both Chinese characters, i.e. not punctuation, digit, or English character, we always regard the punctuation as a word.
- **Consecutive and identical punctuation**: some consecutive and identical punctuation tend to be joined together as a word. For example, "———" represents a Chinese hyphen which consist of three "—", and consecutive punctuations of "." or "。" all presents suspension points. Inspired by this observation, we would like to join some consecutive and identical punctuations as a single word.
- **Dot**: when the character "•" appears in the training data, it is generally used as a connection symbol in a foreign personal name, such as "奥黛丽•赫本". Taking this observation into consideration, we always join the character "•" and its previous and next segment units into a single word. A similar rule is designed to join consecutive digits on the sides of the symbol ".", ex. "0.99".
- **Emotion symbol**: some consecutive punctuations have special meanings. For example, "'^_^" and ":-)" all mean smiling expressions. "T_T" and "Q_Q" all mean sad expressions. This is a kind of network language features. So when we come across these consecutive punctuations, we applied a rule to join them together as a single word.
- **Hyperlink**: MicroBlog corpora contain so many web sites, and there are always than one hyperlinks appear together. Under these circumstances, the CRF-based segementer always has difficulties to separate them. So we get a rule to correct it.
- **Quantifier**: some quantifiers after numbers were connected as one word in our result. Such as "三个", "5 斤", "1cm". So we proposed a rule to split those words whose previous character is a number and next character is a quantifier or a unit. But the word "一个" would be regarded as an exception.
- **Ordinal number**: in Chinese, ordinal numbers are regard as one word such as the word "第一". In MicroBlog corpora, there are many cases that a digit after the character "第" like "第 3", we also regard them as one word. To this end, we join the character "第" with its next segment which consists of digits completely. A similar rule is designed to join integers or decimals with its next character "%".

Table 2 summarizes all the rules we utilized in the post-processing step.

Rule type	Example
Punctuation	你好吗？很好。
Consecutive and identical punctuation	思考中。。。。。。
Dot	奥黛丽•赫本
Emotion symbol	今天很开心^_^
Hyperlink	http://www.taobao.com/
Quantifier	买了 5 斤苹果
Ordinal number	开学的第一天

Table 2 Explaining of post-processing

4 Experiments

For this CIPS-SIGHAN bakeoff, we focus on the Chinese Word Segmentation task on MicroBlog corpora. Before the final test, we use the data provided by SIGHAN 2012 which consists of approximately 500 messages from MicroBlog to test our approaches described in the previous sections. The results are shown in Table 3, where P, R, F represents the precision rate, recall rate and harmonic average measure rate respectively. The approaches we used are:

- **Basic** represents the result of our model using only the corpora of PKU.
- **+Pre** represents the result of our model using the preprocessing rules.
- **+Post** represents the result of our model using the post-processing rules.

- **+Ann** represents the result of our model using the annotated data.

As the table shows, after the use of preprocessing rules, the results are somehow decreased. The reason for a worse performance is that when we use preprocessing rules, we treat all the digits, other types alike, as the same, whereas they are always different in some circumstance. For example, we always regard "一个" as one word, but others like "三个", "五个" all regard as two words. These problems are solved in post-processing, and we can see that the designed post-processing rules are effective and thus could greatly improve the results.

	P	R	F
Basic	0.8959	0.8613	0.8782
+Pre	0.8589	0.8585	0.8587
+Pre +Post	0.9225	0.9153	0.9187
+Pre+Post+Ann	0.9336	0.9224	0.9279

Table 3 Performances tested before final test

P	R	F	CS	CSP
0.9383	0.9346	0.9365	1909	38.18

Table 4 Performance of the final test.

The final test data consists of approximately 5,000 texts from MicroBlog. The performances are shown in Table 4, where CS indicates the sum of correct sentences, and CSP indicates the percentage of correct sentences in all the sentences. The F-score we achieved is 0.9365, which is higher than the results when only 500 texts are used.

5 Conclusion

In this paper, we introduce our Chinese word segmentation system for SIGHAN 2012. The nice performance of system are attributed to three main aspects: the CRF learning algorithm, the newly annotated data on Sina MiroBlog, the preprocessing and post-processing rules.

References

Adwait R. 1996. A Maximum Entropy Part-of-speech Tagger. In Proceedings of the Empirical Method in Natural Language Processing Conference, 133-142. University of Pennsylvania.

Lafferty J., A. McCallum and F. Pereira. 2001. Conditional Random Field: Probabilistic Models for Segmenting and Labeling Sequence Data. In Proceedings of the Eighteenth International Conference on Machine Learning, 282-289. June 28-July 01, 2001.

Li S., G. Zhou, and C. Huang. 2012. Active Learning for Chinese Word Segmentation. In Proceeding of COLING-2012, poster. To appear.

Li S., C. Huang. 2009. Word Boundary Decision with CRF for Chinese Word Segmentation. In proceeding of PACLIC-2009, pages 726-732.

Xue N. 2003. Chinese Word Segmentation as Character Tagging. Computational Linguistics and Chinese Language processing, Vol. 8(1): 29-48.

Xue N. and L. Shen. 2003. Chinese Word Segmentation as LMR Tagging. In Proceedings of the Second SIGHAN Workshop on Chinese Language Processing, in conjunction with ACL'03, 176-179. Sapporo, Japan.

Zhao H. and C. Kit. 2008. Unsupervised Segmentation Helps Superivised Learning of Character Tagging for Word Segmentation and Named Entity Recognition. In Proceedings of SIGHAN-6 2008, pages 106-111.

Zhao H., C. Huang, M. Li and B. Lu. 2006. Effective Tag Set Selection in Chinese Word Segmentation via Conditional Random Field Modeling. In Proceedings of PACLIC-2006, pages 87-94.

CRFs-Based Chinese Word Segmentation for Micro-Blog with Small-Scale Data

Longyue Wang
Natural Language Processing & Portuguese-Chinese Machine Translation Laboratory, Department of Computer and Information Science, University of Macau, Macau S.A.R., China.
vincentwang0229@hotmail.com

Derek F. Wong
Natural Language Processing & Portuguese-Chinese Machine Translation Laboratory, Department of Computer and Information Science, University of Macau, Macau S.A.R., China.
derekfw@umac.mo

Lidia S. Chao
Natural Language Processing & Portuguese-Chinese Machine Translation Laboratory, Department of Computer and Information Science, University of Macau, Macau S.A.R., China.
lidiasc@umac.mo

Junwen Xing
Natural Language Processing & Portuguese-Chinese Machine Translation Laboratory, Department of Computer and Information Science, University of Macau, Macau S.A.R., China.
nlp2ct.anson@gmail.com

Abstract

In this paper, we proposed a Chinese word segmentation model for micro-blog text. Although Conditional Random Fields (CRFs) models have been presented to deal with word segmentation, this is still the first time to apply it for the segmentation in the domain of Chinese micro-blog. Different from the genres of common articles, micro-blog has gradually become a new literary with the development of Internet. However, the unavailable of micro-blog training data has been the obstacle to develop a good segmenter based on trainable models. Considering the linguistic characteristics of the text, we proposed some methods to make the CRFs models suitable for segmentation in the domain of micro-blog. Several experiments have been conducted with different settings and then an optimal tagging method and feature templates have been designed. The proposed model has been implemented for the Second CIPS-SIGHAN Joint Conference on Chinese Language Processing Bakeoff (Bakeoff-2012) and achieves a very high F-measure of 93.38% within the test set of 5,000 micro-blog sentences. One of our main contributions is the online version of toolkit[1], which provides segmentation service for Chinese micro-blog text.

1 Introduction

Unlike Roman alphabetic languages such as English, Portuguese, etc., Chinese has no explicit word delimiters within a sentence. Therefore, word segmentation is the very first step in Chinese information processing. After years of intensive researches, Chinese word segmentation has achieved a very good performance (Huang, 2007). However, the performance of segmentation is not so satisfied for tokenizing micro-blog corpora. The main reason is that traditional segmentation models are often trained from the corpora of news, literatures, etc. due to the availability of the corpora in these domains. When using the trained models to the text which is out of the trained domains (e.g. Internet, vernacular records), the precision and recall rates will decline sharply. Among all the proposed methods, character-based tagging with CRFs models have attracted more and more attention since it is firstly introduced into language processing (Lafferty et al., 2001). Reviewing the recent Bakeoffs, we found that Low et al. (2005) and Tseng et al.

[1] It can be accessed at http://nlp2ct.sftw.umac.mo/views/utility.html.

(2005) in Bakeoff-2005 have obtained the best results based on CRFs. Besides, the model of Zhao and Kit (2008) has been ranked at the top in the closed track of Bakeoff-2008, who integrated unsupervised segmentation and CRFs model. The results fully proved that CRFs can do well for the segmentation task.

In order to solve the segmentation problems with cross-domain data, Qin et al. (2010) proposed novel steps for the first CIPS-SIGHAN segmentation task and achieved 0.9278 of F-measure based on CRFs approach. The result shows that the out-of-domain resources could improve the segmentation performance, especially for the task with small-scale training data.

In our system, we continue to improve the CRFs-based tagging method. Not only the best feature templates are designed, but also that the use of a new 6-tag set, external 1-gram dictionaries and out-of-domain corpus are proposed to further improve the performance of Chinese segmentation for micro-blog. This will be helpful to the research on the tasks of information retrieval, Internet slang analysis and construction of corpus for domain of Chinese micro-blog.

The paper is organized as follows. The linguistics phenomena of micro-blog are analyzed in Section 2. Various tag sets used for segmentation are reviewed and discussed in Section 3. The feature template of the proposed approach is described in Section 4. Results, discussion and comparison between different strategies are given in Section 5 followed by a conclusion to end the paper.

2 Micro-Blogs

From the perspective of linguistics, micro-blog text is a new domain comparing with the common articles. In order to design a good segmentation system targeted for micro-blog text, several found phenomena are summarized in the followings:

2.1 Unknown Words

Similar to the Internet slang, many new words are used to emerge frequently and disseminate rapidly over the Internet. This will result in a lower recall rate of the segmentation system, because these out-of-vocabulary (OOV) words are not easy to be recognized. Here given some new words which occur on the Internet in recent years. "驴友 (*tour pal*)", "正太 (*cute boy*)" and "木有 (*have nothing*)" are all combined with two common Chinese characters and mostly used in the blogs. In order to improve the ability to identify these words, external word list of popular Internet slang are essential and used in our segmentation model.

2.2 Colloquial

Unlike written language which tends to be formal, users often express their moods and viewpoints with spoken language in their blogs. To simplify or personalize the descriptions, it is very common to see some sentences, which are colloquial, incomplete, or ungrammatical. For instance, the sentence "所有的一切，都在乎，真的 (*everything, treasure, really*)" was not only left out the subject "我 (*I*)", but also disrupted the word order (the formal sentence should be "我真的在乎所有的一切" / *I really treasure everything*). So syntax analysis such as part-of-speech etc. is not helpful to the segmentation in the domain of micro-blog and would seriously interfere the segmentation performance. Different from traditional methods for Chinese word segmentation, syntactic information was not used as features in our segmenter.

2.3 Brief

Micro-blogs are famous for its "micro". In another words, every micro-blog has a length limitation for all the users. For example, Sina Micro-Blog requires each blog has no more than 140 characters. Under this restriction, users get used to texting with shorter sentences. Several strategies to deliver more information with fewer words are adopted. For example, contractions (e.g. "女排" is short for "女子排球队" / *women's volleyball team*), idioms (e.g. "一言难尽" / *it is a long story*), classical Chinese texts (e.g. "但愿人长久，千里共婵娟" / *we wish each other a long life so as to share the beauty of this graceful moonlight, even though miles apart*) and foreign words are often used.

2.4 Non-Chinese Characters

The blog texts are nonstandard, because they are usually composed with a mixture of non-Chinese characters for some special purposes. Punctuations, foreign words, numbers and symbols are commonly used in blogs. For example, URLs often occur after reprints to cite them. Furthermore, several common symbols and numbers can be combined as emoticons (e.g. "^0^ (*smiling face*)"). And young people would like to use some foreign words (mostly English) to make their expression outstanding. These make the micro-blog more complex compared to the formal text. Therefore, all of the cases should be well considered during the design of useful features for the proposed segmentation model.

According to the discussed phenomena, we analyzed the training data of the 500 micro-blog texts that are provided by the Bakeoff-2012. The detailed distributions are shown in Figure 1. The average length of blogs is around 64.62, which includes both Chinese and non-Chinese characters. In average, more than 60% of tokens are single character words. The length of most tokens (around 98.54%) is no more than 4. We consider the URLs as a single token, and hence URLs usually consists of multiple characters (the length is usually more than 6). So, there are more tokens of which length are more than six than the ones with less length (the lengths are 4, 5, and 6).

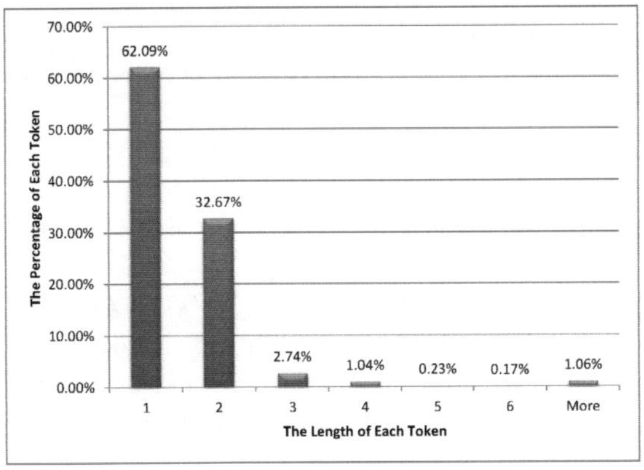

Figure 1. Distribution of token length in micro-blog

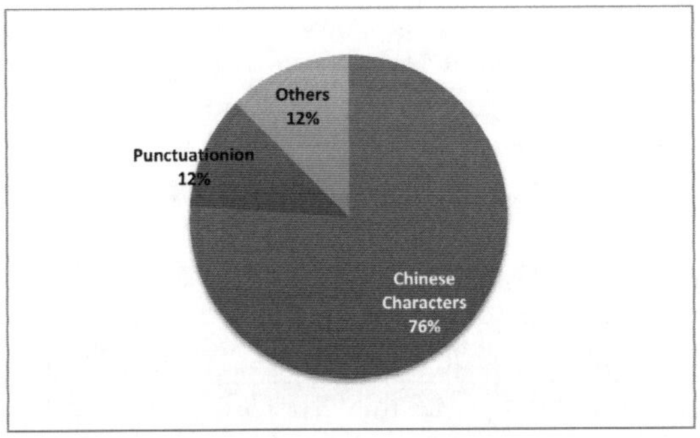

Figure 2. Distribution of different types of characters in micro-blog

Regarding the characters, we found that there are 24% of non-Chinese characters, as shown in Figure 2, which is unusual in comparing with general texts. This fully illustrates its nonstandard phenomena. Among all the non-Chinese characters, half of them are punctuations due to the redundant punctuations used in the blogs for Special expression. So we paid much more attention on those characters during the segmentation.

3 Tag Set

Character based tagging method for Chinese word segmentation, either based on maximum entropy or conditional random fields, views the Chinese word segmentation as a typical sequence labeling problem (Ratnaparkhi, 1996).

There are three kinds of schemes that are commonly used to distinguish the character position in a word, i.e., 6-tag set (Zhao, 2006), 4-tag set (Xue, 2003) and 2-tag set (Tseng, 2005). The details of those schemes are presented in Table 1. A 4-tag set is used for maximum entropy model in (Xue, 2003; Xue and Shen, 2003) and (Low et al., 2005), while a 2-tag set is used for CRFs model in (Peng et al., 2004) and (Tseng et al., 2005). Zhao (2006) extends it into 6-tag set by adding "B2" and "B3" and get a better result in SIGHAN-2006.

6-tag set	
Tag	**Description**
B	First Character (Start of Token)
*B*2	Second Character
*B*3	Third Character
M	The n_{th} Character ($n = 4 \ldots len-1$)
E	Last Character (End of Token)
S	Unit Character
4-tag set	
Tag	**Description**
B	First Character (Start of Token)
M	The n_{th} Character ($n = 4 \ldots len-1$)
E	Last Character (End of Token)
S	Unit Character
2-tag set	
Tag	**Description**
S	First Character (Start of Token)
N	Continuation

Table 1: Various tag sets used for segmentation

Based on Zhao's 6-tag set, we proposed a different tag set which is more suitable for micro-blog text segmentation. The details of the proposed 6-tag set are shown in Table 2. Our system pays more attention to the second last character ("*E2*") of a token, instead of the second one ("*B2*"). In order to evaluate that the proposed 6-tag set is more suitable for micro-blog text, several experiments are conducted to compare between the various schemes used in Chinese segmentation, as described in Section 5.

Proposed 6-tag set	
Tag	**Description**
B	First Character (Start of Token)
B2	Second Character
M	The n_{th} Character ($n = 3...len$-1)
E2	Second Last Character
E	Last Character (End of Token)
S	Unit Character

Table 2: Proposed tag set

4 Feature Template

The selection of feature template is also an important factor. Eight feature templates are selected for this special task.

4.1 Basic features

The basic features of our word segmenter are based on the work of Zhao (2006) and Qin (2010), who achieved very good results in segmentation respectively for common texts and cross domain texts. However, some features are modified to adapt to micro-blog.

The basic feature templates we adopted are given in Table 3. *C* refers to a Chinese character. Templates (a) – (c) refer to a context of three characters (the current character and the proceeding and following characters). C_0 denotes the current character while C_{-1} and C_1 denotes its previous and next character. C_{n-i} (C_{n+i}) denotes the character *i* positions to the right (left) of the current *n*th character. For example, given the character sequence "我成为微博达人 (I become a micro-Bardon)", when considering the character C_0 "微", C_{-1} denotes "为" and C_0C_1 denotes "微博", etc. Different from the previous work (Low, 2005), we reduced the scope of context from 5 to 3. As stated in Section 2, most tokens are 1-character words or 2-character words.

For feature (d), it checks whether C_n is a punctuation symbol (such as "?", "–", ",") or not. In our system, we did not take any special symbols like "#", "@", etc. as punctuations. Because of their specific meanings in micro-blog, for example, "#" is a start or end symbol of a topic and they are often appeared in pairs. This is the main difference in this feature.

No.	Type	Feature
a	Unigram	C_n ,n = 0,-1,1
b	Bigram	$C_n\, C_{n+1}$, n = -1,0
c	Skip	$C_{-1}\, C_1$
d	Punctuation	P_n, n = 0,-1
e	Date, Digit and Letter	$T_{-1}T_0T_1$ T_n, n = -1,-2

Table 3: Basic features (a) to (e)

Besides, we should give an explanation to feature template (e). Based on the 4-classification in (Zhao, 2006), we divided the characters into seven classes. The numbers are represented as Class 1, which both include Arabic numbers and Chinese numbers; alphabetic characters belong Class 2; dates ("日 (*day*)", "月 (*month*)", "年 (*year*)") are Class 3; pound sign (#) and at sign (@) are represented as Class 4 and 5; measure word (e.g. "个 (*ge*)" is a quantifier, which is frequently used in modern Chinese) belongs Class 6, while other characters are Class 7. For example, when considering the character "年" in the sequence "1988 年 Born", the feature $T_{-2}T_{-1}T_0T_1T_2$=11322.

Finally, we did not use the feature of "tone" (Zhao, 2006), because there is no improvement when adopting it in the domain of micro-blog.

4.2 External Dictionary

The use of external dictionary in CRFs models was firstly introduced in (Low et al., 2005). In this approach, each possible subsequence of neighboring characters around C_0 in the sentence is firstly looked up from a dictionary based on maximum match strategy. The longest one *W* in the dictionary will be chosen. Finally, the matched words will be represented in the feature templates. However, there is still a fault in the maximum matching method. For example, given the character sequence "金山石化 (*Golden Hill Petrochemical*)", taking "山 (*hill*) " as the current character C_0, the following candidates of "山 (*hill*)", "金山 (*golden hill*) ", "山石 (*hillstone*) ", "金山石 (*jin shan shi*) ", "山石化 (*shan shi hua*) " and "金山石化 (*Golden Hill Petrochemical*)" can be found. Supposed both "金山" and "山石" are the possible lexicons in the dictionary, it is hard to determine which one is better. The

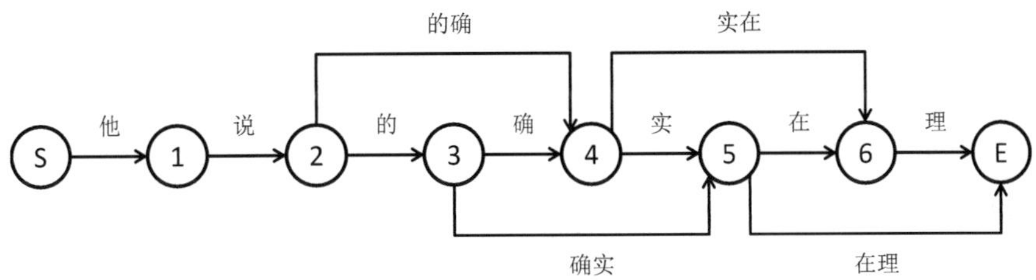

Figure 3. Graph representation of possible segmentations

problem of ambiguity often makes the method fail to determine the correct segmentation, because it does not consider the information of the whole sentence. To solve the conflict, it is used to take the candidate which gives the highest bigram probability in considering of neighboring context.

Therefore, we used the N-Shortest-Paths to fix the ambiguous problems. The details of the approach applied in Chinese word segmentation are discussed in (Leong et al. 2006).

In our system, Google Corpus is used as the external lexicon, which has the 1-gram frequency information of words. As it is the collection of words acquired from online, some popular vocabularies of micro-blog are included. The candidate that gives the highest probability is selected as the final segmentation. In this model, lexicon is represented by a vector of three features and is derived from the used dictionary, as illustrated in Table 4. L_0 is length of current matched word and t_n is position of the nth character in the current matched word. The matching of lexicon is compared against the feature set instead of the lexical item itself.

No.	Type	Feature
f	Length and Position	L_0t_0
g	Character and Position	C_nt_0 (n = -1, 0, 1)
h	Position	t_n (n = -1, 1)

Table 4: Additional features (f) and (g)

Consider the sentence "他说的确实在理 (*what he said is indeed reasonable*)", as shown in Figure 3, it gives several possible segmentation paths, i.e. "他/说/的确/实在/理", "他/说/的确/实/在/理", "他/说/的确/实/在理", "他/说/的/确实/在/理", "他/说/的/确实/在理", and "他/说/的/确/实/在/理". The frequency of each token is treated as the cost of the path. The Dijkstra's algorithm is used for finding optimal path that gives the maximum joint probability. Supposed that the path "他/说/的/确实/在理" is selected and the current character C_0 is "实", the feature templates (f) to (h) are "2E", "实 E" (n = 0) and "S" (n = -1) respectively.

In addition to the Google words, we also include the lists of Chinese idioms, four-word phrases, popular frequently used vocabularies of blogs, and Chinese reduplicating words and emoticons symbols in the proposed system.

4.3 Additional Training Corpus

Corpora in different domains have their own linguistic features and different organizations prepare training corpora in their own standards. These factors mainly limit the amount of training corpora available for micro-blog segmentation. However, the People's Daily Corpus was segmented according to the same segmentation standard (Specification for Corpus Processing at Peking University) (Yu, 2003) as the one adopted by the Bakeoff-2012 for micro-blog. Additionally, Low (2005) presented a method to reduce the OOV problems with additional training corpus. This cross-domain training method is employed in this work to overcome the problem of the micro-blog domain with limited resource.

Therefore, four months of the People's Daily Corpus (1998.01, 1998.09, 2000.03, and 2000.12) were used to extend our limited training data. Several steps are taken for adding additional training corpus:

1. Perform the training step with CRFs models using the original training corpus D_0.
2. Use the trained word segmenter to segment the four-month People's Daily corpus D.
3. Suppose a Chinese character C in D is assigned a boundary tag t by the word segmenter with probability p. If t is identical to the boundary tag of C in the gold-standard annotated corpus D, and p is less than some threshold μ, then the entire correct segment-

ed sentences are added into the original training corpus D_0.

4. Finally, a new word segmenter is trained using the new enlarged dataset.

5 Experiments

In order to obtain the best tag set and best feature templates, we conducted some comparisons with different settings. Due to the limitation of micro-blog corpus, we used a small corpus with 500 sentences, which is released by the CIPS-SIGHAN. 80% of it is used as training data and 20% is for testing set.

	2-Tag Set	4-tag Set	6-Tag Set	Proposed 6-Tag Set
P	0.9199	0.9275	0.9262	**0.9330**
R	0.9275	0.9315	**0.9317**	0.9281
F	0.9237	**0.9295**	0.9289	**0.9305**

Table 5: Evaluation results of various tagging schemes

Firstly, we tested our system with different tag sets. It is found that the model with 4-tag set gives a better result than that of 2-tag set and 6-tag set, while the model with the proposed 6-tag set achieves the best performance among all schemes. The results are shown in Table 4. 6-Tag Set achieves the highest recall value (0.9317), but a little lower than both the proposed tag set and 4-tag set in precision. Although the improvement of the proposed is not very clear, it is only evaluated with 500 sentences. So a good performance of the tag set still can be expected.

Based on the basic feature templates and proposed tag set, three strategies were evaluated. Firstly, there were not any additional dictionaries or corpora involved in the segmented models and this evaluation is the baseline of our experiments. And the Strategy A is applied with all the dictionaries listed in Section 4.2. Finally, both additional dictionaries and corpus were used in Strategy B. As shown in Table 5, the presence of both Strategy A and B achieve much better performance than the baseline proves that additional resources could be helpful to the segmentation for micro-blog. The recall value of Strategy A is higher than that in Strategy B, which prove that additional training corpus do well in reducing the OOV problem. However, the precision declines due to the different domain of data used for training models.

After obtaining the best strategy, a CRFs-based model was trained using the corpus with 500 sentences. And then our Chinese word segmenter was evaluated in an open track, on the test set of 5,000 micro-blog sentences which is released by the second CIPS-SIGHAN.

	Baseline	Strategy A	Strategy B
P	0.8349	0.9330	0.9293
R	0.8284	0.9281	**0.9375**
F	0.8316	**0.9305**	**0.9334**

Table 6: Evaluation results with different strategies

Table 6 shows the official bakeoff results. The column of "Proposed System" shows the precision, recall, F-measure and correct sentence (CS) of our system, which are all very closed to the values of Strategy B in Table 4. This is mainly because a suitable ratio (80% training set and 20% test set) was selected to evaluated presented approach. The third column gives the best value in each measure while Δ stands for the difference between our result and the best one. There is only a gap of 1.4% in F-measure between our system and the best one. The result shows a good performance of the segmentation in the domain of Chinese micro-blog using CRFs-based methods.

	Proposed System	Best Value	Δ
P	0.9294	0.9460	0.0166
R	0.9383	0.9496	0.0113
F	**0.9338**	0.9478	0.0140
CS (%)	37.34%	44.88%	**7.54%**

Table 7: The official bakeoff results

6 Conclusion

This article presents a CRFs-based approach for Chinese micro-blog segmentation. We not only consider the linguistic characteristics of micro-blog, but also solve the problem of small-scale training data with technique to enhance the training corpus. This is the first time to deal with Chinese micro-blog segmentation using CRFs methods. Through the comparison experiments, we found the best tag set, feature template and additional resource for this special task and achieve a good result with a very small training corpus. The performances showed that this method can do a good job of Chinese micro-blog segmentation.

Acknowledgments

This work was partially supported by the Research Committee of University of Macau under grant UL019B/09-Y3/EEE/LYP01/FST, and also supported by Science and Technology Development Fund of Macau under grant 057/2009/A2.

References

Huang C. and Zhao H. 2007. Chinese word segmentation: A decade review. *Journal of Chinese Information Processing*. 21:8–20.

Lafferty J.D., McCallum A., and Pereira F.C.N. 2001. Conditional Random Fields: Probabilistic Models for Segmenting and Labeling Sequence Data. *Proceedings of the Eighteenth International Conference on Machine Learning*. 282–289.

Leong K.S., Wong F., Tang C.W., and Dong M.C. 2006. CSAT: A Chinese segmentation and tagging module based on the interpolated probabilistic model. *Proceedings of the Tenth International Conference on Enhancement and Promotion of Computational Methods in Engineering and Science (EPMESC-X)*. 1092–1098.

Low J.K., Ng H.T., and Guo W. 2005. A maximum entropy approach to Chinese word segmentation. *Proceedings of the Fourth SIGHAN Workshop on Chinese Language Processing*. 161-164.

Qin X., Zong L., Wu Y., Wan X., and Yang J. 2010. CRF-based Experiments for Cross-Domain Chinese Word Segmentation at CIPS-SIGHAN-2010. *In CLP2010*.

Ratnaparkhi A. and others. 1996. A maximum entropy model for part-of-speech tagging. *Proceedings of the Conference on Empirical Methods in Natural Language Processing*. 1:133–142.

Tseng H., Chang P., Andrew G., Jurafsky D., and Manning C. 2005. A conditional random field word segmenter for sighan bakeoff 2005. *Proceedings of the Fourth SIGHAN Workshop on Chinese Language Processing*. vol. 171.

Xue N. 2003. Chinese word segmentation as character tagging. *Computational Linguistics and Chinese Language Processing*. 8:29–48.

Yu S., Duan H., Zhu X., Swen B., and Chang B. 2003. Specification for corpus processing at Peking University: Word segmentation, POS tagging and phonetic notation. *Journal of Chinese Language and Computing*. 13:121–158.

Zhao H., Huang C.N., and Li M. 2006. An improved Chinese word segmentation system with conditional random field. *Proceedings of the Fifth SIGHAN Workshop on Chinese Language Processing*. vol. 1082117.

Zhao H. and Kit C. 2008. Unsupervised segmentation helps supervised learning of character tagging for word segmentation and named entity recognition. *Proceedings of the Sixth SIGHAN Workshop on Chinese Language Processing*. 106–111.

ISCAS: A Cascaded Approach for CIPS-SIGHAN Micro-Blog Word Segmentation Bakeoff 2012 Track

Bei Shi, Xianpei Han, Le Sun
Institute of Software, Chinese Academy of Sciences
HaiDian District, Beijing, China
{shibei, xianpei, sunle}@nfs.iscas.ac.cn

Abstract

The state-of-the-art Chinese word segmentation systems have achieved high performance on well-formed long document. However, the segmentation for microblog is difficult due to the noise problem and the OOV problem. In this paper, we present a Chinese Micro-Blog Segmentation system for the CIP-SIGHAN Word Segmentation Bakeoff 2012 track. The proposed system adopts a cascaded approach which contains three steps, correspondingly the preprocessing, the word segmentation and the post-processing. In the preprocessing step, the noise which contains the special characters is processed and removed. The remaining sentences are segmented in the second step. Finally, we use the dictionary to detect the OOVs which are not correctly segmented. The results show the competitive performance of our approach.

1 Introduction

In recent years, Chinese word segmentation (CWS) has a large of progress on statistical methods (Peng et al., 2004). For instance, character-based tagging method (N Xue et al., 2003) achieves great success in the second International Chinese word segmentation Bakeoff in 2005 (Low et al., 2005). And the state-of-the-art CRF-based systems have achieved great performance using the closed train set and test set. However, the segmentation performance on the web document or on the open set is still low (Huang Changing et al., 2007). Specifically, generated by different kinds of users in the daily life, the micro blogs are noisy and full of OOV (Gustavo et al, 2010). For example, for the brevity and the significance of labels, there are lots of emotion labels, URLs, abbreviations and special characters in the micro-blogs. Otherwise, due to the social property of the micro blogs, there are lots of OOVs (including names of users, stars, locations and organizations), which make it a challenge task for the segmentation of micro blogs.

In this paper, we propose a cascaded approach of Micro-Blog segmentation. Firstly, we use regex expressions to recognize the URLs, English words and Numbers. Some special characters and punctuations are used to split the sentence into pieces. Secondly, the generated components of the sentences are partitioned into smaller pieces which comprise the preliminary result using a segmentation system. Finally, we leverage quantities of dictionaries of OOVs and idioms from the network to merge the words in order to handle the words which are segmented incorrectly. Our system's final F1 score on the test set is 92.73%.

In the rest of this paper, the models and the method used in our tasks are presented in section 2. The experiments and the results are described in section 3. We will discuss the method in section 4. Finally, we give the conclusions and make prospect in the future work.

2 A Cascaded Approach

In this section, we describe our system in detail. The system consists of three steps: preprocessing, HMM-based segmentation (Liu Qun et al., 2004) and post-processing.

2.1 Preprocessing

As mentioned above, the contents of micro blogs is full of noise including special format words and special characters. In order to remove the noise, we preprocess the micro blog content through two steps which are demonstrated below.

Firstly, we recognize and extract the fixed format content types such as date, fraction, and decimals using the regex expressions which are shown in Table 1.

Table 1: The regex expressions for fixed format content extraction

Regex Expression	**Component**
http://[a-zA-Z0-9\/\.]*	URL
www\.[a-zA-Z0-9\/\.]*	URL
[。]+	the sequence of '。'
[￥]{0,}\d+\.\d+	the representation of China Yuan
\d+:\d+[:\d+]	Time
\d+%	Percentage
[\d+\.]%	Percentage
[A-Za-z0-9\-\—_０１２３４５６７８９]+	English words and numbers

Secondly, we split the remaining pieces of sentences using some special characters and punctuations which are shown in Table 2.

Table 2: The split characters

<table>
<tr><th colspan="4">Split characters</th></tr>
<tr><td>Space</td><td>*</td><td>/</td><td>\</td></tr>
<tr><td>[</td><td>]</td><td>《</td><td>》</td></tr>
<tr><td>(</td><td>)</td><td>=</td><td>+</td></tr>
<tr><td>|</td><td>{</td><td>}</td><td>“</td></tr>
<tr><td>#</td><td>:</td><td>!</td><td>@</td></tr>
<tr><td>?</td><td>~</td><td>☆</td><td>◆</td></tr>
<tr><td>【</td><td>】</td><td>→</td><td>◢</td></tr>
</table>

From Table 2, we can see that there are lots of rare characters. It is noteworthy that both the full-width and half-width characters should be used as split characters due to the users' random input in micro blog. In this paper, most of the split characters are extracted from the format reference of the segmentations provided by the organizers.

It may be that a word will be split in-correctly by the split characters. For example, the emotion label '^_^' will be split into '^', '_' and '^'. We will resolve this problem in the step of post processing step.

2.2 Segmentation

Given the split sentences, we segments them into words using two different systems: 1) The first is ChineseNLPTools, a HMM segmentation system trained with Ren Min newspaper corpora; 2) The second is a hierarchical hidden Markov model (HHMM) based system, ICTCLAS (Hua-Ping Zhang et al., 2003), which integrates Chinese word segmentation, Part-Of-Speech tagging, dis-ambulation and unknown words recognition within a uniform framework.

We observed that ICTCLAS is better on recall than ChineseNLPTools in experiments. However, The ChineseNLPTools achieves better performance on named entity reorganization and precision. In order to get better performance, we combine the results of both two tools: we first segment the text using ChineseNLPTools, then the words whose length is greater than four will be segmented again by ICTCLAS and the corresponding results will be replaced.

Because the first name and the last name of people are separated in the format reference, it is important for us to recognize the people name. We use a precision based vote strategy to determine whether a word is named entity using the results of ChineseNLPTools and ICTCLAS.

2.3 Post Processing

In the results produced through the above steps, some words (especially the OOVs) are incorrectly segmented. For example, "盛德利" will be split into "盛" and "德利"。Therefore, we introduce a post processing step which can merge the words into the correct OOVs. Besides, the reduplicated words and the negative words are handled in this step.

We observed that we can better detect the OOVs using more word dictionaries. In this paper, we use the title of Baidu Baike[1], the title of

[1] http://baike.baidu.com

Wikipedia[2], and the list of Chinese and Foreign stars as word dictionaries. We also use the hot topic words in the Feng Yun Bang[3] of Sina Micro Blog. We also use the dictionary of the frequent words of the network which is published by Sogou Labs[4]. The emotion labels will also be extracted in this step.

To merge the different segmentation candidates, we adopt the shortest-path strategy which prefers the long word. In case of the noise in the dictionary, we also filter words whose length is greater than 3 because long words in the dictionary matches will decrease the recall with a fine-grained criterion of segmentation.

After the match of strings, the reduplicated words are merged and handled by rules. Besides, the person names which are voted by the two tokenizers will be split into the first name and the last name in accord with the official format reference.

3 Empirical Results

3.1 Experiment Setup

In the CIPS-SIGHAN track, the train data set consists of 503 sentences. And we mainly do experiments on train data set for evaluating the performance of our tokenizer because of the test data set has not been published.

There are three evaluation metrics used in this bake-off task: Precision (P), Recall (R) and F1, where F1 is calculated as 2RP/(R+P).

3.2 Experimental Results

In this section, we evaluate our methods and discuss the result of each step.

3.2.1 Preprocessing

As mentioned above, we preprocess the sentences to filter out the noise text. We demonstrate the segmentation results with and without preprocessing step in Table 3, where 'With_Pre' denotes the tokenizer with preprocessing and vice versa.

Table 3: Results with and without preprocessing

	Precision	Recall	F1
With_Pre	**0.9367**	**0.9315**	**0.9341**
Without_Pre	0.8898	0.8811	0.8855

From Table 3, we can see that the F score has increased by about 5 percentage points. It means that the step of preprocessing is useful to the word segmentation for micro blogs. And the split characters have a very significance for the noise reduction

We believe this is because the existed tokenizers have worse performance on the words in the format of date, time and so on. Due to the diversity of micro blogs, it is of great difficulty to extract them only through segmentation.

3.2.2 Segmentation

After preprocessing, we compare three tokenizers. The CRF one which uses CRF++ is trained on the corpora of SIGHAN 2005 bakeoff. The ICTCLAS is generated by passing the longer words produced by our model to ICTCLAS. The last one stands for the tokenizer without ICTCLAS.

Table 4: Results of the three tokenizers

	Precision	Recall	F1
CRF	0.8899	0.8679	0.8787
With_ICTCLAS	0.9367	**0.9315**	**0.9341**
Without_ICTCLAS	**0.9375**	0.9233	0.9303

Table 4 shows the results of the three tokenizers. We can see the method of CRF is the worst due to domain variety between the training news document and the test micro blogs. Besides, the tokenizer with ICTCLAS has better performance on Recall and F1. It means ICTCLAS makes a contribution on the recall.

3.2.3 Post-processing

We obtain the preliminary segmentation results through the HHMM model-based segmentation, and then we detect the OOVs using different dictionaries. In order to eliminate as more errors as possible, we demonstrate how adding resources will increase the segmentation performance.

[2] http://zh.wikipedia.org
[3] http://data.weibo.com/top
[4] http://www.sogou.com/labs/dl/w.html

Figure 1: The performance using different resources

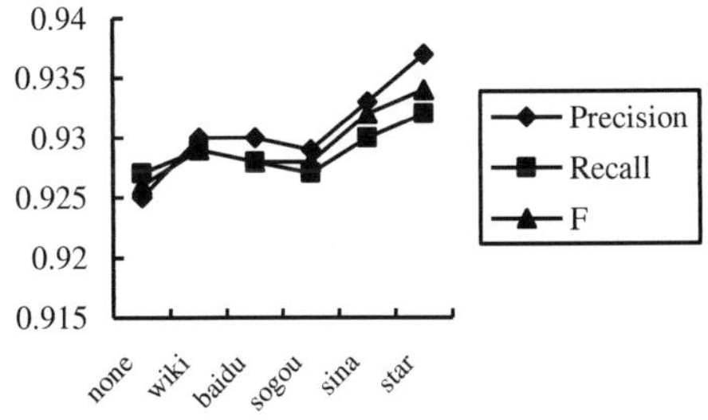

Figure 1 illustrates the quality of the dictionaries. 'None' stands for the system without the OOV dictionary. 'Wiki' stands for the import of the title of wiki. 'Baidu' denotes the title of Baidu Baike. 'Sogou' stands for the frequent words list of web published by Sogou Labs. 'Sina' means the frequent words that appear in micro blog frequently and 'star' means the list of the stars captured on the Internet. The curves decrease at the point of 'baidu' and 'sogou'. It indicates the quality of 'baidu' and 'sogou' is poorer than others due to its consistency with the original micro blog segmentation. For example, the word '打卤面' are merged in the dictionary while '打卤' and '面' are split in the corpus. The growth trend of the whole curve shows that the use of resources can improve the overall segmentation performance.

After processing the reduplicated words, negative words and quantifiers, the final segmentation performance increases 1% in F1.

3.3 Evaluation and Analysis in Test Set

In this task of micro blogs, our final results are showed in Table 5. "CS" denotes the number of the correct sentences; "PCS" denotes the percentage of the correct sentences. The first row is our result and the second row is the best result in this task.

Table 5: Final Result of the Test Set

Precision	Recall	F	CS	PCS
0.9258	0.9288	0.9273	1684	33.68%
0.946	0.9496	0.9478	2244	44.88%

Table 5 indicates that our result (0.9273) of the test set is worse than our result on the train set (0.9341). We believe this is because the resources are not sufficient for the test set.

4 Discussion

In this task, our result is slightly lower than the best performance. The reasons are as follows. First, spelling mistakes and the abbreviations of words which are common in micro blogs make the segmentation more difficult. What is more, the social property of micro blogs also increases the appearance of person names, location names, etc. Second, the quality of the dictionaries we crawl from the Internet is not as high as we expected (For example, Baidu Baike and Sogou). Third, we use the dictionaries determinedly by the shortest path, rather than probabilistically. This will make some mistake since it didn't consider the context of the OOVs. Besides, a large number of OOVs do not exist in our dictionary because of there are not up-to-date. Finally, the criterion of segmentation of our own tokenizer is not in accordance with the official criterion. In a word, the users' imagination and the properties of micro blogs cause difficulties on the segmentation.

5 Conclusions and Future work

In this paper, we have briefly described a cascaded approach for the Chinese word segmentation for micro blogs. A HMM model is implemented and combined with ICTCLAS. In order to solve the noise and the OOV in micro blog, we employ some special strategies. The results on training data set and test data set show that our approach is competitive. However, our method still has much improvement room to resolve the problem of OOVs in micro blog.

Acknowledgements

The work is supported by the National Natural Science Foundation of China under Grants no 90920010 and 61100152.

References

Xue, Nianwen, 2003, Chinese Word Segmentation as Character Tagging, Computational Linguistics and Chinese Language Processing. Vol.8, No.1, pp29-48

Peng, F., F. Feng, and A. McCallum. 2004. Chinese segmentation and new word detection using conditional random fields. Proceedings of the 20th international conference on Computational Linguistics

Low, Jin Kiat et al., 2005, A Maximum Entropy Approach to Chinese Word Segmentation. Proceedings of the Fourth SIGHAN Workshop on Chinese Language Processing, Jeju Island, Korea,. pp161-164

Huang Changning, HaoHai. 2007. Ten Years of Chinese word segmentation. Vol. 21, No. 3. JOURNAL OF CHINESE INFORMATION PROCESSING

Gustavo Laboreiro and Luis Sarmento. 2010. Tokenizing Micro-Blogging Messages using a Text Classification Approach. AND'10, October 26, 2010, Toronto, Ontario, Canada.

Liu Qun, Zhang Huaping, Yu Hongkui. 2004. Chinese lexical analysis using cascaded hidden Markov model. Journal of Computer Research and Development, 2004, 41(8):1421-1429

Hua-Ping Zhang, Hong-Kui Yu, De-Yi Xiong and Qun Liu. 2003. HHMM-based Chinese Lexical Analyzer ICTCLAS. SIGHAN'03 Proceedings of the second SIGHAN workshop on Chinese Language Processing - Volume 17, Pages 184-187

Adapting Conventional Chinese Word Segmenter for Segmenting Micro-blog Text: Combining Rule-based and Statistic-based Approaches

Ning Xi, Bin Li, Guangchao Tang, Shujian Huang, Yinggong Zhao, Hao Zhou, Xinyu Dai, Jiajun Chen
State Key Laboratory for Novel Software Technology,
Department of Computer Science and Technology,
Nanjing University, Nanjing, 210023, China
{xin,lib,tanggc,huangsj,zhaoyg,zhouh,dxy,chenjj}@nlp.nju.edu.cn

Abstract

We describe two adaptation strategies which are used in our word segmentation system in participating the Micro-blog word segmentation bake-off: Domain invariant information is extracted from the in-domain unlabelled corpus, and is incorporated as supplementary features to conventional word segmenter based on Conditional Random Field (CRF), we call it *statistic-based* adaptation. Some heuristic rules are further used to post-process the word segmentation result in order to better handle the characters in emoticons, name entities and special punctuation patterns which extensively exist in micro-blog text, and we call it *rule-based* adaptation. Experimentally, using both adaptation strategies, our system achieved 92.46 points of F-score, compared with 88.73 points of F-score of the unadapted CRF word segmenter on the pre-released development data. Our system achieved 92.51 points of F-score on the final test data.

1 Introduction

Recent years have witnessed the great development of Chinese word segmentation (CWS) techniques. Among various approaches, character labelling via *Conditional Random Field* (CRF) modelling has become a prevailing technique (Lafferty et al., 2001; Xue, 2003; Zhao et al., 2006), due to its good performance in OOV words recognition and low development cost. Given a large-scale corpus with human annotation, the only issue the developer need to focus on is to design an expressive set of feature templates which captures the various characteristics of word segmentation to achieve better performance.

The demand for Chinese micro-blog data mining has been unprecedentedly increased, owing to the growing number of the Chinese micro-blog users in the past few years. In these tasks, Chinese word segmentation plays an important role in correctly understanding the micro-blog text. Chinese word segment on the micro-blog text is a challenging task. On one hand, it is difficult to obtain large-scale labelled corpora of micro-blog domain for CRF-based learning, and the only labelled corpus we have is *People's Daily corpus* (PDC) which comes from the News domain; on the other, compared with the News text, the micro-blog text contains a large number of new words, name entities, URLs, emoticons (such as ":)"), punctuation patterns (such as "...."), as well as structured symbols representing conversation ("@"), repost("//@"), and topic ("#...#") etc. The word distribution and usage of micro-blog text are also much more free than the News text, making things more difficult.

In this paper, we adapt the conventional Chinese word segmenter which is trained on out-of-domain (News domain) labelled corpus using CRF to segment in-domain micro-blog text, without using any information from the labelled in-domain data. We use two adaptation strategies: the first is *statistic-based adaptation*. We incorporate domain invariant information extracted from the in-domain unlabelled corpus as supplementary features to the conventional CRF segmenter, in order to enhance its ability of recognizing domain-specific words. The unlabelled corpus can be conveniently crawled from the web; the other is *rule-based adaptation*. We proposed some heuristic rules to further post-process the word segmentation result in order to enhance to better handle the characters in emoticons, name entities and special punctuation patterns which extensively exist in micro-blog text. Experimentally, using both adaptation strategies, our system achieved 92.46 points of F-score, compared with 88.73 points of F-score of the unadapted CRF word segmenter on the pre-released development data. Our system achieved 92.51 points of F-score on the final test data.

2 System Description

In this section, we describe our adapted CRF-based word segmenter.

2.1 Basic Model

Chinese word segmentation (CWS) was first formulated as a character tagging problem by Xue (2003). This approach treats the unsegmented Chinese sentence as a character sequence. It assigns a label to each Chinese character in the sentence, indicating whether a character locates at the beginning of (label "B") of a word, inside ("M") a word, at the end ("E") of a word, or itself forms a single character word ("S"). An example of the labelled sequence is shown in Table 1, which corresponds to the word segmentation "开/出/一朵朵/红莲".

Sequence	开	出	一	朵	朵	红	莲
Label	S	S	B	M	E	B	E

Table 1: An example of labelled sequence

Conditional Random Field (CRF) (Lafferty et al., 2001) is a statistical sequence labelling model. It assigns the probability of a particular label sequence as follows:

$$P(y_1^T|w_1^T) = \frac{exp(\sum_t \sum_k \lambda_k f_k(y_{t-1}, y_t, w_1^T, t))}{Z(w_1^T)} \quad (1)$$

where $w_1^T = w_1 w_2 ... w_T$ is the Chinese character sequence, y_1^T is the corresponding label sequence, t is the index of the character, y_{t-1} and y_t denote the label of the $t-1$th and the t-th character respectively, f_k is a feature function and k ranges from 1 to the number of features, λ_k is the associated feature weight, and $Z(w_1^T)$ is the normalization factor. λ_ks are trained on *People's Daily corpus* (PDC) which is a out-of-domain labelled corpus. In our implementation, CRF++ package[1] was used.

Without any constraint, the CRF model will label Chinese characters as well as non-Chinese characters in the sentence being segmented, including English letters and numeric characters. These non-Chinese characters are strong indicators of word boundaries. Therefore, we use the following heuristics to pre-group these characters: 1) all consecutive English characters. They often form English words or abbreviations (such as "HTC" in sentence "领取HTC手机"), 2) all consecutive numeric characters. They often form numeric words (such as the "205" in sentence "进入205房间"). Splitting these two kinds of consecutive characters will yield meaningless words. Treating these two kinds of words as single units in implementing CRF will not only speed up the decoding process but also improve the segmentation performance on these kinds of words. Moreover, the characters in a URL are pre-grouped using a simple regular expression, and punctuations representing structure symbols (such as conversation ("@"), repost("//@"), topic ("#...#")) are treated as a single unit.

2.2 Feature Template

The primary art in CRF-based CWS is to design an expressive set of features that captures the various characteristics of CWS. In the next, we will elaborate three kinds of features we adopted in our system, including character-based features (section 2.2.1), word-based features (section 2.2.2) and metric-based features (section 2.2.3).

2.2.1 Character-based Features

The character-based features are extensively used by almost all the CRF word segmenters (Xue, 2003; Zhao et al., 2006). Word segmenters incorporating character features have a good generalization ability in recognizing OOV words. To conveniently illustrate the features we used, we denote the current character token c_i, and its context characters $...c_{i-1}c_ic_{i+1}...$. Moreover, we define $p_i = 1$ if c_i is a punctuation character and $p_i = 0$ otherwise, $n_i = 1$ if c_i is numeric character and $n_i = 0$ otherwise, $a_i = 1$ if c_i is English letter and $a_i = 0$ otherwise. The character-based features template associated with each character type are listed in Table 2.

[1] http://crfpp.googlecode.com/svn/trunk/doc/index.html

Type	Template
surface form	$c_{-1}, c_0, c_1, c_{-1}c_0, c_0c_1, c_{-1}c_1$
number	$n_{-1}, n_0, n_1, n_{-1}n_0, n_0n_1, n_{-1}n_1$
punctuation	p_{-1}, p_0, p_1
English letter	$a_{-1}, a_0, a_1, a_{-1}a_0, a_0a_1, a_{-1}a_1$

Table 2: Character-based feature template.

2.2.2 Word-based Features

Combining word-based features and character-based features has been suggested by (Sun 2010; Sun and Xu, 2011), based on the observation that word-based features capture a relatively larger context than character-based features. We define $c_{[i:j]}$ as a string that starts at the i-th character and ends at the j-th character, and then define $D_{[i:j]} = 1$ if $c_{[i:j]}$ matches a word in a pre-defined dictionary, and 0 otherwise. The word-based feature templates are listed in Table 3.

Template
$D_{[i-5:i]}, D_{[i-4:i]}, D_{[i-3:i]}, D_{[i-2:i]}, D_{[i-1:i]}$
$D_{[i:i+1]}, D_{[i:i+2]}, D_{[i:i+3]}, D_{[i:i+4]}, D_{[i:i+5]}$

Table 3: Word-based feature template.

In order to incorporate word-based features, two dictionaries are constructed. The first dictionary consists of words which were directly extracted from the PDC, and the second dictionary consists of the words in the first dictionary as well as the n-grams with length up to 3 which are extracted from the unsegmented micro-blog corpus and have higher confidence scores than a pre-defined threshold. In our system, we choose *Mutual information* (MI) to measures the association between two consecutive characters. The higher the MI, the more likely these two characters are contained in the same word. We adopted the method of Li and Chen (2006) (Eq. 2) to compute the mutual information of strings with length up to four. In practice, we use 7.0 as the threshold.

$$\begin{aligned} MI(a,b) &= \frac{P(ab)}{P(a)P(b)} \\ MI(a,b,c) &= \frac{P(ab)P(bc)P(ac)}{P(a)P(b)P(c)P(abc)} \end{aligned} \quad (2)$$

2.2.3 Metric-based Feature

We use two metrics to compute the confidence of how likely a string in the unsegmented micro-blog text be a word, they are *Accessor Variety* and *Punctuation Variety*. These metrics can be computed conveniently on large-scale in-domain unlabelled corpus using suffix array (Kit and Wilks, 1999). The values of these metrics can be used as supplementary features to the baseline CRF-based word segmenter. These features are domain-invariant (Gao et al., 2010), therefore, the associated feature weights can be trained on out-of-domain labelled corpus. We call the approach *statistic-based adaptation*.

Accessor Variety (AV) is firstly proposed by Feng et al. (2004) in the task of identifying meaningful Chinese words from an unlabelled corpus. The basic idea of this approach is when a string appears under different linguistic contexts, it may carry a meaning. The more contexts a string appears in, the more likely it is a independent word. Given a string s, we define the *left accessor variety* of s as the number of distinct characters that precede s in the corpus, denoted by $L_{AV}(s)$. The higher value $L_{AV}(s)$ is, the more likely that s can be separated at its start position. Similarly, *right accessor variety* of s is defined as the number of distinct characters that follow s in the corpus, denoted by $R_{AV}(s)$. The higher value $R_{AV}(s)$ is, the more likely that s can be separated at its end position.

Punctuation Variety (PV) is a metric similar to AV, which is used by Sun and Xu (2011). The basic idea is when a string appears many times preceding or following punctuations, there tends to be word-breaks succeeding or preceding that string. We define the *left punctuation variety* of a string s as the number of times a punctuation precedes s in a corpus, denoted by $L_{PV}(s)$, and define the *right punctuation variety* of a string s as the number of times a punctuation follows s in a corpus, denoted by $R_{PV}(s)$.

As the values of AV and PV are integers, when incorporating them as features in CRF, simple discretization method is adopted to deal with data sparseness. For example, the value of PV are binned into two intervals. If it is greater than 30, the feature "$PV > 30$" is set to 1 while the feature "PV(0-30)" is set to 0; if the value is less than 30, the feature "$PV > 30$" is set to 0 while the feature "PV(0-30)" is set to 1; The value of AV are also binned into three intervals: "< 30", "30-50", and "> 50", and is incorporated similarly as PV.

Template
$L_{AV}(c_{[i:i+1]}), L_{AV}(c_{[i+1:i+2]})$
$L_{AV}(c_{[i:i+2]}), L_{AV}(c_{[i+1:i+3]})$
$L_{AV}(c_{[i:i+3]}), L_{AV}(c_{[i+1:i+4]})$
$R_{AV}(c_{[i-1:i]}), R_{AV}(c_{[i-2:i-1]})$
$R_{AV}(c_{[i-2:i]}), R_{AV}(c_{[i-3:i-1]})$
$R_{AV}(c_{[i-3:i]}), R_{AV}(c_{[i-4:i-1]})$
$L_{PV}(c_{[i:i+1]}), L_{PV}(c_{[i:i+2]}), L_{PV}(c_{[i:i+3]}),$ $R_{PV}(c_{[i-1:i]}), R_{PV}(c_{[i-2:i]}), R_{PV}(c_{[i-3:i]})$

Table 4: Feature template of accessor variety and punctuation variety.

2.3 Rule-based Adaptation

We proposed some heuristic rules to further post-process the results given by the word segmenter as described above, in order to better handle the following patterns which are hard to recognize otherwise.

Emoticon In the original output of CRF segmenter, characters representing an emoticon are usually separated by spaces. For example, the emoticon ":-D" is usually segmented as ": - D" which does not preserve the meaning of "smile". To reduce the segmentation errors like this, we collected a list of emoticons from the web. For each emoticon in the list, we create a regular expression which removes any intervening space in this emoticon.

Full Stops In the micro-blog text, consecutive stops such as "..." or consecutive Chinese stops such as "。。。。" are often used to express the meaning of being surprised or embarrassed. We create a rule to group these stops. According to the official pre-released development data (see section 3.1), every three consecutive stops from left to right in the output of CRF segmenter are grouped as a token, the remaining one or two stops are also grouped when necessary.

Name Entities As our system does not have separate modules to recognize name entities, we leverage ICTCLAS[2] to recognize them. We use the ICTCLAS to segment and POS-tag the micro-blog text. If a word is POS-tagged as *nr, ns, nt, nz, nl, or ng* by ICTCLAS, we adjusted our word segmentation to accept this word too.

Setting	P	R	F
CRF	89.18	88.29	88.73
+RB	91.34	91.72	91.53
+RB+WF0	90.67	93.94	92.28
+RB+WF1	91.80	92.26	92.03
+RB+MF	91.99	91.18	91.58
+RB+WF0+MF	91.15	93.82	92.46
+RB+WF1+MF	91.91	92.21	92.06

Table 5: Results of our systems on development data, measured in **P**: precision, **R**: recall, and **F**: F-score. **RB**: rule-base adaptation. **WF0**: word-based feature using dictionary extracted from data (a). **WF1**: word-based feature using dictionary extract from both data (a) and data (b). **MF**: metric-based feature.

3 Experiments

3.1 Data

The following four pieces of data were used in our experiment:

(a) out-of-domain labelled corpus. *People's Daily Corpus* of the first half year in 1998, which is segmented under PKU specification[3]. It was used as CRF training corpus;

(b) in-domain unlabelled corpus. It is a large micro-blog corpus containing 1.9M sentences crawled from the web. It was used to compute word-based features or metric-based features for CRF training;

(c) official pre-released development data. It contains 600 segmented sentences in micro-blog domain under PKU specification. In our experiments, it is only used as **development data** to choose the best setting;

(d) official released test data. It is used for final evaluation.

Full-width characters in all the above data are converted to the corresponding half-width characters. Traditional Chinese characters are also converted to their simplified version.

[2] a well-known Chinese word segmenter/POS-tagger downloaded from www.ictclas.org/

[3] PKU specification is adopted in this track

	P	R	F	CS	CS(%)
Baseline+RB+WF0	0.924	0.9262	0.9251	1628	32.56
Best System	0.946	0.9496	0.9478	2244	44.88

Table 6: Comparison of our system and the best system in the Bake-off on the final test data. **CS**: the number of correct sentences. **CS(%)**: percent of the number of correct sentences.

3.2 Results on development data

We first conducted experiments on the development data to investigate the effectiveness of various features. Table 5 shows the results of seven settings in terms of precision, recall and F-score. **Baseline** represents the setting of the conventional CRF, where only character-based features were incorporated, and no adaptation strategy was used. As we can see, having incorporated rule-based adaptation into the baseline, as shown in **Baseline+RB**, the F-score was significantly improved from 88.73 to 91.53, which achieved a 24.8% reduction of error rate. This improvement shows that rule-based adaptation is an very simple and effective approach in adapting a conventional word segmenter to work on micro-blog domain.

We next investigated incorporating word-based features into **Baseline+RB**. As noted in section 2.2.2, we tried two dictionaries respectively, the first dictionary was extracted from only data (a), denoted by **Baseline+RB+WF0**; and the other dictionary was extracted from both data (a) and data (b), denoted by **Baseline+RB+WF1**. We see that using the first dictionary yielded an improvement of 0.75 points of F-scores, compared to **Baseline+RB**. However, using the second dictionary yielded an improvement of 0.5 F-score only. These results suggest that incorporating word-based features do improve the word segmentation results, however, its effectiveness could rely heavily on the quality of the dictionary. The first dictionary consists of words extracted from from data (a), which is annotated by humans, thus it is of high quality. However, the words extracted from data (b) are not guaranteed to be genuine words because they are included into the second dictionary as long as their confidence scores were higher than the threshold. The noisy words in the second dictionary seem to be blame for the worse results in **Baseline+RB+WF1**.

We then evaluated the impact of incorporating metric-based features. Moving from **Baseline+RB** to **Baseline+RB+MF**, the F-score increased from 91.51 to 91.58. It seems that the metric-based features are not very useful. However, comparing **Baseline+RB+WF0** and **Baseline+RB+WF0+MF**, the improvement increased from 92.28 to 92.46, and **Baseline+RB+WF0+MF** achieved the best performance among all settings, indicating the effectiveness of using metric-based features. Again, **Baseline+RB+WF0+MF** outperformed **Baseline+RB+WF1+MF**, which confirms the conclusion we draw in the last paragraph. Overall, both rule-based adaptation and statistic-based adaptation work well in micro-blog word segmentation.

Finally, we present the results of our system and the best system on the test data in Table 6. Although our results underperformed the best system with a margin of 2.27 points of F-score, we did not use any information extracted from in-domain labelled corpus, i.e. development corpus.

4 Conclusions and Future Works

We describe our Chinese word segmentation systems that we developed for participating the Chinese Micro-blog Word Segmentation Bakeoff. We adapt the conventional Chinese word segmenter which is trained on segmented News domain corpus by Conditional Random Field (CRF) to work on text from the micro-blog domain. Both statistic-based and rule-based adaptation strategies are demonstrated useful in micro-blog word segmentation.

In the future, we will firstly try to investigate how to incorporate more effective domain invariant features to improve the results. We will also try to develop better domain-specific name entity recognition tools to further enhance the performance.

Acknowledgements

We thank anonymous reviewers for their constructive comments. This work is supported by the National Natural Science Foundation of China (No. 61003112 and No. 61170181), the Research Fund for the Doctoral Program of Higher Education of China (Grant No. 20110091110003), China Post Doctoral Fund under contract 2012M510178, and Jiangsu Post Doctoral Fund under contract 1101065C.

References

Weiwei Sun. 2010. Word-based and Character-based Word Segmentation Models: Comparison and Combination. *Proceedings of COLING 2010*, 1211–1219.

Weiwei Sun, Jia Xu. 2011. Enhancing Chinese Word Segmentation Using Unlabelled Data. *Proceedings of the 2011 Conference on Empirical Methods in natural language Processing*, 970–979.

John D. Lafferty, Andrew McCallum, and Fernando C. N. Pereira. 2001. Comditional Random Fields: Probabilistic models for segmenting and labelling sequence data. *Proceedings of ICML 2001*, 282–289.

Haodi Feng, Kang Chen, Xiaotie Deng, Weimin Zheng. 2004. Accessor Variety Criteria for Chinese Word Extraction. *Computational Linguistics*, 30:75–93.

Wenjun Gao, Xipeng Qiu, and Xuanjing Huang. 2010. Adaptive Chinese Word Segmentation with Online Passive-Aggressive Algorithm. *CIPS-SIGHAN Joint Conference on Chinese Language Processing*.

Zhongguo Li and maosong Sun. 2009. Punctuation as Implicit Annotations for Chinese Word Segmentation. *Computational Linguistics*, 35:505–512.

Chunyu Kit and Yorick Wilks. 1998. The Virtual Corpus Approach to Deriving N-gram Statistics from large Scale Corpora. *Proceedings of the 1998 International Conference on Chinese Information Processing*, :223–229.

Nianwen Xue. 2003. Chinese Word Segmentation as Character Tagging. *Proceedings of the International Journal of Computational Linguistics and Chinese Language Processing*.

Bin Li and Xiaohe Chen. 2003. A Human-Computer Interaction Word Segmentation Method Adapting to Chinese Unknown Texts. *Journal of Chinese Information Processing*.

Hai Zhao, Chang-Ning Huang, and Mu Li 2006. An improved Chinese Word Segmentation System with Conditional Random Field.. *Proceeding of SIGHAN-5*, 162–165.

Cascaded Chinese Weibo Segmentation Based on CRFs

Keli Zhong, Xue Zhou, Hangyu Li and Caixia Yuan
School of Computer,
Beijing University of Posts and Telecommunications,
Beijing, 100876 China
zhongkeli@139.com yuancx@bupt.edu.cn
{bupt.zhouxue, hangyuli1209}@gmail.com

Abstract

With the developments of Web2.0, the process for the data on Internet becomes necessary. This Paper reports our work for Chinese weibo segmentation in the 2012 CIPS-SIGHAN bakeoff. In order to improve the recognition accuracy of out-of-vocabulary words, we propose a cascaded model which first segments and disambiguates in-vocabulary words, then recovers out-of-vocabulary words from the fragments. Both the two process are trained by a character-based CRFs model with user-edited external vocabulary. The final performance on the test data shows that our system achieves a promising result.

1 Introduction

Since there are no spaces in Chinese sentences, Chinese word segmentation becomes a vital and fundamental task in Chinese language processing. Many approaches have been implemented in Chinese segmentation, including simple Forward Maximum Match (FMM), statistic based methods like Hidden Markov model, conditional random fields model, along with other learning models(Sproat et al., 1996; Xue and Shen, 2003; Tseng et al., 2005; Song et al., 2006). The main problems of segmentation are word boundary ambiguities and out-of-vocabulary (OOV) word recognition while many researchers have been working on them (Wang et al., 2008; Xu et al., 2010; Koichi et al., 2002).

Recent developments in Web 2.0 have heightened the need for Web text processing (Downey et al., 2007), which makes the problems above more prominent. Being different from traditional texts like news reports and literary works, Web texts like microblogs, tweets tend to be more oral, casual, and have plenty of catchwords, typos and OOVs in them, which bring much challenge to language understanding. For example, "Gelivable" is a Chinglish word coined by Chinese people stands for the word "给力" (awesome), which is a popular Chinese catchword in Web texts. Some users leave the typos deliberately to unique and individual. For instance, "碎叫" (shleep) stands for "睡觉" (sleep). Although human people would understand the meaning of this piece of Chinese tweets, segmenter based on dictionary may never understand how it went wrong (Bian, 2006). In the next place, thousands of new words emerge from current event, social phenomena or even actors' lines. For instance, "喵星人" and "基友" are the new words that emerged from Internet not long ago, which stands for "cat" and "gay friend" respectively. And the sentence patterns like "神马都是浮云" (Everything is nothing.) a prevalent slogan of many people on the Internet. These phenomena exemplified above exacerbate the OOV problem (Xu et al., 2008). Take weibo, a popular Chinese MicroBlog, for example, within a piece of text restricted to 140 Chinese characters, there are 21.7(15.5%) OOV words on average. Finally, the structure of MicroBlog sentences prone to be simple, elliptical, non-predicate and incompleteness. Some of the sentences are mixed with words in foreign languages and emoticons (like :), ToT). Hence the segmenter based on linguistic knowledge would not be efficient enough (Li et al., 1998).

In order to better solve the Web text problems, we propose an efficient Chinese Web text segmentation model based on CRF model with a user-edited dictionary. Specifically, we first conduct a coarse-grained segment for input Web text, then refine the results through models learned from new word vocabulary provided by users.

Following sections describe in detail the proposed method and its results on the SIGHAN 2012 Chinese MicroBlog segmentation task. In section 2 to 4, we introduce the main idea of our method. Section 5 gives experiment results and related analysis, which proves the effectiveness of our model. Section 6 addresses the future work.

2 Our Method

We use a CRF model[1] based on character to implement Chinese MicroBlog segmentation. Following the work of (Qin et al., 2008), we use a BIO style to formulate the word segmentation into a sequence learning task. We define 6 tags in order to distinguish different roles of characters more accurately. The 6 tags and their descriptions are denoted in Table 1.

label	meaning
B	the start of word
E	the end of word
M1	the 1st character of a word
M2	the 2nd character of a word
M	other characters of a word
S	single-character word

Table 1: Labels and their descriptions.

2.1 Basic procedure

The processing of word segmentation is shown in Fig.1.

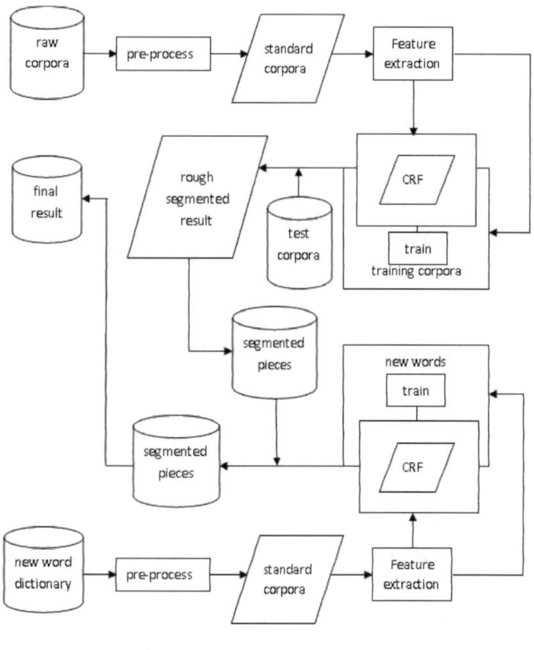

Figure 1: Framework of our segmentation model.

[1]CRF++0.54, http://crfpp.sourceforge.net/

We use 6 months of PKU people's daily data in year 2000 (Yu et al., 2002) as training corpora, in which the sentences in paragraphs have been segmented into words by spaces. In order to construct the character-level based segmenter, we transform the original corpora into the sequential form representing by 6 labels shown in Table 1, and each line only includes one character and its corresponding label.

2.2 Feature selection

As the feature has great influence on the segmentation result, hence what kinds of features should be selected is the key to our task.

We design two classes of feature templates: (1) Unigram feature template, (2) Bigram feature template. Particularly, the Unigram and Bigram that we use here are the count for label that exist in feature, not the count for the character that exist in feature. From this point of view, the meaning of Unigram and Bigram are no longer the same with other existing papers (Jurafsky et al., 2007; Chen et al., 2005).

For character level based Chinese segmentation, character feature is the major concern here. According to the distance from current character, we have features 1-5 respectively as depicted in Table2., and these features belong to Unigram feature templates. The context characters are confined to be two characters around the character at hand. These template features would expand into thousands of features while CRF training, and each feature corresponds to a feature function, which are vital to CRFs model's learning process.Besides the context characters of the current, we also take their bigram sequence into account when designing feature template, which corresponds to features 6-8 in Table 2.

Another critical feature for character tag labeling is the type of the character at hand. We distinguish the character with 4 types including Chinese character, English character, number, punctuation, and add the character type into the feature template as a Unigram feature, which are represented as feature 9 and 10 in Table 2.

The feature templates in Table 2 are basic feature templates designed from character position and their types.

In order to exploit more deliberate properties of how likely a sequence of characters being a word, we investigate the probability of two adja-

No.	feature	feature description
1	C_{-2}	the 2nd lefthand character of C_0
2	C_{-1}	the 1st lefthand character of C_0
3	C_0	current character
4	C_1	the 1st righthand character of C_0
5	C_2	the 2nd righthand character of C_0
6	$C_{-1}C_0$	sequence of C_{-1} and C_0
7	C_0C_1	sequence of C_0 and C_1
8	$C_{-1}C_1$	sequence of C_{-1} and C_1
9	T_0	type of C_0
10	$T_{-1}T_1$	type of C_{-1} and C_0

Table 2: Context features and character type features we used.

cent characters forming a word, that is the cohesion of two characters on word level. Consider the current character C_0, and the probability of being a word with the lefthand character C_{-1} can be computed as:

$$P_{-1,0} = \frac{W(C_{-1}C_0)}{Count(C_{-1}C_0)} \quad (1)$$

in which $W(C_{-1}C_0)$ represents the amount of $C_{-1}C_0$ as a word that exist in the training corpora, and $Count(C_{-1}C_0)$ represents the amount of $C_{-1}C_0$ that appear in a sentence.

For instance:

1) 中国 的 士兵 (China 's soldier)

2) 中国 的士 (China taxi)

W("的士")=1, while Count("的士")=2.

We used 3 levels to represent the cohesion of two characters, and add them into the feature template as uniform features as is shown in Table 3.

No.	feature	feature description
11	S	$P_{-1,0} < 0.2$ the probability of character C_i and C_j being a word is low
12	NS	$P_{-1,0} > 0.75$ the probability of character C_i and C_j of being a word is high
13	N	$0.2 \leq P_{c_ic_j} \leq 0.75$

Table 3: Character cohesion features.

Finally, 13 features are used for CRF model training, including basic Unigram features in Table 2 and the being-a-word features in Table 3. We train a CRFs model using feature templates listed in Table 2 and 3. This model is then used for the first-round segmentation which yields a word and fragment sequence. Our experiment results depicted later show that this model achieves high performance for in-vocabulary words, while most out-of-vocabulary words are segmented as character fragments. Thus we will investigate the improved model for recognizing such OOV words.

3 User Editable Dicitionary

In order to make model exploit external knowledge about OOV words and easily adapt to different user demand, we design a plug-in user dictionary, which is used to refine the segmentation model trained in Section 2. For SIGHAN MicroBlog segmentation task, we collect 278,060 words from Sogou word bank[2]. Due to MicroBlogs are the epitome of people's life, so the new words we collected from Sogou word bank are close to the type that used in MicroBlogs, which consists of newly invented words on the Internet, dishes' name, celebrities' name, online shopping words (product names, brands, etc.) and others that is related with people's daily life.

4 Refined OOV Word Recognition Model

Quite amount of OOV would emerge during the MicroBlog segmentation. Based on the vocabulary collected in Section 3, we refine the segmentation results yielded in the first-round segmentation depicted in Section 2. The refined model is trained on the user-edited vocabulary and is to used for a second-round segmentation. Each word is viewed as a training sample. Besides feature templates listed in Table 2, we design several new features for the refined model which is described in Table 4.

No.	feature	feature description
14	$C_{-2}C_{-1}$	sequence of C_{-2} and C_{-1}
15	C_1C_2	sequence of C_1 and C_2
16	$C_{-1}C_0P_{-1,0}$	sequence of C_{-1}, C_0 and $P_{-1,0}$

Table 4: New context features and character type features in Model 1, while other features are already shown in Table 2.

The function of Model 1 is to segment test corpora for the first time. And the features it uses is shown in Table 4.

[2]http://pinyin.sogou.com/dict/

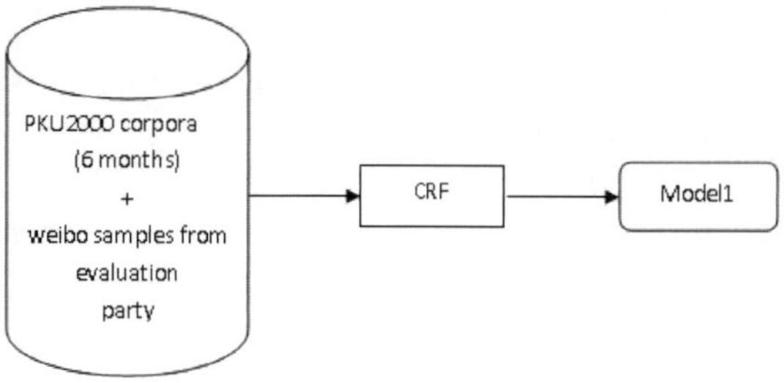

Figure 2: Training process.

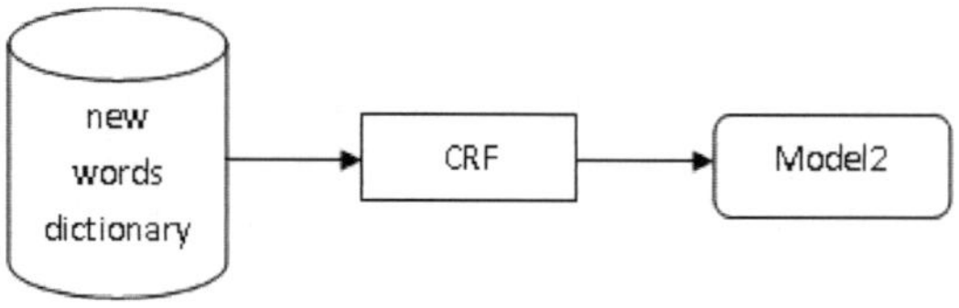

Figure 3: New words training process.

Model2 is trained using new words from user-editable dictionary. Each word is viewed as a training sample and features are extracted according to feature templates shown in Table 2.

The whole structure of the Model is shown in Fig.4.

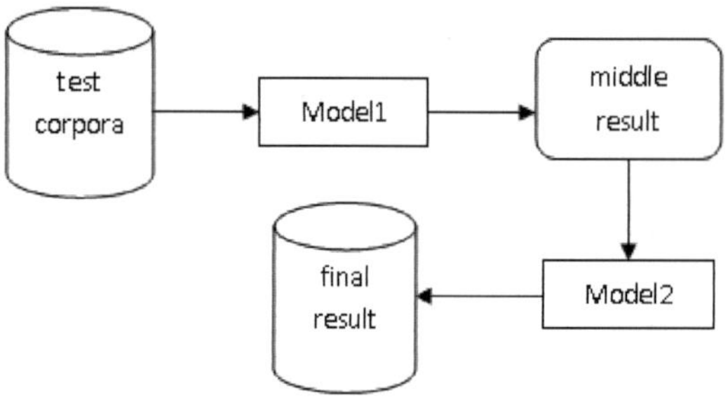

Figure 4: Model predicting process.

5 Experiment

We design 4 experiments to test contributions of different features, and the effectiveness of our proposed model. The comparison of the result is made and shown in Table 5. The base training data we used is 6 months of People Daily in year 2000 built by Peking University (Yu et al., 2002). Experiment 1 uses features listed in Table 2, and experiment 2 adds features listed in Table 3. The test data of experiment 1 and 2 are MicroBlog training samples. In experiment 3, we add half of training samples of SIGHAN, while the rest half is used for test data. Experiment 4 uses base training data and all the MicroBlog training samples provided by SIGHAN, and is evaluated on the test data provided by SIGHAN. From the results of experiment 1 and 2,we can observe that adding cohesion ratio of two characters listed in Table 3 achieves a higher accuracy. The cohesion ratio of characters is a strong sign for them being a word or not. From the result of experiment 2 and 3, we learn that to achieve a better performance in mirco-blog sengmentation, more corpora or features that embody the characteristics of MicroBlog is vitally needed.

No.	**1**	**2**
Training data	PKU	PKU
Features	Feature1-10	Feature1-13
test data	Weibo	Weibo
Recall	0.897	0.925
Precision	0.915	0.927
F1 measure	0.906	0.926
No.	**3**	**4**
Training data	PKU+1/2 Weibo	PKU+Weibo
Features	Feature1-16	Feature1-16
test data	1/2 Weibo	test data
Recall	0.928	0.932
Precision	0.935	0.935
F1 measure	0.932	0.933

Table 5: Experiment results comparison in different data settings, in which Weibo stands for Weibo samples and test data is the given Weibo test data.

No.	**5**	**6**
Training data	PKU	PKU
Features	Feature1-10	Feature1-13
Test data	1 month of PKU	
Recall	0.951	0.962
Precision	0.967	0.973
F1 measure	0.959	0.967
OOV Recall	0.847	0.860
IIV	0.957	0.968

Table 6: Feature used here is the cohesion ratio feature.

Table 6 demonstrates test result on the text from a month of People Daily. We can observe that F score is improved to 0.973 after adding cohesion features of characters, which is consistent with the observation on MicroBlog data in Experiment 2.

6 Future Work

In this paper, we try to implement micro blog segmentation, finding out the cohesion ratio of characters is a crucial feature for them being a word or not. Meanwhile, the user-editable vocabulary can not only provide flexibility for domain adaptation, but also be used as external knowledge to improve OOV recognition rate.

The current system is far from our goal, and there still has a lot of work to do:

(1)We use PKU corpora mainly for training, with a little corpora from micro blogs. Sufficient corpora is needed to extract the cohesion ratio features in MicroBlog. So active-learning (Baldridge et al., 2004; KimS et al., 2006) can be implemented here to achieve better performance through iterative training on relative small scale of manually labeled data.

(2)A method that can express the cohesion ratio feature between characters more efficiently is required. In this paper, we just calculated the probability of being a word between characters in a simple statistical way. Therefore another direction of future work is to explore the relationship between words to reflect the relationship between characters.

Acknowledgement

This research has been partially supported by the National Science Foundation of China (NO. NSFC61202248). We also thank Xiaojie Wang and Huixing Jiang for useful discussion of this work.

References

J. Wang, J. Liu, P. Zhang. 2008. *Chinese Word Sense Disambiguation with PageRank and HowNet.* In Proceedings of the Sixth SIGHAN Workshop on Chinese Language Processing.

X. Xu, M. Zhu, X. Fet, J. Zhu. 2010. *High OOV-Recall Chinese Word Segmenter.* In CIPS-SIGHAN Joint Conference on Chinese Language Processing.

G. Bian. 2006. *Chinese Word Segmentation using Various Dictionaries.* In Proceedings of the Fifth SIGHAN Workshop on Chinese Language Processing.

Z. Xu, X. Qian, Y. Zhang, Y. Zhou. 2008. *CRF-based Hybrid Model for Word Segmentation, NER and even POS Tagging.* In Proceedings of the Sixth SIGHAN Workshop on Chinese Language Processing.

H. Li, B. Yuan. 1998. *Chinese Word Segmentation.* In Language, Information and Computation(PACLIC12), 19-20 Feb, 1998, 212-217.

Y. Qin, X. Wang, Y. Zhong. 2008. *Cascade Identification of Chinese Chunks.* In the Journal of Beijing University of Posts and Telecommunications.

R. Sproat, C. Shin, W. A. Gale, and N. Chang. 1996. *A stochastic finite-state word-segmentation algorithm for Chinese.* In Computational Linguistic, 22(3):337-404.

N. Xue, L. Shen. 2003. *Chinese word segmentation as lmr tagging.* In Proceedings of the 2nd SIGHAN Workshop on Chinese Language Processing, Sapporo, Japan.

H. Tseng, P. Chang, G. Andrew, D. Jurafsky, and C. D. Manning. 2005. *Conditional random field word segmenter.* In Proceedings of the Fourth SIGHAN Workshop on Chinese Language Processing.

D. Jurafsky, James H. Martin 2007. *Speech and Language Processing: An introduction to natural language processing, computational linguistics, and speech recognition.* Prentice Hall.

S. Yu, H. Duan, X. Zhu, B. Sun. 2002. *The Basic Processing of Contemporary Chinese Corpus at Peking University SPECIFICATION.* In Journal of Chinese Information Processing. Vol.15 No.5.

K. Tangigaki, H. Yamamoto, Y. Sagisaka. 2000. *A Hierarchical Language Model Incorporating Class-Dependent Word Models For OOV Words Recognition.* In the Proceedings of the 6th International Conference on Spoken Language Processing.

D. Downey, M. Broadhead, O. Etzioni. 2007. *Locating Complex Named Entities in Web Text.* In IJCAI'07 Proceedings of the 20th international joint conference on Artifical intelligence.

D. Song, Anoop Sarkar. 2006. *Voting between Dictionary-Based and Subword Tagging Models for Chinese Word Segmentation.* In Proceedings of the Fifth SIGHAN Workshop on Chinese Language Processing.

A. Chen, Y. Zhou, A. Zhang, G. Sun. 2005. *Unigram language model for Chinese word segmentation.* In the Fourth SIGHAN Workshop on Chinese Language Processing (Second International Chinese Segmentation Bakeoff)

J. Baldridge, M. Osborne. 2004. *Active learning and the total cost of annotation.* In Proceedings of the Conference on Empirical Methods in Natural Language Processing (EMNLP):9 - 16. ACL Press. 2004.

S. Kim, Y. Song, K. Kim, J. Cha, G. G. Lee. 2006. *MMR-based active machine learning for bio named entity recognition.* In Proceedings of Human Language Technology and the North American Association for Computational Linguistics (HLT-NAACL):69 - 72.ACL Press. 2006.

L. Zhou 2007. *The Recognition Method of Unknown Chinese Words Based on Fragments Segmentation.* In the Journal of Changshu Insititue of Technology(Natural Sciences). Vol 2.

Rules-based Chinese Word Segmentation on MicroBlog for CIPS-SIGHAN on CLP2012

Jing Zhang
Dalian University of Technology,
DaLian, P. R. China.
zhangjingqf@mail.dlut.edu.cn

Degen Huang
Dalian University of Technology,
DaLian, P. R. China.
huangdg@dlut.edu.cn

Xia Han
Dalian University of Technology,
DaLian, P. R. China.
hanxia@mail.dlut.edu.cn

Wei Wang
Dalian University of Technology,
DaLian, P. R. China.
wangwei.dl@263.net

Abstract

In this evaluation, we have taken part in the task of the Word Segmentation on Chinese MicroBlog. In this task, after analysing the feature of the MicroBlog and the result of our original Chinese word segmentation system, four Optimization Rules are proposed to optimize the segmentation algorithm for Chinese word segmentation on MicroBlog corpora. The optimized segmentation system is based on character-based and word-based Conditional Random Fields (CRFs). Experiments show that the optimized segmentation system can obviously improve the performance of CWS on MicroBlog corpora.

1 Introduction

Chinese word segmentation is a crucial fundamental task in Chinese language processing. After years of intensive researches, Chinese word segmentation has achieved a quite high performance. However, it is not so satisfying when the Chinese word segmentation works on MicroBlog corpora. This CIPS-SIGHAN-2012 bake-off task of Chinese word segmentation focuses on the performance of Chinese word segmentation algorithms on MicroBlog corpora. This evaluation is an opened evaluation on simplified Chinese word segmentation task. The task provides no training set, and we are free to use data learned or model trained from any resources.

In this evaluation task, we propose some useful optimization rules for Chinese Word Segmentation (CWS) on MicroBlog corpora, after analysing the results of segmentation on MicroBlog corpora by our original CWS system, which combines character-based and word-based Conditional Random Fields (CRFs).

The rest of this paper is organized as follows. Section II outlines the new Chinese word segmentation algorithm on MicroBlog corpora. Section III reports the results of experiments and some discussions. Finally, some conclusions are presented in Section IV.

2 Word Segmentation Algorithm

2.1 Machine Learning Models

Conditional random fields (CRFs), a statistical model for sequence labeling, was first introduced by Lafferty, McCallum and Pereira (2001). It is the undirected graph theory that CRFs mainly use to achieve global optimum sequence labeling. It is good enough to avoid label bias problem by using a global normalization.

In previous labeling task of character-based CRFs, the number of the characters in the observed sequence is as same as the one in the annotation sequence. However, for CWS task, the input of n-character will generate the output of m-word sequence on such a condition that m is not larger than n. But this problem can be well solved by word-lattice based CRFs, because the conditional probability of the output sequence depends no longer on the number of the observed sequence, but the words in the output path. For a given input sentence, its possible paths may be various and the word-lattice can well represent this phenomenon. A word-lattice can not only express all possible segmentation paths, but also reflect the different attributes of all possible words in the path. Zhang, Chen and Hu (2012) and Nakagawa (2004) have successfully used the word lattice in Japanese lexical analysis.

Our paper adopt the word-lattice based CRFs that combines the character-based CRFs and the word-based CRFs, and specifically, we put the candidate words selected by the character-based CRFs into a word-lattice, and then label all the candidate words in the word-lattice using word-based CRFs model. When training the word-lattice based CRFs model, the maximum likelihood estimation is used in order to avoid over-loading. And Viterbi algorithm is utilized in the decoding process which is similar with (Huang and Tong, 2012).

2.2 Feature Templates

The character-based CRFs in our method adopt a 6-tag set in (Kudo, Yamamoto and Matsumoto, 2004), and its feature template comes from (Huang and Tong, 2010), including C_{-1}, C_0, C_1, $C_{-1}C_0$, C_0C_1, $C_{-1}C_1$ and $T_{-1}T_0T_1$, in which C stands for a character and T stands for the type of characters, such as Number, String. Character and so on, and the subscripts -1, 0 and 1 stand for the previous, current and next character, respectively. Four categories of character sets are predefined as: Numbers, Letters, Punctuation and Chinese characters. The feature templates of the character-based CRFs are described in detail in Table 1.

No.	Feature	Description of Feature
1	C_0	The current character
2	C_1	The later character
3	C_{-1}	The former character
4	$C_{-1}C_0$	The former and the current characters
5	C_0C_1	The current and the later characters
6	$C_{-1}C_1$	The former and the later characters
7	$C_{-1}C_0C_1$	The former, current and the later characters
8	$T_{-1}T_0T_1$	The type of the former, current and the later characters

Table 1: The feature templates of the character-based CRFs

Two kinds of features are selected for the word-based CRFs, like (Huang and Tong, 2012): unigram features and bigram features. The unigram ones only consider the attributes information of current word, and bigram ones are also called compound features, which utilize contextual information of multiple words. Theoretically, the current word's context sliding window can be infinitely large, but due to efficiency factors, we define the sliding window as 2. The specific features are W_0, T_0, W_0T_0, W_0T_1, T_0T_1, W_0W_1, where W stands for the morphology of the word, T stands for the part-of-speech of the words, and subscript 0 and subscript 1, respectively, stand for the former and the latter of two adjacent words. Furthermore, the Accessor Variety (AV) in (Zhao, Huang and Li, 2006) is applied as global feature. The feature templates of the word-based CRFs are shown in Table 2.

No.	Feature	Description of Feature
1	W_0	The current word
2	T_0	The POS of the current word
3	$T_{-1}T_0$	The POS of the former and the current words
4	T_0T_1	The POS of the current and the later words

Table 2: The feature templates of the word-based CRFs

2.3 Optimization Rules

As we all know, there exist plenty of new words, a great variety of symbols, and a good deal of URLs in MicroBlog corpora. Those features bring a big challenge to Chinese word segmentation. Considering the features of MicroBlog corpora and the segmentation result of our original Chinese word segmentation system, we propose several rules to optimize the segmentation result on MicroBlog corpora.

The features of MicroBlog corpora we summarized is as follows:

I. There are a lot of new words in MicroBlog, such as "团购" tuan-gou (online shopping), "点评网" dian-ping-wang (HankowThames), "有木有" you-mu-you (yes or not) and so on.

II. Many kinds of special symbols are used in MicroBlog, and what we deal with is mainly included in the following three cases:

   A. All kinds of combinations of the punctuation, especially, "！", "。", "-", for example, "其实应该很开心的呀！ ！ ！ ！" (Actually we are suposed to be very happy!!!!), "我要虚脱了。。。" (I am exhausted。。。).

   B. The frequently use of "@", e.g. "@姚晨" @-yao-chen.

   C. There also exist large number of emoticon icons, for instance, "^_^", "→_→" and so on.

III. The expression forms of time or date are quite various.

IV. The vast majority of the MicroBlog have URLs.

Our original segmentation system does not solve those problems mentioned above very well. Therefore, considering these characteristics of the MicroBlog, we propose some optimization rules to optimize the original results, which finally improve the segmentation results.

The rules are described in detail as follows:

Optimization Rule 1: With regards to the first feature, we use the contextual information, which is described in detail in (Huang and Tong, 2012) to calculate the frequency of the new words, and then added the high-frequency words to the dictionary.

Optimization Rule 2: According to the second feature, we have collected some commonly used combinations of punctuations to the dictionary.

Optimization Rule 3: Considering the third feature, the original system can not deal with the string of time very well, for instance, "2012年11月 8日" (November 8, 2012), the string of time is segmented as "2012/年/11/月/8/日", while the correct segmentation is "2012年/11月/8日". Under this circumstance, we have built a set of Time Templates. If the string matches any of the Time Templates, it will be segment as Time.

Optimization Rule 4: As to the last point, first, we search for the key word "http", and then we look for the right boundary of the URLs. At last, we merge all the string between the "http" and the right boundary together.

2.4 Word Segmentation Process

The Process of the optimized segmentation system is as follows:

Step1. Collect the commonly used combinations of punctuations to the dictionary which is mentioned in Rule 2.

Step2. Put all the candidate words in 3-Best paths selected by the character-based CRFs model into the word-lattice.

Step3. To build the word-lattice, in other word, give properties and costs to each node, the candidate words selected by character-based CRFs in Step2, in the word-lattice, which is divided into four cases to deal with:

①If the candidate words are in the system dictionary, then assign the properties and cost of the words in the system dictionary directly to the candidate words in the word-lattice.

②If the candidate words are not in the system dictionary, then we use Optimization Rule 1, search the dictionary of contextual information, if it is in there, then the properties of the words in the contextual information dictionary will be assiged to the candidate words, and a weight value, calculated by Eq. (1), will be added to the cost of the candidate words.

$$cost'(w) = \begin{cases} \dfrac{1.0}{rNum+1} \times cost_0(w) & rNum>0 \\ \left(\dfrac{0.2}{\log(frequency+2)} + 0.8\right) \times cost_0(w) & rNum=0 \end{cases} \quad (1)$$

Where w stands for the word, and t on behalf of the Part of Speech (POS), and *Cost* represents the difficulty of the emerging of a candidate word, and *Frequency* delegates the frequency of being a candidate word, and *rNum* is in the name of the frequency of being the node in the final segmentation path. Besides, $cost_0(w)$ stands for the original cost of the words.

③If the candidate words is not in the system dictionary, neither in the contextual information dictionary, then we will search the synonyms forest to find a synonym of the candidate words. If the synonym exits in the system dictionary, we'd like to replace the candidate word with it.

④If the above cases are not suitable for the candidate words, then the candidate words will be classified according to the classification mentioned above.

Step4. To find the optimal path, the least costly path of word segmentation, in the word-lattice using the Viterbi algorithm according to Eq. (4), and the values of $TransCost(t_i,t_{i+1})$ and $Cost(w_i)$ can be calculated by Eq. (2) and Eq. (3), respectively. Since all feature functions are binary ones, the cost of the word is equal to the sum of all the weight of the unigram features about the word, and the transition cost is equal to the sum of all bigram features about the two parts of speech.

$$Cost(w) = -factor * \sum_{f_k \in U(w)} \lambda_{f_k} \quad (2)$$

$$TransCost(t_1,t_2) = -factor * \sum_{f_k \in B(t_1,t_2)} \lambda_{f_k} \quad (3)$$

Where $U(w)$ is the unigram feature set of the current word, $B(t_1, t_2)$ is the bigram feature set of the adjacent words t_1 and t_2. λ_{fk} is the weight of the corresponding feature f_k and factor is the amplification coefficient.

$$Score(Y) = \sum_{i=0}^{Y^{\#}} (TransCost(t_i,t_{i+1}) + Cost(w_i)) \quad (4)$$

It can be seen from the above process that the factors of recognizing the territorial words are considered in Step3. Contextual information as well as synonym information is used to adjust the cost and the properties of the candidate words in the path, which can contribute to the follow-up Step4 to select the best path.

Step5. To optimize the original segmentation results. Optimization Rule 1 and Optimization Rule 2 have been used in the previous steps, while Optimization Rule 3 and Optimization Rule 4 are utilized in the end. The purpose of these two rules is to revise the segmentation results. In another word, some errors in the segmentation results can be corrected by Rule 3 and Rule 4.

3 Experiment Results

3.1 Data Sets

Our method is tested on the simplified Chinese MicroBlog testing data and the training data from the CIPS-SIGHAN-2012 bake-off task. The test corpus consists of approximately 5,000 texts from MicroBlog, and the training data includes 500 texts from MicroBlog with the gold standard result. The experiment results are evaluated by P (Precision), R (Recall) and F-measure. The system dictionary we used is extracted from the People's Daily from January to June, in 2000, containing 85000 words, with the POS. The word-based CRFs model is trained by the corpus with POS tag which is from the People's Daily of January, in 1998).

3.2 Evaluation Metrics

The metrics we used in this bake-off task is as follows:

$$\text{Precision} = \frac{\text{Num1}}{\text{Num2}} * 100\%$$

$$\text{Recall} = \frac{\text{Num1}}{\text{Num3}} * 100\%$$

$$F\text{-}measure = \frac{2 * \text{Precision} * \text{Recall}}{\text{Precision} + \text{Recall}} * 100\%$$

Num1 means the number of words correctly segmented.

Num2 stands for the number of words segmented.

Num3 means the number of words in the reference.

3.3 Experimental Results

Test Track	P	R	F
$Base_{500}$	78.76	88.59	83.39
$Final_{500}$	83.50	89.21	86.26
$Final_{5000}$	83.35	89.43	86.28

Table 3: The result of the experiments

In our experiments, at first, we use our original Chinese word segmentation system as the Baseline, and the 500 MicroBlog corpora provided by the organization are used as the test corpora. The segmentation result is shown in the first row of Table 3.

After that, in order to compare with the Baseline, we use the segmentation system added the optimization rules segments the 500 MicroBlog corpora, and the second row of Table 3 shows the result of this experiment. From the result we can see that our optimization works very well, and the F-measure is promoted obviously.

At last, we use the 5000 MicroBlog corpora to test our Final system, the segmentation system added the optimization rules, and we can see the result from the last row of Table 3, having the similar promotion with the second row.

From the above, we can clearly get that our optimized segmentation system can promote the segmentation performance significantly.

3.4 Error Analysis

Although the optimization rules improve the segmentation performance significantly, several typical errors are observed in the results of the experiment.

First, those problems we mentioned above are not solved thoroughly, especially the variety of punctuation problems. Because the combination is so flexible to sum up, we just summarize some frequently used combinations of punctuations.

Second, there still exist many new words which occur just a few times in the corpora, so they have not been added into the system dictionary eventually.

4 Conclusions

In this evaluation task, according to the features of MicroBlog, we propose several optimization rules of Chinese word segmentation on MicroBlog corpora. In the processing, experiments show that those optimization rules works very well on this task. While there still exit amount of problems need to be solved when Chinese word segmentation works on MicroBlog, and we have a lot of works to do in the future.

Acknowledgments

This work has been supported by the National Natural Science Foundation of China (No.61173100, No.61173101, No.61272375), Fundamental Research Funds for the Central Universities (DUT10RW202). The authors wish to thank Wu Qiong, Wang Dandan and for their useful suggestions, comments and help during the design and editing of the manuscript.

References

Huang Degen and Tong Deqin. 2012. Context Information and Fragments Based Cross-Domain Word Segmentation. J. China Communications, 9 (3): 49-57

Huang Degen, Tong Deqin, and Luo Yanyan. 2010. HMM Revises Low Marginal Probability by CRF for Chinese Word Segmentation. Proc of CIPS-SIGHAN Joint Conference on Chinese Processing. 216-220. ACL, Beijing

Kudo T, Yamamoto K, and Matsumoto Y. 2004. Applying conditional random fields to Japanese morphological analysis. Proc of EMNLP2004. 230-237. ACL, Barcelona

Lafferty J, McCallum A, and Pereira F. 2001. Conditional Random Fields: probabilistic models for segmenting and labeling sequence data. Proceedings of ICML2001. 282-289. Morgan Kaufmann, San Francisco

Nakagawa T. 2004. Chinese and Japanese word segmentation using word-level and character-level information. Proc of COLING 2004. 466-472. ACL, Geneva

Zhang Chongyang, Chen Zhigang, and Hu Guoping. 2012. A Chinese Word Segmentation System Based on Structured Support Vector Machine Utilization of Unlabeled Text Corpus. Proc of CIPS-SIGHAN Joint Conference on Chinese Processing. 221-227. ACL, Beijing

Zhao Hai, Huang Changning, and Li Mu, et al. 2006. Effective tag set selection in Chinese word segmentation via Conditional Random Field modeling. In PACLIC-20. 87-94. ACL, Wuhan

Semi-supervised Chinese Word Segmentation for CLP2012

Sai-ke He
State Key Laboratory of Management and Control for Complex Systems
Institute of Automation,
Chinese Academy of Sciences
Beijing 100190 China
saike.he@ia.ac.cn

Song-xiang Cen
Baidu, Inc Baidu Campus, No. 10,
Shangdi 10th Street Haidian District,
Beijing 100085 China
censongxiang@baidu.com

Nan He
Nuance Software Technology
(Beijing) Co., Ltd.
hn.ft.pris@gmail.com

Jun Lu
State Key Laboratory of Management and Control for Complex Systems
Institute of Automation,
Chinese Academy of Sciences
Beijing 100190 China
lujun_tiger@hotmail.com

Abstract

Chinese word segmentation (CWS) lays the essential foundation for Mandarin Chinese analysis. However, its performance is always limited by the identification of unknown words, especially for short text such as Micro-blog. While local context are helpless in handling unknown words, global context do manifest enough contextual information, and could be used to guide CWS process. Based on this motivation, in this paper, we report our attempt toward building an integrated model in semi-supervised manner. Considering the complexity of model, we design a strategy to manipulate global and local contextual information asynchronously. Though the coverage of unknown words by such integrated model is still small, official results from CLP2012 present promising result.

1 Introduction

Essentially, Chinese is a kind of paratactic language, rather than hypotactic language. This makes it character based, not word based. However, words are the basic linguistic units of natural language. Thus, the identification of lexical words or the delimitation of words in running texts is a prerequisite in Chinese natural language processing (NLP).

Chinese word segmentation can be cast as simple and effective formulation of character sequence labeling. A number of recent papers have examined this problem (Zhang et al., 2003; Xue, 2003; Peng et al., 2004) and could provide relatively good performance. However, these systems are genre or domain specific and use many different segmentation guidelines derived from the training dataset. This characteristic guarantees these systems with good performance on the known words, yet severely deteriorates on unknown words[1] from relatively unfamiliar context. This constitutes the major drawback of supervised segmentation.

In contrast, unsupervised approaches are model-free and more adaptive to unfamiliar context. This provides a potential solution for identify unknown words and have been attracting more attention recent years (Sproat and Shih, 1990; Feng et al., 2004; Goldwater et al., 2006; Mochihashi et al., 2009).

Since super and unsupervised methods excel in different situations, a natural idea would be a combination of these two to overcome drawbacks of both. A myriad of attempts exist and can be roughly categorized into two groups: simultaneous and asynchronous manner.

In simultaneous design, most researchers bind to the theory of transfer learning (or multitask learning, Caruana, 1997), and believe it achieves

[1] Unknown words also refer to out-of-vocabulary (OOV) words in some literature.

more when all the tasks are solved together. Admitted, this may be true in some situations (Gao et al., 2005; Tou Ng and Low. 2004). However, these achievements are often gained in the cost of complex system design. On the other side, asynchronous system moderate well between performance and simplicity. Thus, it is more favorable for large data processing, especially when real time analysis is primal.

In this paper, we report the integrated system designed for CLP2012 Micro-blog word segmentation subtask[2]. Considering simplicity, we are intended to provide a semi-supervised methodology by execute supervised and unsupervised segmentation asynchronously. In addition, we also design strategies to deal with unknown words: (1) beyond the coverage of training dataset (2) or without obvious segmentation guidelines.

The rest of the paper is organized as follows: Section 2 reviews previous work in the literature. Section 3 describes our integrated framework of CWS in detail. Section 4 presents and analyzes our experimental results. Finally, we conclude the work in Section 5.

2 Related Work

There is a line of research on solving Chinese Word Segmentation in supervised manner. Zhang et al. (2003) use a hierarchical hidden Markov Model (HMMs) to incorporate lexical knowledge. As an advance in this area, Xue (2003) uses a sliding-window maximum entropy classifier to label Chinese characters with one of four position tags, and then covert these labels into final segmentation using rules. Recently, Conditional Random Fields (CRFs) (Lafferty et al., 2001) have been successfully employed in CWS and achieve the state-of-the-art performance (Peng et al., 2004).

At the same time, unknown words gradually develop to be a serious problem that curbs the performance of CWS. As supervised method cannot help much in this situation, researchers begin to resort to new approaches.

Since Sproat and Shih (1990) introduced mutual information (MI) to word segmentation, there emerges a new line of research on unsupervised approaches. Unsupervised CWS systems tend to use three different types of information: the cohesion of the resulting units (Sproat and Shih, 1990), the degree of separation between the resulting units (Feng et al., 2004, Zhao and Kit, 2008) and the probability of a segmentation given a string (Goldwater et al., 2006; Mochihashi et al., 2009).

As unsupervised approaches can cooperate with supervised ones to achieve mutual enhancement, combination strategies of these two forms the trend. Gao et al. (2005) believe word boundary disambiguation and unknown word identification are not separable in nature, and solve them simultaneously in a pragmatic framework. Mao et al. solve CWS in a by using CRFs and transformation-based error-driven learning (TBL) in a cascaded manner. Evaluation results from Bakeoff-04[3] demonstrate their approach's effectiveness.

3 Framework of CWS

In this section, we define our framework of CWS in three steps (as shown in Figure 1). First, we train a CRFs model based on dataset from Bakeoff-04. This base model is used to segment known words in traditional manner. Then, we use an unsupervised approach to mine out unknown words from the training dataset. Those words will subsequently be used to adjust the segmentation results from CRFs model. Finally, to meet the need from CLP 2012, we also adjust previously segmentation results in the post-processing phase. Those three steps will be illustrated in detail in the following part.

Figure 1: Flow chart of CWS system

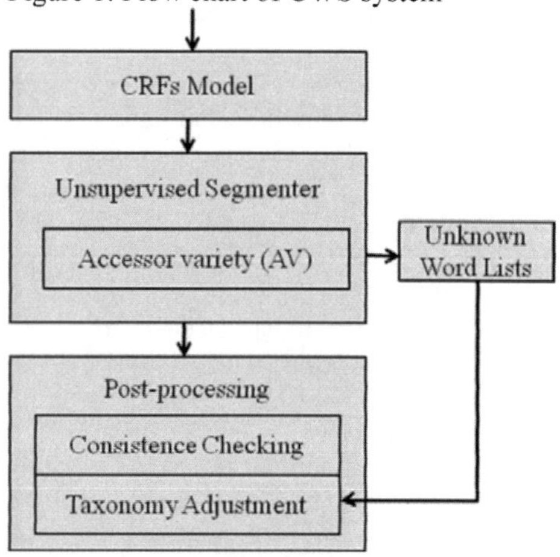

3.1 Conditional random fields

Although Chinese Word Segmentation can be solved in many ways, for sequence labeling,

[2] http://www.cipsc.org.cn/clp2012/task1.html

[3] http://www.china-language.gov.cn/bakeoff08/bakeoff-08_basic.html

conditional random fields offer advantages over both generative models like HMMs and classifiers applied at each sequence position (Sha and Pereira, 2003). CRFs are an undirected graph established on G = (V, E), where V is the set of random variables $Y = \{Y_i | 1 \leqslant i \leqslant n\}$ for each the n tokens in an input sequence and $E = \{(Y_{i-1}, Y_i) | 2 \leqslant i \leqslant n\}$ is the set of (n-1) edges forming a linear chain. Following (Lafferty et al., 2001), the conditional probability of the state sequence $(s_1, s_2 \ldots s_n)$ given the input sequence $(o_1, o_2 \ldots o_n)$ is computed as follows:

$$P_\Lambda(s|o) = \frac{1}{Z_o} \prod_{c \in C(s,o)} exp\left(\sum_{t=1}^{T}\sum_{k=1}^{K} \lambda_k f_k(s_{t-1}, s_t, o, t)\right) \quad (1)$$

where f_k is an arbitrary feature function; and λ_k is the weight for each feature function; it can be optimized through iterative algorithms like GIS (Darroch and Ratcliff, 1972). Recent research indicates that quasi-Newton methods such as L-BFGS (Byrd and Schnabel, 1994.) are more effective than GIS.

3.2 Tag set

As justified in (Zhao et al., 2007; Zhao et al., 2008), a 6-tag set enables the CRFs learning of character tagging to achieve a better segmentation performance than others. So we adopt this tag set in our CWS framework, namely, B, B2, B3, M, E and S, which respectively indicates the start of a word, the second position within a word, the third position within a word, other positions within a word, and the end of a word. An example is illustrated in Table 1.

Word Length	Tag sequence for a word
1	S
2	BE
3	BB2E
4	BB2B3E
5	BB2B3ME
>=6	BB2B3M … ME

Table 1: Illustration of 6-tag format in CWS

3.3 Feature templates

Table 2 illustrates the features we used in our CWS systems. Where *C* represents character; subscript *n* indicates its relative position taking the current character as its reference; *Pun* derives from the property of the current character: whether it is a punctuation; *T* describes the type of the character: numerical characters belong to class 1, characters whose meanings are date and time represent class 2, English letters represent class 3, punctuation labels represent class 4 while other characters represent class 5. In addition, the tag bi-gram feature is also employed.

Type	Feature
Unigram	C_n(n=-2,-1,0,1,2)
Bigram	C_nC_{n+1}(n=-2,-1,0,1)
Jump	$C_{-1}C_1$
Punctuation	Pun(C0)
Date,Digit,letter	$T_{-1}T_0T_1$

Table 2: The features used in CWS systems

3.4 Unsupervised segmentation

Due to the inherent Markovian assumption, sequence models, including CRFs, could only capture local structure, and thereby encode local context, i.e. labels directly depend only on the labels and observations within small window around them. This constraint hinders us from exploiting the global contextual information presents in natural language, such as information concerning label assigned at a long distance from a given character string, or even crucial textual information from the whole text.

Such global contextual information play key roles in two-fold: (1) serves to warrant that same or similar character sequences receive the same segmentation label; (2) enhance weak context by leveraging contextual information globally – essential to unknown word detection. Thus, to capture and utilize global contextual information, we employ an unsupervised segmentation approach in our system, as described below.

In Chinese text, each substring of a whole sentence can potentially form a word, but only some substrings carry clear meanings and thus form a correct word. Accessor variety (AV), sparked by (Feng, 2004) is used to evaluate how independent a string is from the rest of the text. The more independent it is, the higher the possibility that it is a potential word carrying a certain kind of meaning. The accessor variety value (AV value) of a string s is defined as:

$$AV(s) = \min\{Lav(s), Rav(s)\} \quad (2)$$

where Lav(s) is the left accessor variety of s, which is defined as the number of its distinct predecessors, plus the number of distinct sentences in which s appears at the beginning, while Rav(s) is the right accessor variety of s, which is defined as the number of its distinct successors, plus the number of distinct sentences in which s appears at the end.

Given the definition in formula (2), the segmentation problem is then cast as an opti-

LW	Lexical Word	教授,朋友,高兴,吃饭
MDW	Morphologically Derived Word	
MP_, MS_	Affixation (Prefix, Suffix)	朋友们
MR_	Reduplication	高高兴兴
ML_	Splitting	吃了饭
MM_	Merging	上下班
MHP_	Head + Particle	走出去
FT	Factoid word	
Dat	Date	1983年, 10月11日
Dur	Duration	2个月
Tim	Time	12点30分
Per	Percent and fraction	百分之十, 1/4
Mon*	Money	1000(美元)
NUMBER*	Frequency, integer, decimal, ordinal, rate, etc.	(每秒)5(次), 33.8, 第一(届), 三比三
MEASURE*	Age, weight, length, area, capacity, speed, temperature, angle, etc.	二十二(岁), 19(摄氏度), 360(米), 600(公顷)
Ema	E-mail	annoymous@sina.com
Pho	Phone, fax, telex	(0086)12345678
WWW	WWW	http://weibo.com
NE*	Named Entity	
P	Person name	白(岩松) 杨(幂)
L	Location name	天河(体育场)
O	Organization name	新闻(纵横), 百度
NW	New Word	三通, 非典

Table 3: Taxonomy of Chinese words used in CLP2012
* indicates adjustment specified for CLP2012 subtask. Note, pair-wised brackets represent delimitation among character strings here, yet such delimitation rule may not hold under other segmentation guidelines.

Category	Original Words	Gazetter Words		Volume	
		First Name	Last Name	First Name	Last Name
Person name	刘翔, 吴奇隆, 司马义 …	吴, 刘,司马, 吴刘, 刘吴 …	翔, 奇隆, 义 …	4138	7326
Location name	涿州市, 广西壮族自治区 …	涿州, 市, 广西, 壮族, 自治区 …		66461	
Organization name	剑桥大学, 社区管理委员会 …	剑桥, 大学, 社区, 管理, 委员会 …		21351	

Table 4: Gazetteer collected for
For person names, we mainly statistic elites from China, Japan, Europe, and Northern America.

mization problem to maximize the target function of the AV value over all word candidates in a sentence. The target function takes two factors: the segment length and the corresponding AV value. Theoretically, the choice of target function is arbitrary. Here, we choose polynomial function for its simplicity yet good generalize ability.

Since the value of each segment can be computed independently from the other segments in the same sentence, the optimal segmentation strategy for a sentence can be computed using a dynamic programming technique, in which the time complexity is linear to sentence length. After this procedure, we can obtain a plausible segmentation of the text as well as candidate unknown word lists.

3.5 Post-processing

In the pos-processing phase, we mainly utilize two techniques: consistence checking and taxonomy adjustment.

Consistence Checking: Label inconsistency is ubiquitous in context with great variance, especially in short text scenarios. To solve this problem, we use consistency checking inspired by (Ng and Low, 2004). The mechanism is to guarantee same word stings occur at different places labeled consistently. To this aim, we design the following rule：

Class-majority: Assign the majority label to the token sequence which is matched with the potential word list exactly. This rule enables us to capture the long distance dependencies between identical words, so that the same candidate words of different occurrences can be recalled favorably.

Taxonomy Adjustment: In taxonomy adjustment, we develop a taxonomy redefined from (Gao et al., 2005) where Chinese words are categorized into five types: lexicon words (LW), morphologically derived words (MDW), factoids (FT), named entities (NE), and new words (NW)[4]. The detail is shown in Table 3.

In taxonomy adjustment, we carry out a fine-tuned design.

For words following into category LW, MDW, and NW, we mainly use the semi-supervised method introduced previously.

For those belongs to FT, we rely on rule-based method, which could be considered as a simplified version of deterministic finite automaton (DFA) approach (Sipser, 1997). For each subgroup from FT, we design segmentation rules accordingly. To avoid conflicts among these rules, they are launched in a cascaded manner with dedicatedly specified execution order.

For those belong to NE, we use a dictionary matching method and collect word lists for each subgroups from NE category accordingly. However, words collected in this manner could not be used directly in exact matching way, for this is not the segmentation granularity needed for CLP2012. To solve this conflict, we further segment the collected words into more subtle linguistic units, as exemplified in Table 4.

4 Evaluation Results

This section reports the experiment result based on CWS corpora from CLP2012 Micro-blog word segmentation subtask. The corpora consists of 5000 messages crawled from Sina Weibo[5], a Twitter-like Micro-blog system in China. All the corpora are simplified Chinese text encoded in UTF-8 format. Table 5 lists the official results.

Results / Run ID	Precision Rate	Recall Rate	F Score	#Total Correct Sentences	Ratio of Correct Sentences
Our Result	0.9195	0.9085	0.914	1414	28.28%
Best	0.946	0.9496	0.9478	2244	44.88%

Table 5: Evaluation Results
'Best' indicate the high score achieved in CLP2012 Micro-blog word segmentation subtask.

5 Conclusions

In this paper, we report our work on CLP2012 Micro-blog word segmentation subtask. Specific to the characteristics of short text, we design our system in three steps. First, we train a statistical model to mainly segment known words. Then, we utilize an unsupervised segmentation method to indentify unknown words. Third, for the words beyond knowledge of the training data, we employed a dictionary based approach. Generally, our system design is easy to implement and presents good segmentation results.

References

Haodi Feng, Kang Chen, Xiaotie Deng, and Weiming Zheng. 2004. Accessor variety criteria for Chinese word extraction. *Computational Linguistics*, 30(1):75–93.

Jianfeng Gao, Mu Li, Changning Huang, Andi Wu. 2005. Chinese Word Segmentation and Named Entity Recognition: A Pragmatic Approach. *Computational Linguistics*, 31(4): 531-574.

Sharon Goldwater, Thomas L. Griffiths, and Mark Johnson. 2006. Contextual dependencies in unsupervised word segmentation. In *Proceedings of the*

[4] New words are identical to unknown words, but more suitable in the taxonomy. These words are identified in the unsupervised segmentation phase.

[5] http://weibo.sina.com/

21st International Conference on Computational Linguistics and the 44th annual meeting of the Association for Computational Linguistics, page 673–680.

J. Lafferty, A. McCallum, and F. Pereira. 2001. Conditional Random Fields: Probabilistic Models for Segmenting and Labeling Sequence Data. In *Proceedings of the 18th International Conf. on Machine Learning*, pages 282–289.

Xinnian Mao, Yuan Dong, Saike He, Sencheng Bao, and Haila Wang. 2008. Chinese word segmentation and named entity recognition based on conditional random fields. In *Proceedings of IJCNLP 2008*.

Daichi Mochihashi, Takeshi. Yamada, and Naonori Ueda. 2009. Bayesian unsupervised word segmentation with nested Pitman-Yor language modeling. In *Proceedings of the Joint Conference of the 47th Annual Meeting of the ACL and the 4th International Joint Conference on Natural Language Processing of the AFNLP*: Volume 1-Volume 1, page 100–108.

Hwee Tou Ng and Jin Kiat Low. 2004. Chinese Part-of-Speech Tagging: One-at-a-Time or All at Once? Word-based or Character based? In *Proceedings of the Conference on Empirical Methods in Natural Language Processing*, Spain.

Fuchun Peng, Fangfang Feng, and Andrew McCallum. 2004. Chinese segmentation and new word detection using conditional random fields. In *COLING 2004*, pages 562–568, Geneva, Switzerland, August 23-27.

Caruana, R. 1997. Multitask Learning. Ph.D. thesis, School of Computer Science, CMU.

Sproat, Richard and Chilin Shih. 1990. A statistical method for finding word boundaries in Chinese text. *Computer Processing of Chinese and Oriental Languages*, 4(4):336–351.

F. Sha and F. Pereira. 2003. Shallow parsing with conditional random fields. In *Proceedings of HLT/NAACL-2003*, 134-141. Edmonton, Canada.

Michael Sipser. 1997. Introduction to the Theory of Computation. PWS, Boston. Section 1.1: Finite Automata, pp.31–47.

N. Xue. 2003. Chinese Word Segmentation as Character Tagging. *International Journal of Computational Linguistics and Chinese Language Processing*, 8(1).

H. Zhang, Q. Liu, X. Cheng, H. Zhang, and H. Yu. 2003. Chinese Lexical Analysis Using Hierarchical Hidden Markov Model. *In Proceedings of the Second SIGHAN Workshop,* pages 63–70, Japan.

Hai Zhao, Chang-Ning Huang, Mu Li, and Bao-Liang Lu. 2006. Effective tag set selection in Chinese word segmentation via conditional random field modeling. In *PACLIC-20*, pages 87–94, Wuhan, China, November 1-3.

Hai Zhao and Chunyu Kit. 2008. Unsupervised Segmentation Helps Supervised Learning of Character Tagging for Word Segmentation and Named Entity Recognition, *The Sixth SIGHAN Workshop on Chinese Language Processing (SIGHAN-6)*, pp.106-111, Hyderabad, India, January 11-12.

Micro blogs Oriented Word Segmentation System

Yijia Liu[†]**, Meishan Zhang**[†]**, Wanxiang Che**[†]**, Ting Liu**[†]**, Yihe Deng**[‡]
[†] Research Center for Social Computing and Information Retrieval
Harbin Institute of Technology, China
{yjliu,mszhang,car,tliu}@ir.hit.edu.cn
[‡] School attached to Huazhong University of Science and Technology
Wuhan, 430074
brooklet60@gmail.com

Abstract

We present a Chinese word segmentation system submitted to the first task on CLP 2012 back-offs. Our segmenter is built using a conditional random field sequence model. We set the combination of a few annotated micro blogs and People Daily corpus as the training data. We encode special words detected by rules and information extracted from unlabeled data into features. These features are used to improve our model's performance. We also derive a micro blog specified lexicon from auto-analyzed data and use lexicon related features to assist the model. When testing on the sample data of this task, these features result in 1.8% improvement over the baseline model. Finally, our model achieves F-score of 94.07% on the bake-off's test set.

1 Introduction

Chinese word segmentation is the initial step of many NLP tasks, includes information retrieve, dependency parsing and semantic role labeling. Previous studies focus on word segmentation problem on standard data set, of which the training and testing data are drawn from same domain. However it's not always true when it comes to micro blogs. As a new source of information, micro blogs produce rich vocabulary ranging over many topics and changing with the times. Words like "给力" never appear in traditional data set, but occur frequently in micro blogs. At the same time, owing to the informal nature of micro blog, new type of words, such as URL, smiley and even the misspelled words, also make it very different from traditional task.

According to empirical analysis, one challenge of word segmentation on micro blogs is the sparsity issue resulting from lack of micro blog specified data. Current systems trained on standard data set perform poorly on micro blogs, because of domain mismatch. However, building a micro blogs specific word segmenter in standard supervised manner requires a lot of annotated data. Mannually creating them is a tedious and time-consuming work. Semi-supervised approaches, which make use of large scale unlabeled data is a promising solution to this issue. It enhances the segmenter with micro blog information and thus reduces sparsity in labeled training data. Recent studies have adopted semi-supervised approaches in word segmentation system(Wang et al., 2011; Sun and Xu, 2011), and improvement over the traditional supervised approach is observed.

Another challenge is the special word's detection. Due to the character of micro blogs, there are plentiful special words, such as hash tag, username, URL. Here is an example of micro blog entry: "[音乐] #我正在听# @MCHOTDOG熱狗《差不多先生》http://t.cn/h0VJQ （分享自@微博音乐盒）/ [music] #I'm listening# @MCHOTDOC *Mr. Ordinary* http://t.cn/h0VJQ (share from @weibomusicbox)". Words surrounded by "#" are hash tag, usually indicating the topics of the micro blog. "@MCHOTDOC熱狗" represent user names, and "http://t.cn/h0VJQ" is a shortened URL link. It's usually difficult for a word segmentation model to learn these changeable words from the training data. However, some certain type of special word can be detected by some rules easily and unambiguously. In this paper, we introduce some regular expressions to match special words in micro blog. The matching results, along with information extracted from unlabeled data, are integrated into a CRF sequence model to learn a robust and high performance segmenter. We also derive a lexicon from auto-analyzed micro blog data and enhance our model with the lexicon information.

The reminder of this paper is organized as follows. Section 2 describes the details of our system. Section 3 presents experimental results and empirical analysis. Section 4 concludes this paper.

2 System Architecture

In this section, we describe the details of our system. We use some regular expressions to detect special words in micro blog. The detected word boundary of *URL*, *English word* and *special punctuation*, along with other information from unlabeled data, are integrated into a CRF sequence model as features. We build our first segmenter with information mentioned above and use this segmenter to parse large scale unlabeled data. After that, we extract a lexicon from auto-analyzed data and retrained the CRF model with information provided by the lexicon. The architecture of our system is illustrated in Figure 1.

2.1 Model and Basic Features

We employ a character-based sequence labeling model for word segmentation, which assign labels to the characters indicating whether a character is the beginning(B), inside(M), end of a word(E) or a unit-length word(S). A linear chain CRFs is used to learn model from annotated data. When considering the candidate character token c_i, the basic types of features of our model are listed below.

- character unigram: c_s $(i-2 \leq s \leq i+2)$
- character bigram: $c_s c_{s+1}$ $(i-2 \leq s \leq i+1)$, $c_s c_{s+2}$ $(i-2 \leq s \leq i)$
- character trigram: $c_{s-1} c_s c_{s+1}$ $(s = i)$
- repetition of characters: is c_s equals c_{s+1} $(i-1 \leq s \leq i)$, is c_s equals c_{s+2} $(i-2 \leq s \leq i)$
- character type: is c_i an *alphabet*, *digit*, *punctuation* or *others*

2.2 Rule Detection Features

We introduce regular expressions to detect three kinds of special words in micro blog, *URL*, *English word* and *Irregular suspension*. These three type of words are demonstrate as below.

- URL: "来看华硕新版U36首发评测吧！http://t.cn/aBPi3D / Come and see the reviews of newly released ASUS U36! http://t.cn/aBPi3D"
- English word: "分享Colbie Caillat 的歌曲/ Share Colbie Caillat's song"
- Irregular suspension: "非常的期待....... / I'm expecting ...."

We encode word boundary detected by the regular expressions into a new type of preprocessing features. If the candidate character token c_i, the following features about URL is extracted.

- beginning of a URL: $URL(c_i) = B$
- inside of a URL: $URL(c_i) = M$
- end of a URL: $URL(c_i) = E$

Features of *English word* and *irregular suspension* can be represented in same manner.

We expect that CRF model learns from these matching results and this information assists the CRF model to detect special words and words surrounding them.

2.3 Semi-supervised Features

Information of unlabeled data can be easily computed and benefit the word segmentation model. When integrated into machine learning framework, it will help reduce sparsity issue caused by the out of vocabulary words.

2.3.1 Mutual Information

In probability theory, mutual information measures the mutual dependency of two random variables. Empirical study shows that observation of high mutual information between two characters may indicates real association of these two characters in a word, while low mutual information usually means they belongs to different words.

In this paper, we follow Sun and Xu (2011)'s definition of mutual information. For a character bigram $c_i c_{i+1}$, their mutual information is computed as follow:

$$MI(c_i c_{i+1}) = \log \frac{p(c_i c_{i+1})}{p(c_i)p(c_{i+1})}$$

For each character c_i, $MI(c_i c_{i+1})$ and $MI(c_{i-1} c_i)$ are computed and rounded down to integer. We incorporate these values into our model as a type of features.

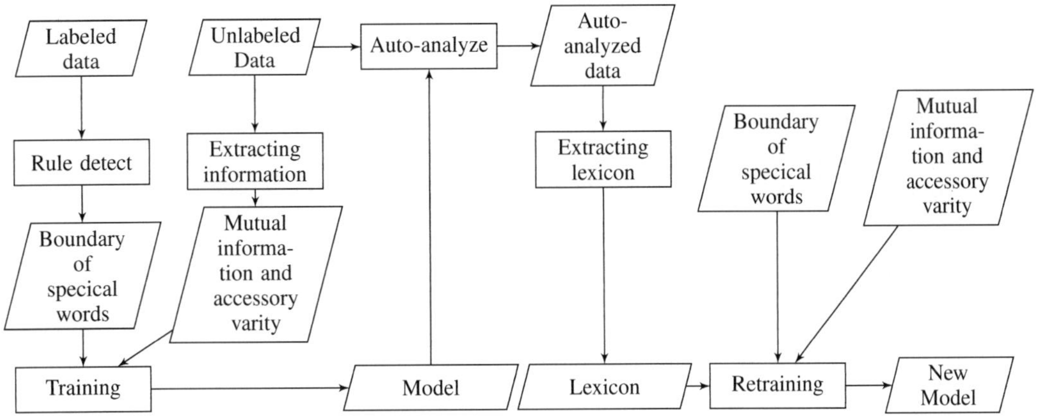

Figure 1: System architecture

2.3.2 Accessory Variety

Another empirical study of word segmentation boundary is that if some n-gram appears in many different environments, it's more likely that this n-gram be a real word. Sun and Xu (2011) introduce a criterion *Accessory Variety* to evaluate how independently a n-gram is used. In this paper, we follow this study and incorporate the following features $L^l_{AV}(c_{[i:i+l-1]})$, $L^l_{AV}(c_{[i+1:i+l]})$, $R^l_{AV}(c_{[i-l+1:i]})$, $R^l_{AV}(c_{[i-l:i-1]})$ $(l = 2, 3, 4)$ into our model. Here $L^l_{AV}(c_{[s:e]})$ and $R^l_{AV}(c_{[s:e]})$ means accessor variety of strings with length l, $c_{[s:e]}$ means the character sequence starts from c_s and ends with c_e.

2.4 Extracting Lexicon

Study has shown that CRF model can benefit from lexicon features(Zhang et al., 2010). Micro blog specified lexicon provides a clue for detecting words in unfamiliar context. In this paper, we try to extract a micro blog specified lexicon from auto-analyzed data to improve our model's performance.

Firstly, we train a CRF model with features described in 2.2 and 2.3. We use this model to parse large scale unlabeled data, and a list of word is obtained. Intuitively, high frequency word in the auto-analyzed results is more likely to be real word. Therefore, we collect words that never occur in the training data and rank them in order of frequency. A lexicon of words whose frequency is higher than a threshold is extracted. In this paper, top 80% most frequent words is extracted. We drop the tokens with more than 5 characters, and then build the lexicon.

After the lexicon D is built, we encode the information of lexicon into a type of features. We follow Zhang et al. (2010)'s work on utilization of lexicon When considering c_i, the lexicon feature we extract is shown below:

- $match\_prefix(c_i, D)$ the length of longest word in lexicon D which starts with c_i
- $match\_mid(c_i, D)$ the length of longest word in lexicon D which contains with c_i
- $match\_suffix(c_i, D)$ the length of longest word in lexicon D which ends with c_i

3 Experiments

3.1 Data Preparation and Setting

We crawl some micro blog from September 1st, 2011 to September 5nd, 2011, and drop the entries which not contains simplified Chinese characters. We got 1 million entries and use them as unlabeled data. From these micro blog entries, we randomly sampled 1,442 entries and manually annotated their segmentation. This set of corpus is use as one part of the labeled data. There are 23.3 words each entry in the annotated micro blogs on average. At the same time, 183,630 lines of sentences from People daily is also used as labeled data. All of the character in training and testing data is convert from single-byte character to double-byte character.

We use a toolkit - CRFSuite(Okazaki, 2007) to learning the sequence labeling model for segmentation. L-BFGS algorithm is set to solve the optimization problem.

We conclude our experiments result on the sample data of the bake-off task. There are 503 entries in the test data set, with 38.9 words each entry. Recall(R), precision(P) and F_1 is used as evaluation metrics of system performance. We also report the recall of out of vocabulary(OOV) words(R_{oov}).

3.2 Effect of Annotated Micro blog

In this set experiments, we test performance of standard supervised learning on different training data. As mentioned above, we have a large set of annotated corpus on newswire and a small set of micro blogs. We expected that a combination of these two corpus will help promote the performance.

We extract basic features from this two data and trained two CRF model BL^{pd} and BL^{mb}. Then we combine two data and trained another CRF model BL^{comb}. Performance of these three models is shown is Table 1.

Model	P	R	F
BL^{pd}	0.8820	0.8694	0.8757
BL^{mb}	0.8903	0.8925	0.8914
BL^{comb}	0.9161	0.9098	0.9130

Table 1: Effect of different annotated corpus

In previous study, the state-of-the-art word segmentation system can achieve F-score of about 97%(Che et al., 2010) when tested in-domain data. However, Table 1 shows that when applied to micro blogs, traditional word segmentation system's performance drops severely.

Experiment result also shows that, a small set of annotated micro blog corpus can achieve better performance than the traditional newswire corpus. And the model trained with combination of two corpus out performance the others. In the following section, all of our models are built on the combination of these two corpus.

3.3 Effect of Rule Detection Features

Table 2 compares the baseline model with model that integrates rule detection features.

Model	P	R	F	R_{oov}
BL	0.9161	0.9098	0.9130	0.5763
+PRE	0.9216	0.9178	0.9197	0.6715

Table 2: Effect of preprocessing

We can see that rule detection features improve the model's performance, especially the recall of OOV. To give a farther analysis of rule detection features' effect, we categorized words in test set into four sort: *URL*, *English word*, *Punctuation*, *Others* and evaluate the recall of certain type of word. Table 3 shows the experiment result.

Model	R_{URL}	R_{Punc}	R_{Eng}	R_{Others}
BL	0.8940	0.9857	0.6018	0.8997
+PRE	0.9536	0.9862	0.9227	0.9040

Table 3: Recall of preprocessing on four sort of words

The experiment result shows that rule detection features improves the recall of special word type, especially the English words occur in micro blog. With more accurate detection of sepecial words, accuracy on ordinary words is also improved.

3.4 Effect of Semi-supervised Features

Table 4 summarizes the experiment result on different combination of semi-supervised features.

Model	P	R	F	R_{oov}
BL+PRE	0.9216	0.9178	0.9197	0.6715
+MI	0.9282	0.9220	0.9251	0.7046
+AV	0.9309	0.9231	0.9270	0.7250
+MI+AV	0.9304	0.9231	0.9268	0.7123

Table 4: Effect of semi-supervised features

It can be seen that two types of semi-supervised features both result in improvement on performance. However, when two types of feature combined, the performance drops slightly. Empirically, we consider that the effect of these two type features overlaps due to they share some common property.

3.5 Effect of Lexicon

We also compare our model integrating lexicon features and without lexicon features. The results are shown in Table 5.

Model	P	R	F	R_{oov}
BL+PRE+MI+AV	0.9304	0.9231	0.9268	0.7123
+Lexicon	0.9352	0.9275	0.9314	0.7337

Table 5: Effect of lexicon features

As expected, lexicon features result in improvement over performance.

3.6 Final System

Our final system is set as the configuration of "BL+PRE+MI+AV+Lexicon". Our experimental results show that our final system achieves an F-score of 93.14% and an improvement of 1.8% comparing to our baseline model. On the evaluation data of the bake-off, the F-score of our system is 94.07%.

4 Conclusion

In this paper, we describe our system of *Chinese Word Segmentation on MicroBlog Corpora*. We exploit a single model enhanced by preprocessing, semi-supervised and lexicon features. These features improve the model's performance. Our model achieve an F-score of 94.07% on the bake-off's test data.

Acknowledgments

This work was supported by National Natural Science Foundation of China (NSFC) via grant 61133012, the National "863" Major Projects via grant 2011AA01A207, and the National "863" Leading Technology Research Project via grant 2012AA011102.

References

W. Che, Z. Li, and T. Liu. 2010. Ltp: A chinese language technology platform. In *Proceedings of the 23rd International Conference on Computational Linguistics: Demonstrations*, pages 13–16. Association for Computational Linguistics.

Naoaki Okazaki. 2007. Crfsuite: a fast implementation of conditional random fields (crfs).

W. Sun and J. Xu. 2011. Enhancing chinese word segmentation using unlabeled data. In *Proceedings of the Conference on Empirical Methods in Natural Language Processing*, pages 970–979. Association for Computational Linguistics.

Y. Wang, Y.T. Jun' ichi Kazama, W. Chen, Y. Zhang, and K. Torisawa. 2011. Improving chinese word segmentation and pos tagging with semi-supervised methods using large auto-analyzed data. In *Proceedings of the Fifth International Joint Conference on Natural Language Processing (IJCNLP-2011)*.

M. Zhang, Z. Deng, W. Che, and T. Liu. 2010. Combining statistical model and dicitionary for domain adaptation of chinese word segmentation. *Journal of Chinese Information Processing*, 26(2):8–12.

Rules Design in Word Segmentation of Chinese Micro-Blog

Zong Hao **Derek F. Wong** **Lidia S.Chao**
NLP²CT Research Group, Department of Computer and Information Science, University of Macau, Macau SAR, China
{MB15463, DerekFw, Lidiac}@umac.mo

Abstract

This paper proposed a Hidden Markov Model (HMM) based tokenizer for Chinese micro-blog texts. Comparing with normal Chinese texts, micro-blog texts contain more uncertainties. These uncertainties are generally aroused by the irregular use of bloggers (such as network words, dialect words, wrong written characters, mixture of foreign words and symbols, etc.). Besides the lack of the annotated training corpus is also a restriction in solving this task. Hence the segmentation for micro-blogs is much more difficult than that of general text, we present an HMM based segmentation model integrated with a pre and post correction module. The evaluation results show that the proposed approach can achieve an F-measure of 90.98% on test set of 5,000 sentences.

1 Introduction

Word segmentation is a common task in Chinese information processing. This task is to split a character sequence into many small groups by inserting a space between two neighbor groups. Each group, as a Chinese word, represents an independent meaning. For example, given a character sequence "李明是个好人" (*Li Ming is a good man*); the segmentation result will be "李明 /是/个/好人" . We select this task as our research target because it is a very common task and many scholars had done a lot of experiments on it. We can easily compare our method with others', more importantly, segmentation is normally the first step to process the Chinese text. The quality of it may seriously affect on the later processing.

Micro-blog has more uncertainties than normal Chinese text. For instance, the micro-blog texts contain a large number of *network words* like "打酱油" and "楼主" which are easily to be mis-segmented due to the arbitrary nature of language. The dialect words and wrong written words are also easily to be mis-segmented according to a limited knowledge of these.

To accomplish this task, many approaches had been proposed. The first adapted and efficient approach is the Maximum Matching (Wong & Chan, 1996). Its segmentation accuracy is depending on the quality of system dictionary. System dictionary is a manual defined lexicon that it contains the majority of standardized words. However, with the development of language, new words are springing up. The system dictionary cannot track of newly born vocabularies. Several years later machine learning approaches had been applied. The Maximum Entropy (Shi, 2005) achieved the highest accuracy among most of the tasks in SIGHAN-2005 Bake-off[1] Segmentation contest. During the same contest Conditional Random Fields (CRFs) (Zhou et al, 2005) has the best performance in solving the out-of-vocabulary (OOV) problem. Hidden Markov Model (HMM) (Zhang et al, 2003) is another efficient approach in Chinese segmentation. It has an efficient approach in handling the word ambiguity[2] issue. Furthermore it achieved the best result in the first Chinese segmentation competition[3].

The most two common issues in Chinese segmentation are OOV and ambiguity. In this word we assume that the some existing segmentation

[1] http://www.sighan.org/swclp4/

[2] Example: "长春市长春饭店" can be segmented as "长春市长 春 饭店" or "长春市 长春 饭店". So this sentence is ambiguity.

[3] Proceedings of the Second SIGHAN Workshop on Chinese Language Processing task2: Chinese segmentation.

tool is already very good. Based on this tool we designed several rules to modify the segmentation result to overcome its inadaptation for this domain.

2 Task Specialty

Comparing with normal Chinese text segmentation, micro-blog text segmentation has to overcome more difficulties due to the arbitrary nature of language. We will show this in detail in the following sections.

Network words: thanks to the speed of spread in the internet age, a large amount of irregular words had been widely emerged and accepted. These words such as "屌丝" (*diao si*) usually have the rich connotation and can represent the heartfelt idea. Therefore although the network words are irregularly written and some of them even are not grammatical, they are still widely used.

Accent words: accent words such as "木有" (*mu you*) and "酱紫" (*jiang zi*) are nonstandard pronounced words. These words are widely used because it can show their accent and sounds cute.

Wrong written words: these words such as " 戒子" (*jie zi*) (refer to "戒指" (*ring*)) and "针贬" (*zhen bian*) (refer to "针砭" (*zheng bin*)) are very are hard to be recognized by the current segmentation approaches.

The mixture of foreign words: many people like to write with foreign words such as words or phrases of "打 (*da*) ball" (*play basketball*) and " 很 (*hen*) down" (*very disappointed*). It is very popular and common in some specific topic. Using these words can express the richest meaning with the less characters.

3 Rules design for Chinese micro-blog segmentation

Chinese micro-blog texts are unrestrained. In this task we followed the tagging schema of "Specification for Corpus Processing at Peking University"[4] in the design of our model.

In this word, under the assumption that a segmentation system for general text is already good , for a special domain we only need to do some modification to make the segmentation result better. The main frame of this system is using ICTCLAS[5] as the segmentation tool. Based on it result, we do a group of preprocessing and post-processing to get a better result.

After analyzed the 500 sentences train corpora, we found that there are some rules in the segmentation that it is very difficult to use other approaches to recognize them. Therefore we designed rules as the pre-processing and post-processing of this system.

Pre-processing rules

The rules designed for preprocessing are the URL and E-mail address. In ICTCLAS, URL and E-mail address cannot be segmented at all and these mis-segmented URL and E-mail address may encounter more segmentation errors later.

This system used regular expression[6] to define the segmentation rules for URL and E-mail address. Figure 1 showed the improvement after applying the preprocessing rules.

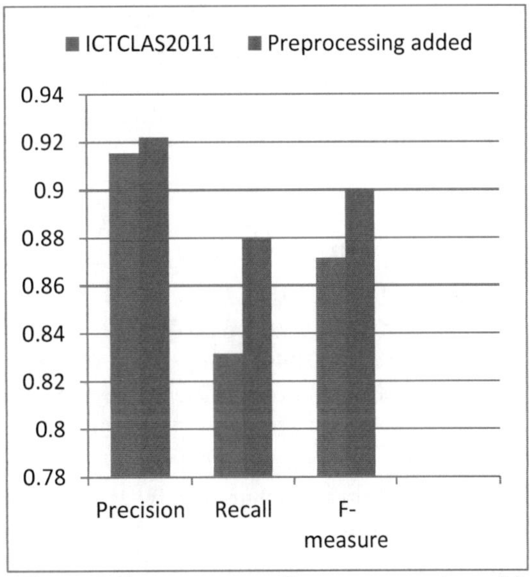

Figure 1. Improvement after preprocessing added.

Postprocessing rules

These rules are generated after analyzing the fragments of ICTCLAS2011's segmentation result. The fragments revealed that the ICTCLAS2011 cannot segment the roll-call system in micro-blog which will frequently occur in micro-blog texts. For instance, "@一移已易-YEE33333" will be segmented as "@/一/移/已/易/-YEE33333" while the right segmentation is "@/一移已易/-/YEE33333". Error about this is complicated and we believed that if the system

[4] http://www.icl.pku.edu.cn/icl_groups/corpus/coprus-annotation.htm

[5] http://www.ictclas.org/index.html

[6] Regular expression referenced from http://en.wikipedia.org/wiki/Regular_expression

use rules as the segmentation constrain, this error will be totally correct.

The detail of this roll-call system rules is followed:

1. If the text starts with a group of meaningful Chinese words, use normal segmentation strategy (ICTCLAS). For example, "@花心女想要去流浪 1989" should be segmented as "@/花/心/女/想/要/去/流浪/1989"
2. If the text starts with a group of meaningless Chinese characters, group these characters together. For example, "@一移已易-YEE33333" should be segmented as "@/一移已易/- /YEE33333" rather than "@/一/移/已/易/ - /YEE33333".
3. If the text starts with an account ID, the ID characters should be grouped together. Example: "@super_lv" should be segmented as "@/super_lv".
4. When the symbol "-" or "_" is between English and Chinese. If the left is Chinese and the right is English the symbol should be segmented alone. Else it should group to the English. Example: "@一移已易-YEE33333" should be segmented as "@/一移已易/-/YEE33333", "@小丁_Vic" segmented as "@/小丁/_/Vic", "@12th_章" segmented as "@/12th_/章", "@BETTY-萍萍" segmented as "@/BETTY-/萍萍"
5. If the roll-call system contains Chinese personal name, the surname should be separated. Example: "@刘彦友 2527" should be segmented as "@/刘/彦友/2527".

Beside the roll-call system, two other rules are also applied in this system.

1. For continuous symbols "." And "。", every three of them should be a group. For instance, "….." should be segmented as ".../.." and "。。。。。。" should be segmented as "。。。/。。。".
2. For continuous mimetic words, they should grouped together. For example "哈哈哈哈哈哈哈" should be segmented as "哈哈哈哈哈哈哈" and "呵呵呵呵呵呵" should be segmented as "呵呵呵呵呵".

Figure 2 showed the improve after postprocessing added.

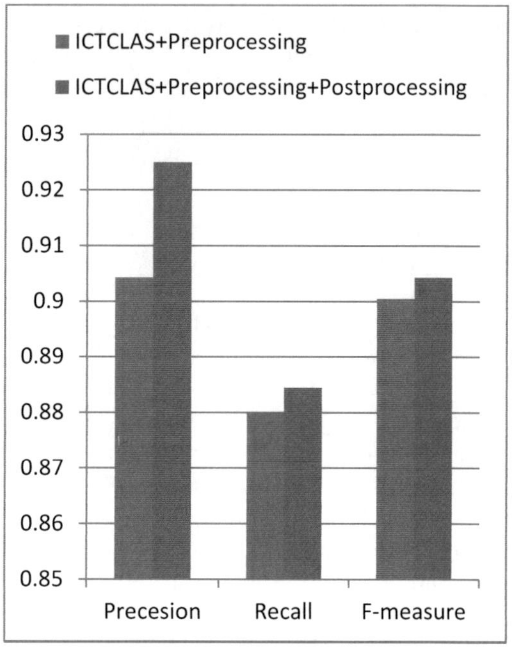

Figure 2. Improvement after postprocessing added

Although the improvement is not very obvious, we can ensure that all the special case covered by these rules will be completely correct.

4 External Dictionary

In order to overcome the sparsity of training data, an external dictionary is necessary.

To get a micro-blog related dictionary we referenced a famous Chinese Input Method: Sougou[7] Input. We got the network dictionary (9850 words) and applied in this system. But mechanically added this network dictionary did not improve the result a lot. Therefore we analyzed the detail terms in this dictionary. We found that many terms like "祝妈妈身体健康"(*wish mom healthy*) did not be segmented. Then we use ICTCLAS again to segment the terms in this dictionary and group all singer character together. For example: "醉驾" (*drunk driving*) will be segmented as "醉/驾", then we group these two singer characters together as "醉驾".

Figure 3 showed the improvement after applied the external dictionary.

[7] http://pinyin.sogou.com/

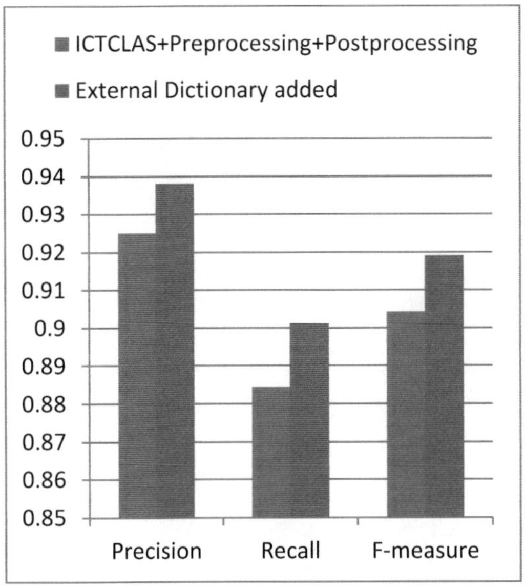

Figure 3. Improvement after external dictionary added

5 Named Entity Recognition

After applied all approaches above the evaluation result still can not reach the state-of-the-art, the segmentation error showed that the named entities encountered much error. Then named entity recognition procedure imported into this system.

Chinese Named Entity Recognition (NER) is more complex than English Named Entity Recognition because it contains a segmentation step before. In this system NER is playing a very important role. For those unlabeled data, it will do NER first. If this system recognizes that the name in this text is not a Named Entity (NE), it will directly assert that this text belongs to the OTHER class. If the name in the text is a NE, we will then mark all the NE in this text to help the later work.

Before we do NER we have to do the Chinese segmentation and Part-of-Speech (POS) tagging. Here this system used ICTCLAS 2011 with additional user dictionary to improve the segmentation and POS tagging accuracy.

Conditional Random Fields (CRFs) is the most popular approach to do NER task. This approach is easy to implement and usually achieve a very high accuracy. A Study on Features of the CRFs-based Chinese Named Entity Recognition (Duan & Zheng, 2011) did a lot of work on this task and gave a conclusion of the feature selection. This system also used CRFs to do the NER. The CRFs toolkit adopted in this system is CRF++[8] toolkit and used feature is three single characters (before, current, after), three POS tags (before, current, after), some suffix and prefix (s/f) information and three segmentation label sets (before, current, after). The training data set is January-June People's Daily 1998. We get F-measure 91.4% from our test set.

Figure 4 showed the improvement of NER added into this system.

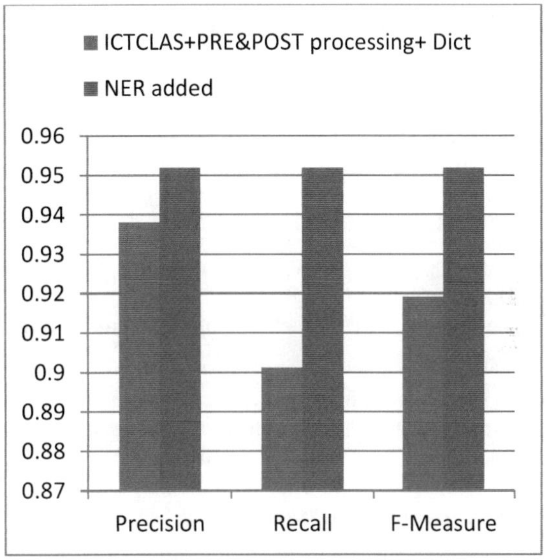

Figure 4. Improvement after NER added

6 Conclusion

This paper proposed a modification of ICTCLAS a basic segmentation tool for the Chinese microblog segmentation. These modifications contain preprocessing, postprocessing in rule level, an external network dictionary with a little amelioration and a named entity recognition. All these modifications improved the original segmentation result in 8.4 percent which is a very obvious improvement in Chinese segmentation. However due to the time limit, there are still some other issues we had not considered such as wrong written error and the mixture of foreign words.

Table 1 showed our final evaluation result in SIGHAN-2012 Bake-off Task 1.

Precision	0.9000
Recall	0.9199
F-measure	0.9098
All right sentences	1,388
All right sentence rate	27.76%

Table 1. Final evaluation result

[8] CRF++: Yet Another Toolkit [CP/OL]. http://crfpp.googlecode.com/svn/trunk/doc/index.html

The reason why we get a large decrease may be that the train corpora is so small that we have not anticipated any other error in the test set.

Acknowledgments

This work was partially supported by the Research Committee of University of Macau under grant UL019B/09-Y3/EEE/LYP01/FST, and also supported by Science and Technology Development Fund of Macau under grant 057/2009/A2.

References

Wong, P. & Chan, C. 1996. *Chinese word segmentation based on maximum matching and word binding force,* Proceedings of the 16th conference on Computational linguistics-Volume 1, 200–203.

Shi, W. 2005. *Chinese Word Segmentation Based On Direct Maximum Entropy Model,* Proceedings of the Fourth SIGHAN Workshop on Chinese Language Processing.

Zhang, H.P. and Liu, Q and Cheng, X.Q and Zhang, H and Yu, H.K 2003. *Chinese lexical analysis using hierarchical hidden markov model,* Proceedings of the second SIGHAN workshop on Chinese language processing-Volume 17, 63-70.

Duan, H. and Zheng, Y. 2011. *A study on features of the CRFs-based Chinese Named Entity Recognition,* International Journal of Advanced Intelligence-Volume 3, 287-294.

A Comparison of Chinese Word Segmentation on News and Microblog Corpora with a Lexicon Based Method

Yuxiang Jia[1], Hongying Zan[1], Ming Fan[1], Zhimin Wang[2]
1. School of Information Engineering, Zhengzhou University, China
2. College of Chinese Studies, Beijing Language and Culture University, China
{ieyxjia,iehyzan,iemfan}@zzu.edu.cn,wangzm000@gmail.com

Abstract

Microblog is a new and important social media nowadays. Can traditional methods deal well with Chinese microblog word segmentation? We adopt the forward maximum matching (FMM) method and design rules to recognize words with non-Chinese characters. We focus on comparing results between news text and microblog. The lexicon based method allows us to investigate well new words emerging in microblog by comparing with lexicon words. Experimental results show that the performance on microblog outperforms that on news text under the same setup, which may be a signal that microblog word segmentation is not as hard as expected.

1 Introduction

Chinese is writtern as a sequence of characters, with no boundary between words. Word segmentation or word breaking is a task to recognize words and turn a sequence of characters into a sequence of words. Because word is the basic unit of a language, word segmentation is considered as the first step of Chinese language processing.

Extensive work has been done on Chinese word segmentation. Word segmentation methods can be divided into two categories. The first category is lexicon based method. This method needs a predefined lexicon or word list. Solely based on the lexicon, maximum matching method can be used for word segmentation. Combined with labeled corpus, statistical methods can be applied (Huang and Zhao, 2007). The other category is character tagging method (Xue, 2003). This method considers word segmentation as a character position classification problem or sequence labeling problem, and applies related machine learning models.

Supervised machine learning methods need labeled data. In order to alleviate human labeling labor and utilize large scale unlabeled data, semi-supervised (Sun and Xu, 2011) and unsupervised methods (Wang et al., 2011) are also studied.

SIGHAN has organized several bakeoff tasks for Chinese word segmentation on news corpora (Emerson, 2005; Zhao and Liu, 2010), which has greatly pushed the advancement of Chinese word segmentation. This year it turns to microblog word segmentation, in the face of the great development of microblog and social network in Chinese.

Compared with news text, microblog has more words containing non-Chinese characters, like numbers, alphabets, symbols, etc. Such words are of great number but can be classified into different types and recognized respectively based on rules. Chinese character sequences in microblog are relatively shorter than those in news text. So a traditional segmenter enhanced by a special process of non-Chinese characters may have a good performance.

In this paper, we propose a lexicon and rule based method, using forward maximum matching (FMM) method to recognize Chinese words and regular expressions to recognize words with non-Chinese characters. FMM is simple and fast implemented, and is always taken as a baseline method. Here we take FMM to compare the baseline performance on corpora of different styles.

The rest of this paper is organized as follows. Section 2 describes the word segmentation process. Section 3 gives experimental results and analysis, including comparison of different lexicons, comparison of different corpora, and comparison of experimental results. Conclusions are given in section 4.

2 Segmentation Method

The word segmentation process is shown in figure 1. Preprocessing step combines non-Chinese character sequence as one character, just like a Chinese character.

FMM step takes forward maximum matching method for word segmentation. The maximum word length is set to be 7. The lexicons used here will be discussed in the next section.

Chinese character words are recognized in the FMM step. In the next step, with a rule based method, non-Chinese character sequences are divided into meaningful words, such as URLs, Emails, English words, numbers, etc.

In the postprocessing step, some words need to be combined to make a final word. For example, word sequence "一" (one), "九" (nine), "九" (nine), "八" (eight), "年" (year) should be combined as a word "一九九八年" (the year 1998). Other processes can also be added into this step.

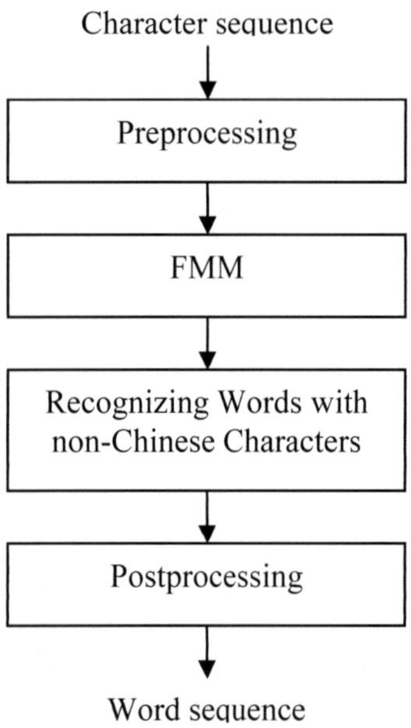

Figure 1. Word segmentation process

3 Experiments and Analysis

Several popular Chinese lexicons are compared to explore the impact of lexicons on the FMM method. Word distributions are compared between news and microblog corpora. Experimental results with respect to different metrics are compared and analyzed.

3.1 The Lexicons

The Chinese lexicons used here are as follows:

1. The Grammatical Knowledge-base of Contemporary Chinese (GKB) (Yu et al., 2003). GKB organizes words into different categories and provides comprehensive grammatical knowledge for each word. The version of GKB used here has a vocabulary of 74188 word types.

2. HowNet (HN) (Dong and Dong, 2006). HowNet encodes relations between concepts into a semantic network. It provides a definition for each concept as a combination of basic sematic units. HowNet version 2000 has a vocabulary of 55496 word types.

3. TongYiCiCiLin (CiLin) (Che et al., 2010). CiLin is a semantic lexicon. A concept is represented as a synonym set, and all concepts are organized into trees of the same height. CiLin has a vocabulary of 77457 word types.

4. Lexicon of Common Words in Contemporary Chinese (LCW) (Li et al., 2008). LCW is a list of words frequently used in various corpora, including news, literature, etc. LCW has a vocabulary of 55731 word types.

The sizes of vocabulary intersection of different lexicons are shown in table 1. We can see that the vocabularies are different greatly from each other. There are only 41419 words in common in the first three lexicons and 34540 words in common in all the four lexicons, while there are 104150 distinct words in total in the four lexicons.

	GKB	HN	CiLin	LCW
GKB	74188	43740	61780	45780
HN	-	55496	45652	37601
CiLin	-	-	77457	45612
LCW	-	-	-	55731
CGH	41419			-
CGHL	34540			

Table 1. Size of vocabulary intersection of different lexicons

3.2 Data Sets

The data sets used here are as follows:

News corpus. We choose Peking university test set of the 2nd International Chinese Word Segmentation Bakeoff as the news corpus. This corpus contains 1944 sentences and 104372 words (13148 types).

Microblog corpus. We choose the sample corpus of the bakeoff task this year as the test set, which contains 503 sentences and 20058 words (5047 types).

Statistics about the two corpora are shown in table 2. Column names are out-of-vocabulary rate (OOVR), average word length (AWL), rate of words with non-Chinese characters (RWNC). Let the union of the above four lexicons as our lexicon (104150 word types), we can see that microblog text contains more out-of-vocabulary words and much more words with non-Chinese characters. The average word length is shorter in microblog text.

	OOVR	AWL	RWNC
News	9.61%	2.13(type)/ 1.61(token)	2.61%
Microblog	13.91%	1.79(type)/ 1.38(token)	7.98%

Table 2. Statistics of news and microblog corpora

3.3 Results

Metrics used to evaluate system performance are Precison (P), Recall (R), F1-mearsure (F1), R_{IV}, R_{OOV}. R_{IV} is the recall of in-vocabulary word, and R_{OOV} is the recall of out-of-vocabulary word.

	P	R	F1	R_{OOV}	R_{IV}
GKB_m	87.20	**91.71**	**89.40**	79.30	**96.22**
GKB_n	85.31	91.01	88.07	73.37	96.10
$CiLin_m$	87.40	90.69	89.01	**81.44**	93.95
$CiLin_n$	86.61	90.06	88.30	77.76	93.37
HN_m	83.48	88.56	85.94	58.45	94.69
HN_n	82.19	88.09	85.04	42.22	94.98
LCW_m	83.50	89.13	86.22	74.51	95.12
LCW_n	79.60	87.62	83.42	65.35	95.55
$Union_m$	**87.67**	89.49	88.57	70.44	92.56
$Union_n$	86.60	88.32	87.45	57.28	91.62

Table 3. Experimental results

Experimental results are shown in table 3. The numbers in bold indicate the highest values of each metric. GKB_m and GKB_n mean that we use GKB as the lexicon. $Union_m$ and $Union_n$ mean that we use the union of all the four lexicon as the lexicon. The subscript "m" denotes result on microblog and "n" denotes result on news corpus. We can see that the all the results on microblog outperform those on news corpus. The results of the metric R_{IV} indicate that even in-vocabulary words are better recognized in microblog. GKB and CiLin achieving better results than lexicon union shows that the lexicon is not the larger the better for FMM. Lexicon needs filtering.

The official test data contains 5000 pieces of microblog. The evaluation metrics are Precision (P), Recall (R), F1-measure (F1), number of correct sentence (CS), correct sentence rate (CSR). The lexicon for our submitted system is composed of the union of the above four lexicons and the word list of the sample data. The official result is shown in table 4.

P	R	F1	CS	CSR
89.84	90.83	90.33	1256	25.12%

Table 4. The official result

4 Conclusions

This paper proposes a simple, lexicon based method for Chinese microblog word segmentation. By comparing results on news and microblog corpora, we find that this baseline method achieves better performance on microblog corpus. This may be a signal that microblog word segmentation is not as hard as expected. In addition, lexicon based method makes it easy to investigate new words emerging in the new media. Lexicon quality is an important factor influencing the performance.

The performance can be improved by adding more rules and carefully enlarging lexicon vocabulary. This simple and labeled-corpus-free method can provide a baseline for statistical methods, which may better utilize contextual information to tackle OOV and ambiguity.

Acknowledgements

This work is partially supported by grants from the National Natural Science Foundation of China (No.60970083, No.611700163), the China Postdoctoral Science Foundation (No.2011M501184), the Postdoctoral Science Foundation of Henan Province, China (No.2010027), the Outstanding Young Talents Technology Innovation Foundation of Henan Province, China (No.104100510026), and the Open Projects Program of National Laboratory of Pattern Recognition (No.201001116). We are grateful to the bakeoff organizers who provide such a good opportunity for research on Chinese word segmentation on microblog corpora.

References

Wanxiang Che, Zhenghua Li, and Ting Liu. 2010. *LTP: A Chinese Language Technology Platform.* In Proceedings of the COLING 2010: Demonstrations, pp. 13-16.

Zhendong Dong and Qiang Dong. 2006. *HowNet and the Computation of Meaning.* World Scientific.

Thomas Emerson. 2005. *The Second International Chinese Word Segmentation Bakeoff.* In Proceedings of the Fourth SIGHAN Workshop on Chinese Language Processing, pp. 123-133.

Changning Huang and Hai Zhao. 2007. *Chinese Word Segmentation: A Decade Review.* Journal of Chinese Information Processing, 21(3): 8-19.

Xingjian Li, et al. 2008. *Lexicon of Common Words in Contemporary Chinese.* The Commercial Press.

Weiwei Sun and Jia Xu. 2011. *Enhancing Chinese Word Segmentation Using Unlabeled Data.* In Proceedings of the EMNLP2011, pp. 970-979.

Hanshi Wang, et al. 2011. *A New Unsupervised Approach to Word Segmentation.* Computational Linguistics, 37(3): 421-454.

Nianwen Xue. 2003. *Chinese Word Segmentation as Character Tagging.* International Journal of Computational Linguistics and Chinese Language Processing, 8(1): 29-48.

Shiwen Yu, et al. 2003. *The Grammatical Knowledge-base of Contemporary Chinese, AComplete Specification (2nd edition).* Tsinghua University Press.

Hongmei Zhao and Qun Liu. 2010. *The CIPS-SIGHAN CLP2010 Chinese Word Segmentation Backoff.* In Proceedings of the CIPS-SIGHAN CLP2010, pp. 199-299.

A MMSM-based Hybrid Method for Chinese MicroBlog Word Segmentation

Xiao Sun*, Chengcheng Li, Chenyi Tang, Jiaqi Ye
AnHui Province Key Laboratory of Affective Computing and Advanced Intelligent Machine,
School of Computer and Information, Hefei University of Technology
Hefei, Anhui China, 230009.
School of Computer Science and Engineering, Dalian University of Technology
Dalian, Liaoning China, 116023.
sunx@hfut.edu.cn

Abstract

After years of researches, Chinese word segmentation has achieved quite high precisions for formal style text. However, the performance of segmentation is not so satisfying for MicroBlog corpora. In this paper we describe a scheme for Chinese word segmentation for, MicroBlog which integrates the character-based and word-based information in the directed graph generated by MMSM model. Word-level information is effective for analysis of known words, while character-level information is useful for analysis of unknown words. A multi-chain unequal states CRF model is proposed. The proposed multi-chain unequal states CRF has two state chains with unequal states which can recognize the POS tag simultaneously. The hybrid model was effective and adopted in real-world system.

1 Introduction

MicroBlog is an emerging application in the Web 2.0 era. On MicroBlog websites, users are able to post short messages less than a certain length, e.g., 140 English or Chinese characters, to communicate and share information with each other. After obtaining cleaned messages for a given user, we perform word segmentation for messages. In this paper, we use the system developed by Affective Computing and Natural Language Processing Group in Hefei University of Technology.

The system performs word segmentation and POS tagging simultaneously using a word lattice based re-ranking method proposed by Sun et al. [1]. Microblogs contain many out-of-vocabulary (OOV) words. To address the OOV problem, we also maintain a large up-to-date external vocabulary for word segmentation and POS tagging. To keep the vocabulary up-to-date, we import new words from two sources. The first is the Sogou New Word Dictionary which is updated weekly, and the second is the Sina Popular Word List, which is updated daily. The hybrid model for Chinese MicroBlog morphological analysis includes Chinese word segmentation, unknown word recognition and POS tagging. The foundation of the model is a directed segmentation graph based on the maximum matching and second-maximum matching (MMSM) model. Based on a known words system dictionary trained from the corpus, the MMSM model tries to build a directed graph with the candidate words and their parts-of-speech. In the directed graph, the character-level information and word-level information are combined, the HMM model is used to process the known words (words in system dictionary) using the word-level information; the proposed multi-chain unequal states CRF model is adopted to process the unknown words and their parts-of-speech using character-level information. Meanwhile, for the unknown word, which is the main difficulty in Chinese morphological analysis, both the word boundary and the parts-of-speech of the unknown words are unknown.

A multi-chain unequal states (MUS) CRF model is proposed here to process the unknown word segmentation and POS tagging. The proposed multi-chain CRF model has multi states chains for multi tasks. In our system, we adopted two states chains in which one states chain for the unknown words recognition and the other states chain for the unknown words POS tagging. The proposed MUS CRF model recognizes the unknown words from the sentence together with their POSs in one step, without using two separate linear-chain CRF models. The unknown words with their part-of-speech recognized by the multi-chain are added into the directed graph as candidates. With the directed segmentation graph and the proposed multi-chain CRF, the word-level information and character-level information are combined, Chinese word segmentation, unknown word recognition and POS tagging can be accomplished simultaneously.

2 The MMSM Directed Graph

The MMSM model acts as the basic framework in the hybrid model. The MMSM model (Huang and Sun, 2007) is a segmentation method that keeps the maximum and second-maximum segmentation result from a certain position in a sentence, and store the candidates of segmentation and POS tagging results in a directed graph, then some decoding algorithm is adopted to find the best path in the directed graph. With the MMSM model, all the possible segmentation paths and most lexical information like the POS information can be reserved for further use; little space cost is guaranteed by using the directed graph to store the segmentation paths; the context spaces are extended from single-dimension to multi-dimension; the MMSM model is also easy to be extended and add some new models in it.

The MMSM model is applied to build the original directed graph. Given a sentence, from a certain place if there are some candidates of segmentation words from the system dictionary, the MMSM model is applied to build the directed graph. Take the sentence “出生在聊城镇(Born in Liaocheng Town)” for example, the segmentation directed graph generated by the MMSM model is shown in figure 1. The labels after the words are POSs(parts-of-speech) defined in the PKU corpus.

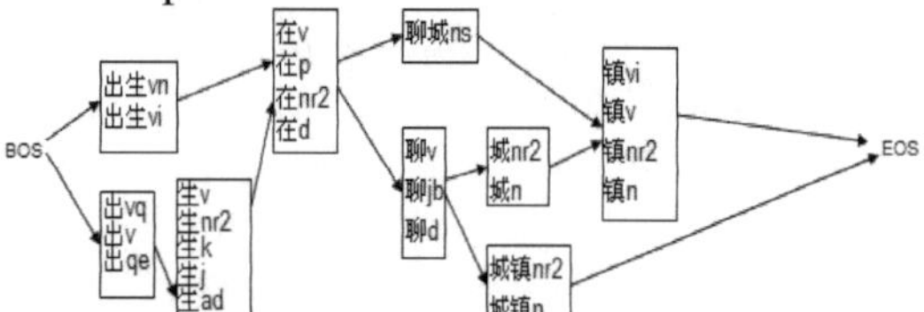

Figure 1. Segmentation directed graph by MMSM model

The word-based HMM model is trained and applied to assign cost for the nodes and edges in the directed graph by the MMSM model. The word-based HMM models were first used in English part-of-speech (POS) tagging (Charniak et al., 1993; Brants, 2000). This method identifies POS tags $T = t_1,..., t_n$, given a sentence as a word sequence $W = w_1,...,w_n$, where n is the number of words in the sentence. In Chinese language processing, the method is used with some modifications. Because each word in a sentence is not separated explicitly in Chinese, both segmentation of words and identification of the POS tags of the words must be done simultaneously. Given a sentence S, its most likely word sequence $\hat{\mathrm{W}}$ and POS sequence $\hat{\mathrm{T}}$ can be found as follows where W ranges over the possible segments of S ($w_1,...,w_n = S$):

$$(\hat{\mathrm{W}},\hat{\mathrm{T}}) = \underset{\mathrm{W,T}}{\operatorname{argmax}} P(\mathrm{W,T}\,|\,\mathrm{S})$$

$$= \underset{\mathrm{W,T}}{\operatorname{argmax}} \frac{P(\mathrm{W,T,S})}{P(\mathrm{S})} = \underset{\mathrm{W,T}}{\operatorname{argmax}} P(\mathrm{W,T}) \qquad (1)$$

$$\approx \underset{\mathrm{W,T}}{\operatorname{argmax}} \prod_{\mathrm{i=1}}^{\mathrm{n}} P(\mathrm{w_i}\,|\,\mathrm{t_i}) P(\mathrm{t_i}\,|\,\mathrm{t_{i-1}})$$

$P(w_i|t_i)$ represents the cost of nodes, while $P(t_i|t_{i-1})$ represents the cost of edges in the directed graph. When building the directed graph, there could be some positions where exists no candidates of segmentation words and corresponding parts-of-speech. The MUS CRF model is applied from such positions to recognize the unknown words and their corresponding POS and then adds them to the directed graph.

3 Multi-chain Unequal States CRF Model

Conditional Random Fields (CRFs) (J. Lafferty et al, 2001) is considered as one of the best sequence labeling classifier. A sequence labeling problem can be viewed as following: given an observed sequence $\vec{\mathrm{x}}$, we hope to get a corresponding label sequence $\vec{\mathrm{y}}$ with maximum probability. All possible y_i in $\vec{\mathrm{y}}$ are assumed from a finite label set Y. For example, in a part-of-speech tagging problem, given a sentence $\vec{\mathrm{x}}$, the corresponding POS labels $\vec{\mathrm{y}}$ are hoped to be gotten. CRF is a kind of discriminative model, which aims to estimate the probability $p(\vec{\mathrm{y}}\,|\,\vec{\mathrm{x}})$ directly without estimating the marginal $p(\vec{\mathrm{x}})$. The Linear-chain CRF is,

$$P_\theta(\vec{y}\,|\,\vec{x}) = \frac{1}{Z_\theta} \prod_{t=1}^{T-1} \Phi_t(y_t, y_{t+1}, \vec{x}, t) \qquad (2)$$

Where

$$\Phi_t(y_t, y_{t+1}, \vec{x}, t) =$$
$$\exp(\sum_k \lambda_k f_k(y_t, y_{t-1}, \vec{x}, t))$$

The boundary and POS of the unknown word are both unknown. In order to solve the unknown word recognition and POS tagging, instead of adopting two separate linear-chain CRF models, a MUS CRF model is proposed in this paper. The multi-chain CRF includes one observe chain and two state chains. It is defined as follows:

Let $\vec{X}$ be an observed sequence, $\vec{Y}$ be a set of corresponding labels, and $\vec{W}$ be a set of higher-level labels. Then the distribution p is a multi-chain conditional random field if each state $\vec{x}_i$ in $\vec{X}$ corresponds to one state $\vec{y}_i$ in $\vec{Y}$ while each state $\vec{w}_i$ in $\vec{W}$ corresponds to several contiguous states in $\vec{X}$, the distribution is as follows:

$$P_\theta(\vec{y}\mid\vec{x}) = \frac{1}{Z_\theta}\left(\prod_{t=1}^{T-1}\Phi_t(y_t, y_{t+1}, \vec{x}, t)\Psi_t(y_t, w_k, \vec{x}, t)\right) * \left(\prod_{k=1}^{K-1} T_k(w_k, w_{k+1}, k)\right) \quad (3)$$

Where

$$\Psi_t(y_t, w_k, \vec{x}, t) = \exp\left(\sum_i \lambda_i f_i(y_t, w_k, \vec{x}, t)\right)$$

$$T_k(w_k, w_{k+1}, k) = \exp\left(\sum_j \lambda_j f_j(w_k, w_{k+1}, k)\right)$$

$$Z_\theta = \sum_{\vec{y}}\left\{\prod_{t=1}^{T-1}\Phi_t(y_t, y_{t+1}, \vec{x}, t)\Psi_t(y_t, w_k, \vec{x}, t)\right) * \left(\prod_{k=1}^{K-1} T_k(w_k, w_{k+1}, k)\right\}$$

In Chinese word segmentation and POS tagging, the $\vec{x}$ in the multi-chain CRF equation represents sequence of the Chinese characters, the x_i represents the *ith* character in the sentence. The $\vec{y}$ represents the positional tag sequence of $\vec{x}$, the y_i represents the positional tag of x_i. The $\vec{w}$ represents the POS tagging sequence of the sentence, the w_i represents the POS of the *ith* word in the sentence. Thus the MUS CRF can perform the Chinese word segmentation and POS tagging simultaneously without having to build two separate linear-chain CRF models. The feature functions f in equation (3) represents the features obtained from the contexts. The features templates will be discussed in the next subsection. The equations of MUS CRF can be easily derived from DCRF (Dynamic CRF) (Charles Sutton et al., 2006) and the parameter estimation for multi-chain CRF is almost the same as linear-chain CRF. The structure of the MUS CRF is shown in the following figure 2. The lines in the figure present the features between the nodes.

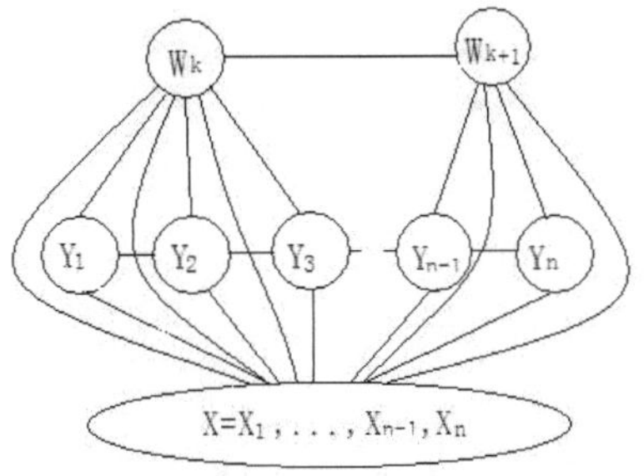

Figure 2, Multi-chain Unequal States CRF

The different between the DCRF and the proposed MUS CRF is that the top state chain in the MUS CRF does not have the same number of states as the bottom states chain. Just take the Chinese word segmentation and POS tagging for example. We should give each character in a sentence a corresponding label (Y_i) to mark its position in a word, a sequence of characters that form a word share a single POS label (W_k). The top state chain does not need so many states as the bottom state chain, so the complexity of computational cost drops down.

Given an input sentence, from the position that cannot be segmented, the multi-chain CRF is applied to recognize the unknown words and their related POSs. In our system, a 6-tag label set(Zhao,2006) is applied for Chinese word segmentation, which is shown in Table 1. Each character in the sentence is assigned a tag from the 6-tag label set to mark their position in a word.

Label	Position
B	The first position in a word
B_2	The second position in a word
B_3	The third position in a word
M	Other positions in a word with more than five characters except the last
E	The last position in a word
S	Single character word

Table 1. 6-tag label set for the Chinese word segmentation

The probability model and corresponding feature function is defined over the set H×T, where H is the set of possible contexts (or any predefined condition) and T is the set of possible tags. Generally, a feature function can be defined as follows

$$f(h,t) = \begin{cases} 1 & \text{if } h = h_i \text{ and } t = t_i \\ 0 & \text{else} \end{cases} \quad (5)$$

Where $h_i \in H$ and $t_i \in T$. For convenience, features are generally organized by some groups, which used to be called feature templates.

A feature template set for observe chain is shown in Table 2. C_i means the character at the *ith* poison. The C_iC_{i+1} means the combination of two characters C_i and C_{i+1}. The $C_{i-1}C_iC_{i+1}$ means the combination of three characters C_{i-1}, C_i, and C_{i+1}. In the table, $S(C_0)$ stands for predefined class of the character C_0. There are five classes predefined: numbers represent class 1, English letters represent class 2, punctuation represents class 3, Chinese characters represent class 4, and other characters represents class 5. We also import some outer lexical information like the outer dictionary to build the outer information template. The outer information template is derived from an outer lexical dictionary, which contains words and their lexical information selected from the internet and other formatted corpus. The words together with their POSs are stored in the dictionary. The maximum length of the word in the dictionary is five characters. The $T(C_0)$ represents the POS of the C_0 if C_0 exists as a word in the outer dictionary. The $L(C_0)$ represents the maximum length of word in the sentence around C_0 that exist in the outer dictionary. The $P(C_0)$ represent the position of the C_0 in the word exist in the outer dictionary.

Type	Label	Position
Unigram	1) C_{-2} 2) C_{-1} 3) C_0 4) C_1 5) C_2	The current character and characters around it.
Bigram	1) $C_{-2}C_{-1}$ 2) $C_{-1}C_0$ 3) C_0C_1 4) C_1C_2	The combination of two characters.
Trigram	1) $C_{-2}C_{-1}C_0$ 2) $C_{-1}C_0C_1$ 3) $C_0C_1C_2$	The combination of three characters
Style	1) $S(C_0)$	The predefined type of the current character
Outer Info.	1) $T(C_0)$ 2) $L(C_0)$ 3) $P(C_0)$	The information from outer dictionary.

Table 2. Feature templates

The proposed feature template is applied to train the MUS CRF model and recognize the unknown words together with their POSs. After the recognition, the unknown words are added into the directed graph. Take the "庄炎林担任庄希泉基金会主席(Yanlin Zhuang act as chairman of the Xiquan Zhuang Fund)" for example, The person name "庄炎林(Yanlin Zhuang)" and "庄希泉(Xiquan Zhuang)" do not exist in the system dictionary. The word-based MMSM model can not segment and POS tag them correctly. The MUS CRF is applied to recognize the unknown person name from the position where word-based model does not work. After the recognition, the two unknown person names are recognized together with their POSs(nr means person name) and added into the directed graph as shown in figure 3.

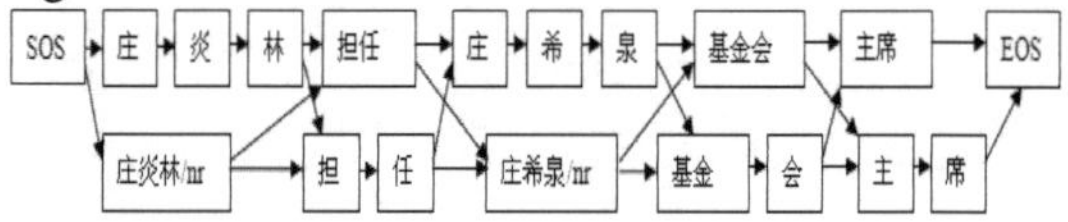

Figure 3. The directed graph after the unknown word recognition

4 Experimental and Results

We trained the hybrid model on the PKU2002 corpus, the PKU2002 corpus have 12 months corpus of Peoples' Daily News of year 2002 that have been annotated. As the corpus are different from MicroBlog, so the final test result are not quite satisfying. The evaluation tools and standards for SIGHAN6 are adopted in the experiments. We present the results of our experiments in recall, precision and F-measure, which are defined in the equations below, as usual in such experiments.

$$recall = \frac{\#\text{ of correctly extracted words}}{\text{total }\#\text{ of words}}$$

$$precision = \frac{\#\text{ of correctly extracted words}}{\text{total }\#\text{ of recognized words}}$$

$$F-measure = \frac{2 \times recall \times precision}{recall + precision}$$

First the hybrid model was tested by using different size of training corpus with the same outer lexical dictionary (with the maximum length of word of five). The test corpus in our experiment is randomly selected 500KB raw corpus from the PKU corpus except the training corpus. The result is shown in table 3. The R in the table means recall; The P in the table means precision; The F in the table means F-measure. The R, P, F in the following tables has the same meaning. The IVR means recall of in-vocabulary words. The IVP means precision of in-vocabulary words. The IVF means F-measure of in-vocabulary words. The OOVR means recall of out-of-vocabulary words. The OOVP means precision of out-of-vocabulary words. The OOVF means F-measure of out-of-vocabulary words.

Train corpus	R	P	F
One month	0.9820	0.9853	0.9837
Two months	0.9829	0.9854	0.9841
Three months	0.9849	0.9879	0.9864
	IVR	IVP	IVF
One month	0.9838	0.9903	0.9870
Two months	0.9847	0.9894	0.9871
Three months	0.9859	0.9915	0.9887
	OOVR	OOVP	OOVF
One month	0.9456	0.8891	0.9165
Two months	0.9426	0.9027	0.9222
Three months	0.9574	0.8989	0.9272

Table 3. Chinese word segmentation result by using different size of training corpus.

In the experiments, as the size of training corpus increases, the training cost increases exponentially. It costs too much memories and time to train the model on four months corpus, so we only tested on one month, two months and three months corpus. We can see as the size of training corpus increases, the F-score of our model increases simultaneously.

We also tested the model using different outer dictionary. We adopted two different outer dictionaries, the maximum length of word in one dictionary is 4(DIC4), and the other is 5(DIC5). The first dictionary has about 100,000 words. The other has more than 300,000 words. The words in the dictionary are collected from the internet using our internet crawler. The training corpus in this experiment is the three months training corpus. The test corpus is randomly selected 500KB raw corpus. The result is shown in the following Table 4

Outer	R	P	F
DIC4	0.9784	0.9794	0.9789
DIC5	0.9849	0.9879	0.9864
	IVR	IVP	IVF
DIC4	0.9816	0.9859	0.9837
DIC5	0.9859	0.9915	0.9887
	OOVR	OOVP	OOVF
DIC4	0.8948	0.8227	0.8572
DIC5	0.9574	0.8989	0.9272

Table 4. Chinese word segmentation result by using different outer dictionary

The result of DIC5 is much better than the DIC4 because of the increasing of the maximum length of the word in the dictionary and the size of the dictionary.

We tested our POS tagging result using two training corpus. In the first experiment we trained one month corpus and in the second we trained two months corpus. The test corpus is randomly selected 500KB raw corpus. The result of POS tagging is in Table 5. The A in Table 5 means total accuracy of POS tagging. The IV-R means the POS tagging recall of in-vocabulary words. The OOV-R means the POS tagging recall of out-of-vocabulary words. The MT-R means POS tagging recall of multi-tag words.

Corpus	A	IV-R	OOV-R	MT-R
One month	0.9329	0.9518	0.6441	0.8972
Two months	0.9463	0.9711	0.6751	0.9064

Table 5. POS tagging result by using different size of training corpus.

We also deleted the outer dictionary for the multi-chain model and tested our model using the close test of SIGHAN6. We compared the Chinese word segmentation and POS tagging result with other participators' result (F-measure rank one in each corpus). We only adopted the close test of SIGHAN6 because we wanted to evaluate the model only. The Chinese word segmentation result is shown in Table 6

		R	P	F
CTB	Our	0.9620	0.9653	0.9636
	Rank1	0.9583	0.9596	0.9589
NCC	Our	0.9458	0.9329	0.9393
	Rank1	0.9402	0.9407	0.9405
SXU	Our	0.9658	0.9589	0.9623
	Rank1	0.9622	0.9625	0.9623

Table 6. Chinese word segmentation result of SIGHAN2007

We can see from the table that the hybrid model achieves competitive F-score and all the R-scores of the hybrid model are better than the rank one score in SIGHAN6. This is because the hybrid model combines the HMM model and CRF model together.

The POS tagging result on close test of SIGHAN6 is shown in Table 7

		A	IV-R	OOV-R	MT-R
CTB	Our	0.9456	0.9591	0.8032	0.9241
	Rank1	0.9428	0.9557	0.7522	0.9197
NCC	Our	0.9632	0.9801	0.7021	0.9340
	Rank1	0.9541	0.9738	0.5998	0.9195
PKU	Our	0.9503	0.9680	0.7102	0.9411
	Rank1	0.9411	0.9622	0.6057	0.9200

Table 7. POS tagging result of SIGHAN 2007

The hybrid model gets the highest score in Chinese POS tagging especially the OOV-R score in all corpuses. The MUS CRF in the hybrid model devotes a lot to this. The MUS CRF can recognize the POS of the unknown word and increase the performance of the whole model.

5 Conclusions

The MMSM model is adopted to combine the word-based HMM model and character-based

CRF model together. The word-based information is for known words segmentation and POS tagging while the character-based information is for the unknown words recognition and their POSs tagging. The MUS CRF is proposed to solve the unknown words recognition and their POS tagging synchronously. The adoption of the MUS CRF model decreases the computational cost of Dynamic CRF. Also it avoids using two separated linear-chain CRF models for the unknown word recognition and POS tagging. The hybrid model also decreases the computational cost without having to tagging all the characters in a sentence for Chinese word segmentation and POS tagging. Experimental results showed that the method achieves high accuracy compared to the state-of-the-art methods in both Chinese word segmentation and POS tagging.

The costs in the directed graph are encoded by the HMM model. We will adopted the CRF model to encode the cost in the directed graph, which will get rid of the limitations of hypothesis in the HMM model and combine more lexical information from the context in the directed graph to get higher precision.

Acknowledgments

The work is supported by the 863 National Advanced Technology Research Program of China (NO. 2012AA011103), and also supported by the Funding Project for AnHui Province Key Laboratory of Affective Computing and Advanced Intelligent Machine(1206c0805039), HeFei University of Technology. This project is also supported by the National Science Foundation for Post-doctoral Scientists of China (Grant No. 2012M511156) and China Postdoctoral Science Foundation(2012M511156).

References

Asahara, M. and Matsumoto, Y., 2003, Unknown Word Identification in Japanese Text Based on Morphological Analysis and Chunking, In *IPSJ SIG Notes Natural Language*, 2003-NL-154:47–54.

A. Berger, S. D. Pietra, and V. D. Pietra, A Maximum Entropy Approach to Natural Language Processing, *Computational Linguistics*, (22-1), March 1996.

Charles Sutton, Andrew McCallum and Khashayar Rohanimanesh. Dynamic Conditional Random Fields: Factorized Probabilistic Models for Labeling and Segmenting Sequence Data. *Journal of Machine Learning Research*. 2007:693-723

C. Sutton, A. McCallum, and K. Rohanimanesh, Dynamic Conditional Random Fields: Factorized Probabilistic Models for Labeling and Segmenting Sequence Data, *Journal of Machine Learning Research,* 2007(3):694-723.

E. Charniak, Hendrickson C., Jacobson N., and Perkowitz M. 1993. Equations for part of speech tagging. *In Proceedings of the Conference of the American Association for Artificial Intelligence.* 1993:784-789.

Gao J., Wu A., Li M., Huang C. N., Li H., Xia X., and Qin H. 2004. Adaptive Chinese word segmentation. *In Proceedings the 41st Annual Meeting of the Association for Computational Linguistics,* 2004:21-26.

Huang Degen and Sun Xiao. 2007. An Integrative Approach to Chinese Named Entity Recognition. *In Proceedings of Sixth International Conference on Advanced Language Processing and Web Information Technology*. 2007:171-176

H. T. Ng and J. K. Low. 2004. Chinese Part-Of-Speech Tagging: One-at-a-Time or All-at-Once? Word-Base or Character-Based? *In Proceedings of Conference on Empirical Methods in Natural Language Processing.* 2004.

J. Lafferty, A. McCallum, and F. Pereira, Conditional random fields: Probabilistic models for segmenting and labeling sequence data. *International Conference on Machine Learning,* 2001.

K. P. Murphy, Y. Weiss, and M. I. Jordan. Loopy belief propagation for approximate inference: An empirical study. *In Conference on Uncertainty in Artificial Intelligence,* 1999:467-475.

Lafferty, J., McCallum, A., and Pereira, F. 2001. Conditional Random Field: Probabilistic models for segmenting and labeling sequence data. *In Proceedings of the International Conference on Machine Learning*. 2001:282-289

Lance A. Ramshaw and Mitchell P. Marcus. 1995. Text chunking using transformation-based learning. In Proceedings of the 3rd Workshop on Very Large Corpora, 1999:82-94.

Masayuki Asahara and Yuji Matsumoto. 2000. Extended Models and Tools for High-performance Parts-of-Speech Tagger. *In Proceedings of the 18th International Conference on Computational Linguistics*, 2000:21–27.

Masayuki Asahara, Chooi Ling Goh, Xiaojie Wang, and Yuji Matsumoto. 2003. Combining Segmenter and Chunker for Chinese Word Segmentation. *In Proceedings of the 2nd SIGHAN Workshop on Chinese Language Processing*, 2003:144–147.

Nianwen Xue. 2003. Chinese Word Segmentation as Character Tagging. *International Journal of Computational Linguistics and Chinese*, 8(1):29–48.

Peng, F., Feng, F., and McCallum, A. 2004. Chinese segmentation and new word detection using conditional random fields. *In Proceedings of the Computational Linguistics*, 2004:562-568.

Richard Sproat and Thomas Emerson. 2003. The First International ChineseWord Segmentation Bakeoff. *In Proceedings of the Second SIGHANWorkshop on Chinese Language Processing*, 2003:133–143.

S. M. Aji, G. B. Horn, and R. J. McEliece, On the convergence of iterative decoding on graphs with a single cycle. *In Proc. IEEE Int'l Symposium on Information Theory*, 1998.

Shi, W. 2005. Chinese Word Segmentation Based On Direct Maximum Entropy Model. *In Proceedings of the Fourth SIGHAN Workshop on Chinese Language Processing.*

Thorston Brants, 2000. TnT A Statistical Parts-of-Speech Tagger. *In Proceedings of Sixth Applied Natural Language Processing Conference.* 2000:224-231.

Tatsumi Yoshida, Kiyonori Ohtake, and Kazuhide Yamamoto. 2003. Performance Evaluation of Chinese Analyzers with Support Vector Machines. *Journal of Natural Language Processing*, 10(1):109–131.

Wu Y. C., Chang C. H. and Lee Y. S. 2006a. A general and multi-lingual phrase chunking model based on masking method. *Lecture Notes in Computer Science: Computational Linguistics and Intelligent Text Processing*, 3878: 144-155.

Wu Y. C., Fan T. K., Lee Y. S. and Yen S. J. 2006b. Extracting named entities using support vector machines, *Lecture Notes in Bioinformatics: Knowledge Discovery in Life Science Literature*, 3886: 91-103.

Wu Y. C., Lee Y. S., and Yang J. C. 2006c. The Exploration of Deterministic and Efficient Dependency Parsing. *In Proceedings of the 10th Conference on Natural Language Learning.*

Y. Shi, M. Wang, A Dual-layer CRFs Based Joint Decoding Method for Cascaded Segmentation and Labeling Tasks. *In International Joint Conferences on Artificial Intelligence*, 2007.

Zhao Hai, Huang Chang-Ning, and Li Mu, An Improved Chinese Word Segmentation System with Conditional Random Field, *In Proceedings of the Fifth SIGHAN Workshop on Chinese Language Processing*, 2006:162-165.

Chinese Tweets Segmentation based on Morphemes

Chaoyue Wang
Heilongjiang University
Harbin, China.
chaoyue.wang@yahoo.cn

Guohong Fu
Heilongjiang University
Harbin, China.
ghfu@hlju.edu.cn

Abstract

Chinese tweets segmentation is a critical problem in natural language processing area. While segmentation of in-vocabulary words is well studied to date, few research findings are yet available concerning the prediction of new words on twitter. In this paper, we attempt to exploit multiple features for segmenting tweets in real text. To this end, we first take morpheme as the basic component units of Chinese words and thus investigate the relationship between Chinese new words and their internal morphological structures. Then, we explore both word internal cues and word external contextual features, and combine them for segmentation of Chinese new words using conditional random field. Our experimental results show that the incorporation of multiple features, especially the word-internal morphological features is of great value to Chinese tweets segmentation.

1 Introduction

Chinese word segmentation is one of the important steps in natural language processing. Essentially, segmentation is trying to determine the boundary of the word. As a fundamental natural language analysis task, word segmentation plays a key role in many natural language processing applications.

Different from the traditional word segmentation, many new words exist in the segmentation on twitter. Traditional methods can't deal with this problem well, especially the dictionary based method. In this paper, we use statistical method to solve this problem.

In previous study, most researchers used word as the basic unit; however, this method is fatigue on addressing the new words detection. To address this problem, in this paper, we use morpheme as the basic unit under the Conditional Random Filed (CRF). Fu et al. proved that morphemes were informative for unknown words processing.

2 Approach

In this paper, we take word segmentation as sequence labeling. Given an input sequence of words, our approach for word segmentation consists of three main parts: First, a word decomposition module is employed to decompose unknown words within the input sentence into a sequence of morphemes. Then the extended BIO tagset is used to represent the position patterns of morphemes within words. Finally, CRF is used to predict the corresponding label.

2.1 Chinese Morphemes

In the present study we consider two major types of morphemes, namely free morphemes and bound morphemes (viz. affixes). A free morpheme can stand by itself as a word, whereas an affix can show up if and only if being attached to other morphemes to form a word.

To explore word-internal clues for segmentation of Chinese new words, we employ the extended IOB tagset to represent the position patterns of Chinese morphemes in word formation. Table 1 presents the detailed definition of the extended IOB tags and the correspondence between IOB tags and morpheme types.

Tag	Definition
O	A morpheme as a word by itself
I	A morpheme inside a word
B	A word-initial morpheme
E	A word-final morpheme

Table1 The extended IOB tagset for the representation of component morphemes within Chinese word

2.2 Word decomposition

Word decomposition is the process of decomposing a word to a sequence of morphemes associated with their IOB tags defined in Table 1. For example, the word “不安全感”(the sense of insecurity) should be decomposed as “不/O 安/B 全/E 感/O”.

2.3 Features

Feature selection plays a critical in CRF. In the present study, we consider two main groups of features for Chinese word segmentation, namely contextual features around words and word-formation features within words. We choose the part of speech (POS) of the morpheme as the internal feature; the table2 shows our feature template.

```
# Unigram
    U00:%x[-1,0]
    U01:%x[0,0]
    U02:%x[1,0]
    U03:%x[-1,1]
    U04:%x[0,1]
    U05:%x[1,1]
    U06:%x[-1,0]/%x[0,0]
    U07:%x[0,0]/%x[1,0]
    U08:%x[-1,1]/%x[0,1]
    U09:%x[0,1]/%x[1,1]
    # Bigram
    B
```

Table 2 Feature template for morpheme-based CRFs

3 Experimental result

Table 3 shows the result. The ‘Best’ indicates the high score achieved in CLP2012 Micro-blog word segmentation subtask.

Results	Precision Rate	Recall Rate	F Score	Total Correct Sentences	Ratio of Correct Sentences
Our Result	0.8451	0.8437	0.8444	750	15.0%
Best	0.946	0.9496	0.9478	2244	44.88%

Table 3 Evaluation Results

4 Conclusions

In this paper, we have attempted to explore word internal morphological clues within Chinese words, and incorporate them with word-external contextual features for segmentation of Chinese words. Due to the lack of large scale corpus and deep morphological knowledge for Chinese, in the present study we only took into account surface morphological clues, namely the position patterns of morphemes in word formation. In future work we intend to explore systematically deep morphological knowledge.

References

Ruiqiang Zhang, Keiji Yasuda, Eiichiro Sumita. 2008. Improved statistical machine traslantion by multiple Chinese word segmentation. Proceedings of the 3rd workshop on statistical machine translation, 216-223.

S. Foo, H. Li. 2004. Chinese word segmentation and its effect on information retrieval. Information Processing and Management, 40(1): 161-190.

Guohong Fu, Kang-Kwong Luke. 2006. Chinese POdisambiguation and unknown word guessing with lexicalized HMMs. International Journal of Technology and Human Interaction, Vol.2, No.1, pages 39-50.

Guohong Fu, Chunyu Kit, Jonathan J. 2008. Webster. Chinese word segmentation as morpheme-based lexical chunking. Information Sciences, Vol.178, No.9, pages 2282-2296.

The Task 2 of CIPS-SIGHAN 2012
Named Entity Recognition and Disambiguation in Chinese Bakeoff

Zhengyan He Houfeng Wang [*] Sujian Li
MOE Key Lab of Computational Linguistics, Peking University
hezhengyan.hit@gmail.com, {wanghf, lisujian}@pku.edu.cn

Abstract

The CIPS-SIGHAN 2012 Chinese Named Entity Recognition and Disambiguation (NERD) bake-off was held in the summer of 2012. Named entity recognition and disambiguation is an important task in natural language processing and knowledge base construction. It aims at detecting entity mentions in raw text, followed by pointing the detected mentions to real world entities. Often, real world entities can be found on online encyclopedia like Wikipedia and Baike. This task focuses on NERD in Chinese Language, and presents some challenges unique to Chinese, namely the confusion of named entity with common words, and lack of capital clues as in English. We manually construct query names and a knowledge base from Baike. Evaluation results show promising future of this field.

1 Overview

Named Entity Recognition and Disambiguation (NERD) is the task of detecting entity mentions from raw text and classifying each mention to its real world entity. NERD is a fundamental problem in Natural Language Processing (NLP), and the first step towards many higher level tasks, such as constructing knowledge bases, populating entities with attributes, social analysis, information extraction and question answering.

NERD in Chinese has posed some unique challenges. First, common words can be used as named entities. For example, 高明(brilliant), a common adjective, is also a person name in China. Therefore, it is challenging to distinguish common words which function as named entities, given that Chinese words have less morphology variations than many other languages. Second, different types of named entities can use the same names. For example, 金山(Gold Hill) can be used as the name of persons, locations and organizations. Finally, it is typical in China that many persons share the same name. For instance, there are many persons having the name 王刚(Wang Gang) in China. To investigate these issues, SIGHAN 2012 establishes a task for Named Entity Recognition and Disambiguation (NERD task).

Similar tasks in English have been studied for several years. Related events include Knowledge Base Population (KBP) track of Text Analysis Conference (TAC) (Ji and Grishman, 2011; Ji et al., 2010), Web People Search (WePS) (Artiles et al., 2007). In WePS, the task is person name clustering, in which there is no knowledge base available. In TAC-KBP, the task is called entity linking, where the knowledge base is constructed with a subset of Wikipedia, and an entity linking system should output the correct entity id in knowledge base or "NIL" if the entity is not present in the knowledge base . It is also closely related to cross-document coreference resolution. Some other names like entity disambiguation (Kataria et al., 2011) and Wikification (Mihalcea and Csomai, 2007) are also used.

In the SIGHAN 2012 NERD task, 8 teams has successfully submitted their results and several approaches have proved to be quite effective and promising.

[*]corresponding author

2 Task Definition and Evaluation Metrics

2.1 Task description

The participants are provided with a collection of web documents (the Source) and a Knowledge Base (KB) which contains the targets of disambiguation. One needs to find for each mention the target entity it refers to, according to the context in which it appears.

Table 1 is a sample of the knowledge base. Each one is an XML document, in which there are several candidate entities with the same name, and each entity has a short description. Each ambiguous name has a collection of test text. For each test text, one should determine which real entity the name refers to, if it presents in the knowledge base, output the id in the KB; or if it is a common word, output "Other"; or if it is an entity outside the KB, group them into different clusters, output "Out_n".

2.2 dataset preparation

The query person names are manually selected to reflect both the variation of this name and the confusion with common words. knowledge base is constructed from Baidu Baike entries according the person names. Source texts are selected by 20 student querying the search engine. The students are advised to crawl web document with as many variation of persons for each name as possible, and also with common words. The crawled documents for one query are splitted into folders for each real person in Baike, and reviewed by the advisor.

The query names are chosen to reflect some commonly observed in Chinese person name recognition and disambiguation, such as common words ("张扬" "田野" "高明"), entity type variation ("沈阳" "金山" "黄河").

The entire dataset contains 32 names in Chinese. Table 2 gives an overview of the dataset.

2.3 Evaluation

For each name, there is a collection of test documents for evaluation. Evaluation is carried out on a per document basis. Let T denote the document collection for one name (e.g. "雷雨"), for each query document $t \in T$, the system output may fall into three classes, namely: SL_XX, SOther and SOut_XX, representing in-KB id, a common word,

```
<?xml version='1.0' encoding='UTF-8'?>
<EntityList name="雷雨">
  <Entity id="01">
    <text>通江县第二中学教师, 男, 大学本
科, 西华师范大学英语语言文学专业毕业。高
    二英语备课组长。自参工以来一事从事高中英
语教学工作, 长期从事班主任工作, 所任
    班级历届成绩显著。...
    </text>
  </Entity>
  <Entity id="02">
    <text>重庆市黔江区太极乡党委副书记、乡
长。主持政府全面工作, 主管财政、金融、
    审计、统计、非公有制经济、城乡统筹、乡镇
企业、招商引资、烤烟、蚕桑工作。
    </text>
  </Entity>
  <Entity id="03">
    <text>罗源县中房镇下湖村人。1978年8月
加入中国共产党。1981年, 毕业于上海同济大
    学规划专业。同年起, 任福州市城乡设计院规
划室主任、工程师, 兼任福州市土木建筑
    学会秘书长。...
    </text>
  </Entity>
  <Entity id="04">
    <text>男, 汉族, 硕士研究生学历, 出生
于1961年9月, 陕西 中共商南县委书记, 商州
    人, 1980年8月参加革命工作, 1982年7月加
入中国共产党, 现任中共商南县委书记。曾
    任任共青团商洛地委副书记; 洛南县政府副县
长; 任中共商南县委副书记; 中共山阳县
    委常委、县政府常务副县长, 等。
    </text>
  </Entity>
  <Entity id="05">
    <text>四川省蒲江县教育局党组书记、局
长。主持县教育局全面工作。主管教育督导、
    计财、基建和教仪电教等工作。
    </text>
  </Entity>
  <Entity id="06">
    <text>女, 1975年8月生, 回族, 广西南宁
人, 中共党员, 1997年7月广西师范大学汉语
    言专业毕业, 2006年获教育硕士学位, 中学
中级教师, 1997年7月进入桂林中学任教语文
    至今。
    </text>
  </Entity>
</EntityList>
```

Table 1: Sample of Knowledge Base. Each entry contains a short description of the real world entity.

Name	in-KB					not-in-KB					Other
	#text	#cluster	max	min	avg	#text	#cluster	max	min	avg	
丛林	81	5	20	7	16.0	14	9	3	1	1.0	24
严明	37	12	13	2	3.0	0	0	0	0	0.0	10
华山	109	9	18	7	12.0	19	4	6	3	4.0	0
华明	55	4	19	6	13.0	10	5	3	1	2.0	0
吉祥	56	8	19	1	7.0	1	1	1	1	1.0	19
张弛	202	27	24	1	7.0	52	12	7	2	4.0	26
张扬	145	19	15	1	7.0	0	0	0	0	0.0	14
方正	115	12	18	1	9.0	12	4	5	1	3.0	4
李晓明	416	33	33	2	12.0	86	15	9	2	5.0	0
杜鹃	155	13	21	2	11.0	12	8	5	1	1.0	12
杨柳	210	15	25	1	14.0	22	5	9	2	4.0	18
江涛	248	28	26	1	8.0	16	6	6	1	2.0	17
汪洋	181	12	37	1	15.0	21	4	8	1	5.0	21
田野	258	34	21	1	7.0	11	2	8	3	5.0	20
白云	244	19	28	2	12.0	16	2	9	7	8.0	18
白雪	116	9	19	5	12.0	0	0	0	0	0.0	17
秦岭	78	12	15	1	6.0	22	2	16	6	11.0	0
约翰逊	254	15	20	3	16.0	74	18	11	2	4.0	12
胡琴	43	3	22	7	14.0	7	3	3	2	2.0	24
金山	115	8	17	9	14.0	5	1	5	5	5.0	5
雷雨	56	6	17	3	9.0	7	1	7	7	7.0	23
马啸	57	6	18	2	9.0	9	2	6	3	4.0	3
高山	126	19	19	1	6.0	4	1	4	4	4.0	20
高峰	200	37	19	1	5.0	3	1	3	3	3.0	24
高明	195	22	20	1	8.0	16	3	11	1	5.0	23
高超	88	13	19	2	6.0	13	7	3	1	1.0	15
高雄	78	4	29	10	19.0	6	2	4	2	3.0	0
黄梅	150	13	22	3	11.0	3	2	2	1	1.0	19
黄河	156	14	26	1	11.0	22	4	8	4	5.0	0
黄海	108	19	15	1	5.0	20	3	8	5	6.0	0
黄莺	80	9	16	4	8.0	15	4	5	2	3.0	24
黄龙	129	14	21	1	9.0	23	4	7	3	5.0	9

Table 2: Statistics of dataset. Each column in in-KB and not-in-KB means number of texts in total, number of entities in total, max/min/average number of texts containing the name. The last column is number of texts classified as "Other" in gold standard.

or a out-of-KB cluster id respectively; the gold label is L_XX, Other and Out_XX. We compute the precision and recall for this query as follows:

1. if t in T is predicted as SL_XX, we use the following formulae.

$$Pre(t) = \frac{|SL\_XX \cap L\_XX|}{|SL\_XX|} \quad (1)$$

$$Rec(t) = \frac{|SL\_XX \cap L\_XX|}{|L\_XX|} \quad (2)$$

2. if t in T is predicted as SOther, we use the following formulae.

$$Pre(t) = \frac{|SOther \cap Other|}{|SOther|} \quad (3)$$

$$Rec(t) = \frac{|SOther \cap Other|}{|Other|} \quad (4)$$

3. if t in T is predicted as SOut_XX, we use the following formulae.

$$Pre(t) = \frac{|SOut\_XX(t) \cap Out\_YY(t)|}{|SOut\_XX|} \quad (5)$$

$$Rec(t) = \frac{|SOut\_XX(t) \cap Out\_YY(t)|}{|Out\_YY|} \quad (6)$$

4. Accorting to all the instance documents of 雷雨, the overall precision and recall are calculated as follows.

$$Pre(n) = \frac{\sum_{t \in T} Pre(t)}{|T|} \quad (7)$$

$$Rec(n) = \frac{\sum_{t \in T} Rec(t)}{|T|} \quad (8)$$

5. The overall precision and recall for all test names are calculated as follows (the set of all the test names are notated as N, each name is represented as n in N)

$$Pre = \frac{\sum_{n} Pre(n)}{|N|} \quad (9)$$

$$Rec = \frac{\sum_{n} Rec(n)}{|N|} \quad (10)$$

$$F = \frac{2 \times Pre \times Rec}{Pre + Rec} \quad (11)$$

Organization	Contact
NLP group at the University of Macau(I)	Longyue Wang
NLP group at the University of Macau(II)	Hao Zong
Shenzhen Graduate School, Harbin Institute of Technology & Hong Kong Polytechnic University	Jian Xu
Kunming University of Science and Technology	Zhengtao Yu
Institute of Automation, Chinese Academy of Sciences	Tao Zhang
Beijing University of Posts and Telecommunications	Caixia Yuan
Zhengzhou University	HongyingZan
Institute of Software, Chinese Academy of Sciences	Le Sun

Table 3: List of participants

3 Participants of this task

Table 3 lists the 8 teams of the bake-off task.

4 Results, System Comparison and Discussion

4.1 Basic steps of recognition and disambiguation

There are several common components shared by many teams, which is determined by the task requirements:

- preprocessing: the KB and Source text are segmented into Chinese words, and other processing like POS-tagging and named entity recognition are alternatively used;

- information extraction: keywords, entities and relevant attributes are extracted, to construct a vector representation of KB and Source text;

- similarity calculation: the similarity is computed with feature vector, and entities in KB is generated by the rank score. Most teams use simply the unsupervised method to rank candidates, and some teams use semantic resources like Tongyici Cilin (Tian et al., 2012) or the Web for a better scoring;

- "NIL" entity clustering: maximum similarity score below a threshold is a good sign of determining if the entity is in the KB. Hierarchical clustering method is used by many teams to group NIL entities (Peng et al., 2012; Zhang et al., 2012).

- a separate common word detection step is used after the first entity recognition step, or after the knowledge base linking phase.

There are several features which proves useful for accurate disambiguation. The features are listed as follows:

- keywords: one team report extracting discriminative keywords from the KB to represent the target entities, besides using bag-of-word feature vector, and the performance is good (Zong et al., 2012).

- entity of different types: person, organization, location, and other types are used by many teams (Qing-hu et al., 2012; Peng et al., 2012; Zong et al., 2012; Wang et al., 2012). One team reports cooccuring persons more discriminative than other types (Zong et al., 2012). This is reasonable since a person is largely influenced by its social relations.

- entity attributes: several teams (Tian et al., 2012; Wang et al., 2012; Wei et al., 2012) extract attribute of many types, such as title, occupation, gender, nationality, graduate school, education background, publication, etc. Whether the performance is good is largely determined by the extraction technique.

- representation of pseudo-entities (i.e. "Other" and "Out_n"): one team benefits from a explicit representation of common words and out-of-KB entities (Peng et al., 2012), rather than using same set of feature for classification and clustering. They leverage the Web to discover keywords frequently occurring with common names. They further make the assumption that if all the entities in test document do not appear in the entries of KB, then it is likely to be an out-of-KB entity.

Feature weighting tuning: with those diverse kinds of representative features, the NERD system has to determine which feature is more important. One team uses supervised method to tune the weight of different features (Tian et al., 2012), while another team uses the information gain criterion (Wei et al., 2012).

Besides a good representation of both source text and knowledge base entities, there are other aspects that may benefit a NERD system. One team use model combination method: there are several rank score and each with different feature input; a classification model finally determine the relative importance of each scoring (Liu et al., 2012). Training set can be used to decide the threshold in NIL linking and tune the weight of different features and models. One team also uses the extended version of KB from Baidu Baike to enrich the feature set (Liu et al., 2012), and constructs a one-to-one mapping from Baike to KB, because most of the entities is constructed from Baike.

4.2 Analysis of difficult queries

Table 4 shows detailed top/median precision/recall/f-score across all teams, for each query name. The result shows that the performance is good for most of the queries, except for a few, like "田野" "黄河" "黄莺" "黄龙". As we did not have the named entity recognition result, we detect it is due to their so common usage in Chinese Language as a common word. It is even harder for the detection system to consider it as a named entity without strong clues.

Table 5 shows detailed median score for in-KB, NIL clustering, and common word detection results. We can see that the precision and recall of in-KB entities are generally much higher than the NIL clustering. This is reasonable because the entities in KB are almost famous people and rich in attributes and cooccurence entities, as most systems use these attributes as strong indicator of specific person.

Moreover, there is general trend that the recall of NIL clustering is higher than precision. That is to say most of the systems tend to put entities into separate clusters. The reason may be that most NIL entities are so rarely observed and have fewer clues like social relations. They are in most situations dissimilar to each other, if the system uses attribute or cooccuring entities, simply because the features of these types have a small opportunity to match.

Finally, the "Other" class performance differs a lot across different queries. We deduce this is caused by the difficulty level of the query document. As this part is closely related to the segmentation and entity recognition processing step, it is hard to tell which aspects are more important, the recognition or segmentation.

It is interesting to see that with so many difficulty discussed, there are general clues which indicate a good performance of an NERD system. Most systems use fine-grained keywords, attributes, and cooccurence entities, which gives competitive performance. One team exceeds over 80% total F-score, and 3 teams at around 75%. We can expect better performance with better recognition tools and even large collections of Source and KB information.

name	precision	recall	f-score
丛林	0.867/0.806	0.916/0.783	0.883/0.778
严明	0.972/0.798	0.885/0.724	0.920/0.777
华山	0.809/0.722	0.863/0.723	0.792/0.697
华明	0.969/0.837	0.905/0.866	0.936/0.822
吉祥	0.934/0.833	0.955/0.882	0.938/0.842
张弛	0.750/0.615	0.905/0.830	0.820/0.692
张扬	0.907/0.786	0.915/0.824	0.904/0.807
方正	0.860/0.792	0.926/0.797	0.885/0.738
李晓明	0.859/0.618	0.871/0.720	0.812/0.674
杜鹃	0.870/0.749	0.852/0.793	0.853/0.759
杨柳	0.868/0.785	0.890/0.808	0.855/0.797
江涛	0.836/0.661	0.825/0.778	0.830/0.709
汪洋	0.866/0.675	0.837/0.736	0.847/0.684
田野	0.734/0.649	0.791/0.718	0.761/0.683
白云	0.813/0.660	0.867/0.697	0.819/0.694
白雪	0.925/0.839	0.929/0.846	0.927/0.839
秦岭	0.817/0.680	0.861/0.715	0.837/0.699
约翰逊	0.734/0.621	0.890/0.719	0.804/0.685
胡琴	0.973/0.890	1.000/0.843	0.978/0.850
金山	0.937/0.777	0.925/0.809	0.931/0.767
雷雨	0.942/0.796	0.898/0.766	0.847/0.802
马啸	0.930/0.868	0.911/0.826	0.893/0.843
高山	0.880/0.763	0.874/0.804	0.867/0.796
高峰	0.916/0.746	0.848/0.755	0.880/0.759
高明	0.861/0.709	0.899/0.748	0.871/0.721
高超	0.806/0.672	0.894/0.769	0.822/0.703
高雄	0.917/0.765	0.966/0.732	0.843/0.722
黄梅	0.822/0.803	0.857/0.815	0.831/0.786
黄河	0.729/0.667	0.875/0.727	0.740/0.690
黄海	0.891/0.690	0.929/0.757	0.892/0.738
黄莺	0.783/0.660	0.922/0.760	0.781/0.665
黄龙	0.528/0.340	0.681/0.477	0.447/0.411
total	0.795/0.702	0.856/0.732	0.802/0.721

Table 4: analysis of queries. Each cell gives the maximum/median score over all teams.

5 Conclusion

The Chinese named entity recognition and disambiguation task for CIPS-SIGHAN 2012 has raised the problem in Chinese NERD. Besides the basic difficulty of detection, classification, and NIL clustering , there are other difficulties like common words detection, disambiguation across entity types. 8 teams have submitted their results, and address the difficulties in different ways. Most teams use simple unsupervised scoring metrics, with careful design of feature representation. Some of the techniques prove effective and the result is promising.

Acknowledgment

This work was partially supported by National High Technology Research and Development Program of China (863 Program) (No. 2012AA011101), National Natural Science Foundation of China (No.91024009, No.60973053), the Specialized Research Fund for the Doctoral Program of Higher Education of China (Grant No. 20090001110047)

References

J. Artiles, J. Gonzalo, and S. Sekine. 2007. The semeval-2007 weps evaluation: Establishing a benchmark for the web people search task. *Proceedings of Semeval*, pages 64–69.

Name	in-KB p/r	Out_n p/r	Other p/r
丛林	0.85/0.77/5	0.71/0.83/9	0.93/0.74/24
严明	0.91/0.82/7	1.00/0.00/0	0.76/0.79/6
华山	0.77/0.76/9	0.59/0.87/4	0.00/0.00/0
华明	0.95/0.89/4	0.71/0.85/5	0.00/0.00/0
吉祥	0.81/0.92/8	1.00/1.00/1	1.00/0.73/19
张弛	0.63/0.82/27	0.69/0.77/12	0.83/0.69/26
张扬	0.77/0.83/19	0.79/0.00/0	0.89/0.65/14
方正	0.81/0.82/12	0.71/0.66/4	0.38/0.77/4
李晓明	0.69/0.74/32	0.50/0.66/15	0.00/0.00/0
杜鹃	0.80/0.79/13	0.67/0.83/8	0.88/0.70/12
杨柳	0.82/0.83/15	0.68/0.68/5	0.65/0.65/18
江涛	0.70/0.78/27	0.71/0.83/6	0.21/0.76/17
汪洋	0.69/0.75/12	0.46/0.69/4	0.69/0.59/21
田野	0.66/0.75/32	0.73/0.80/2	0.66/0.54/20
白云	0.77/0.71/19	0.51/0.71/2	0.75/0.59/18
白雪	0.86/0.90/9	0.79/0.00/0	0.89/0.68/17
秦岭	0.81/0.83/10	0.89/0.77/2	0.00/0.00/0
约翰逊	0.72/0.79/15	0.45/0.66/18	0.03/0.62/12
胡琴	0.86/0.97/3	0.69/0.79/3	0.95/0.73/24
金山	0.92/0.83/8	0.53/0.80/1	0.50/0.70/5
雷雨	0.84/0.76/6	0.85/0.69/1	0.93/0.78/23
马啸	0.89/0.85/6	0.78/0.73/2	0.53/0.56/3
高山	0.79/0.85/17	0.85/0.81/1	0.73/0.66/20
高峰	0.78/0.79/31	0.87/0.71/1	0.69/0.64/22
高明	0.81/0.80/18	0.70/0.74/3	0.70/0.65/19
高超	0.69/0.79/12	0.83/0.79/7	0.74/0.75/14
高雄	0.89/0.75/4	0.77/0.72/2	0.00/0.00/0
黄梅	0.82/0.82/13	0.61/0.96/2	0.72/0.63/19
黄河	0.77/0.81/13	0.55/0.88/4	0.00/0.00/0
黄海	0.80/0.80/18	0.55/0.82/3	0.00/0.00/0
黄莺	0.75/0.78/9	0.55/0.74/4	0.59/0.62/24
黄龙	0.34/0.44/15	0.47/0.52/4	0.52/0.65/9

Table 5: Statistics of in-KB, out-of-KB, other class performance; the score is median of precision, recall; and number of types of entity for in-KB and out-of-KB, number of Other documents in gold standard.

H. Ji and R. Grishman. 2011. Knowledge base population: Successful approaches and challenges. In *Proceedings of the 49th Annual Meeting of the Association for Computational Linguistics: Human Language Technologies*, volume 1, pages 1148–1158.

H. Ji, R. Grishman, H.T. Dang, K. Griffitt, and J. Ellis. 2010. Overview of the tac 2010 knowledge base population track. In *Proceedings of the Third Text Analysis Conference*.

S.S. Kataria, K.S. Kumar, R. Rastogi, P. Sen, and S.H. Sengamedu. 2011. Entity disambiguation with hierarchical topic models. In *Proceedings of KDD*.

Jie Liu, Ruifeng Xu, Qin Lu, and Jian Xu. 2012. Explore chinese encyclopedic knowledge to disambiguate person names. In *The 2nd CIPS-SIGHAN Joint Conference on Chinese Language Processing (CLP-2012)*.

R. Mihalcea and A. Csomai. 2007. Wikify!: linking documents to encyclopedic knowledge. In *Proceedings of the sixteenth ACM conference on Conference on information and knowledge management*, pages 233–242. ACM.

Zehuan Peng, Le Sun, and Xianpei Han. 2012. Sirnerd: A chinese named entity recognition and disambiguation system using a two-stage method. In *The 2nd CIPS-SIGHAN Joint Conference on Chinese Language Processing (CLP-2012)*.

FAN Qing-hu, ZAN Hong-ying, CHAI Yu-mei, JIA Yuxiang, and NIU Gui-ling. 2012. Chinese personal name disambiguation based on vector space model. In *The 2nd CIPS-SIGHAN Joint Conference on Chinese Language Processing (CLP-2012)*.

Wei Tian, Xiao Pan, Zhengtao Yu, Yantuan Xian, Xiuzhen Yang, Yu Qin, and Wenxu Long. 2012. Chinese name disambiguation based on adaptive clustering with the attribute features. In *The 2nd CIPS-SIGHAN Joint Conference on Chinese Language Processing (CLP-2012)*.

Longyue Wang, Shuo Li, Derek F. Wong, and Lidia S. Chao. 2012. A joint chinese named entity recognition and disambiguation system. In *The 2nd CIPS-SIGHAN Joint Conference on Chinese Language Processing (CLP-2012)*.

Han Wei, Liu Guang, Mao Yuzhao, and Huang Zhenni. 2012. Attribute based chinese named entity recognition and disambiguation. In *The 2nd CIPS-SIGHAN Joint Conference on Chinese Language Processing (CLP-2012)*.

Tao Zhang, Kang Liu, and Jun Zhao. 2012. The nlpr entity linking system at clp 2012.

Hao Zong, Derek F. Wong, and Lidia S. Chao. 2012. A template based hybrid model for chinese personal name disambiguation. In *The 2nd CIPS-SIGHAN Joint Conference on Chinese Language Processing (CLP-2012)*.

SIR-NERD: A Chinese Named Entity Recognition and Disambiguation System using a Two-Stage Method

Zehuan Peng Le Sun Xianpei Han
Institute of Software, Chinese Academy of Sciences
HaiDian, Beijing, PRC.
{zehuan, sunle, xianpei}@nfs.iscas.ac.cn

Abstract

This paper presents our SIR-NERD system for the Chinese named entity recognition and disambiguation Task in the CIPS-SIGHAN joint conference on Chinese language processing (CLP2012). Our system uses a two-stage method and some key techniques to deal with the named entity recognition and disambiguation (NERD) task. Experimental results on the test data shows that the proposed system, which incorporates classifying and clustering techniques, can achieve competitive performance.

1 Introduction

Named entity recognition and disambiguation (NERD) is an important task in information retrieval (IR) and natural language processing (NLP). Given a set of documents, a NERD system should recognize all named entities within them, and disambiguate them by either linking them to knowledge base entries or grouping names into clusters, with each resulting group a specific entity. Compared with the English NERD, the Chinese NERD has some special challenges: Firstly, many common words can often be used as named entities, too. For example, both the common adjective word "高明 (brilliant)" and the common noun "高峰(peak)" are also common male names in China. In these situations, it is challenging to distinguish common words from named entities, and the lack of morphology information in Chinese (such as the Capital word for named entity) further increases the difficulty. Secondly, the Chinese entity name is usually highly ambiguous on entity types, i.e., the same name may refer to many different types of named entities. For example, 金山(Gold Hill) can be used as the name of persons, locations and organizations; 黄河 (Yellow River) can be used as name of persons or rivers. Thirdly, it is common that many persons share the same name. For example, the name 李明(Li Ming) or 高峰(Gao Feng) is very popular in China.

In recent years, NERD has attracted a lot of research attention, and most of the research work focus on clustering the observations of a specific name, with each resulting cluster corresponding to a specific entity. Song et al. 2009 proposed a locality-based *tfidf* framework for document representation and similarity measure for webpages clustering. Chen et al. 2007 proposed several token-based and phrase-based features for clustering webpages containing the same person, and achieved a significant improvement of disambiguation performance for web people search.

In the SIR-NERD system, we adopt a two-stage method which can incorporate classifying and clustering techniques for the personal name entity disambiguation task. In the first stage, the system preprocess the corpus through, word segmentation, general named entity recognition, and calculate the similarity between two documents. In the second stage, we group documents into clusters using the agglomerative hierarchical clustering approach, so that each cluster corresponds to a specific entity.

The paper is organized as follows. Section 2 describes the task; Section 3 describes the SIR-NERD system in detail; Section 4 describes the experiments and discusses the results; finally we give a conclusion.

2 Task Description

The named entity recognition and disambiguation task in CIPS-SIGHAN 2012 is a combination of classifying and clustering tasks. There are 16 names in the training data and 32 names in the test data. For each name *N*, there is a document collection *T* and knowledge base (KB) which contains several persons, organizations or locations who share the same name *N*. For each document in *T* (the name *N* in a document is supposed only refer to one entity), the task is to find the target entity of the name *N* in KB; if the target entity of the name *N* in document is not contained in KB, then the system needs to determine whether *N* is a common word or not; if not, we need to cluster these documents into subsets, each of which refers to one single entity. Table 1 shows a KB example for the name 白雪, which contains seven entities. For each entity, a detailed introduction is given.

Id	Introduction
1	*A singer come from Zhejiang* "祖籍浙江省温州市...歌手...浙江军区文工团...歌唱演员..马剑"
2	*A famous actress* "白百何...女演员...白雪...中央戏剧学院...《幸福在哪里》...《与青春有关的日子...《失恋 33 天》...电影"
3	*A woman marathon champion* "女子马拉松冠军得主"
4	*A woman dubber* "女性配音演员...毕业于北京电影学院....黄渤、边江、邱秋、孟宇、张磊、王凯、刘特、褚珺...女性角色"
5	*A famous painter* "陈大威...白雪...河北省涿州市...画家...教授...人民日报社...编委...副院长...北京国际奥林匹克书画院名誉院长..."
6	*A famous after-80s writer* "80 后唯美派和悲情派...作家...雪...吉林，满族人...陕西省安康市，后随父母搬往河南省新乡市"
7	*A heroine in a novel* "孙皓晖...《大秦帝国之黑色裂变》...女主角。白雪...政商白圭之女...智慧胆识..."

Table 1: A KB example for the name 白雪

Table 2 gives three documents containing the name 白雪. If 白雪 in a document refers to an entity in KB, the system should identify its target entity *id* in KB; if 白雪 in a document is a common word with the meaning of "white snow", the system should classify the document into class *other*; if 白雪 refers to an entity not in KB, the system classifies the document into class *out*.

Doc	Content	Target Entity ID
007	"...女子马拉松白雪突破历史..."	3
031	"...天空飘着白雪，四川汶川..."	other
050	"... 白雪 ... 《橘子红了》..."	out

Table 2: three typical document examples

3 SIR-NERD system

According to the task requirements, the SIG-NERD system divides the NERD task into two subtasks. Given a document containing name *N*, the first subtask is to classify the document into *id, out* or *other*, correspondingly means refering to an entity in KB, an entity not contained in KB and a common word; the second subtask is to cluster documents which are classified as *out* in the first subtask. The two-stage NERD framework of SIR-NERD is illustrated as Figure 1.

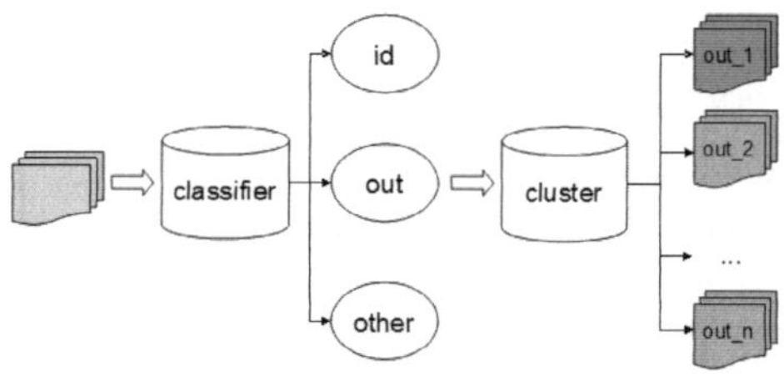

Figure 1: the two-stage NERD framework

In the classification subtask, we first preprocess the corpus through four steps: data clearing, word segmentation and initial named entity recognition, representing documents and entities with selected features, similarity calculation. The steps are described in detail as follows:

- **Data clearing.** In this step, we clear the data by removing XML tags and some unrecognizable characters.

- **Initial NER.** In this step, we use the SIG-NER tool to do the initial word segment and named entity recognition
- **Representing Document**. In this step, we represent each document or entity with some selected features in the context, such as person names, location names, organization names and occupation words
- **Similarity calculation**. In this step, we calculate the similarity between documents and entities based on cosine similarity

In the clustering subtask, we split it into two steps: document representation and hierarchical clustering. The main work is as follows:

- Representing the documents to be clustered with some selected features in the context.
- Using hierarchical clustering method to cluster documents with class label *out*

3.1 Classification

In order to avoid the cascaded error propagation, we determine the class label of a document in one step. For example, in order to process the name 白雪, we use the 7 entities named 白雪 in KB, and treat the *other* and the *out* classes as two pseudo-entities. Each entity is viewed as a class, so 白雪 has 9 classes and now the problem is how to represent these classes. With the document representation, a document containing 白雪 is classified into class with the highest similarity score. As shown above, our SIR-NERD system divides the subtask into four steps: preprocessing, initial NER, documents or entities representation, similarity calculation.

3.1.1 Preprocessing

We are provided with the following data:

- Knowledge base, providing a XML file for each name, the file is named as N.xml, for example 白雪.xml.
- Document collection, for each name N there are a group of xxx.txt files, each of which contain the name N at least once, xxx is a unique document id.
- Answer file, for each name N a answer file with the name N.ans is provided, which records the class label of each document in the document collection.

We use *python xmlparser* to remove all XML tags in XML files and unrecognizable characters in documents.

3.1.2 Initial NER

We use the SIR-NER tool to do the initial named entity recognition. SIR-NER is a Chinese NER tool developed by the SIR laboratory,[1] which does well in general named entity recognition tasks. Taking the following sentence for example:

"足球运动员，曾效力青岛贝莱特，长春亚泰足球俱乐部队。07 赛季租借到广州医药"

The NER result is as follows:

"足球/n 运动员/n ，/w 曾/d 效力/v 青岛/LOC 贝莱特/PER ，/w 长春/LOC 亚泰/nz 足球/n 俱乐部队/n 。/w 07/NUM 赛季/n 租借/v 到/v 广州/LOC 医药/n"

Named entities like 长春, 青岛 and 广州 can be recognized easily, but for the NRED task in CIPS-SIGHAN 2012, the performance is bad because most names in this task are also common words. For example, SIR-NER system regards the word 白雪 as a common word "snow white" without considering the context. The precision of other words in training data is showed in Table 3.

word	precise	word	precise
丛林	0.0	华山	1.0
方正	0.0	杜鹃	0.0
白云	0.0	雷雨	0.0
高山	0.133	高峰	0.0
高明	0.067	黄河	1.0
...	...	...	...

Table 3: the precision of recognizing the target name as a NE by SIR-NER

3.1.3 Document and entity representation

After the initial NER processing, vector space model is used to represent documents in collection *T* and entities in KB. Different from the traditional *BoW* (bag of words) model, our system use entities to represent the document.

[1] Storage & Information Retrieval, ISCAS. www.icip.org.cn

That is because if we use all words, a lot of noise will be introduced. Experimental results show that using words within the following tags in Table 4 as features achieves encouraging performance.

ORG	A NE, an organization name
LOC	A NE, location name
PER	A NE, a personal name
n	Not a NE, a common noun
vn	Not a NE, a noun-verbs
nz	Not a NE, a proper noun

Table 4: tags used to represent documents and entities

In Table 4, a NE with tag like ORG, LOC and PER contributes 80 percent of the NED precision. The potential reason is that an entity usually semantically related with other entities in the same document.

Furthermore, the occupation description of a person plays an important role in distinguishing different people. For example, a person with the occupation of 教授 *professor* and a person with occupation of 歌手 *singer* tend to be two different people. Therefore, our SIR-NERD system maintains an occupation dictionary, which is built as follows:

- Select 30 occupation words as seeds , such as 总统, 教授, 歌手, 画家, 演员, 局长...
- Use the seeds to expand the occupation dictionary with HIT synonyms dictionary[2] .
- Repeat step two twice, at last we get 1078 occupation words, the new added occupation words are 骑手, 庄园主, 名家, 农民工, 针灸师, 学者, and so on.

In our system, the occupation features are given a higher weight compared with other features when represent documents or entities.

Entities representation

For each name, entities in KB are represented using features with tags in Table 4 and features in the occupation dictionary. Each entity is represented as a vector, in which the features weight with *tfidf* value. *tf* is the times of a word appears in the entity description, *idf* is the number of the entities whose descriptions contain the word.

As described above, we have defined two pseudo entities for each name. The *other* pseudo entity describes the situation that the name is used as a common word and the *out* pseudo entity represents the target entities which are not contained in KB.

In order to represent the *other* pseudo entity, we use nouns which have a high co-occurrence rate with the common word *N*. The co-occurrence rate is calculated as formula (1):

$$co(name, word) = \frac{d(name, word)}{d(name) + d(word)} \quad (1)$$

$d(name, word)$ is the number of documents which contain both *name N* and *word*. $d(name)$ is the number of documents which contain *name*, $d(word)$ is the number of documents which contain *word*. Because the given dataset is not big enough to given a robust co-occurrence estimation, we use the Web as the external source for estimation. The candidate nouns come from two sources: for a name in the training data, document labels are given so we can randomly pick one document with label *other* and use nouns in the document as candidates; also we can search the whole internet with the name as a query, nouns in the top returned documents can be used as candidates. We choose top 20 nouns with high rate. For example for the name 白雪, we get the following list:

"雪,公主,树,草,山,玉,花,叶,心,光,马,天空,气,人间,大地,生命,微笑,白色,水,心灵,地,深处,太阳,雪花,脚步,月光,光芒,森林,明月,天,灵魂,风景"

Intuitively, if used as a common word "snow white", 白雪 has a strong semantic association with words like *风景, 公主, 树, 雪花,白色* and so on. So the word lists for 白雪 is reasonable. The weight of each noun in the vector can be computed with the co-occurrence rate.

The representation of the second pseudo entity is also challenging, it describes entities which are not in KB. As discussed above an entity usually has a strong relation with NE like persons, locations and organizations, so when NEs in a document are all not in the NE set in KB, then the document tends to describe an entity not in KB. Based on the hypothesis, we represent the second pseudo entity as follows:

- For each name, we pick out several documents from the doc collections. The

[2]http://ir.hit.edu.cn/phpwebsite/index.php?module=pagemaster&PAGE_user_op=view_page&PAGE_id=162

documents chosen should not contain any NE which appears in KB NE set.

- Select words from the chosen documents with tags in the Table 4 as features, features weight using *tfidf* as above.

Till now we have proposed vector representation methods for three typical entities. Features of different types usually provide different ability for name disambiguation. In order to measure the ability, we define a parameter for each word with tags in Table 4 and each feature in the occupation dictionary. Experiments on the training data show that the weight in Table 5 will result the best performance.

Label	Para name	weight
LOC	v_1	0.715
ORG	v_2	0.429
PER	v_3	0.358
n	v_4	0.191
vn	v_5	0.239
nz	v_6	0.286
occupati-on dict	v_7	1.80

Table 5: parameter values of word labels

Based on the initial weight in Table 5, the weight of the feature words can be calculated as formula (2):

$$w = v_i \times tf \times idf \tag{2}$$

If the words appear in the occupation dictionary the weight can be computed as formula (3):

$$w = v_7 \times v_i \times tf \times idf \tag{3}$$

Document representation

Different from the entity representation in KB, a document is represented using NE words in the document and features in the context instead of using all features in the document. The features should have tags in Table 4, and the weight of each feature is calculated as the same as entity representation.

3.1.3 Similarity Calculation

With the above three steps, we represent each entity as a vector E and each document as a vector D, then the similarity between the two vectors is calculated as formula (4) :

$$sim(e,d) = \frac{\sum_{i=0}^{n} e_i \times d_i}{\sqrt{\sum_{i=0}^{n} e_i^2}\sqrt{\sum_{i=0}^{n} d_i^2}} \tag{4}$$

According to the similarity measure, the document is labeled as the entity label with the highest score.

4 Clustering

Because the number of clusters is not clear, we use agglomerative hierarchical clustering method to divide documents with class label *out* into clusters. Each cluster corresponds to a specific named entity. The algorithm of the bottom-up method is as follows:

1. Treat each document as a single cluster.
2. Calculate the similarity between any two clusters.
3. Merge the two clusters with the highest similarity score into a new cluster.
4. Repeat step 2 and 3 until that any similarity is small than a threshold which is calculated in the training data.

There are three methods to compute similarity between two different clusters: single linkage clustering, group-average linkage clustering and complete linkage clustering. The first step is all the same: calculating the similarity between a document in one cluster and a document in the other cluster. Single linkage clustering uses the largest similarity between data points as clusters similarity; group-average linkage clustering uses the average similarity as clusters similarity; while complete linkage clustering uses the smallest similarity as clusters similarity. In our experiments, we use the group-average linkage methods.

5 Experiment and evaluation

We experiment our system on the training data. The evaluation method is given in the task description in the official website. Precision, recall and F1 value are used as the measurements to evaluate the system performance. Experiment result on the training data is shown in Table 6:

	precision	recall	F1
白雪	0.8152	0.8670	0.8403
白云	0.6491	0.8112	0.7212
丛林	0.9143	0.8731	0.8932
杜鹃	0.8942	0.8791	0.8866
方正	0.8818	0.8674	0.8745
高超	0.8455	0.9005	0.8721
高峰	0.7937	0.8313	0.8121
高明	0.7795	0.8904	0.8313
高山	0.8804	0.9401	0.9093
高雄	0.8305	0.9401	0.9093
胡琴	0.9623	0.9748	0.9685
华明	0.9716	0.9605	0.9660
华山	0.7721	0.8761	0.8208
黄海	0.7919	0.8426	0.8165
黄河	0.6638	0.8400	0.7416
雷雨	0.8852	0.9263	0.9053
total	0.8332	0.8790	0.8555

Table 5: experiment results on training data

The performance of SIR-NERD system on the test data set is as follows: the precision is 0.7948, the recall is 0.8098 and the F1 value is 0.8022.

6 Conclusion

This paper presents the SIR-NERD system for task 2 in CIPS-SIGHAN 2012. We proposed a two-stage named entity recognition and disambiguation framework, in the first stage we classify the documents into three categories, in the second stage we use the agglomerative hierarchical cluster algorithm to divide the documents with class label *out* into subsets, each resulting cluster corresponds to a specific entity. The key techniques of the SIR-NERD system are:

- We identify that occupation is a discriminant feature for name disambiguation, so we build an occupation dictionary for capturing such features.
- Instead of using all words in a document, we use only entities and occupations for document representation and entity representation, which reduces the noise in representation.

Acknowledgments

The work is supported by the National Natural Science Foundation of China under Grants no. 90920010 and 61100152.

References

Fei song, Robin cohen, Song Lin, Web People Search Based on Locality and Relative Similarity Measures, Proceedings of WWW 2009.

Ying Chen and Martin J.H. CU-COMSEM: Exploring Rich Features for Unsupervised web Personal Name Disambiguation, Proceedings of ACL Semeval 2007.

E. Elmacioglu, Y. F. Tan, S. Yan, M.-Y. Kan, and D. Lee. Psnus: Web people name disambiguation by simple clustering with rich features. In SemEval, 2007.

R. Guha and A. Garg. Disambiguating people in search. In Stanford University, 2004.

A Template Based Hybrid Model for Chinese Personal Name Disambiguation

Zong Hao	Derek F. Wong	Lidia S. Chao
NLP[2]CT Research Group Department of Computer and Information Science, University of Macau, Macau SAR, China		
MB15463@umac.mo	derekfw@umac.mo	lidiac@umac.mo

Abstract

This paper proposes a template based hybrid model for Chinese Personal Name Disambiguation (CPND). The template makes use of the features of personal role such as discriminating personal name (nickname, stage name), together with the specific context of most frequent words, personal name nearest words named entities, date and time that are effective for this disambiguation task, as well as surrounding context of nominal, verbal and adjectival constituents. The construction of the templates is automatically derived from the articles that maximizes the deviation of different categories of personal names. The extraction algorithm of keyword features based on the distribution of unlabeled data is also proposed in this paper for this challenging task. In addition, an augmented similarity measure for the CPND model has been designed to calculate the similarity between a standard template and an unlabeled text. The final evaluation reveals that the proposed model can achieve the F-measure of 75.75% on the test data.

1 Introduction

The We participated in the CIPS-SIGHAN Joint Conference on Chinese Language Processing and focus on task 2: Chinese Personal Name Disambiguation.

This task is a little different from 2010 SIGHAN task 3[1]. It has given a short description of a certain personal name (here we call this standard classes), and each unlabeled text may belong to three main categories which respectively are a **standard class**, **OUT** class and **OTHER** class.

This task is a little more challenging than 2010 SIGHAN Bake-off task 3, because this task has given us a standard class which usually has less information than an unlabeled text.

This task is very similar to a text clustering problem. Usually most people will use some clustering algorithm, like Xiamen University (Zhu, et al., 2010) and Dalian University (Wang & Huang, 2010) in 2010 SIGHAN Bake-off task3, both of them used Hierarchical Agglomerative Clustering (HAC) algorithm (Jain et al., 1999) to do the clustering. As a conclusion, the most dissimilar in SIGHAN 2010 task3 is that they used different feature set.

For this task, we have a referenced standard class; the clustering for this standard class may not have a good effect. The shortage for this clustering algorithm is that the text must be large enough for this algorithm to extract useful feature, and more importantly the clustering algorithm is very time consuming and highly rely on the feature set. This feature set will add much human effort inside, such as the university name selection, gender selection, job title selection, work experience selection. For this specific task these information may not be enough to distinguish standard classes. Because two standard classes many have some common features. That is the last we want to see. Therefore we design a

[1] http://www.cipsc.org.cn/clp2010/task3_en.html

similarity formula to handle the clustering time consuming problem. We pruned most unnecessary calculation. For example, we first calculate the unlabeled text's keyword similarity to each standard class; then further calculate good feature similarity if there is more than one standard has the same keyword similarity. For feature selection, we also design an algorithm to extract the most discriminating words. This original idea of this algorithm is to extract the primitive name or used name. However this personal name information is limited, so we try to use other information as our text feature. Here we proposed a word distribution concept. This word distribution concept refers to the distribution in the whole unlabeled texts. We suppose there is a group of existing words in the standard classes that their sum of distribution is **close to 1**. Since the classification has OTHER and OUT class, we set the expected sum of all distribution is **0.75**. So we suppose the total **OTHER** and **OUT** unlabeled texts are less than 25% of entire texts.

The following sections include Keyword extraction, named entity recognition, model construction, similarity calculation, OUT class solution and other issues. Then we will show the evaluation and conclusion.

2 General Instructions

The keyword extraction in standard class is different from the key word extraction in unlabeled text. Since the words in the standard classes are rare, we have to make full use of these words. In standard classes we extract the personal name (primitive name, used name (name ever used before), stage name, pen name, nickname and so on), organization name (university, company, government organization), other name entity (such as film name, song name, etc.) and other discriminating word as the keyword. In unlabeled text we only extract the named entities as the keywords.

2.1 Keyword Extraction Algorithm

ACL-2010 Keyword extraction is the most significant procedure in our system. We utilize keyword as the most efficient word to associate the unlabeled text with its corresponding standard class.

Many scholars use the bag of words as their keyword, such as AIDA (Yosef et al., 2011), Collective Annotation of Wikipedia Entities in Web Text (Kulkarni et al., 2009), both of them used bag of word strategy. However in this task, we anticipate that there may have some very similar standard classes which are very difficult to distinguish with this bag of words. We suppose that if we use as less keywords as possible, we can distinguish those similar standard classes more easily.

This algorithm is based on this idea, and usually each standard class will have no more than 3 keywords. Using the most discriminating words as our keywords usually gets the best result. We then proposed an algorithm to extract the keywords automatically.

Algorithm 1 Keyword Extraction

Input:
1. ***SCT***: Standard classes text;
2. $T_{unlabeled\ text}$: unlabeled text

Output:
1. ***Kwd***: Keywords for all standard classes text;

Variables:
$Frag$: segmentation result appending POS;
$Dist$: Distribution of keywords in unlabelled text;

```
Begin:
For each SC ∈ SCT
    Frag ← SEG_WITH_POS(SC)
    Kwd ← CHOOSE_ONE_KWD(Frag)
    Count[SC] ← 0
    For each u ∈ T_unlabeled text:
        If {∃w|w ∈ u, w ∈ keyword}
            Count[SC] ← Count[SC] + 1
            Break
        End if
    End for
End for
Dist ← SUM(Count)
While Dist< 0.75 * COUNT (T_unlabeled text)
    T ← GET_CLASS(MIN(Count))
    Frag ← SEG_WITH_POS (T)
    Kwd ← CHOOSE_ONE_KWD(Frag)
    For each u ∈ T_unlabeled text
        If {∃w|w ∈ u, w ∈ keyword}
            Count[T] ← Count[T]+1
            Break
        End If
    End For
    Dist ← SUM(Count)
End While
Return Kwd
End;
```

Algorithm 1. Keyword Extraction Algorithm

This algorithm shows the basic strategy of extract keyword. We always follow a rule which is making the distribution keep reasonable. We suppose the distribution should be flat (evenly distributed), hence we got a bad performance on overbalance unlabeled texts.

By this algorithm we can extract really useful keyword. For example, in the test data, after we run this algorithm, we get all keywords as Table 1 below for personal name "白雪 (*Bai Xue*)". Considering the probability of overbalance, not only the keyword but also other useful features together which make the performance of this system much better should be taken into account.

This keyword extraction is only for the standard class, not for the unlabeled texts. It is because that we assume that most of the unlabeled texts have a corresponding standard class, and based on this we design this algorithm, and for the OUT unlabeled texts, we have not figured out a solution.

Standard Class **No.**	**Keyword**
Standard class 1	越剧 (*Shaoxing opera*)
Standard class 2	白百合 (*Bai Baihe*)
Standard class 3	马拉松(*Marathon*)
Standard class 4	配音(*Dub*)
Standard class 5	陈大威 (*Chen Dawei*)
Standard class 6	作家(*Writer*)
Standard class 7	大秦帝国 (*The great Qin empire*)

Table 1: Keywords of Personal Name 白雪 (*Bai Xue*)

2.2 Keyword priority

We set different priority corresponding to different kind of keywords. We consider that the most discriminating words are personal names. When trying to distinguish someone with a same name, other personal titles (such used name, pen name, stage name, etc.) are always the most effective. For example, in standard class 白雪 (*Bai Xue*), 白百合 (*Bai Baihe*) and 陈大威 (*Chen Dawei*) can distinguish these two standard classes efficiently. In Table 2 we list our priority setting for different types of keyword.

Keyword type	**Priority**
Personal name	High
Other named entity	Mid
Other discriminating words	Low

Table 2: Keyword priority

Here all the other discriminating words refer to nouns, and the chosen condition is the distribution of these words in unlabeled text.

3 Named Entity Recognition

Chinese Named Entity Recognition (NER) is more complex than English Named Entity Recognition because it contains a segmentation step before. In this system NER is playing a very important role. For those unlabeled data, it will do NER first. If this system recognizes that the name in this text is not a Named Entity (NE), it will directly assert that this text belongs to the OTHER class. If the name in the text is a NE, we will then mark all the NE in this text to help the later work.

Before we do NER we have to do the Chinese segmentation and Part-of-Speech (POS) tagging. Here this system used ICTCLAS[2] 2011 with additional user dictionary to improve the segmentation and POS tagging accuracy.

Conditional Random Fields (CRFs) is the most popular approach to do NER task. This approach is easy to implement and usually achieve a very high accuracy. Hence this system also used CRFs to do the NER. The CRFs toolkit adopted in this system is CRF++[3] toolkit and used feature is three single characters (before, current, after), three POS tags (before, current, after), some suffix and prefix (s/f) information and three segmentation label sets (before, current, after). The training data set is January-June People's Daily 1998. We get F-measure 91.4% from our test set.

4 Model Construction

We propose a hierarchical personal model for each standard class and unlabeled text. Basically this model consists of four parts:

1. The Keyword, it has the highest priority (K).
2. The second is good features (G), it contains other NE except the keyword, the nearest 10 words and the most frequently used 10 words.
3. The date information word (D).
4. The other information (O) contains all noun, verb and adjective.

In this system, all these features are in different level, we divide features in four levels, and each level's word contributes different weight to the final classification result.

Basically we rule the weight from great to less is K, G, D, O. The keyword in standard class is different from unlabeled text. In the standard class, we use the keyword extraction algorithm,

[2] http://www.ictclas.org/

[3] CRF++: Yet Another Toolkit [CP/OL]. http://crfpp.googlecode.com/svn/trunk/doc/index.html

but in unlabeled text, we check whether this text contains the keyword in standard class is, if it contain, we add this keyword to it K set, otherwise K set will empty.

In this task, the majority of unlabeled texts will have a richer model than standard class, because unlabeled texts have a very high probability of containing a larger size of texts. In some standard class it even contains several single words. Hence, This system also tried to balance the model between the standard class and the unlabeled text. It is defined that if a standard class contains less than 10 words, all this standard class text's words will be added in its model.

5 Similarity Calculation

Most scholars will choose to use cosine similarity between two candidate models as the final similarity between two documents. This method is a measure of similarity between two vectors of an inner product space that measure the cosine of the angle between them. Its value range is from -1 to 1, which is a very good range (no need to do the normalization). Here is an example to explain this method: when calculating the cosine similarity of two candidate documents, firstly convert these two documents into a vector space A and B, the use θ represent the angle between A and B. The similarity then can be calculated using the following equation:

$$similarity = \cos(\theta) = \frac{A*B}{||A||\,||B||} = \frac{\sum_{i=1}^{n} A_i \times B_i}{\sqrt{\sum_{i=1}^{n}(A_i)^2} \times \sqrt{\sum_{i=1}^{n}(B_i)^2}} \quad (1)$$

Some common vector units are the *tf-idf* words, some user defined useful information (such as university name, job title, age, gender, hometown, etc.).

The biggest advantage of this similarity is its result is already normalized. And the shortage is when converting the model to vector space, and during this procedure some character information will be abandoned. Furthermore this calculation can't solve unsymmetrical length problem (the standard class is usually much shorter than unlabeled text). Therefore we define a formula to overcome its shortage. The formula takes this form:

$$Similarity = \sum_{i=0}^{n} weght * t_i - P \quad (2)$$

t_i Denotes the ith matched word between standard class model and unlabeled model. $Weight$ Denotes a balance factor for different types of words. P Denotes penalty, it depends on the length of the unlabeled text. For each unlabeled text, we will calculate the similarity for each named standard class, and choose the one with largest similarity as its corresponding standard class. When the largest similarity is less than a threshold we will label this text as an OUT class.

6 Out Class Solution

The OUT class enlarged the complexity of this task. The OUT categories are not limited and they are full of uncertainty. Some OUT texts may be very similar to a standard class related text. In this section we defined a formula. It can basically distinguish the OUT class.

To handle the OUT class, we need clustering algorithm. The basic idea is still using the Similarity formula. The detail algorithm is following:

Algorithm 2 OUT Classification

Input:
    O : All potential OUT class text
Output:
    Label : Label for each OUT class text
Begin
Variables:
$Model$: Consist of a group of features extracted from text;
$Threshold$: A threshold used to determine whether this model is belong to a certain model or not;
For each O ∈ $\{OUT\ text\}$
    If Order$_O$ = 1
        $Label \leftarrow OUT\_01$
        $Model \leftarrow$ EXTRACT_FEATURE(O)
    Else
        $T_{model} \leftarrow$ EXTRACT_FEATURE(O)
        $Max \leftarrow -1$
        $Label \leftarrow default$
        For each M ∈ Model
            $Simi \leftarrow$ SIMILARITY$(Tmodel, M)$
            If $Simi < Max$
                $Max \leftarrow Simi$
                $Label \leftarrow M_{label}$
            END If
        End For
            If $Max > Threshold$
                MERGE_MODEL(T_{model}, M)
            Else
                $Label$
                $\leftarrow OUT_($MAX$(Model_{label}) + 1)$
    Return Label
End For
End;

Algorithm 2. OUT classification Algorithm

7 System Architecture

Our system involves the following steps to do the personal name disambiguation.
For the standard class:

1) Extract keyword and other useful information. Utilize this information to build a model for this standard class.

For the unlabeled text:

1) Do named entity recognition, label all the named entity in this text, if the certain name is not a named entity, marked it as the **OTHER** category.
2) Extract keyword and other useful information (good feature, date information and other nouns, verbs, adjectives).
3) Calculate the similarities against the standard class.

The main architecture of this system is shown in Figure 1.

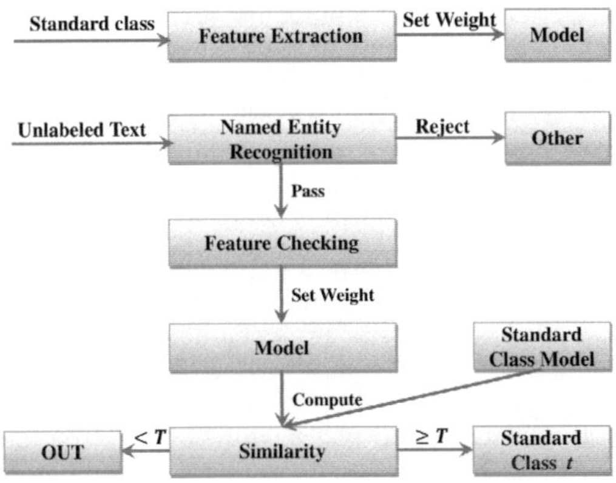

Figure 1: Main workflow. T denotes a threshold.

8 Other Issues

There are some other issues about this task, firstly we think the word match method should not be completely matched, we should use a similarity instead. Since our matching approach did not contain large information about the word position. We get a bit lower F-measure after applying a TongYiCiCiLin(同义词词林) based similarity calculation.

We also tried to add the information about the distance to the headword which is the certain personal name by setting weight. Due to the complexity of the unlabeled text, this approach did not show a better result.

9 Evaluation

We followed the formula given by the organizers to calculate the precision rate, recall rate and FB1[4].

We directly list the best test result based on the given so called train set (Table 3):

Personal Name	P	R	FB1
白雪(*Bai Xue*)	0.7447	0.7944	0.7687
白云 (*Bai Xun*)	0.5333	0.7526	0.6243
从林 (*Cong Lin*)	0.7738	0.8956	0.8303
杜鹃(*Du Juan*)	0.7143	0.9010	0.7969
方正 (*Fang Zheng*)	0.6064	0.9135	0.7289
胡琴 (*Hu Qin*)	0.7577	0.9131	0.8282
华明(*Hua Ming*)	0.8511	0.9770	0.9097
华山 (*Hua Shan*)	0.5062	0.7332	0.5989
Total	0.6859	0.8600	0.7632

Table 3: The evaluation of the training data

And for the competition, our result is in Table 4:

Precision	Recall	FB1
0.7256	0.7923	0.7575

Table 4: The official evaluation of final test.

We only get overall score, not in detail. All these data show that our recall rate is obviously larger than the precision rate. Which means our system is better at detecting the OUT and the OTHER class.

10 Conclusion

We designed an approach for this Chinese Personal Name Disambiguation task. In our approach we firstly removed the OTHER class and then using a name model to distinguish the unlabeled text. We designed a keyword extraction algorithm which is significantly useful in this task. Furthermore, since the recall rate is always larger than the precision rate, our designed formula is also vital.

We implement this system in Python, and our system is highly efficient, in the so called train set, our whole classification procedure cost only 5 seconds, and for the final test set it cost 55 seconds (experiment environment: Inter Core i5 760 CPU and 8GB DDR3 1333 memory).

Acknowledgments

[4] http://www.cipsc.org.cn/clp2012/task2.html

This work was partially supported by the Research Committee of University of Macau under grant UL019B/09-Y3/EEE/LYP01/FST, and also supported by Science and Technology Development Fund of Macau under grant 057/2009/A2.

References

Jain, A. K., Murty, M. N. & Flynn, P. J. 1999. *Data clustering: a review,* ACM computing surveys (CSUR),31(3),264–323.

Kulkarni, S., Singh, A., Ramakrishnan, G. & Chakrabarti, S. 2009. *Collective annotation of Wikipedia entities in web text,* Proceedings of the 15th ACM SIGKDD international conference on Knowledge discovery and data mining, 457–466.

Wang, D. & Huang, D. 2010. *DLUT: Chinese Personal Name Disambiguation with Rich,* CIPS-SIGHAN Joint Conference on Chinese Language Processing.

Yosef, M. A., Hoffart, J., Bordino, I., Spaniol, M. & Weikum, G. 2011. *Aida: An online tool for accurate disambiguation of named entities in text and tables*, Proceedings of the VLDB Endowment, 4(12).

Zhu, X., Shi, X., Liu, N., Guo, Y. M. & Chen, Y. 2010. *Chinese Personal Name Disambiguation: Technical Report of Natural Language Processing Lab of Xiamen University,* CIPS-SIGHAN Joint Conference on Chinese Language Processing.

Duan, H. & Zheng, Y. 2011. *A study on features of the CRFs-based Chinese Named Entity Recognition,* International Journal of Advanced Intelligence, 3(2), 287–294.

Attribute based Chinese Named Entity Recognition and Disambiguation

Wei Han, Guang Liu, Yuzhao Mao, Zhenni Huang
School of Computer,
Beijing University of Posts and Telecommunications,
Beijing, 100876 China
{hanw,liug,maoyz}@bupt.edu.cn, liangsi07@gmail.com

Abstract

In this paper, we briefly report our system for Chinese Named Entity Recognition and Disambiguation task in CIPS-SIGHAN joint conference. We first present a method to extract different types of target person attributes from text documents with multiple techniques. Then we use these attributes to disambiguate different entities. Finally a classifier is used to distinguish entities in the knowledge base, and a cluster to recognize entities out of the knowledge base.

1 Introduction

Named Entities are meaningful units in texts. The ability to identify the named entities (such as people and locations) especially person name has long been an important task in natural language processing and text mining. And it is of great significance in the field of Web information extraction, machine translation, information retrieval, etc.

Generally speaking, a particular occurrence of a name string is insufficient to uniquely identify the corresponding entity. This is due to the fact that, in natural language, the same name string can refer to more than one entity. For example "George Bush" can refer to the former president of United States, or the real estate developer. In web search, 15-21% of the queries contain person names (11-17% of the queries are composed of a person name in web search, with additional terms and 4% are identified simply as person names). So it will be greatly improved to identify the entity that corresponds to a particular occurrence of a name string in the text document for many applications.

And it is especially important and challenging in Chinese. As there are less morphology variations than many other languages, it is challenging to distinguish common words from named entities in Chinese such as 高明 (brilliant), a common adjective and also a common person name. In addition, different types of named entities can use the same names and many persons may share the same name. For this reason, SIGHAN 2012 proposed the task, Named Entity Recognition and Disambiguation in Chinese.

Similar tasks have been explored previously. The KBP task and WePS task are public evaluation campaigns for entity disambiguation, providing annotated datasets for training and testing. During these tasks, it was noticed that attributes (such as birthday, occupation, affiliation, nationality, birth place, relatives, etc.) are very important clues for disambiguation. In fact, every person has his own attributes, and we believe that it is the right direction to study such problem. So in this work, we introduce an entity disambiguation system based on attribute extraction for the Named Entity Recognition and Disambiguation in Chinese task.

The overview of our system is as follows. We split this task into five parts: preprocessing, attribute extraction, similarity measures and document clustering, document classification and remained document clustering.

The remainder of this paper is organized as follows. Section 2 explains our task and describes related work, respectively. Section 3 explains our framework. Section 4 evaluates our framework with a dataset. Section 5 summarizes our work.

2 Named Entity Recognition and Disambiguation Task

2.1 Task definition

The formal definition is described in a web page, available at the following URL.
http://www.cipsc.org.cn/clp2012/task2.html

In the Named Entity Recognition and Disambiguation Task, given a query that consists of a name string-which can be a person (PER), organization (ORG), location (LOC) or just common words- and a background knowledge base, the system is required to provide the ID of the KB entry to which the name refers; or OTHER if it is not an entity, or OUT if there is no such KB entry. In addition, the system is required to cluster together documents referring to the same entity not present in the KB and provide a unique ID for each cluster.

For example, the knowledge base is as follows:

```
<?xml version="1.0" encoding="UTF-8" ?>
- <EntityList name="雷雨">
- <Entity id="01">
<text>重庆市黔江区太极乡党委副书记、乡长。主持政府全面工作，主管财政、金融、审计、统计、非公有制经济、城乡统筹、乡镇企业、招商引资、烤烟、蚕桑工作。</text>
</Entity>
<Entity id="02">
<text>四川省蒲江县教育局党组书记、局长。主持县教育局全面工作。主管教育督导、计财、基建和教仪电教等工作。
</text>
</Entity>
- <Entity id="03">
<text>女，1975 年 8 月生，回族，广西南宁人，中共党员，1997 年 7 月广西师范大学汉语言专业毕业，2006 年获教育硕士学位，中学中级教师，1997 年 7 月进入桂林中学任教语文至今。</text>
</Entity>
</EntityList>
```

Given a set of documents containing the targeted name, we should give the corresponding results. For example, the document about the middle school teacher should be linked to the KB entry 03; and the document which has no corresponding KB entries should be clustered into a cluster with a unique ID such as "Out_01"; the document that describe the weather such as "雷雨天气" should be marked as "Other".

2.2 Related Work

Personal name ambiguity is so common in the web that most previous disambiguation systems choose to work on personal name disambiguation. The related task has been addressed by several researchers starting from Bagga and Baldwin in 1998. They first selected tokens from local context as features to tackle the problem of cross-document co-reference by comparing, for any pair of entities in two documents, the word vectors built from all the sentences containing mentions of the targeted entities. Niu et al. (2004) extended Bagga's method by presenting an algorithm that uses information extraction results in addition to co-occurring words. Mann and Yarowsky (2003) proposed a bottom-up agglomerative clustering algorithm based on extracting local biographical information as features.

Bekkerman and McCallum (2005) focused on social network to find the documents that refer to a particular person using two methods: one based on the link structure and the other used agglomerative/conglomerate double clustering. But their scenario focuses on simultaneously disambiguating an existing social network of people who are known to be connected. Bunescu et al. (2006) used the category information from Wikipedia to disambiguate names. However, due to the limitation of the coverage of the Wikipedia entries of people, this method cannot be applied to resolve the people who are not famous enough to be included in Wikipedia.

Ying Chen et al. (2009) used a Web 1T 5-gram corpus released by Google to extract additional features for clustering. Masaki Ikeda et al. (2009) proposed a two-stage clustering algorithm. In the first stage, reliable features such as named entities are used to find documents that refer to the same person. Then some new features are extracted from the clustered documents and bootstrapping algorithm is used in the second stage.

3 Methodology

In this section, we present our proposed named entity disambiguation approach, which consists of five main steps. The overview of our approach will be provided first, followed by detailed steps.

1. First, the given documents are processed to decide if the name string in the document is an entity.
2. Then, both the documents and the texts in KB entries are converted into an attribute vector based on the attributes extracted from the text.
3. After that, the similarity score between KB entries and documents containing the same name string is calculated through their attribute vectors as well as the similarity score between each document. And the based on these score, some of documents are clustered.
4. Then, a classifier is trained to classify the remained documents.
5. Finally, remained documents referred to the same entity are clustered.

3.1 Preprocessing

As not all the documents containing the name string are about an entity, they may just an adjective, an adverb or something else. And through the dataset, we found most of the documents that contain the targeted string but not an entity are collocation commonly used in the Web data. For example, to the name string 高明, it is often used as an adjective such as “手段高明”. These documents need to be filtered out. So we first use word segmentation and part-of-speech tagging tools to process the given dataset. We use a Web 1T 5-gram corpus released by Google to calculate the most frequent word collocations containing the targeted name. For each document, if the name string is used in the collocation we got, it is very likely to refer to a non-entity. Using these word collocations as well as part-of-speech results and some simple but efficient rules, we are able to mark those documents as other. And these documents will not be processed in the following steps.

3.2 Attribute Extraction

In order to extract the attributes, the first challenge is to define what “the attributes of people” are. These have to be general enough to cover most people, meaningful and useful for disambiguation. We first looked at the attributes used in the WePS task and then took an empirical approach to define them; we extracted possible attributes from the training set and web pages and created a set of attributes which are frequent and important enough for the evaluation. We looked at the documents from the SIGHAN corpus, and found many kinds of attributes very useful and meaningful. Finally we made up 19 attribute classes, as shown in Table 1.

Attribute Class	Examples of Attribute Value
外文名	Christina
别名	小丽
性别	男
机构	黄海医院
出生日期	1987 年 3 月
血型	A 型
星座	狮子座
身高	190cm
出生地	北京市海淀区
民族	苗族
作品	大秦帝国
国籍	美国
政治面貌	党员
关系	张三
学校	北京邮电大学
公司名	某某集团公司
现居地	北京
学历	硕士研究生
职业	记者

Table 1: Definition of 19 attributes of Person

We extract attribute candidates by using processing pipelines with multiple techniques including traditional NER, regular expression patterns, gazetteer-based matching, and manually constructed rules and so on.

First, we extract the attributes based on bootstrapping method which is a machine learning method that automatically gather information. With some seed words and patterns, we can get a lot of attribute extraction template. The implement procedure is as follows:

1. get attribute value from new pattern;
2. calculate the score of attribute value;
3. put the top 5 attribute values into the attribute value dictionary;
4. get the context of the new attribute value and make it a candidate template;
5. calculate the score of pattern;
6. Put the top 3 patterns into the pattern dictionary.

We use some texts from web pages as the training set and repeat 10 times to get patterns.

The score of value and pattern is calculated as follows:

$$\mathrm{score}(\mathrm{value_i}) = \frac{\mathrm{R\_pattern}}{\mathrm{ALL\_pattern}} * \log_2(\mathrm{R_{pattern}}) \quad (1)$$

$$\mathrm{score}(\mathrm{pattern_i}) = \frac{\mathrm{R\_value}}{\mathrm{ALL\_value}} * \log_2(\mathrm{R\_value}) \quad (2)$$

Then we use some dictionaries to match some attributes such as job. And use NER tools to get the attributes like relatives. Finally, we use hownet to extend some synonyms.

As these methods we used are no good enough that some documents we can’t extract the attributes or they may not contain any attributes we defined at all, so we can’t only use the attributes to finish the task. So we first use the attributes to get some results in step 3. Then remained documents are processed in step 4 and 5 with some other techniques to finish the task.

3.3 Similarity measures and document clustering

We can see that different attributes have different influence on the disambiguation task. For example, the job and date of birth attribute are obvious more important and useful than the nationality attribute.

To assign weights to the attributes those indicate their contribution in resolving the person name's identity, we utilized information gain method. It is an algorithm that measures the discrimination performance. Information gain value of an attribute can be expressed as the desired reduction in the entropy of the attribute partition data sets caused.

The information gain formula is as follows:

$\mathrm{Gain}(S, A) \equiv \mathrm{Entropy}(S) - \sum_{v \in \mathrm{Value}(A)} \frac{|S_v|}{|S|}$ Entropy (S_v) (3)

Attribute Class	Weights of attribute
外文名	0.323
别名	0.677
性别	0.842
机构	0.922
出生日期	0.988
血型	0.226
星座	0.420
身高	0.644
出生地	0.990
民族	0.659
作品	0.655
国籍	0.385
政治面貌	0.792
关系	0.512
学校	0.950
公司名	0.994
现居地	1
学历	0.821
职业	0.908

Table2: The weights of 19 attributes of Person

The similarity is calculated based on these weights. If the value on a certain attribute is the same, then the weight of that attribute is added to a score called right score. If it's not same, then the weight of that attribute is added to a score called wrong score.

We first calculate the similarity between each document and the corresponding KB entries. Then we clustered the documents based on these similarities. If the right score and wrong score is in the threshold, we link it to the corresponding KB entry. In order to ensure the correctness of these results, we manually annotate some of the documents which are very ambiguous according to the similarity score.

3.4 Classification

After the previous steps, we've already got some documents linked to their corresponding KB entry or some clustered with a unique ID that is out if the KB entry. For the remained documents, it's hard to get the result only through their attributes. So we trained a classifier using the results from previous steps as training set.

We use SVM tools to train the classifier and tf-idf as the feature. If the score is beyond the threshold we set, we would link it to the corresponding KB entry. Otherwise, the documents would be considered as out of the KB entry and be processed in the following step.

3.5 Clustering

The remained documents are all regarded as out of the KB entry. All features are represented in vector space model. Every document is modeled as a vertex in the vector space. So every document can be seen as a feature vector. Before clustering, the similarity between documents is computed by cosine value of the angle between feature vectors. We cluster these documents into a cluster with a unique ID. Till now, all the documents have their own labels.

4 Evaluation

The dataset for Chinese Named Entity Recognition and Disambiguation task contains training data and testing data. The training data contains 16 names. Every name folder contains 50-300 articles. The testing data contains 32 names. The thresholds we used are obtained from the training data.

The evaluation method is based on precision, recall and F-measure. The overall precision and recall for all test names are calculated as follows (the set of all the test names are notated as N, each name is represented as n in N)

$$\mathrm{Pre} = \frac{\sum_n \mathrm{Pre}(n)}{|N|}$$

$$\mathrm{Rec} = \frac{\sum_t \mathrm{Rec}(t)}{|N|}$$

$$F = \frac{2 * \mathrm{Pre} * \mathrm{Rec}}{\mathrm{Pre} + \mathrm{Rec}}$$

Precision	Recall	F-measure
67.18	85.62	75.29

Table 3: Official Results

The official results show that our method performs not very well, the precision score is a little low. That is because the method we used relies on the performance of the third step which has impact on the following results.

5 Conclusion

In this paper, we report our named entity recognition and disambiguation system and a framework which integrates AE approaches.

In the future, we will attempt to use better methods to improve the performance of the attribute extraction. And consider how to combine the disambiguation part and the AE part to complement each other.

References

Javier Artiles, Julio Gonzalo, and Satoshi Sekine. The semeval-2007 weps evaluation: Establishing a benchmark for the web people search task. In the Fourth International Workshop on Semantic Evaluations (SemEval-2007). ACL, June 2007.

Bagga, Amit. & Baldwin, Breck. (1998). Entity-based cross-document co-referencing using the vector space model. In Proceedings of the 17th international conference on computational linguistics.

C. Niu, W. Li, and R. K. Srihari. 2004. Weakly Supervised Learning for Cross-document Person Name Disambiguation Supported by Information Extraction. In Proceedings of ACL 2004.

Gideon S. Mann and David Yarowsky. Unsupervised personal name disambiguation. In HLT-NAACL, pages 33–40, May 2003.

Ron Bekkerman and Andrew McCallum. Disambiguating web appearances of people in a social network. In WWW, pages 463–470, May 2005.

Lan, M., Zhang, Y.Z., Lu, Y., Su, J. & Tan. C.L. (2009). Which who are they? People attribute extraction and disambiguation in web search results. In 18th WWW Conference 2nd Web People Search Evaluation Workshop (WePS 2009).

Minkov, E., Wang, R. & Cohen, W. (2005). Extracting personal names from emails: applying named entity recognition to informal text. In Proceedings of HLT/EMNLP .

Rao, Delip., Garera, Nikesh & Yarowsky, David (2007). JHU1: An unsupervised approach to person name disambiguation using web snippets. In Proceedings of semeval 2007, association for computational linguistics .

Watanabe, K., Bollegala, D., Matsuo, Y. & Ishizuka, M. (2009). A two-step approach to extracting attributes for people on the web in web search results. In 18th www conference 2nd web people search evaluation workshop (WePS 2009),.

Xianpei Han and Jun Zhao. 2009. CASIANED:Web Personal Name Disambiguation Based on Professional Categorization. In 2nd Web People Search Evaluation Workshop (WePS 2009), 18th WWW Conference.

Xianpei Han and Le Sun. 2011. A Generative Entity-Mention Model for Linking Entities with Knowledge Base. Proc. ACL2011.

Heng Ji and Ralph Grishman. 2011. Knowledge Base Population: Successful Approaches and Challenges. Proc. ACL2011.

Heng Ji, Ralph Grishman, Hoa Trang Dang, Kira Griffitt and Joe Ellis. 2010. An Overview of the TAC2010 Knowledge Base Population Track. Proc. Text Analytics Conference (TAC2010).

Minoru Yoshida, Masaki Ikeda, Shingo Ono, Issei Sato, and Hiroshi Nakagawa. Person name disambiguation on the web by two-stage clustering. In WWW, April 2009.

Minoru Yoshida, Masaki Ikeda, Shingo Ono, Issei Sato, and Hiroshi Nakagawa. Person name disambiguation by bootstrapping. In SIGIR, July 2010.

Bunescu, R., & Pas, M. (n.d.). Using Encyclopedic Knowledge for Named Entity Disambiguation, In EACL, pages 17–24, April 2006.

Chinese Name Disambiguation Based on Adaptive Clustering with the Attribute Features

Wei Tian, Xiao Pan, Zhengtao Yu, Yantuan Xian, Xiuzhen Yang
School of Information Engineering and Automation,
Kunming University of Science and Technology, Kunming, China.

Abstract

To aim at the evaluation task of CLP2012 named entity recognition and disambiguation in Chinese, a Chinese name disambiguation method based on adaptive clustering with the attribute features is proposed. Firstly, 12-dimensional character attribute features is defined, and tagged attribute feature corpus are used to train to obtain the recognition model of attribute features by Conditional Random Fields algorithm, in order to do the attribute recognition of given texts and knowledge bases. Secondly, the training samples are tagged by utilizing the correspondences of the text attribute and answer, and attribute feature weight model is trained based on the maximum entropy model and the weights are acquired. Finally, the fuzzy clustering matrix is achieved by the correlation of Knowledge Base(KB) ID attributes and text attributes for each KB ID, the clustering threshold is selected adaptively based on the F statistic, and clustering texts corresponding to ID are obtained, thus the texts corresponding to each ID are gained followed. For the texts not belong to KB, Out and Other types are obtained by fuzzy clustering to realize name disambiguation. The evaluation result is: P = 0.7424, R = 0.7428, F = 0.7426.

1 Introduction

Person search is an information retrieval way for a specific person, due to the phenomenon of name repetition, therefore, name disambiguation problem becomes more and more important. In recent years, various types of evaluation tasks related to name disambiguation have been launched successively at home and abroad. One task is WPS (Web People Search). WPS is aimed at English names and does not provide any knowledge base, instead it require names referring to the same entity to be clustered together. Another related is the KBP (Knowledge Base Population) task in TAC (Text Analysis Conference) has a named entity disambiguation task, which they use the term entity linking. KBP provides a knowledge base (KB) of named entities. The KB provides a mapping from names to entities. One name can be mapped to many entities. The goal of KBP is to link names occurring in the document to the corresponding entities in KB and to cluster names referring to the same entity, if this entity is not included in the KB. The 2nd task of the CIPS-SIGHAN2012 (CLP2012) [1]—-Named Entity Recognition and Disambiguation in Chinese, can be seen as combination of related tasks in WPS and KBP: First the test names in the document should be judged to be common words or named entities; if a name is predicted as a named entity, participants should further determine which named entity in the KB it refer to; finally, if some names are predicted as named entities that do not occur in the KB, participants should instead cluster these names by the named entities they refer to.

For the name disambiguation, most of the work is concentrated on unsupervised-based or semi-supervised clustering disambiguation method, such as Wang proposed to use the vector space model of web content to do expert evidence-pages clustering disambiguation to solve the multi-document coreference resolution problem to some extent [2]. Bollegala put forward the experts clustering disambiguation solution on key phrases extraction automatically in the context and computing similarity, particularly keyword extraction method depended mainly on the individual information, and the entire extraction process was prone to error cascade phenomenon [3]. Zhou presented a two-stage method for name disambiguation based on exclusive and non-exclusive character attributes, which can improve the disambiguation effect to some extent, but it did not give a clear explanation for threshold selection on the improvement of the hierarchical clustering [4]. Zhang used hierarchical clustering algorithm to solve the multi-text ambiguity issue of Chinese names, though it can better distinguish the names' features, considering verb information as features led to a larger noise introduction without making noise reduction processing [5]. Through the analysis of a large number of name texts, the names' attributes in the text have an important impact on name disambiguation. Therefore, this paper uses the training corpus of the CLP2012 name disambiguation to establish the model of attribute recognition and weight distribution, and applies adaptive clustering method, which can automatically select clustering threshold, to achieve the Chinese name disambiguation.

2 Chinese Name Disambiguation Based on Adaptive Clustering with the Attribute Features

2.1 Corpus Preparation

We must first define the ambiguous name before the name disambiguation. As same as the definition of ambiguous names in CLP2010, the CLP2012 is based on the assumption that "one text corresponds to one person name", that is, supposing a text corresponds to only one person's name, there is no one-to-many problem between the text and the name.

According to text analysis of the CLP2012 training corpus, we found that not all text content is to play a significant role in name disambiguation, but the momentous attributes related to the person appearing in the text is very important to distinguish the persons, for example, there are some sentences about the sports figure inserting into the text of the artistic literature topic, and a few words in above sentences written to the attribute information, such as character's career, just plays the important role in the name disambiguation. Therefore, we need to select the attributes related to the character as the name disambiguation features, which can be named as character attribute features, including 12-dimension, respectively, the person's name (rm), place (dm), organization(jg), career(zy), position(zw), awards (ry), gender (xb), nation(mz), education background(xl), graduate school(byyx), birthday(csrq), works(zp). KB files corresponding to each name must be analyzed to extract ID number and corresponding text messages. And mark the relevant features and do attribute recognition.

2.2 Attribute Recognition

Attribute recognition based on Conditional Random Fields (CRFs) achieves very good recognition effect [6]. Therefore, the CRFs Tools package is used to train on the marked attribute features to obtain the recognition model of 12-dimension attribute feature. The texts and KB files of the CLP2012 test corpus are respectively done the attribute feature recognition by using the recognition model.

Due to the feature of an attribute may be repeated many times, the duplicate must be removed after text recognition completed. Corresponding to each text, there is a feature set $N = \{a_i | i = 1, 2, ..., 12\}$, which N represents the text number, a_i is the ith dimensional feature. According to the feature dimension defined the feature set will be organized into the form of the feature vector. Similarly, each ID which each xml file of knowledge base contained is corresponding to a set of attribute features. As the 001th text and to the xml ID = 01 of "白雪(Xue Bai)" for examples, the attribute features of specific text and Knowledge Base as shown in Table 1.

2.3 Attribute Feature Weighting

After obtaining the attribute feature vector of text file, use the answer corresponding to the text to mark the answer category which the text belongs to, and then consider the category number as one new feature to add to the attribute feature vector to form a new feature vector, which is regarded as weight training corpus. Then employ the weight training command of the maximum entropy model for training the weights of feature functions on the corpus, namely the attribute weights $W_{oi}\,(i = 1, 2, ..., 12)$ for the corresponding dimension.

After getting the weight of each attribute feature, the next is matching calculation of the attribute features, that is similarity calculating between the attribute feature set of texts and the KB feature collection on the test corpus. The attribute feature matching problem is considered as the words' matching. The existing matching methods mainly for Chinese words are "HowNet",

Table 1: The representation examples of the attribute feature set and vector of "白雪（Xue Bai）".

Document Type	Text	KB
attribute feature set representation	001={白雪（Xue Bai），浙江（Zhejiang），浙江代表团（delegation of Zhejiang），歌手（singer），无（null），无（null），无（null），无（null），无（null），无（null），无（null），无（null）}	01={白雪（Xue Bai），浙江温州（Wenzhou Zhejiang），浙江军区文工团（Military district enter-tainment regi-ment in Zhejiang），歌手（singer），无（null），无（null），无（null），无（null），无（null），浙江温州清县小百花越剧团（Xiaobaihua Yueju regiment in Qingxian, Wenzhou Zhejiang），1975年2月28日（birthday），无（null）}
feature vector representation	（001 白雪（Xue Bai）浙江（Zhejiang）浙江代表团（delegation of Zhejiang）歌手（singer）无（null）无（null）无（null）无（null）无（null）无（null）无无（null））	（01白雪（Xue Bai）浙江温州（Wenzhou Zhejiang）浙江军区文工团（Military district entertainment regiment in Zhejiang）歌手（singer）无（null）无（null）无（null）无（null）无（null）浙江温州清县小百花越剧团（Xiaobaihua Yueju regiment in Qingxian, Wenzhou Zhejiang）1975年2月28日无（null））

"Tongyici Cilin" and "Chinese Concept Dictionary" [7]. Word similarity calculated by "Tongyici Cilin" is the closest to the similarity of people's thinking, so Cilin is selected to calculate the similarity. On the basis of analyzing the classification mode and the word-coding table of Cilin [7] and related theory of meanings, the meaning similarity of the two words is calculated according to their meanings coding and the maximum is taken as the similarity finally, the calculating method is shown as follows:

Assume $Sim(x, y)$ is the similarity of the two meanings, if the first letter of the two words' meaning code is the same, then in the same tree$T$, where $T \in \{A, B, C, D, E, F, G, H, I, J, K, L\}$. The formula of $Sim(x, y)$ is shown as follows:

$$Sim\,(x,y) = \begin{cases} f, (x \in T_1, y \in T_2) \\ \delta \times \cos\left(n \times \frac{\pi}{180}\right)\left(\frac{n-k+1}{n}\right) \\ ,(x, y \in T_1, C_x \neq C_y) \\ e, \begin{pmatrix} C_x = C_y, \\ C_{xend} = C_{yend} =' \#' \end{pmatrix} \\ 1, \begin{pmatrix} C_x = C_y, \\ C_{xend} = C_{yend} ='=' \end{pmatrix} \end{cases} \quad (1)$$

Where$\delta \in \{a, b, c, d\}$, and if x and y branches at the second layer, then the coefficient$\delta = a = 0.65$, similarly, the third$\delta = b = 0.8$, the fourth $\delta = c = 0.9$, the fifth $\delta = d = 0.96$. In order to control the similarity between 0 and 1, a parameter $\cos\left(n \times \frac{\pi}{180}\right)$ is introduced, where n is the total number of nodes of branch layers, the control parameter $\left(\frac{n-k+1}{n}\right)$ and $k$is the distance between two branches. Define C_x, C_y as the meaning code of x, y, and C_{xend}, C_{yend} is respectively the end symbol of x, y. Take $f = 0.1, e = 0.5$ as a matter of experience.

A large number of statistical results show that two words with the similarity above 0.7 are generally considered to have a similar meaning in people's thinking, so defined that if $Sim\,(x, y) \geq 0.8$, then the attribute features in the same dimension is perceived as matching successful. The weight of the vector matching successful is regarded $W_{oi}{*}10$ as matching weight $W_{mi}\,(i = 1, 2, ..., 12)$, and the matching weight becomes 0 if the matching is not successful.

2.4 Fuzzy Clustering Matrix Construction

After matching the attribute features between each text and any one ID (short text) in the knowledge base, the matching weight vector of each text corresponding to the above ID gotten by matching, is the row vector of initial matrix. Since the initial matrix is not square, which is the product of attribute feature matching and not the similarity of the texts in the true sense. All above makes that the adaptive clustering can not work. Therefore transform and adjust on the initial matrix by the cosine of the angle is to make it become the fuzzy clustering matrix of fuzzy clustering.

Assume text set$U = \{x_1, x_2, ..., x_n\}$, where $x_i = \{x_{i1}, x_{i2}, ..., x_{im}\}$ $(m = 12)$ is the attribute feature vector, build the fuzzy clustering matrix. The similarity between x_i and x_j is:

$$A = r_{ij} = \frac{\sum_{k=1}^{m} x_{ik} \cdot x_{jk}}{\sqrt{\sum_{k=1}^{m} x_{ik}^2}\sqrt{\sum_{k=1}^{m} x_{jk}^2}} \quad (2)$$

Where x_{ik}, x_{jk} represents the feature vector in the same dimension between texts, and calculate to obtain the similarity matrix, that is fuzzy clustering matrix$A$.

2.5 The Adaptive Clustering Based on the Attribute Features

The Adaptive Algorithm Thought and the Process Description. The fuzzy clustering is a common clustering method in pattern recognition, and has achieved very good effect on pre-classification of characters in Chinese character recognition [8] and classification and matching of speech recognition [9]. Aiming at the task characteristics, different text may has different attribute feature relationships with the knowledge base. If we use the same clustering threshold, it may cause one ID-type clustering better, while another is not good consequences. Thus this paper selects fuzzy clustering method to do name disambiguation processing, according to the difference between the fuzzy clustering matrix generated each time and the content of knowledge base ID, adjust the clustering threshold dynamically and adaptively, and then cluster for each ID of the Knowledge Base through adaptive clustering way. The main idea is to make the classical partition definition fuzzification and dynamically adjust the threshold, which can be solved effectively that 0,1 binary membership can not fully reflect the actual relationship between the data points and the cluster center.

Different thresholds$\lambda \in [0, 1]$can lead to different classifications in Fuzzy clustering analysis, in order to form a dynamic clustering diagram, which makes the classification of the sample image and intuitive. We need to find the optimal λ to effectively cluster some texts with their corresponding ID of KB, and then the clustering result corresponding to λ now is the best result. In this paper, the$F$statistic is used to determine the optimal λ.

Set the text set $U = \{x_1, x_2, \ldots x_n\}$ is the text sample space, and each text$x_i$has $m$features:$x_i = (x_{i1}, x_{i2}, ..., x_{im})$ $(i = 1, 2, ..., n)$.Thereby the initial matrix is obtained, where $\overline{x_k} = \frac{1}{n}\sum_{i=1}^{n} x_{ik}\,(k = 1, 2, \ldots, m)$, and $\overline{x}$ represents the center vector of the overall sample, that is any one ID of KB. Set the number of categories is r corresponding to λ , the number of texts is n_j in the jth cluster, $x_1^{(j)}, x_2^{(j)}, ..., x_{n_j}^{(j)}$ is denoted. The cluster center, that is the jth ID of K-B, of the$j$th cluster is $\overline{x}^{(j)} = \left(\overline{x}_1^{(j)}, \overline{x}_2^{(j)}, ..., \overline{x}_m^{(j)}\right)$, where$\overline{x}_k^{(j)}$is the average of the$k$th features, namely $\overline{x}_k^{(j)} = \frac{1}{n_j}\sum_{i=1}^{n_j} x_{ik}^{(j)}\,(k = 1, 2, ..., m)$.

The F statistic is shown as follow:

$$F = \frac{\sum_{j=1}^{r} n_j \left\|\overline{x}^{(j)} - \overline{x}\right\|^2 \Big/ (r-1)}{\sum_{j=1}^{r}\sum_{i=1}^{n_j} \left\|x_i^{(j)} - \overline{x}^{(j)}\right\|^2 \Big/ (n-r)} \quad (3)$$

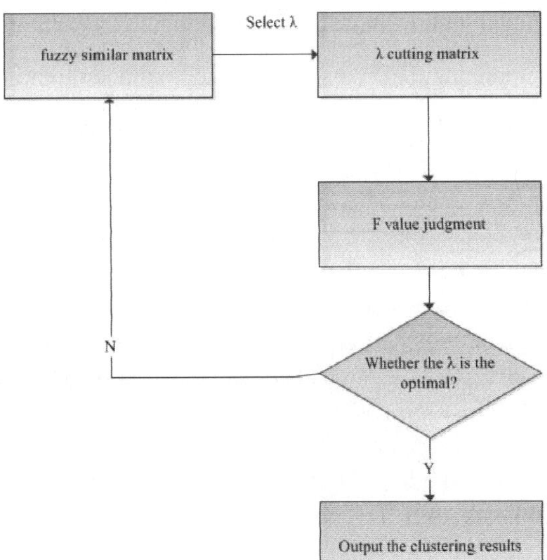

Figure 1: The flowchart of adaptive clustering for name disambiguation

Where $\left\|\overline{x}^{(j)}-\overline{x}\right\| = \sqrt{\sum_{k=1}^{m}\left(\overline{x}_k^{(j)}-\overline{x_k}\right)^2}$ is the distance between $\overline{x}^{(j)}$and $\overline{x}$, $\left\|x_i^{(j)}-\overline{x}^{(j)}\right\|$ shows the distance of $x_i^{(j)}$ and the center $\overline{x}^{(j)}$ in the jth sample. The formula (1) is named F statistic, which follows a Fdistribution with the degree of freedom$r-1, n-r$. For the F statistic, the distance between clusters is represented by the numerator while the distance in one cluster, the denominator. So the larger$F$statistic, the larger distance between clusters, that is the larger distance is inferred between the texts not related to the ID and the texts corresponding to, which shows out a better clustering result.

It can be known that the difference between clusters is significant and illustrates a more reasonable classification result according to the theory of mathematical statistics and analysis of variance, if $F > F_\alpha(r-1, n-r)\,(\alpha = 0.05)$. If there are more than one F statistics meeting the requirements, $(F-F_\alpha)/F_\alpha$must be examined further, and we can get the maximum of F, which the λcorresponding to is the optimal threshold.

The Realization of the Adaptive Clustering. According to the evaluation task of CLP2012 Chinese name disambiguation, the final answer to the clustering usually consists of three types, namely one is the ID type marked in the "KB", another is the "out" type, which contains not only text attribute features but also not appeared in the Knowledge Base. Besides, there is an "other" type not containing entities and considered as ordinary word. So each type is processed respectively in this article.

For "KB" type, firstly the attribute feature correlation of KB ID and text is used to obtain fuzzy clustering matrix for each KB ID. Secondly adaptive clustering threshold is adaptively selected based on the Fstatistic, and the clustering result corresponding to the threshold is acquired, that is, the texts corresponding to the above threshold. Finally these texts clustered should exclude, and then the rest of the texts and the next ID is used for clustering. Repeat the above process until the rest of the text can not be clustered into a group with the KB ID. For the "other" type, if the texts not related to the KB are extracted no attribute features, and then these texts are regarded as "other" type. For the "out" type, clustering, , a text in the texts excluded the "KB" type and the "other" is randomly selected as a basis for the matching of attribute features, and fuzzy clustering matrix is obtained, then clustering threshold is adaptively chosen to get the clustering result according to the F statistic.

3 Experiments

3.1 Experimental Data

Table 2: Experimental data statement.

Experimental Data	The number of text set	The number of text in each text
training data	16	50-200
test data	32	50-500

There are two types of data given in the evaluation. One is knowledge base, NameKB. A XML file for each test name is provided. This file contains several entries describing the name. The file is named as Name.xml, where Name is the test name. For example, the file for 雷雨(Yu Lei) is 雷雨(Yu Lei).xml. Another is text collection, T for each test name. All texts containing the name N are placed under the folder N. For example, all text containing 雷雨(Yu Lei) are under the folder 雷雨(Yu Lei). Every file in the folder is a plain text file, named as XXX.txt, where XXX is three numbers.

The evaluation tool used in the experiment is provided by the evaluation project group of CLP2012. The overall evaluation indexes are precision, recall and F-value for all test names.

3.2 Experiment Results and Analysis

Do the experiment on the test data by using our approach. The evaluation results are given as follows:

Table 3: The evaluation index comparisons of training data and test data.

DataSets	Precision	Recall	F-value
training data	0.9256	0.9032	0.9143
test data	0.7424	0.7428	0.7426

As can be seen from the results, the attribute recognition model for name disambiguation has taken good effect. The identification effect is better on training data than the test data. Analyzing the reasons, the recognition errors may be caused by a variety of reasons. For example, the error that the original text is related with name but identified to common word that accounted for 1/2 of the error portion. According to the statistics, the error distribution is shown in the following table.

Table 4: The distribution of the attribute feature recognition errors.

Error Types	**Error Proportion**
names are recognized to common words	0.5162
only recognized a part of names	0.1956
common words are recognized to names	0.0659
the most important attribute is not identified	0.2223

4 Conclusion

For the characteristics of the evaluation task CLP2012 named entity recognition and disambiguation in Chinese, a Chinese name disambiguation method based on adaptive clustering with the attribute features is proposed, which will resolve this complex disambiguation task into KB type, out and other three types for processing. Do the attribute recognition of given texts and knowledge bases, using the recognition model of attribute features trained by Conditional Random Fields algorithm. Then the attribute feature weight model is trained by utilizing the corresponding attribute feature with answer tag based on the maximum entropy model. After that, the initial matrix is obtained by matching and weighting on the attribute features, on which the fuzzy clustering matrix is generated by transforming, and then clustering by the adaptive method. The algorithm is characterized in automatically finding the optimal clustering threshold to realize name disambiguation according to the different contents of the text and knowledge base. Further research will focus on non-attribute feature selection and the clustering method optimization.

Acknowledgments

This paper is supported by National Nature Science Foundation (No.61175068), and the Open Fund of Software Engineering Key Laboratory of Yunnan Province (No.2011SE14), and the Ministry of Education of Returned Overseas Students to Start Research and Fund Projects. We appreciate the help and assistance of Yu Qin and Wenxu Long.

The corresponding author is Zhengtao Yu(ztyu@hotamil.com).

References

CIPS, SIGHAN. 2012. *http://www.cipsc.org.cn /clp2012/task2.html*. Tianjin, China.

Houfeng Wang, Zheng Mei. 2005. Chinese multi-document person name disambiguation. *High Technology Letters*, 11(3):280–283.

Bollegala D, Matsuo Y, Ishizuka M. 2006. Disambiguation person names on the Web using automatically extracted key phrases. *Proceedings of the 17th European Conference on Artificial Intelligence*, 553–557. Riva del Garda, Italy.

Xiao Zhou, Chao Li, Minghan Hu, Huizhen Wang. 2006. Chinese Name Disambiguation Based on Exclusive Character Attributes. *The 6th CCIR Conference Proceedings*, 2010:333–340. Harbin, China.

Shunrui Zhang, Lianghong You. 2010. Chinese People Name Disambiguation by Hierarchical Clustering. *New Techology of Library and Information Service*, 2010(11):64–68.

John L., Andrew M., Fernando P.. 2001. *The ICML2001 Proceedings*, 2001:282–289.

Jiule Tian, Wei Zhao. 2010. Word Similarity Algorithm Based on Tongyici Cilin in Semantic Web Adaptive Learning System. *Journal of Jilin University (Information Science Edition)*, 2010,28(6):602–608.

Da Lu, Mingpei Xie, Wei Pu. 2000. A Character Preclassification Method Based on Fuzzy Structure Analysis of Typographical Characters. *Journal of Software*, 2000,11(10):1397–1404.

Xiangdong Yu, Xiuyun Suo, Jianren Zhai. 2002. Speech Recognition Based on Fuzzy Clustering. *Fuzzy Systems and Mathematics*, 2002,16(1):75–79.

Explore Chinese Encyclopedic Knowledge to Disambiguate Person Names

Jie Liu*   Ruifeng Xu*   Qin Lu† Jian Xu†
Key Laboratory of Network Oriented Intelligent Computation,
Shenzhen Graduate School, Harbin Institute of Technology, China*
{lyjxcz, xuruifeng.hits}@gmail.com
Department of Computing, Hong Kong Polytechnic University, Hong Kong†
{csluqin, csjxu}@comp.polyu.edu.hk

Abstract

This paper presents the HITSZ-PolyU system in the CIPS-SIGHAN bakeoff 2012 Task 3, Chinese Personal Name Disambiguation. This system leveraged the Chinese encyclopedia Baidu Baike (Baike) as the external knowledge to disambiguate the person names. Three kinds of features are extracted from Baike. They are the entities' texts in Baike, the entities' work-of-art words and titles in the Baike. With these features, a Decision Tree (DT) based classifier is trained to link test names to nodes in the NameKB. Besides, the contextual information surrounding test names is used to verify whether test names are person name or not. Finally, a simple clustering approach is used to group NIL test names that have no links to the NameKB. Our proposed system attains 64.04% precision, 70.1% recall and 66.95% F-score.

1 Introduction

With the development of the Internet and social network, more and more personal names appear on the web. However, many people share the same namesake, thus causing name ambiguities in online texts. A useful approach for disambiguating the person names is of great benefit to the information extraction and other natural language processing problems.

Worse still, Chinese personal name disambiguation is much more challenging. This is because it is difficult to locate the boundaries for Chinese personal names. In example 1,

Both "朱方勇/ZhuFangyong" and "朱方/ZhuFang" can be identified as named entities since the word "勇/Yong" (meaning "bravely") can be placed together with the word "闯/pass" to form a phrase.

Example 1: **朱方勇**闯三关 (ZhuFangyong passed three barriers)

In addition, some Chinese surnames are a combination of parents' family names. Take "张包子俊/Zhang-Bao Zijun" for example, the surname "张包/Zhang-Bao" was made by combining two signal-syllable family names "张/Zhang" and "包/Bao". This combination also makes the situation more complex. Moreover, some person names are simply common words. For example, "白雪/BaiXue" can refer to "white snow" when it doesn't refer to a person.

In recent years, many researches have been conducted on person name disambiguation. Web People Search (Artiles et al., 2009, 2010) provides a benchmark evaluation competition. In this task, a lot of approaches resolve personal name ambiguity by clustering approaches. Disambiguating personal names generally involved two steps: feature extraction step and document clustering. In terms of extracted features, Bagga et al. (1998) used the within-document coreference approach to extract the most relevant context for test names. Xu et al. (2012) added the key phrases as the features. Other researchers have also used URLs, title words, ngrams, snippets and so on (Chen et al., 2009; Ikeda et al., 2009; Long and Shi, 2010). To group text documents into different clusters, Hierarchical Agglomerative Clustering (HAC) is commonly used. Gong et al. (2009) proposed a method to train a classifier to select the best HAC cutting point. Yoshida et al. (2010) used a two-stage clustering by bootstrapping to improve the low recall values created in the first stage. Besides, some researchers incorporated the social networks of the test names to do person name disambiguation. Tang et al. (2011) established a bipartite graph by extracting named entities that co-occur with the test names and then resolute the person name ambiguity based on graph similarity. Lang et al. (2009) proposed to extend the social networks by using the search engine to achieve a better performance.

Similarly, the TAC-KBP entity-linking task has been held four times (McNamee et al. 2009, Chen et al. 2010, Zhang et al. 2011, Xu et al. 2012). A general architecture consists of three modules: candidate generation, candidate selection, NIL entities clustering.

In the candidate selection step, some researchers viewed it as an information retrieval task. Varma et al (2010) ranked the candidates with a TF-IDF weighting scheme. Fern et al. (2010) used the PageRank approach to rank the entities. Zhang et al. (2010) proposed a compound system by using the Lucene-based ranking, SVM-rank and binary SVM classifier. To rank the candidates, different features are used. Zhang et al. (2011) used surface features, contextual features and semantic features. In addition, they calculated the contexts' probability distribution over the Wikipedia categories to measure the topics' similarity. Chang et al. (2010) extracted anchor text strings as features. Lehmann et al. (2010) and Mcnamee (2010) utilized the Wikipedia links. In our system, a Decision Tree classifier has been used with four kinds of features: the entities' texts in NameKB, the entities' texts in Baike, the entities' work-of-art words and titles in the Baike.

Some test name may have no corresponding links to the entities in the knowledge base (KB) and will be classified as NIL queries. To detect these NIL queries, Chen et al. (2010) simply marked the queries without candidate as NIL. Lehmann et al. (2010) trained a classifier to find NIL queries.

Similar to the WePS and TAC-KBP tasks, the CIPS-SIGHAN CLP2012 bakeoff task was held to promote the Chinese personal name disambiguation. In this task, our system leveraged the Chinese encyclopedia Baidu Baike (Baike) as the external knowledge to disambiguate the person names, resulting in an F1 score of 66.95%.

The rest of the paper is organized as follows. Section 2 describes person name disambiguation task. Section 3 presents the design and implementation of our system for this task. Section 4 gives the performance achieved by our system. Section 5 gives the conclusion and future work.

2 Task Description

CIPS-SIGHAN bakeoff on person name disambiguation is an Entity-Linking task. In the task, 32 test names and a document collection for each test name are provided. Each document contains at least one test name mention. NameKB is also provided to describe entities related to the test name. Each entity with the short description is about one person in reality.

The systems are required to link documents to the corresponding entities in NameKB. Some test names are not named entities but common words. Documents containing these test names should be classified as "other". Other test names that cannot be linked to the NameKB are required to be clustered.

3 Person Name Disambiguation System

In our system, disambiguating personal names is conducted in five steps. In the first step, some preprocessing work will be done, for example, getting the information from encyclopedia, establishing one-to-one mapping between entities in Baike and in NameKB. In the third step, we will link test names mentions in documents to the entities in NameKB. As there is just a short description for each entity in the NameKB, we proposed to enrich the entities' description text by using four kinds of information. Finally, a DT based classifier trained was used to determine which result should be adopted. Then, documents in which the test name mentions have no linking to the entities in NameKB were decided whether their test name mentions refer to some person or just are the common words. In this common words identification step, the test names were judged whether there are the words describing people around them. Finally, simple clustering for the NIL documents was done by considering whether the words set around the test name mentions were sharing the words describing people.

3.1 Preprocessing

In order to use the rich information of the encyclopedia in the Baike, the 32 pages referring to the 32 test names are downloaded for the Internet. In each page, there are several subpages referring to same number of entities. As the Table 1 shown blow, there are 16 entities for the test name "白雪/BaiXue". For each subpage, there is rich information about the corresponding entity. We extract entities' titles, entities' contents and the entities' work-of-art names. In addition, all the texts used in our system are segmented.

1.歌手/singer
2.演员/actor
3.运动员/athlete
4.配音演员/dubbing speaker
5.画家/painter
6.作家/writer
7.《海豚湾恋人》插曲/interlude song of *Love at Dolphin Bay*
8.snowhite 文具/ stationery
9.小说《大秦帝国》女主角/heroine of the novel named *The Qin empire*
10.动漫人物/ cartoon character
11.布袋戏人物/ glove puppetry character
12.《活佛济公》角色/role in *The Legends of Ji Gong*
13.柯南主题曲/the theme song of Conan
14.南京籍演员/actor born in Namjing
15.《金陵十三钗》演员之一/one of the actor in *The Flowers of War*
16.汉语词汇/ word in Chinese

Table 1: Titles of entities in page describing person "白雪/BauXue"

3.2 Map the Baike to the NameKB

Though the various kinds of information were extracted from the Baike, we cannot directly use them in the task because we don't know which entity the information belongs to. In order to solve this problem, the one-to-one mapping between entities in Baike and entities in NameKB is established. For most test names the number of entities in Baike is bigger than the one in NameKB. But it is not always true for all test names that the entity set in Baike contains all the entities in the NameKB.

In this step, VSM is used to represent the entities' contents in both Baike and NameKB. The the nouns found in all the contents are selected as the features and weighted with the TF-IDF score. We then use the cosine metric as similarity calculation function.

It is not simply to select the most similar entity in NameKB for a given entity in Baike. We also must select the most similar entity in Baike for a given entity in NameKB to make the mapping be one-to-one. After establishing the mapping the additional entities both in Baike and in NameKB will be discarded. In the training dataset, this simple method gets the very higher precision.

3.3 Entity-Linking System

In this section, the entity-linking method is described. Entity-Linking system links the documents to the entities in NameKB. Our entity-linking method is a compound one. We built four entity-linking sub-systems by using different kinds of information. Each system gives an entity-linking result. The machine learning method is trained to get a classifier which will help us do better decision with the four entity-linking results given by the sub-systems.
The four entity-linking subsystems (S1, S2, S3 and S4) are described separately.

S1. Using the entity content in NameKB
In the NameKB, a short description is given for each entity. In this subsystem, the similarity between the descriptions in NameKB and the documents in collections was measured to determine whether there is a link between them. In this subsystem, a vectorial representation of document with the test name is compared with the vectorial representations of the entities' descriptions in NameKB. The features used in these vectorial representations are all nouns with assigned TF-IDF scores. The subsystem chooses the NameKB entity which has the maximum similarity with the document as the output. The threshold for the minimum similarity value is set empirically to get the higher accuracy. The documents with similarity being less than a given threshold (0.27 in this task) will be classified as NIL queries, indicating that they have no link to the entities in NameKB.

S2. Using the entity content in Baike
There is richer information in the Baike than in the NameKB. Baike has information box, events list, work-of-art words and so on. These are very useful to disambiguate the test names. Like the S1 subsystem, the similarity between the entities' contents in Baike and the documents in collections was measured to get the most similar entity for each document. The threshold for the minimum similarity value is set empirically, too. Like the S1, the documents less than the given threshold (0.15) will be classified as NIL queries. The result is intermediate one. Then, it is used as the input to get the final result by leveraging the mapping established in 3.2.

S3. Using the work-of-art name string in Baike

The entities in the NameKB are mostly famous person, such as artists, government officials, authors, actors, singers, researchers and so on. There are a lot of work-of-art names marked as "《" and "》" in their descriptions. These names are the names of books, songs, movies, conferences, journals and so on. In most cases we can identify which entity the test name mentioned in a document refers to. It is difficult to make decision when there are more than one entities sharing the same work-of-art names, for example, "EI" is shared by many professors. In order to avoid misjudging in that case, duplicates are removed to get the work-of-art names lists for each entity.

Because most of the work-of-art names will be segmented into several words, we avoid this issue by directly looking up the name strings in each document. The farther away from the test names, the less relevant to them. Based on that observation the boundary for looking up is set to get the better result. Our system just looks up the string names in the substrings containing the test names. The looking up windows is set as 40 characters centered in the test names. If finding, the document will be marked with the corresponding entity. This result is also the intermediate one. Mapping will be done to get the final one. The documents in which the name strings ware not found will be marked with a special tag.

S4. Using the entity title in the Baike

In the Baike, for each entity there is a title to give a very short and exact description, such as "柔道运动员/judo artist", "南京大学副教授/associate professor of Nanjing University". With these short titles we can get some very useful information about the entities. For example we can get entities' organizations, occupations and so on. In this subsystem, the ending words of the titles are used only since for most titles the ending words are the occupations of the entities. We just simply look up the occupation words extracted from the titles in the documents. Similar to the S3 subsystem, the looking up boundary is set to get the better result. The mapping the intermediate result to the final one is also needed.

From four subsystems described above, we get four results which tell us how to link the documents in the collections to the entities in NameKB. In order to combine these results, machine learning method is used to get the best final result. With the training set, a DT based classifier is trained. Features for the DT classifier is shown blow in Table 2. For example, the value S1 will be Y if the subsystem S1 finds a link between the document and some entity in NameKB. Otherwise, N will be assigned to it if S1does not find a link for the document. The value for S12 is if the subsystems S1 and S2 both find the same link for the document. Similarly, the value of feature S1234 indicates whether the four subsystems S1, S2, S3, S4 find the same link for the document. Five classes are trained for classification. They are shown in Table 2. This classifier is applied to determine which result should be adopted.

Feature	**Value**
S1,S2,S3,S4	Y: find a link by Si N: find not link by Si
S12,S13,S14,S23,S24,S34	Y: find the same link by Si and Sj N: other
S123,S124,S134,S234	Y: find the same link by Si, Sj and Sk N: other
S1234	Y: find the same link by S1, S2, S3 and S4 N: other

Table 2: The features in the DT classifier

Classes	**Remark**
AS1, AS2, AS3, AS4	Find the link and the result of Si is adopted
N	There is not link

Table 3: Five classes in the DT classifier

For each document in test set, the four subsystems give four results. The classifier trained in training set tells which subsystems' result should be adopted. For example, some document is labeled by the classifier as the S2, which means the classifier tells us that the link is found and the result of S2 (by using the entities' text in Baike) should be adopted. The documents which are classified in the class N are told that there is no corresponding entity in NameKB.

3.4 Identifying Common Words

The test name words (the words exactly matching the test names and mentioned in the documents) do not always refer to person or named entity. In some documents they are common words. For the test name "白雪/BaiXue", in Example 1, "白雪/BaiXue" is a person name and refers to a marathoner while in Example 2, "白雪/BaiXue" is a common words meaning "white snow" rather than a person name.

Example 1: 白雪获女子马拉松冠军(BaiXue won the women's marathon champion)
Example 2: 海拔 5100 米的玉树雪山披着白雪 (The Yushu snow mountain with the altitude of 5100 meters is covered with white snow)

In this task, the systems are required to find out these common words and to mark them as "other". But in the NameKB of the training set, some test names have the common word entities, such as "黄海/HuangHai", "黄河/HuangHe", "华山/HuaShan", "华明/HuaMing", "方正/FangZheng" and so on. And the documents referring to these common word entities were marked as the entities numbers rather than "other". So "other" is only be labeled on the documents in which the test names don't refer to the entities in NameKB and refer to common words. Base on that observation, our system just identify whether the test names are the common words after entity linking. That means the common words identification is just for those documents which have no links to the NameKB entities.

In this step, the words surrounding the test names within a given window size are collected to identify the common words. If the surrounding words contain person names or occupations, the test names will be identified as the person name. Otherwise, test names will identified as common words and the corresponding document will be marked with "other".

Take the test name "丛林/LinCong" for example, in example 3, the surrounding word set is {"流沙/ShaLiu", "李世荣/ShirongLi", "毋巨龙/JulongWu", "王珍祥/ZhenxiangWang"} when the window size is set to 2 noun. In the word set, "李世荣/ShirongLi", "毋巨龙/JulongWu", and "王珍祥/ZhenXiangWu" are person names, but "流沙/ShaLiu" is not recognized as person name by the POS tagging tools. So the document document is expected to refer to some people. In the Example 4, because the surrounding word set {"厅/department", "厅/director", "印花/print", "基地/base"} contains {"厅长/director"}--an occupation word, the test name string in the document will also denote a person. In the Example 5, the corresponding document will be marked as "other" because the test name mention's surrounding word set {"两岸", "峰峦", "河道", "水流"} contains neither person name nor occupation word. A simple dictionary-based occupation word identification is developed in this step
Example 3: 【作者】陈亮；流沙；李世荣；丛林；毋巨龙；王珍祥；(Authors: Liang Chen, Shan Liu, Shirong Li, Lin Cong, Julong Wu, Zhenxiang Wang)
Example 4: 福建省科技厅厅长丛林来访"冷转移印花示范基地" (Lin Cong, the director of the Science and Technology Department of Fujian Province, visited the cold transfer printing model base)
Example 5: 两岸峰峦竞秀，丛林密布，河道曲折迂回，水流缓急有致 (River twists and turns across the rising mountains which are covered with dense jungles)

After this step, the documents in which the test name mentions are just the common words will be selected and marked as "other". All other documents will be clustered in next section.

3.5 NIL Document Clustering

The documents without the mark "other" are required to be clustered together based on the underlying entities.

In our system, a simple clustering is done among these documents. The words around the test names within a certain window (2 words) are collected as the documents' words sets. All the person words (person names and the occupations words) in the words sets are picked upchosen to measure whether these documents share the same person wordshave words in common. If so, The the documents share the same person words will be clustered togethergrouped into clusters.

For the test name "李晓明/XiaomingLi", because the doc405 and the doc332 will be grouped since they have the same word share the person name "董事长/chairman", they will be clustered together. For the test name "李晓明/XiaomingLi", because the doc405 and the doc332 share the person name "董事长/chairman", they will be clustered together.
Doc 405 : 秦/Qin 龙/Long （国际/international ）集团/Group 董事长/chairman 李晓明/LiXiaoming 到/go to 黑龙江/Heilongjiang Province 交通职业技术学院

/Communication Polytechnic college 参观/visit 考察/inspect

Doc 332: 市委/ municipal Party committee 书记 /secretary 杨信/XinYang 陪同/together 北京 /Beijing 秦/Qin 龙/Long 国际/international 公司 /company 董事长 /chairman 李晓明 /XiaomingLi 一/one 行/coming 来到/go to 扎龙 /Zhalong

Doc 405: personal words set { "董事长 /chairman"}

Doc 332: personal words set { "董事长 /chairman"}

4 Performance Evaluations

This section shows evaluations of our system for the CIPS-SIGHAN bakeoff 2012 Task 3 in training set and the final test set. The results are shown in Table 4.

Data set	Precision	Recall	F1
Training set	0.6761	0.7277	0.7010
Test set	0.6404	0.7013	0.6695

Table 4: The performance of our system

It is shown that our system achieves the higher recall performance than the precision. In addition, the result on the training set is higher than the one on the testing set both in the precision and recall.

To validate the usefulness of the leveraging the encyclopedia, we conducted an experiments with and without using the encyclopedia. Experimental result in Table 5 shows that leveraging the encyclopedia Baike gives remarkable improvement.

Runs	Precision	Recall	F1
Without Baike	0.6399	0.5973	0.6179
With Baike	0.6761	0.7277	0.7010

Table 5: Performance evaluation by leveraging the Encyclopedia Baike

In addition, three sets of experiments are conducted separately on the training dataset to measure the effectiveness of our system in entity linking, common word identification, and document clustering. They are denoted as PureEL, PureCWI and PureCluster, respectively. In the golden answer of the training dataset, there are three types of documents: documents that can be linked to the NameKB, documents that are classified as "other" and documents which are categorized as "NIL" for clustering. PureEL simply considers documents that can be linked to nodes in the NameKB. Our system evaluates the performance in linking these documents to the NameKB in Table 6. Experimental results show that our system achieves a high precision (87.5%) and F-score (82.3%) in linking documents to nodes in NameKB.

PureCWI takes into account documents that are classified as "other" and "NIL" categories in the golden answer for training dataset. Documents of "NIL" categories are introduced as noises to testify the robustness of our system in identifying names as common words. Experimental results in Table 6 indicate a high recall but at the cost of low precision, implying that documents of "NIL" categories affect the performance of common word identification.

PureCluster simply uses the documents of "NIL" categories. Results in Table 6 shows our system achieves a high precision in clustering documents, indicating that our system introduces less noise in clustering solutions. However, our system has a low recall in clustering, implying that the number of clusters produced by our system is less than that of the manually assigned categories in the golden answer. Through further analysis, we found that most of documents of "NIL" categories are placed into a singleton clusters.

Runs	Precision	Recall	F1
PureEL	0.875	0.777	0.823
PureCWI	0.231	0.762	0.355
PureCluster	0.917	0.456	0.609

Table 6: The performance data of the subsystems

5 Conclusions and Future Work

The HITSZ-PolyU system enriches the information of the entities in given NameKB by leveraging the encyclopedia Baike. Experiments have shown that it is very helpful in the task. For the entity linking, four results are got by using different information. A DT based classifier was used to combine the four results to get the final one. A simple approach to predict whether the test name mentions is common words is used but not very useful. More powerful common words identification method will be considered to get better performance. The words matching based clustering does achieve the good performance.

Better clustering approach should be applied to improve the performance. In addition, the using of the Baike in our system is very simple. The new way how to make better use of it should be considered in the future researches. Furthermore, in mapping establishing step the additional entities in Baike was discarded directly. However, those additional entities should be used before the clustering step to filter out the documents which has the link to them, which can alleviate the clustering problem.

References

Amit Bagga, Breck Baldwin. 1998. Entity-Based cross-document coreferencing using the vector space model. In *Proceedings of the 36th Annual Meeting of the Association for Computational Linguistics and 17th International Conference on Computational Linguistics* v.1, pp: 79-85.

Angel X. Chang, Valentin I. Spitkovsky, Eric Yeh, Eneko Agirre and Christopher D. Manning. 2010. Stanford-UBC Entity Linking at TAC-KBP. In *Poceedings of the Third Text Analysis Conference (TAC 2010).*

Chong Long and Lei Shi. 2010. Web person name disambiguation by relevance weighting of extended feature sets. In *Third Web People Search Evaluation Forum (WePS-3), CLEF 2010.*

Ergin Elmacioglu, Yee Fan Tan, Su Yan, Min-Yen Kan and Dongwon Lee. 2007. PSNUS: Web People Name Disambiguation by Simple Clustering with Rich Features. In *Proceedings of the Second Text Analysis Conference (TAC 2007).*

Elena Smirnova, Konstantin Avrachenkov, and Brigitte Trousse. 2010. Using web graph structure for person name disambiguation. In *Third Web People Search Evaluation Forum (WePS-3), CLEF 2010.*

Javier Artiles, Julio Gonzalo, Satoshi Sekine. 2009. Weps 2 evaluation campaign: overview of the web people search clustering task. In *2nd Web People Search Evaluation Workshop (WePS 2009), 18th WWW Conference, 2009.*

Javier Artiles, Andrew Borthwick, Julio Gonzalo, Satoshi Sekine, and Enrique Amigo. 2010. WePS-3 evaluation campaign: overview of the web people search clustering and attribute extraction tasks. In *Third Web People Search Evaluation Forum (WePS-3), CLEF 2010.*

Jian Xu, Qin Lu, Jie Liu, Ruifeng Xu. 2012. NLP-Comp in TAC 2012 Entity Linking and Slot-Filling. In *Proceedings of the Fourth Text Analysis Conference (TAC 2012).*

Jian Xu, Qin Lu, Zhengzhong Liu. 2012. Combining classification with clustering for web person disambiguation. *In Proceedings of the 21st International Conference Companion on World Wide Web*, pp: 637-638.

Jintao Tang, Qin Lu, Ting Wang, Ji Wang, and Wenjie Li. 2011. A Bipartite Graph Based Social Network Splicing Method for Person Name Disambiguation. In *SIGIR 2011*, pp. 1233-1234.

John Lehmann, Sean Monahan, Luke Nezda, Arnold Jung and Ying Shi. 2010. LCC Approaches to Knowledge Base Population at TAC 2010. In *Proceedings of the Third Text Analysis Conference (TAC 2010).*

Jun Gong, Douglas W. Oard. 2009. Selecting hierarchical clustering cut points for web person-name disambiguation. In *Proceedings of the 32nd International ACM SIGIR Conference on Research and Development in Information Retrieval*, pp: 778-779.

Jun Lang, Bing Qin, Wei Song, Long Liu, Ting Liu, Sheng Li. 2009. Person Name Disambiguation of Searching Results Using Social Network. *Chinese Journal of Computers*, No.7, pp: 1365-1374.

Krisztian Balog, Jiyin He, Katja Hofmann, Valentin Jijkoun, Christof Monz, Manos Tsagkias, Wouter Weerkamp and Maarten de Rijke. 2009. The University of Amsterdam at WePS2. In *2nd Web People Search Evaluation Workshop (WePS 2009), 18th WWW Conference, 2009.*

Masaki Ikeda, Shingo Ono, Issei Sato, Minoru Yoshida and Hiroshi Nakagawa. 2009. Person name disambiguation on the web by two-stage clustering. In *2nd Web People Search Evaluation Workshop (WePS 2009), 18th WWW Conference, 2009.*

Minoru Yoshida, Masaki Ikeda, Shingo Ono, Issei Sato, Hiroshi Nakagawa. 2010. Person name disambiguation by bootstrapping. In *Proceedings of the 33rd International ACM SIGIR Conference on Research and Development in Information Retrieval*, pp: 10-17.

Norberto Fernández, Jesus A. Fisteus, Luis Sánchez, and Luis Sánchez. 2010. WebTLab: A cooccurrence-based approach to KBP 2010 Entity-Linking task. In *Proceedings of the Third Text Analysis Conference (TAC 2010).*

Paul McNamee, Mark Dredze, Adam Gerber, Nikesh Garera, Tim Finin, James Mayfield, Christine Piatko, Delip Rao, David Yarowsky and Markus Dreyer. 2009. HLTCOE approaches to knowledge base population at TAC 2009. In *Proceedings of the Second Text Analysis Conference (TAC 2009).*

Paul McNamee. 2010. HLTCOE Efforts in Entity Linking at TAC KBP 2010. In *Proceedings of the Third Text Analysis Conference (TAC 2010).*

Sanyuan Gao, Yichao Cai, Si Li, Zongyu Zhang, Jingyi Guan, Yan Li, Hao Zhang, Weiran Xu and Jun Guo. 2010. PRIS at TAC2010 KBP Track. In *Proceedings of the Third Text Analysis Conference (TAC 2010).*

Vasudeva Varma, Praveen Bysani, Kranthi Reddy, Vijay Bharath Reddy, Sudheer Kovelamudi, Srikanth Reddy Vaddepally, Radheshyam Nanduri, Kiran Kumar N, Santhosh Gsk and Prasad Pingali. 2010. IIIT Hyderabad in Guided Summarization and Knowledge Base Guided Summarization Track. *In Proceedings of the Third Text Analysis Conference (TAC 2010).*

Wei Zhang, Jian Su, Bin Chen, Wenting Wang, Zhiqiang Toh, Yanchuan Sim, Yunbo Cao, Chin Yew Lin and Chew Lim Tan. 2011. I2R-NUS-MSRA at TAC 2011: Entity Linking. *In Proceedings of the Fourth Text Analysis Conference (TAC 2011).*

Ying Chen, Sophia Yat, Mei Lee and Chu-Ren Huang. 2009. PolyUHK: A robust information extraction system for web personal names. *In 2nd Web People Search Evaluation Workshop (WePS 2009), 18th WWW Conference, 2009.*

Zheng Chen, Suzanne Tamang, Adam Lee, Xiang Li, Wen-Pin Lin, Matthew Snover, Javier Artiles, Marissa Passantino and Heng Ji. 2010. CUNY-BLENDER TAC-KBP2010 Entity Linking and Slot Filling System Description. In *Proceedings of the Third Text Analysis Conference (TAC 2010).*

A Joint Chinese Named Entity Recognition and Disambiguation System

Longyue Wang
Natural Language Processing & Portuguese-Chinese Machine Translation Laboratory, Department of Computer and Information Science, University of Macau, Macau S.A.R., China.
vincentwang0229@hotmail.com

Shuo Li
Natural Language Processing & Portuguese-Chinese Machine Translation Laboratory, Department of Computer and Information Science, University of Macau, Macau S.A.R., China.
leevis1987@gmail.com

Derek F. Wong
Natural Language Processing & Portuguese-Chinese Machine Translation Laboratory, Department of Computer and Information Science, University of Macau, Macau S.A.R., China.
derekfw@umac.mo

Lidia S. Chao
Natural Language Processing & Portuguese-Chinese Machine Translation Laboratory, Department of Computer and Information Science, University of Macau, Macau S.A.R., China.
lidiasc@umac.mo

Abstract

In this paper we describe an integrated approach for named entity recognition and disambiguation in Chinese. The proposed method relies on named entity recognition (NER), entity linking and document clustering models. Different from other tasks of named entities, both classification and clustering are considered in our models. After segmentation, information extraction and indexing in the preprocessing step, the test names in the documents would be judged to be common words or named entities based on hidden Markov model (HMM). And then each predicted entity should be linked to the category in the given knowledge base (KB) according to the character attributes and keywords. Finally, the named entities which have no reference in KB would be clustered into a new category based on singular value decomposition (SVD). An implementation of our presented models is described, along with experiments and evaluation results on the Second CIPS-SIGHAN Joint Conference on Chinese Language Processing Bakeoff (Bakeoff-2012). Named entity recognition F-measure reaches up to 76.67% and named entity disambiguation F-measure up to 69.47% within the test set of 32 names.

1 Introduction

The ability to identify the named entities has been established as an important task in several areas, including topic detection and tracking, machine translation, and information retrieval (Cucerzan, 2007). NER is the first step that seeks to locate and classify atomic elements in text into predefined categories such as the names of persons, organizations, locations, etc.. Another big issue in this area is based on a factor that millions of names (especially for person names) and references appear on the Internet, which raises the problem of co-reference resolution, also called name disambiguation (Wu, 2010). Therefore, named entity recognition and disambiguation are both important in Natural Language Processing (NLP), especially in Chinese language.

Unlike Roman alphabetic languages such as English, Portuguese, etc., Chinese named entity recognition and disambiguation are more difficult due to the unavailability of morphology variations, explicit word delimiters etc.. For example, given a word "温馨 (*warm*)", it is hard to determine whether it is a common adjective or a person name. Besides, different types of named entities can use the same names. For instance, "金山 (*Gold Hill*)" can be used as the name of persons, locations and organizations. Finally, it is typical that many persons share the same name.

It is reported that, nearly 300,000 persons have the same name of "张伟 (*Zhang Wei*)" in China.

To further investigate these issues, SIGHAN 2012 establishes a more difficult task, which can be seen as combination of related tasks in KBP (Knowledge Base Population) and WPS (Web People Search). It is divided into three parts and described as follows:

- **Named Entity Recognition**. The test names in the document should be judged to be common words or named entities.
- **Entity Linking**. Each predicted named entity should be further determined which named entity in the KB it refer to.
- **Unlinked Name Clustering**. Some predicted named entities that do not have references in the KB, should be clustered into new categories.

For these three sub-tasks, we presented a PRLC approach, which integrates with named entity **P**re-processing, **R**ecognition, **L**inking and **C**lustering modules. Word segmentation, keywords generation and character attributes extraction are ential for all the documents both in test name set and KB. And then given a test name document, recognition module will determine whether it is a name of person, place, organization or non-entity. Besides, the linking module adopts the technology of information retrieval (IR) to find the category in the indexed KB. Finally, all the unlinked documents would be classified by the named entities they refer to. Different from the traditional methods, we divided our model into four independent parts but all work together to deal with named entity recognition, linking and clustering. The word segmentation and indexing were well conducted in the preprocessing step. And both keywords and character attributes were extracted as quires. In addition, the problem is transformed from named linking to similarity calculation, where conventional IR techniques can be used. So the similarity between each document in KB and a certain query on a test name document can be evaluated to obtain best reference. Finally, an SVD-based method was adopted to group the unlinked entities by the named entities they refer to.

The paper is organized as follows. The related works are reviewed and discussed in Section 2. The proposed PRLC approach based on four models is described in Section 3 and 4. Results, discussion and comparison between different strategies are given in Section 5 followed by a conclusion and future improvements to end the paper.

2 Related Work

The issues of named entity recognition and disambiguation have been discussed from different perspectives for several decades. In this section, we briefly describe some related methods.

NER has been widely addressed by symbolic, statistical as well as hybrid approaches. Its major part in information extraction (IE) and other NLP applications has been stated and encouraged by several editions of evaluation campaigns such as MUC (Marsh and Perzanowski, 1998), the CoNLL-2003 NER shared task (Tjong Kim Sang and De Meulder, 2003) or ACE (Doddington et al., 2004), where NER systems show near-human performances for the English language. However, Chinese NER is far from mature (Wu, 2005). Recent years, a lot statistic-based methods including hidden Markov models (HMMs) (Zhou, 2002; Fu, 2005) have been applied. Comparing with rule-based NER, statistic-based methods utilize the human labeled corpus as the training set, and it doesn't require the extensive knowledge of linguistics when labeling the corpus. Carpenter (2006) presented the character language models with a good accuracy of 97.57% (precision 81.88, recall 80.97 and F-measure 81.42) in the closed track of the 3rd SIGHAN bakeoff. The results show that HMMs can perform well both in accuracy and speed.

With the development of NER, there have been some researches on combining this component with entity linking (EL). Stern et al. (2012) introduced a system based on a joint application of NER and EL, where the NER output is given to the linking component as a set of possible mentions, preserving a number of ambiguous readings. Although the system achieved a high linking accuracy (87%), it is only evaluated in French language. Regarding the Chinese person name disambiguation, Xu et al. (2010) described a system incorporating person name recognition, identity and an agglomerative hierarchical clustering. And finally his proposed method achieves encouraging recall and good overall performance for the task in the CIPS-SIGHAN 2010, which is simpler than the one we tackled.

In order to extract useful information from the descriptive documents, a method named "bags of words" is widely used to find the keywords based on Term Frequency–Inverse Document Frequency (TF-IDF) or Term Frequency (TF). Additionally, the vector space model is usually used to represent the documents and calculated the similarities (Bollegala, 2006). Although the keyword has more relationship to the document itself instead of the information of the person, the contents of the documents in this task are mainly the description of persons. Mann and Yarowsky (2003) proposed another approach which used character attributes to build a person model and achieved a good performance.

3 Pre-processing

Different from the other languages such as English, Portuguese etc., pre-processing like word segmentation is the foundation for Chinese named entity recognition and disambiguation. In order to reduce the search space during entity linking and clustering, both keywords and character attributes are also extracted to represent the documents. We mainly completed the works as follows.

3.1 Word Segmentation

Our task is thought to be more challenging due to the need for word segmentation which could bring errors into the subsequent processes.

After years of intensive researches, Chinese word segmentation has achieved a quite high performance (Huang, 2007). Among all of them, the ICTCLAS (developed by Chinese Academy of Sciences) is currently the best one both in accuracy and speed. This Chinese lexical analysis system combines part-of-speech (POS) tagging, word segmentation and unknown word recognition.

Therefore, ICTCLAS 2007[1] is involved to deal with word segmentation and POS tagging for the documents both in the knowledge base and in the test name set. In order to make all the names segmented correctly, all the test names are collected manually as the external dictionary, Furthermore, persons often have much to do with corresponding works, books etc.. So all these segmented titles should be re-combined for further extraction.

3.2 Character Attributes Extraction

After segmentation, character attributes are extracted by some simple matching rules. According to the character categories in WPS and the contents of the documents in this task, nine kinds of attributes such as gender, political status, educational background etc. were defined to describe a person. The detailed character attributes used in our system are shown in Table 1.

No.	Attributes	Description
1	Gender	Male, female or not mentioned
2	Date	Dates of the events
3	Nation	Like Miao, Han etc.
4	Political Status	Like party members etc.
5	Educational Background	The degrees such as master, PhD etc.
6	Occupation	Name of job or titles
7	Publications	Name of books, films etc.
8	Other Names	Names of other persons, locations and organizations
9	Foreign Words	English words like names of foreigners

Table 1: Character attributes used in our system

3.3 Keywords Generation

After selecting the attributes from the documents of the test name set and KB, the keywords will be selected from the common words (not attributes). Keywords can be supplemented for some documents, which are limited with character information. Therefore, a keywords generation model was designed according the POS, TF-IDF and positions.

Based on the classical algorithm of TF-IDF (Ramos, 2003), a weight is added to obtain the words, which have more relations to the test names. Given a document collection D (e.g. test name set or KB), a word w, and an individual document $d \in D$, we calculate

$$P(w,d) = \frac{\alpha}{Dis} \times f(w,d) \times \log \frac{|D|}{f(w,D)} \quad (1)$$

where $f(w,d)$ denotes the number of times w that appears in d, $|D|$ is the size of the corpus, and $f(w,D)$ indicates the number of documents in which w appears in D. Firstly, nouns and verbs have more ability of describing than other words. In implementation, α should be set as 1 for the nouns and verbs while others as 0. Besides, the words around the entities also have more relation to the person. Therefore, the Dis is used to caculate the distance between a certain word and the closest test name. Division of Dis means that the words with longer distance to the test name should be less important. Finally, all the common words will be ranked by the values of $P(w,d)$

[1] ICTCLAS can be download from http://www.ictclas.org/ictclas_download.aspx

and the best *N*th words will be selected as keywords.

3.4 Query and Indexing

For the document in KB, each character attribute is indexed in respective field and all the keywords are indexed in another filed together. For the test name set, both attributes and keywords of each test name document are combined as a query for retrieving the indexed KB.

4 Proposed Approach

In addition to the pre-processing, the approach relies on three models: recognition model which judges the test name whether name entity or not; linking model which determines which named entity in the KB the test name refer to; and clustering model, which groups the same unlinked entities according by the entities they refer to. The workflow of the approach for PRLC is shown in Fig. 1.

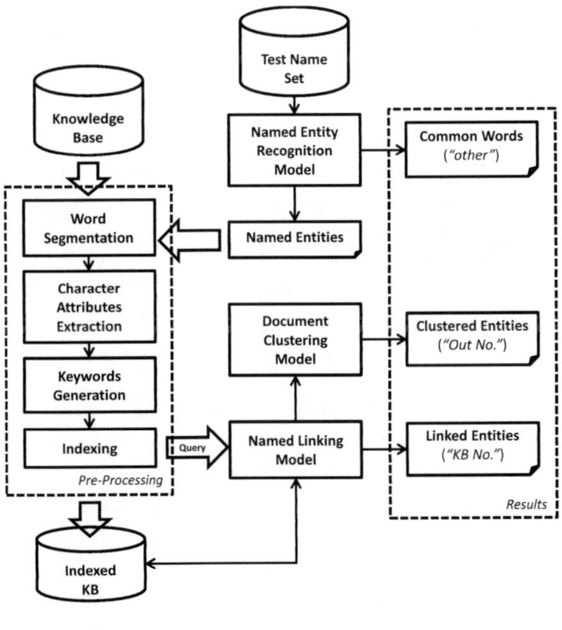

Figure 1. Approach for PRLC.

4.1 Named Entity Recognition

Proper noun of persons (PER), locations (LOC) and organizations (ORG) are included by name entities. Each sentence consists of a single character, a single space character and a tag with BIO coding scheme.

An open source NLP toolkit, LingPipe[2] was utilized to deal with the NER task, which depends on *n*-gram based character language model with the Witten-Bell smoothing (Witten et al., 1991). Regarding training phrase, the model provides a probability distribution of strings over a fixed Chinese character. The recognizer introduced an HMM interface with *n*-best decoder. The approach proposed by Carpenter (2006) was referred in the implementation of the model: the transition between tags is modeled by a maximum likelihood estimate over the training corpus. Therefore, a bounded character language model is trained to estimate the tags.

During decoding, a Chinese chunking implementation was introduced. The chunking utilizes a refinement of the standard "BIO" coding scheme (Culotta and McCallum, 2004), which means more tags were defined to label the Chinese character instead of the original tags. So the confidence estimation of Chinese characters was simplified and the probabilities will be normalized to model the joint probabilities of the Chinese character or tag (Carpenter, 2006). For example, the person's name can be generated with a tag in a person model which is built based on n-best chunker, in which each Chinese word is scored. Finally, a new output is returned with a best score by a re-scoring model.

In summary, the NER model is helpful to distinguish the name entity and none name entity. The performance of this model will be evaluated and shown in Section 5.

4.2 Entity Linking

After indexing the KB and generating the queries, the problem of entity linking is transformed into information retrieval. The core algorithm of the retrieval model is derived from the Vector Space Model (VSM). Our system takes this model to calculate the similarity between each indexed KB and the input query. The final scoring formula is given by:

$$Score(q,d) = coord(q,d)\sum_{t_{in}q} tf(t,d)\times idf(t)\times bst\times norm(t,d) \quad (2)$$

where *tf(t,d)* is the term frequency factor for term *t* in document *d*, *idf(t)* is the inverse document frequency of term *t*, while *coord(q,d)* is frequency of all the terms in query occur in a document. *bst* is a weight for each term in the query. *Norm(t,d)* encapsulates a few (indexing time)

[2] http://alias-i.com/lingpipe/web/download.html

boost and length factors, for instance, weights for each document and field. As a summary, many factors that could affect the overall score are taken into account in this model.

The model can return *N*-best candidates with the scores. In our system, only if the size of candidate set is more than 1 and the highest score is more than a threshold, the top candidate will be linked to the category in the KB. Otherwise, the test name will be treated as unlinked one.

4.3 Document Clustering

In the clustering model, a snippet-based clustering engine named Carrot2[3] was applied for the task. It can automatically organize small collections of documents (search results but not only) into thematic categories. Lingo is one of the algorithms in Carrot, which constructs a "term-document matrix" where each snippet gets a column, each word a row and the values are the frequency of that word in that snippet. It then applies a matrix factorization called singular value decomposition (SVD). All the documents of unlinked test names were group by the toolkit according to the queries.

5 Evaluation and Discussion

A number of experiments have been conducted to investigate our proposed method on different settings. In order to evaluate the performance of the recognition model, we tested it respectively with external corpus.

Measurement	Values	Average
R_{PER}	**0.8540**	
R_{LOC}	0.6823	0.7220
R_{ORG}	0.6123	
P_{PER}	**0.8868**	
P_{LOC}	0.8411	0.8173
P_{ORG}	0.6642	
F_{PER}	**0.8701**	
F_{LOC}	0.7534	**0.7667**
F_{ORG}	0.6372	

Table 2: The NER result

Two years of People's Daily (PD) corpus is used for training data, which are manual segmented and tagged with POS with high quality by Peking University. And then the test set of Microsoft Research in the 3rd SIGHAN Bakeoff was used to evaluate. The results of the person, location and organization are shown in Table 2. Although the total F-measure is only 0.7667, a large amount of test names are person name. With the high F-measure of 0.8701 in person, it fully illustrates the effectiveness of the NER model.

We also use a small test set within 6 test names, which is released by the Second CIPS-SIGHAN. The results in Table 3 show that the proposed method gives an average precision of 74.41%. However, the recall value is not ideal and the distribution is not balanced. It is unmoral that the lowest recall is 0.5925 while the highest is 0.9154. Through analyzing the data, the main reason is that the clustering model is not good enough to group the documents together based SVD. This leads to a not very high F-measure totally. The encouraging results in precision prove a good ability to distinguish categories in KB. Therefore, the technology of information retrieval using the character information or keywords is more useful to named disambiguation.

Personal Name	P	R	FB1
白雪 (*Bai Xue*)	0.8191	0.6684	0.7361
白云 (*Bai Xun*)	0.7796	0.6090	0.6839
丛林 (*Cong Lin*)	0.7024	0.7551	0.7278
杜鹃 (*Du Juan*)	0.8651	**0.5925**	0.7033
方正 (*Fang Zheng*)	0.6378	0.6051	**0.6210**
胡琴 (*Hu Qin*)	0.6604	0.9154	**0.7673**
Total	**0.7441**	0.6909	0.7165

Table 3: The result with a small test set

Finally, we evaluated our system, on the test set of 32 test names. Table 4 shows our official CIPS-SIGHAN bakeoff results. It shows the average precision, recall and FB1[4] of our system. The results show that we still can improve the clustering model to obtain a higher recall. On the whole, the presented PRLC approach is suitable to task of Chinese named entity recognition and disambiguation, but still should be improved in the future.

6 Conclusion

This article presents an integrated approach for the special task in Chinese personal name recognition and disambiguation. We divided our model into four independent parts but all work together and are easy to improve each model independently. In implementation, we combined the

[3] http://project.carrot2.org/download.html

[4] http://www.cipsc.org.cn/clp2012/task2.html

pre-processing, named entity recognition, named linking and document clustering modules into our system. Besides, the character attributes and TF-IDF keywords are both used to build person model for entity linking and clustering. Finally, we simplified the problem of named linking with the technology of information retrieval, which obtains a high precision in the task..

Precision	Recall	FB1
0.7885	0.6209	0.6947

Table 4: The official results

Acknowledgments

This work was partially supported by the Research Committee of University of Macau under grant UL019B/09-Y3/EEE/LYP01/FST, and also supported by Science and Technology Development Fund of Macau under grant 057/2009/A2.

References

Bollegala D., Matsuo Y., and Ishizuka M. 2006. Extracting key phrases to disambiguate personal name queries in web search. *Proceedings of the Workshop on How Can Computational Linguistics Improve Information Retrieval*. 17–24.

Carpenter B. 2006. Character language models for Chinese word segmentation and named entity recognition. *Proceedings of the Fifth SIGHAN Workshop on Chinese Language Processing*. 169–172.

Cucerzan S. 2007. Large-scale named entity disambiguation based on Wikipedia data. *Proceedings of EMNLP-CoNLL*. 6:708–716.

Culotta A. and McCallum A. 2004. Confidence estimation for information extraction. *Proceedings of HLT-NAACL 2004: Short Papers*. 109–112.

Doddington G., Mitchell A., Przybocki M., Ramshaw L., Strassel S., and Weischedel R. 2004. The automatic content extraction (ACE) program-tasks, data, and evaluation. *Proceedings of LREC*. 4:837–840.

Fu G. and Luke K.K. 2005. Chinese named entity recognition using lexicalized HMMs. *ACM SIGKDD Explorations Newsletter*. 7:19–25.

Huang C. and Zhao H. 2007. Chinese word segmentation: A decade review. *Journal of Chinese Information Processing*. 21:8–20.

Mann G.S. and Yarowsky D. 2003. Unsupervised personal name disambiguation. *Proceedings of the Seventh Conference on Natural Language Learning at HLT-NAACL* 2003-Volume 4. 33–40.

Marsh E. and Perzanowski D. 1998. MUC-7 evaluation of IE technology: Overview of results. *Proceedings of the Seventh Message Understanding Conference (MUC-7)*. 20.

Ramos J. 2003. Using tf-idf to determine word relevance in document queries. *Proceedings of the First Instructional Conference on Machine Learning*.

Tjong Kim Sang E.F. and Meulder F. De. 2003. Introduction to the CoNLL-2003 shared task: Language-independent named entity recognition. *Proceedings of the Seventh Conference on Natural Language Learning at HLT-NAACL* 2003-Volume 4. 142–147.

Witten I.H. and Bell T.C. 1991. The zero-frequency problem: Estimating the probabilities of novel events in adaptive text compression. *Information Theory, IEEE Transactions On*. 37:1085–1094.

Wu C., Gong L., and Zeng J. 2010. Multi-document Chinese name disambiguation based on Latent Semantic Analysis. *Fuzzy Systems and Knowledge Discovery (FSKD), 2010 Seventh International Conference On*. 5:2367–2371.

Wu Y., Zhao J., Xu B., and Yu H. 2005. Chinese named entity recognition based on multiple features. *Proceedings of the Conference on Human Language Technology and Empirical Methods in Natural Language Processing*. 427–434.

Zhou G.D. and Su J. 2002. Named entity recognition using an HMM-based chunk tagger. *Proceedings of the 40th Annual Meeting on Association for Computational Linguistics*. 473–480.

Chinese Personal Name Disambiguation Based on Vector Space Model

Qing-hu Fan
College of Information Engineering,
Zhengzhou University, Zhengzhou,
Henan ,China
fanqinghude@163.com

Hong-ying Zan Yu-mei Chai
Yu-xiang Jia
College of Information Engineering,
Zhengzhou University, Zhengzhou,
Henan ,China
{iehyzan, ieymchai, ieyx-jia}@zzu.edu.cn

Gui-ling Niu
Foreign Languages School,
Zhengzhou University, Zhengzhou,
Henan ,China
mayerniu@163.com

Abstract

This paper introduces the task of Chinese personal name disambiguation of the Second CIPS-SIGHAN Joint Conference on Chinese Language Processing (CLP) 2012 that Natural Language Processing Laboratory of Zhengzhou University took part in. In this task, we mainly use the Vector Space Model to disambiguate Chinese personal name. We extract different named entity features from diverse names information, and give different weights to various named entity features with the importance. First of all, we classify all the name documents, and then we cluster the documents that cannot be mapped to names that have been defined. Eventually the results of classification and the clustering are combined. In the test corpus experiments, the accuracy rate is 0.6778, the recall rate is 0.7205 and the F value is 0.6985 for all names.

1 Introduction

Named Entity is the fundamental information elements in text, and is the basis for understanding the text correctly. Named Entities include person names, organization names, place names, time, date, and digital. Named Entity Recognition is to identify the entities in the text and determine what category it is. Such as 方正 fang-zheng 'Fang Zheng', maybe the name is an associate professor at the Department of Mechanical and Electrical Engineering, Physics and Electrical and Mechanical Engineering College of Xiamen University, or it may be Peking University Founder Group Corp that was established by Peking University. It needs to associate with context for disambiguating the entity Fang Zheng. For example, Fang Zheng who is an associate professor at Xiamen University can be extracted with the feature that Xiamen University, Mechanical and Electrical Engineering College or associate professor, which can eliminate ambiguity.

2 Related Research

In the early stages of Named Entity Disambiguation, Bagga and Baldwin (1998) use Vector Space Model to resolve ambiguities between people having the same personal name. Han and Zhao (2010) proposed a knowledge-based method that captures structural semantic knowledge in multiple knowledge sources to disambiguate personal entities. Han and Sun (2011) proposed a generative Entity-Mention model that leverages heterogeneous entity knowledge for the entity linking task. In Chinese person name disambiguation, Li, et al (2010) carried out the first conference, Chinese Language Processing (CLP-2010), which contains Chinese person names disambiguation task. In this task Shi, et al (2011) proposed a post-processing method that is based on multiple entity recognition system integration and heuristic rules, Zhang, et al (2010) proposed a method that extracts various person features to identify different person names, and according to the Chinese word segmentation, we constructed artificially rules that identify the names correctly. We propose a method that is based on various entities recognition and initialize evaluation for the features that are the common characteristics of different names, and then take Vector Space Model to calculate it. In the end, the documents that cannot be mapped to names that have been defined in the knowledge base are clustered into different types.

CLP2012 Named Entity disambiguation is a task pre-classification and later clustering problems. The task provides a knowledge base of Chinese names which include multiple definitions of personal names, and some documents about person names. It is the purpose of the task that makes each name that appears in documents to link corresponding definition of the knowledge base, and makes the documents that cannot link to corresponding definition of the knowledge base to cluster which two documents have the same named Entity feature. Task input: Names knowledge base of named Entity, text set corresponding each name. Task output: if the name of each text links to the knowledge base of a definition, then output the corresponding id, if the name of each text is ordinary words, then output "other", if the name of each text does not belong to the above two kinds, then output Numbers: Out_XX that have been put into.

This paper is organized as follows: in section 3 we will introduce the method that extract the named entities related to figures. In section 4 we will introduce the calculation model of the named entities. In section 5 we will describe experiments and results. In the last section we will make conclusions and future work.

3 Extract the Named Entities Related to Figures

3.1 Character works

Works have the originality and are the intellectual creations that can be copied in a certain physical form in the field of literature and science.[1] Works include literature works, music, drama, folk art forms, dance works, photographs, films, television, video works, etc. Character works is the significant characteristic to identify figures. In evaluation corpus, it is generally that a character works correspond to one specific character. Therefore, it is character works that plays an important role to eliminate name disambiguation.

Extraction method: we extract character works from each figure corpus; in other words, we extract all the contents of quotation marks.

Format the character works:

1) If there is 之 Zhi that appears in the work, then we split the work with 之 Zhi.

For example:

白云(孙皓晖先生的长篇小说《大秦帝国之黑色裂变》中所虚构的女主角)

Bai-Yun(Sun-hao-hui-xian-sheng-de-chang-pian-xiao-shuo-da-qin-di-guo-zhi-hei-se-lie-bian-zhong-suo-xu-gou-de-nv-zhu-jiao)

Bai-Yun(she is the fictional actress in the Danqin Empire with The Black Fission that is Mr.Sun Haohui's novel)

We will extract 大秦帝国之黑色裂变 da-qin-di-guo-zhi-hei-se-lie-bian 'Danqin Empire with The Black Fission' that is the work, however the work cannot be identified. As 大秦帝国之黑色裂变 da-qin-di-guo-zhi-hei-se-lie-bian 'Danqin Empire with The Black Fission' is only the first novel of 大秦帝国 da-qin-di-guo 'Danqin Empire' in literature works.[2] We split 大秦帝国之黑色裂变 da-qin-di-guo-zhi-hei-se-lie-bian 'Danqin Empire with The Black Fission' into 大秦帝国 da-qin-di-guo 'Danqin Empire' and 黑色裂变 hei-se-lie-bian 'The Black Fission'with 之 Zhi, and then they can be identified correctly.

2) If the length of works' name is less than 2, it is required to extract works and quotation marks.

Eg:马啸担任河南卫视《旅游》栏目主持人. Ma-xiao-dan-ren-hen-nan-wei-shi-lv-you-lan-mu-zhu-chi-ren 'Ma Xiao is appointed host of Traveling program in Henan TV'In this sentence 旅游 lv-you 'Traveling' is the work name. It is known that Traveling has different part of speech, which can be a verb or noun. The Traveling is a TV program in the sentence, which is a noun. It will reduce accuracy rate that we take Traveling as the feature.

3.2 Character Aliases

Aliases are the names other than the formal or specific. They are used in writing, oral.[3] Character aliases are an essential feature for eliminating

[1] http://baike.baidu.com/view/94574.htm

[2] http://baike.baidu.com/view/525001.htm

[3] http://baike.baidu.com/view/343250.htm

the disambiguation. We define that each file-name in KB folder is the figure's original name, others are character aliases. We use the methods that are based on pattern matching to extract character aliases Lu and HOU (2006), as is shown below following methods:

1) Synonymy keywords + Synonyms + End identifier

Synonymy keywords: 本名｜别号｜，字｜^(字)｜，号｜^(号)｜又号｜^(名)｜笔名｜自号｜又名｜乳名｜别名｜原名｜艺名｜本名｜曾用名｜俗称｜亦称｜又称, the symbol "|"means choose, "^"means that matches the beginning of the string.

End identifier: it means the end of extracting the synonyms, the end signs are always (，or,) and (。or .), which mean comma symbol and full stop. If we extract character aliases equal with original names, then we should use the feature that synonyms combine with synonymy.

Eg: 白云(原名杨维汉，广东省潮安县人) Bai-Yun(Yuan-ming-yang-wei-han-guang-zhou-chao-an-xian-ren) Bai-Yun(Her original family name is Yang Weihan and she was born in ChaoAn Guangdong Province).

According to the first method that we could extract 杨维汉 yang-wei-han 'Yang Weihan' that it is character aliase. However, the content of 白雪 bai-xue 'Bai Xue' that 白百何，中国内地女演员，别名白雪 Bai-bai-he-zhong-guo-nei-di-nv-yan-yuan-bie-ming-bai-xue 'Bai baihe is Chinese mainland actress and her aliase is Bai Xue' and 陈大威，号白雪，碧松斋主人 chen-da-wei-hao-bai-xue-bi-song-zhai-zhu-ren 'Chen Dawei's art-name is Bai Xue and he is the host of Bi-Song-Zhai', we could extract 白雪 Bai Xue that it is character aliase, which we cannot make a distinction between the two characters. As a result we take 别名白雪 bie-ming-bai-xue 'aliase is Bai Xue' and 号白雪 hao-bai-xue 'art-name is Bai Xue' as the features to eliminate disambiguation.

2) (Original family name|^(Chinese surnames))+ name+ end identifier

Original family name: we take original family name as prefix.

^ (Chinese surnames): it means the beginning of the Chinese; Zhang, et al (2008) found out that the top 400 Chinese surnames have covered 99%.

End identifier: it is the same define as the first method.

If the length of character aliases are less than 2 or more than 3, and then they will be extracted.

Eg1: the content of 白雪 Bai Xue that 白百何，中国内地女演员，别名白雪 Bai-bai-he-zhong-guo-nei-di-nv-yan-yuan-bie-ming-bai-xue 'Bai baihe is Chinese mainland actress and her aliase is Bai Xue' in the sentence the family name of Bai Xue is Bai. End identifier is "," ,then we could extract "白百何" as character aliase from the first method.

Eg2: the content of Baixue that 陈大威，号白雪，碧松斋主人 chen-da-wei-hao-bai-xue-bi-song-zhai-zhu-ren 'Chen Dawei's art-name Bai Xue and he is the host of Bi-Song-Zhai', in this sentence the family name of Bai Xue is Bai,and we know that 陈大威(Chen Dawei) is character aliase, the family Bai is different from 陈 Chen. Therefore, according to second method we use the family name Chen. End identifier is "," ,then we extract character aliase as Chen Dawei.

3.3 Named Entity

Named Entity is the feature to discriminate figures. The features related to figure, Learning Unit, organizations, living space, and other entities, can mark different figures. In this task, we primarily extract features learning unit, organizations, living space, and other entities.

1) Learning unit

Learning unit include university and college.

Extraction rules: (prefix end identifier | ns) + University name+ (University| college)

Prefix end identifier: it means the prefix end identifier of extracting learning unit; the same methods are used in character aliases.

Ns: it means place name.

Extraction process is shown as the following:

First, we use Peking University participle software to segment the character information corpora Yu, et al (2002).

Second, in order to judge the beginning of string we add "#" to the beginning of each character definition.

Third, we index the keywords "University" or "college" in the corpora.

Fourth, it is the direction that university's or college's prefix to loop for each participle units.

Fifth, if the next participle units contain "ns" or "#", the loop will stop.

Sixth, get the Chinese string that is between the beginning and the end index.

2) Organization and other entities

We use "nt" to express organization, and use "nz" to express other entities Yu, et al (2002). Then the Chinese words contain "nt" and "nz" will be extracted.

3) Living space

We mainly extract the highest frequency Chinese words in participle information; the word frequency determines the related degree about figure.

3.4 Figure Title

Title is the name that is set up, which refers to marriage, social relations, the status, and occupation. Such as professor, chief, director, etc. Title can help to distinguish different profession and status, which is essential for distinguishing various figures.

The figure title resource is part of Hownet[4] in this task, which contains 240 titles. We delete 28 titles that they reduce accuracy rate from title resource and add 8 titles that increase accuracy rate as title resources. As is shown in table 1:

Type	Titles
Be Deleted	代表 演员 领导 教授 组长 记者 委员 主任 黄河 书记 主席 姑娘 居民 老人 朋友 亲属 学生 儿子 夫人 父亲 继母 母亲 小姑娘 毕业生 村民 分子 专家 学员
Be Added	歌手 副教授 副主任 配音演员 喜剧演员 影视演员 相声演员 快板演员

Table 1: The titles of be deleted and added

Finally, we get a title resource that contains 220 titles. We will extract the titles that appear in title resource and in figures' definition, which will be title features, or it will be null.

4 Calculation Model

4.1 Vector Space Model

Vector Space Model (VSM) is algebraic model for representing text documents as vectors of identifiers. It is using vectors of identifiers that greatly improve computability of documents. In VSM each document can be expressed as N-dimensional vectors of identifiers, each dimensional can be chosen keywords as vector, which is shown as the following:

$$D_T =< T_1, T_2, T_3, \cdots, T_n >$$

T_i represents the ith item in document. ω_i represents weight of T_i, which is shown as the following:

$$D_\omega =< \omega_1, \omega_2, \omega_3, \cdots, \omega_n >$$

4.2 Feature Weight Calculation

Feature weight is used to reflect the importance for feature item in the document. Originally we calculate feature weight with Boolean weight that if the feature appears in the document, then the feature weight is 1, otherwise 0. However, this calculation method cannot reflect the importance of feature, and then we use Term Frequency (TF) and Relative Word Frequency to calculate, TF is the method that get frequency of feature item. Relative Word Frequency refers to the TF-IDF method.

But owing to the fact that each character information text is short, the above three kinds of feature weight calculation methods cannot effectively reflect importance of different characters. According to the section 3 that there are seven character information features: character works, character aliases, learning unit, organization, other entities, living space, and character title, which face the different importance of character features, we initialize weight for each character features. λ_i represents weight of the ith character feature. Each document can be expressed as seven character features in the following:

$$D_\lambda =< \lambda_1, \lambda_2, \lambda_3, \lambda_4, \lambda_5, \lambda_6, \lambda_7 >$$

Generally, the experience parameters are for: $\lambda_1=10$, $\lambda_2=6$, $\lambda_3=3$, $\lambda_4=2$, $\lambda_5=2$, $\lambda_6=5$, $\lambda_7=3$, we use two methods to disambiguate Chinese personal name.

1) Term Frequency (TF):

$$D_{Out\_num} = MAX\left\{ \underset{num=1}{\overset{n}{D}} \left\{ \sum_{i=1}^{7} \lambda_i \cdot TF_i \right\} \right\}, \quad (1)$$

In formula (1), D_{Out_num} presents the definition that the character id is num in each document. If $D_{Out\_num} = 0$, then the document presents other. $\sum_{i=1}^{7} \lambda_i \cdot TF_i$ represents product weight-sum that initial weight and absolute frequency. $\underset{num=1}{\overset{n}{D}}$ represents the num($1 \le num \le n$) for each defi-

[4] http://www.keenage.com/

nition in each character information, n represents the total number of id for each character.

2) Vectorial Angle Cosine

$$Sim(D_i, D_j) = \frac{\sum_{k=1}^{t} W_{ik} \cdot W_{jk}}{\sqrt{\sum_{k=1}^{t} (W_{ik})^2 \cdot \sum_{k=1}^{t} (W_{jk})^2}}, \quad (2)$$

In formula (2), t represents vector dimension of each document features. W_{ik} represents the kth vector dimension weight of the document D_i.

4.3 Documents Clustering

We cluster the documents from the number results of section 4.2 are "other". The steps are shown as the following:

- We extract the documents from the classification number results of section 4.2 as "other".
- We extract the character features, character work, character aliases, learning unit, and character title, from the documents by using the same method in section three.
- Boolean weighting

If two documents have the same feature that it is one of all, we cluster the two documents to one kind; otherwise, the document corresponds to the classification number of "other".

- Merge the results of section 4.2 and the results of section 4.3.In other words, the results of section 4.3 replace the classification number of "other" of the results of section 4.2.

5 Experiments

5.1 Experimental Data

We use the texts in the training corpus and test corpus of CLP2012. There are 16 character names and 1634 documents in training corpus, and 32 character names and 5503 documents in test corpus. The corpus has two kinds:

1) Knowledge base of named entity

It will provide a knowledge base for each name. For example, the name Fang Zheng refers to 12 entities, some of them are shown below:

- Fang Zheng(Comedian)
- Fang Zheng(Peking University Founder Group Corp)
- Fang Zheng (Associate professor)

2) It will provide a text set for each Name

5.2 Evaluation Method

We still take Fang Zheng as an example. It is defined as 12 kinds of entity in a knowledge base. The test document set that contain Fang Zheng is T. The reference answer marks the texts that contain Fang Zheng:

There are kinds of definition for Fang Zheng in the knowledge base. Each definition belongs to a class, which is expressed as L_XX(01≤XX ≤12), "XX" represents the definition of the XXth entity.

If Fang Zheng is not an entity name but a common word, it belongs to the class of "other".

Fang Zheng is an entity name, but it has no definition in the knowledge base, then it belongs to Out_XX, XX represents id. Out_XX represents respectively Out_01, Out_02...

We always assume that when Fang Zheng appears in a text many times and their mark is the same. Therefore, a text is only given a marked result. This system marks the results that contain Fang Zheng with SL_XX, SOther, and SOut_XX respectively, and each text is only marked by one class. Then we calculate the precision rate and recall rate for each text are as follows:

1) If Fang Zheng that includes t is divided to SL_XX, then it is taken as definition of the knowledge base to calculate precision rate and recall rate are as follows:

$$\mathrm{Pr}\,e(t) = \frac{|SL\_XX \cap L\_XX|}{|SL\_XX|}$$

$$\mathrm{Re}\,c(t) = \frac{|SL\_XX \cap L\_XX|}{|SL\_XX|}$$

2) If Fang Zheng that includes t is divided to SOther, it is taken as a common word to calculate precision rate and recall rate are as follows:

$$\mathrm{Pr}\,e(t) = \frac{|SOther \cap Other|}{|SOther|}$$

$$\mathrm{Re}\,c(t) = \frac{|SOther \cap Other|}{|SOther|}$$

3) If Fang Zheng that includes t is put into SOut_XX, but t belongs to Out_YY in reference answer, the precision rate and recall rate are as follows:

$$\Pr e(t) = \frac{|SOut\_XX(t) \cap Out\_YY(t)|}{|SOut\_XX|},$$

$$\mathrm{Re}\, c(t) = \frac{|SOut\_XX(t) \cap Out\_YY(t)|}{|SOut\_XX|}$$

1) For a name that it is Fang Zheng, and then the precision rate and recall rate are as follows:

$$\Pr e(Fang\ Zheng) = \frac{\sum_{t \in T} \Pr e(t)}{|T|}$$

$$\mathrm{Re}\, c(Fang\ Zheng) = \frac{\sum_{t \in T} \mathrm{Re}\, c(t)}{|T|}$$

2) For all names, the precision rate and recall rate are as follows:

$$\Pr e = \frac{\sum_{n} \Pr e(n)}{|N|}, \mathrm{Re}\, c = \frac{\sum_{t} \mathrm{Re}\, c(t)}{|N|}$$

$$F = \frac{2 \times \Pr e \times \mathrm{Re}\, c}{\Pr e + \mathrm{Re}\, c}$$

5.3 Experimental Results

We use two methods that Term Frequency (TF) and Vectorial Angle Cosine (VAC) to disambiguate Chinese personal name. Two methods results are shown in Table 2.

Method	Pre	Rec	F
TF	0.6399	0.6795	0.6590
VAC	0.5972	0.6079	0.6025

Table 2: The results of two methods

We can see that TF method is superior to Vectorial Angle Cosine (VAC) method from table 2. Therefore, we mainly use TF method to eliminate discrimination on test corpus. The results are shown as table 3:

Method	Pre	Rec	F
TF	0.6778	0.7205	0.6985

Table 3: The results of test corpus

First, we can see the recall rate of the test corpus is not ideal from table 3. The problem is that we cannot extract enough named entity features in the content. Such as company name, and verb structures, etc. Second, the precision rate is low. The problem is that the estimation of initial weight of each named entity features and the clustering algorithm.

6 Conclusions and Future work

In this task we extract different named entities features from diverse names information, and give different weights to various named entities features with the importance of various named entities. Firstly, we classify each name documents. Secondly, we cluster the documents that cannot be mapped to names that have been defined. Finally, the results of classification and the clustering are combined. However, it is only the experience weight for the estimation of initial weight of each named entity features, then different weights have different effects. The Boolean method cannot fully reflect the importance of all kinds of named entities features.

In the future, we can expand the named entity features, such as company name, verb structures, and the noun near character name in the documents. Then we choose more effective named entity initial weights, and use various clustering methods for character documents (Sun, et al2008).

References

Bagga, A. and Baldwin, B. 1998. Entity-Based Cross-Document Coreferencing Using The Vector Space Model. Proceedings of the 17th international conference on Computational linguistics-Volume 1, pp.79-85.

Han Xianpei and Zhao Jun. 2010. Structural Semantic Relatedness: A Knowledge-Based Method to Named Entity Disambiguation. In: Proceedings of the 49th ACL.

Han Xianpei and Sun Le. 2011. A Generative Entity-Mention Model for Linking Entities with Knowledge Base. In: Proceedings of ACL-HLT.

Li Wenjie, Huang Juren, Chen Ying and Jin Peng.2010. Chinese Person Name disambiguation. Http://www.cipsc.org.cn/clp2010/task3_ch.htm.

Lu Yong and Hou Hanqing.2006.Automatic Recognition of Chinese Synonyms Based on Pattern Matching Algorithm. Journal of The China Society For Scientific and Technical Information, 25(6):720-724.

Shi Yingchao, Wang Huizhen, Xiao Tong and Hu Minghan.2011.Personal Name Recognition for Multi-Document Personal Name Disambiguation Task .Journal of Chinese Information Processing, 25(3):17-22.

Sun Jigui, Liu Jie and Zhao Lianyu.2008.Clustering Algorithms Research. Journal of Software, 19(1):53-54.

Yu Shiwen, Duan Huiming, Zhu Xuefeng and Sun Bin.2002. The Basic Processing of Contemporary Chinese Corpus at Peking University SPECIFICATION. Journal of Chinese Information Processing, 16(6):58-64.

Zhang Shunrui and You Hongliang.2010.Chinese People Name Disambiguation by Hierarchical Clustering. Modern library and information technology, 11:64-68.

Zhang Zhufei, Ren Feiliang and Zhu Jinbo.2008.A Comparative Study of Features on CRF-based Chinese Named Entity Recognition. The fourth national conference of information retrieval and content security: 111-117.

Evaluation Reportof the third Chinese Parsing Evaluation: CIPS-SIGHAN-ParsEval-2012

Qiang Zhou
Center for Speech and Language Technology
Research Institute of Information Technology
Tsinghua National Laboratory for Information
Science and Technology
Tsinghua University, Beijing 100084, China.
zq-lxd@mail.tsinghua.edu.cn

Abstract

This paper gives the overview of the third Chinese parsing evaluation: CIPS-SIGHAN-ParsEval-2012, including its parsing sub-tasks, evaluation metrics, training and test data. The detailed evaluation results and simple discussions will be given to show the difficulties in Chinese syntactic parsing.

1 Introduction

The first and second Chinese parsing evaluations CIPS-ParsEval-2009(Zhou and Li, 2009) and CIPS-SIGHAN-ParsEval-2010 (Zhou and Zhu, 2010) were held successfully in 2009 and 2010 respectively. The evaluation results in the Chinese clause and sentence levels show that the complex sentence parsing is still a big challenge for the Chinese language.

This time we will focus on the sentence parsing task proposed by the second CIPS-SIGHAN-ParsEval-2010 to dig out the detailed difficulties of Chinese complex sentence parsing in the respect of two typical sentence complexity schemes: event combination in the sentence level and concept composition in the clausal level. We will introduce a new lexicon-based Combinatory Categorical Grammar (CCG) (Steedman1996, 2000) annotation scheme in the evaluation, and make a parallel comparison of the parser performance with the traditional Phrase Structure Grammar (PSG) used in the Tsinghua Chinese Treebank (TCT) (Zhou, 2004).

This evaluation includes two sub-tasks, i.e. PSG parsing evaluation and CCG parsing evaluation. For each sub-task, there are two tracks. One is the Close track in which model parameter estimation is conducted solely on the train data. The other is the Open track in which any datasets other than the given training data can be used to estimate model parameters. We will set separated evaluation ranks for these two tracks.

In addition, we will evaluate following two kinds of methods separately in each track.

1) Single system: parsers that use a single parsing model to finish the parsing task.

2) System combination: participants are allowed to combine multiple models to improve the performance. Collaborative decoding methods will be regarded as a combination method.

2 Evaluation Tasks

Task 1: PSG Parsing Evaluation

Input: A Chinese sentence with correct word segmentation annotation. The word number is more than 2. The following is an example:

- 小型(small) 木材(wood) 加工场(factory) 在(is) 忙(busy) 着(-modality) 制作(build) 各 (several) 种 (-classifier) 木制品 (woodwork) 。(period) (A small wood factory is busy to build several woodworks.)

Parsing goal: Assign appropriate part-of-speech (POS) tags tothe words in the sentence and generate phrase structure tree for the sentence.

Output: The phrase structure tree with POS tags for the sentence.

- (zj (dj (np (b 小型) (np (n 木材) (n 加工场))) (vp (d 在) (vp-LW (ap (a 忙) (uA

着)) (vp (v 制作) (np (mp (m 各) (qN 种)) (n 木制品)))))) (wE 。))

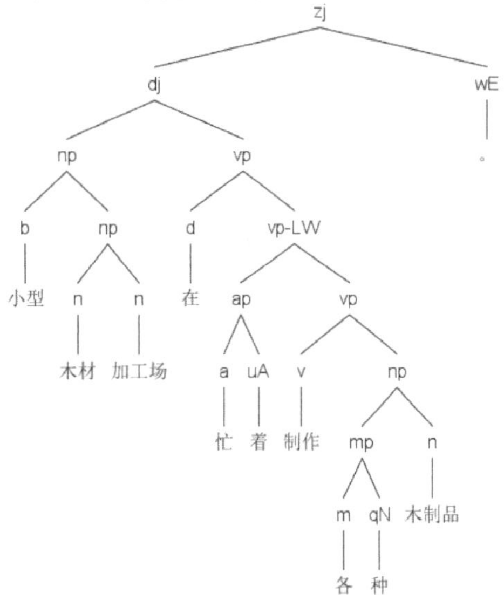

Task 2: CCG Parsing Evaluation

Input: Same with task 1.

Parsing goal: Assign appropriate CCG category tags tothe wordsin the sentence and generate CCG derivation tree for the sentence.

Output: The CCG derivation tree with CCG category tags for the sentence.

- (S{decl} (S (NP (NP/NP 小型) (NP (NP/NP 木材) (NP 加工场))) (S\NP ([S\NP]/[S\NP] 在) (S{Cmb=LW}\NP (S\NP (S\NP 忙) ([S\NP]\[S\NP] 着)) (S\NP ([S\NP]/NP 制作) (NP (NP/NP ([NP/NP]/M 各) (M 种)) (NP 木制品)))))) (wE 。))

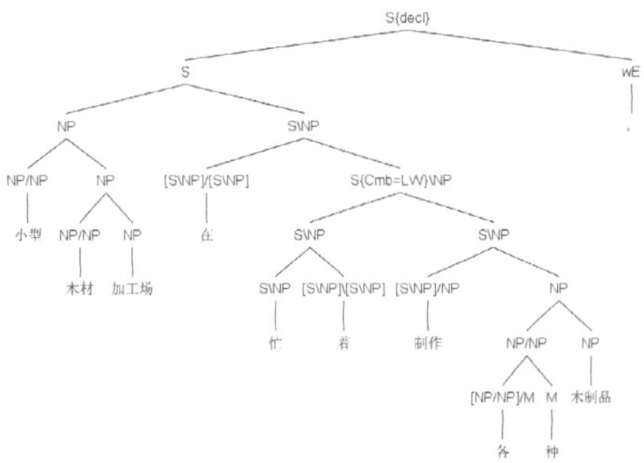

3 Evaluation metrics

There are two parsing stages for the PSG and CCG parsers. One is the stage of syntactic category assignment, including POS tag and CCG category. The other is the stage of parse tree generation, including PSG parsing tree and CCG derivation tree. So we design two different sets of metrics for them.

3.1 Syntactic category evaluation metrics

Basic metrics are the syntactic category tagging precision (SC_P), recall (SC_R) and F1-score(SC_F1).

- SC_P= (#of correctly tagged words) /(# of automatically tagged words) * 100%
- SC_R= (#of correctly tagged words) /(# of gold-standard words) * 100%
- SC_F1= 2*SC_P*SC_R / (SC_P + SC_R)

The correctly tagged words must have the same syntactic categories with the gold-standard ones.

To obtain detailed evaluation results for different syntactic categories, we can classify all tagged words into different sets and compute different SC_P, SC_R and SC_F1 for them. The classification condition is as follows.

If (SC_Token_Ratio>=10%) then the syntactic tag will be one class with its SC tag, otherwise all other low-frequency SC-tagged words will be classified with a special class with Oth_SC tag. Where, SC_Token_Ratio= (word token # of one special SC in the test set) / (word token # in the test set) * 100%.

3.2 Parsing tree evaluation metrics

Basic metrics are the labeled constituent precision (LC_P), recall (LC_R) and F1-score (LC_F1).

- LC_P = (#of correctly labeled constituents) /(# of automatically parsed constituents) * 100%
- LC_R= (# of correctly labeled constituents) / (# of gold-standard constituents) * 100%
- LC_F1= 2*LC_P*LC_R / (LC_P+LC_R)

The correctly labeled constituents must have the same syntactic tags and left and right boundaries with the gold-standard ones.

To obtain detailed evaluation results for different syntactic constituents, we can classify them into 6 sets and compute different LC_P, LC_R and LC_F1 for them.

(1) Clausal and phrasal constituents
(2) Complex event constituents
(3) Concept compound constituents
(4) Single-node constituents
(5) Complementary parsing constituents
(6) All other constituents

The classification is based on the syntactic constituent tags annotated in the automatically parsed results. Please refer next section for more detailed information.

We compute the labeled F1-scores of the first four sets (Tot4_LC_F1) to obtain the final ranked scores for different proposed systems. For comparison analysis, we also list the F1-scores of all six sets for ranking reference.

To estimate the possible performance upper bound of the automatic parsers, we also design the following complementary metrics:

(1) Unlabeled constituent precision (ULC_P)= (# of constituents with correct boundaries) / (# of automatically parsed constituents) * 100%

(2) Unlabeled constituent recall (ULC_R)= (# of constituents with correct boundaries) / (# of gold standard constituents) * 100%

(3) Unlabeled constituent F1-score (ULC_F1)= 2*ULC_P*ULC_R / (ULC_P + ULC_R)

(4) Non-crossed constituent precision (NoCross_P)= (# of constituents non-crossed with the gold standard constituents) / (# of automatically parsed constituents) * 100%

4 Evaluation data

We used the annotated sentences in the TCT version 1.0 (Zhou, 2004) as the basic resources and designed the following automatic transformation procedures to obtain the final training and test data for the two parsing tasks.

Firstly, we make binary for all TCT annotation trees[1] and obtain a new binarizated TCT version. Two new grammatical relation tags RT and LT are added to describe the inserted dummy nodes with left and right punctuation combination structures. They can provide basic parsing tree structures for PSG and CCG parsing evaluations.

Secondly, we classify all TCT constituents into 6 sets, according to the syntactic constituent (SynC) and grammatical relation (GR) tags annotated in TCT[2].

1. Clausal and phrasal constituents, if all the following two conditions are matched
   a) TCT GR tag ∈{ZW, PO, DZ, ZZ, JY, FW, JB, AD}
   b) TCT Sync tag ∈{dj, np, sp, tp, mp, vp, ap, dp, pp, mbar, bp}
2. Complex event constituents, if one of the following conditions is matched.
   a) TCT SynC tag=fj and TCT GR tag ∈{BL, LG, DJ, YG, MD, TJ, JS, ZE, JZ, LS}
   b) TCT SynC tag=jq
3. Concept compound constituents, if all the following two conditions are matched
   a) TCT GR tag ∈{LH, LW, SX, CD, FZ, BC, SB}
   b) TCT Sync tag ∈{np, vp, ap, bp, dp, mp, sp, tp, pp}
4. Single-node constituents, if TCT SynC tag=dlc
5. Complementary parsing constituents, if TCT GR tag ∈{RT, LT, XX}
6. All other constituents

They will provide basic information for detailed parsing tree evaluation metrics computation.

Finally, we build the evaluation data sets for two parsing tasks through the following approaches:

1. For PSG parsing evaluation, we automatically transform the TCT annotation data through:
   a) For the syntactic constituents belong to the above class 2-3 and 5-6, we retain the original TCT two tags;
   b) For the syntactic constituent belong to the above class 1-4, we only retain the original TCT SynC tags.
2. For CCG parsing evaluation, we automatically transform the TCT annotation data into CCG format by using the TCT2CCG tool (Zhou, 2011).

5 Evaluation Results

5.1 Training and Test data

All the news and academic articles annotated in the TCT version 1.0 (Zhou, 2004) are selected as the basic training data for the evaluation. It consists of about 480,000 Chinese words. 1000 sentences extracted from the TCT-2010 version are used as the basic test data.

Table 1 shows the basic statistics of the training and test set. Figure 1 and Figure 2 list the distribution curve of the annotated sentences with different lengths (word sums) in the training and test set. They show very similar statistical

[1] TCT binarizationalgorithm and TCT2CCG tool were finished during the author visited Microsoft Research Asia (MSRA) in April, 2011. The visiting project was supported by the MSRA research foundation provided by Prof. Ming Zhou and Prof. Changning Huang.

[2]Please refer (Zhou, 2004) for more detailed descriptions of these syntactic constituent and grammatical relation tags.

characteristics. Their peaksare located in the region of 14 to 23. More than 75% annotated sentences have 15 or more Chinese words. The average sentence length is about 26. All these data show the complexity of the syntactic parsing task in the Chinese real world texts.

Table 1 Basic statistics of the training and test data: Average Sentence Length(ASL)=Word Sum/ Sent. Sum)

	Sent. Sum	Word Sum	Char. Sum	ASL
Training Set	17558	473587	762866	26.97
Test Set	1000	25226	39564	25.23

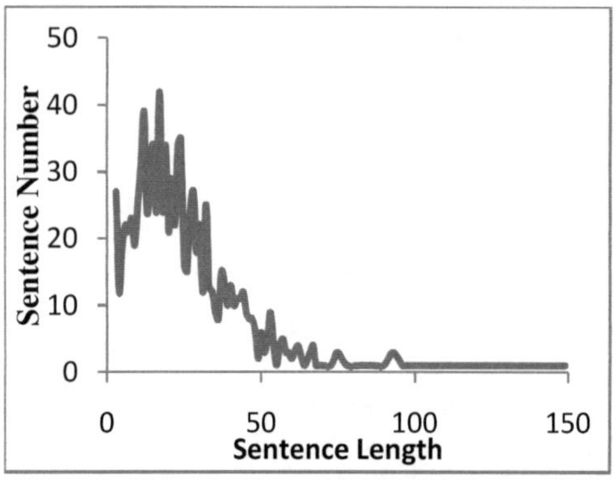

Figure 2 Sentence Length Distribution of the Test Set

Table 2 shows the statistics of different annotated constituents in the training and test set. We can find than about 68% constituents among

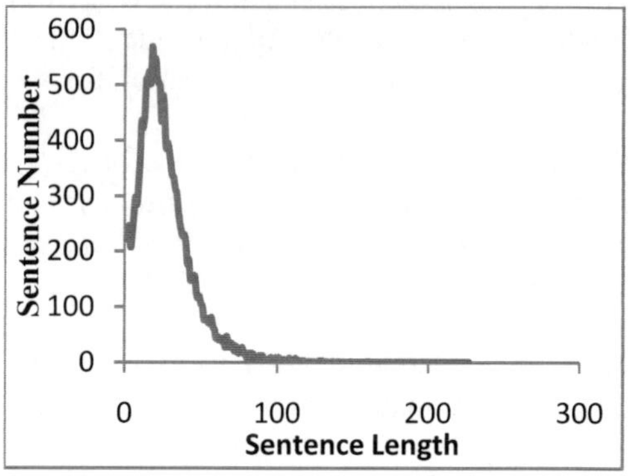

Figure 1 Sentence Length Distribution of the Training Set

them are clausal and phrasal constituents (class 1). They are the backbones of the syntactic parsing trees of Chinese sentences. About 20% constituents are complementary parsing constituents (class 5). It shows the importance of the punctuations in Chinese syntactic parsing. They can provide useful segmentation information to select suitable syntactic structures. About 12% constituents are complex event constituents (class 2) and concept compound constituents (class 3). They are the main points to determinate the parsing complexity of Chinese sentences. Few annotated examples in the training set will bring in more difficulties for feature extraction and parameter training in the statistics-based parsing models.

Table 2 Different annotated constituents in the training and test set

	Class 1	Class 2	Class 3	Class 4	Class 5	Class 6	Total
Training set	310394	24239	30719	2735	89836	316	458239
Test set	16617	1578	1224	53	4746	50	24268

Table 3 Participant information for ParsEval-2012

ID	Participants	Registered Tasks	Proposed Tasks	Systems (Open/Close)
1	Institute of Automation, Chinese Academy of Science	PSG/CCG	/	/
2	Dalian University of Technology	PSG	/	/
3	Nanjing Normal University	PSG	/	/
4	Beijing Information Science and Technology University	PSG	PSG	1/0
5	Harbin Institute of Technology	PSG/CCG	PSG	3/0
6	Speech and Hearing Research Center, Peking University	PSG/CCG	PSG	1/1
7	University of Macau	PSG	PSG	0/1
8	Japan Patent Information Organization	PSG/CCG	PSG	0/1*

5.2 General results

8 participants proposed the registration forms, including 8 for PSG parsing and 4 for CCG parsing subtasks. Among them, 5 participants proposed the final evaluation results of 8 systems. All of them are for PSG parsing task. Table 3lists the basic information of these participants. Because the proposed result of the ID No. 8 gave very little standard binarizated parsing trees and lot of multiple-node constituents, after modifying current evaluation tool, we also include its result in the following evaluation performance tables.

Table4 and Table 5 show the ranked results of the proposed systems in the Open track and Close track respectively. We can find that the best parsing performances (Tot4_LC_F1) of the single model systems in the Open and Close track of the PSG parsing task is about 76-77%, which are similar with the best evaluation results in the task 2-2 of CIPS-SIGHAN-ParsEval-2010. In the respect of the unlabeled constituents, most single model systems can achieve about 87% F1 score, which are 10% better than that of the labeled constituents. After model combination, the F1 score of the best multiple model system can be improved to 90.3% (ID=05). We think it possibly reach the upper bound of boundary identification in the Chinese syntactic parsing task.

As we expected, the parsing performances of the clausal and phrasal constituents (class 1) and the complementary parsing constituents (class 5) are better than the overall results. The best labeled constituent F1 score of the single model system listed in Table 9 is 80.72%, which is about 4% better than the overall F1 score. Due to their simple internal structures, the complementary parsing constituents (class 5) obtain better parsing performances than that of the class 1 (+about 1-2%). The parsing performances of the complex event constituents (class 2) and the concept compound constituents (class 3) are much lower than the overall results with about 20-30% drops in the labeled constituent F1 score. Between them, the LC_F1 of constituents in class 2 is about 8-10% lower than that of class 3. A possible reason is that they may need more long-distance dependency features that are very difficult to be extracted through current statistical parsing model. The same trend can be also found in the performance data in the Open track listed in Table 7.

Unlike the labeled constituents, the parsing performances of the unlabeled constituents of different classes in the Open and Close Track didn't show such larger differences (Table 6 and Table 8). Only the concept compound constituents (class 3) show lower F1 scores (-about 8-10% lower). The main reason is there are lots of crossed coordination constituents in the automatic parsing trees. It is still a big problem to identify the correct boundaries of the coordination constituents in the complex structures.

5.3 Detailed results

To evaluate the effect of different training corpus scale for parser performance, we divide all training data into N parts. In each training round, the n parts ($n \in [1,10]$) annotation corpora can be used to train N different parsing models with incremental training data. Based on them, N different test results can be obtained on the same test data set. Therefore, several variation trend diagrams of different kinds of evaluation metrics on different training corpus can be built. In the evaluation, we set N=10.

2 participants provided their incremental training test results, including 1 system in the Open track and 2 systems in the Close track.Figure 3, Figure 4 and Figure 5 show their general results. We list the following four main evaluation metrics in the figures for reference: syntactic category tagging F1 score (SC_F1), unlabeled constituent F1 score (ULC_F1), labeled constituent F1 score (LC_F1) and the labeled F1-scores of the first four constituent sets (Tot4_LC_F1).

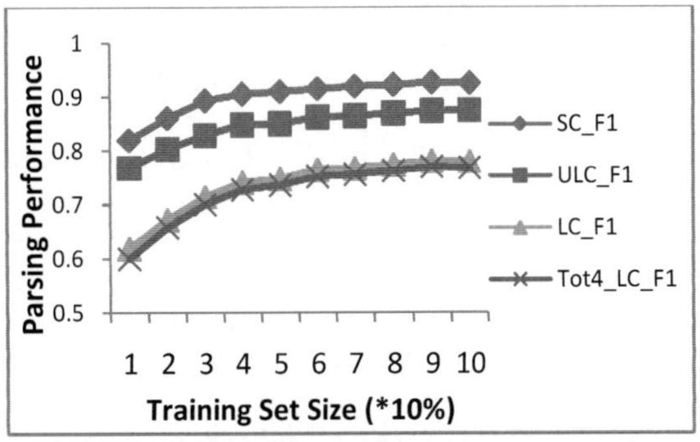

Figure 3 General performance improvement curve under different training data (ID=06, Open Track)

To find the performance improvement trend under different training data more clearly and detailed, we also collect the corresponding data of different class constituents. Figure 6, Figure 7 and Figure 8 show the results. In these figures, we select the labeled constituent F1 score (LC_F1) for reference.

From these figures, we can find that all the parsing performances are gradually improved after using more annotated data for training. It indicates the importance of large-scale annotated sentences for Chinese parser development. But the effects of the annotated sentences for different constituents and parsing stages are different and variable. We need to design new treebank building strategy to annotate more effective sentences with little manual workloads.

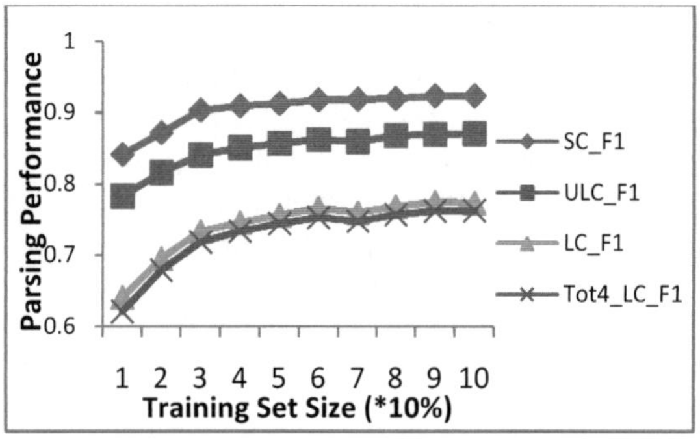

Figure 4General performance improvement curve under different training data (ID=06, Close Track)

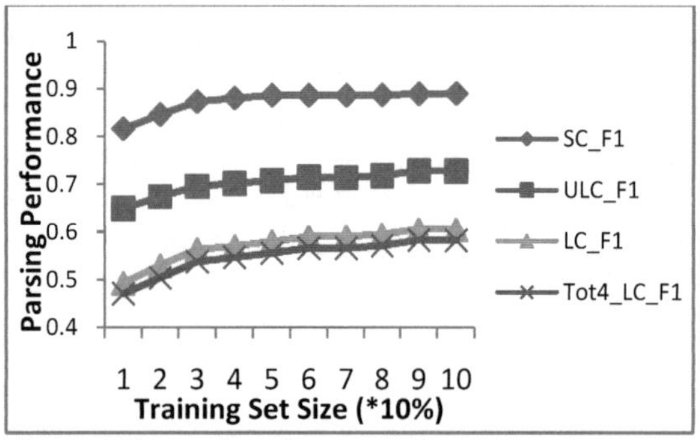

Figure 5General performance improvement curve under different training data (ID=07, Close Track)

For the syntactic category assignment stage (POS tagging in the PSG parsing subtask), after using all the training data, the SC_F1 still show some improvement trend. So we can expect to use more POS annotated sentences to obtain better POS tagging performance. 96% SC_F1 in the 4thSigHan bakeoff evaluation (Jin and Chen, 2008) under about 1M Chinese words training data proves the feasibility of this approach.

For the parse tree generation stage, we can find the different improvement effects of the training data for different kinds of constituents. For the clausal and phrasal constituents (class 1) and the complementary parsing constituents (class 5), more than 60% current training data may be enough to train a better parsing model. But for the complex event constituents (class 2) and the concept compound constituents (class 3), the fluctuated performance curves show the deficiency of current training data. How to select and annotated enough annotated sentences for them is still an open question need to be explored in the future.

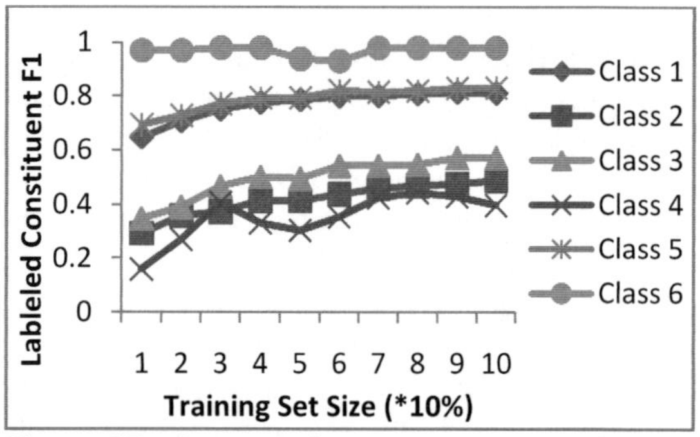

Figure 6 Performance improvement curve of different class of constituents under different training data (ID-06, Open Track)

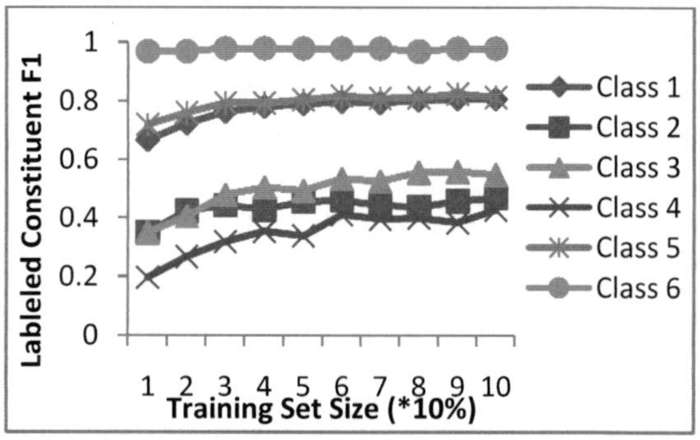

Figure 7 Performance improvement curve of different class of constituents under different training data (ID-06, Close Track)

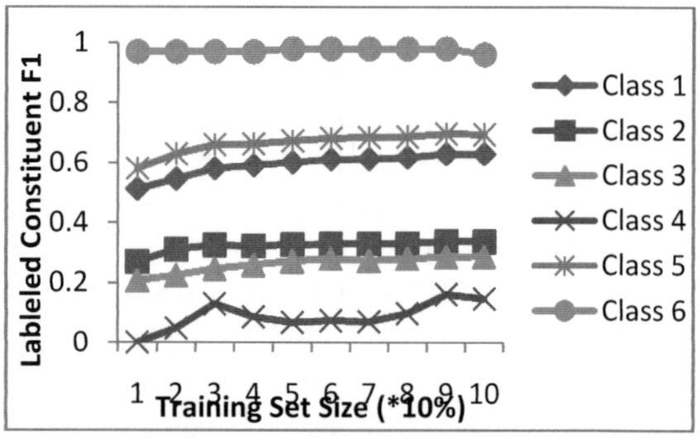

Figure 8 Performance improvement curve of different class of constituents under different training data (ID-07, Close Track)

5.4 Different parsing systems

4 participants proposed 5 technical reports to describe their parsing systems. In the section, we will briefly introduction some key techniques used in these systems.

(Zhang et al., 2012) proposed a bagging method to combine different parsers trained on different treebanks. They adopted Berkeley parser to train two different sub-models based on the TCT and CTB data, and then combined their outputs through CKY-parsing algorithm.

(Li and Wu, 2012) proposed a multilevel coarse-to-fine scheme for hierarchically split PCFGs. After automatically generating a sequence of nested partitions or equivalence classes of the PCFG non-terminals, the parsing model can start from a coarser level to prune the next finer level.

(Huang et. all, 2012) adopted a factored model to parse the Simplified Chinese. The factored model is one kind of combined structure between PCFG structure and dependency structure. It mainly uses an extremely effective A* parsing algorithm which enables to get a more optimal solution.

(Wang et al., 2012) presented a challenge to parse simplified Chinese and traditional Chinese with a same rule-based Chinese grammatical resource---Chinese Sentence Structure Grammar (CSSG).The experiments show that the CSSG that was developed for covering simplified Chinese constructions can also analyze most traditional Chinese constructions.

6 Conclusions

Parsing evaluation under standard benchmark can provide objective research platform for parsing model development and language resource construction. The expected theme of the 3rd Chinese parsing evaluation is to dig out the detailed difficulties of complex sentence parsing. So we design new tag set and propose two different parsing subtasks for performance comparison.

Although there are not any CCG evaluation results proposed, more than 5 PSG parsing results still give us enough evaluation data to verify our preliminary assumptions. Due to their complex internal structure, long-distance dependency and little annotation examples in real world annotated texts, the concept compound constituents and complex event constituents show extremely lower parsing performance than that of most clausal and phrasal constituents. How to collect enough annotated examples for them and explore new feature extraction method will be new research topic in the future.

Acknowledgments

The research was supported by National Basic Research Program of China (Grant No.: 2013CB329304) and National Science Foundation of China (Grant No.: 60873173). Thanks Mr. Qiu Han to develop the evaluation tools and manage all the evaluation results.

References

Clark, S., Copestake, A., Curran, J.R., Zhang, Y., Herbelot, A., Haggerty, J., Ahn, B.G., Wyk, C.V., Roesner, J., Kummerfeld, J., Dawborn, T.: 2009 Large-scale syntactic processing: Parsing the web. *Final Report of the 2009 JHU CLSP Workshop*

QiupingHuang, Liangye He, Derek F. Wong and Lidia S. Chao. 2012. A Simplified Chinese Parser with Factored Model. In *Proc. of CLP-2012*.

Guangjin Jin and Xiao Chen.2008.The Fourth International Chinese Language Processing Bakeoff: ChineseWord Segmentation, Named Entity Recognition and Chinese POS Tagging. In *Proc. of Sixth SIGHAN Workshop on Chinese Language Processing*, P69-81

Dongchen Li and Xihong Wu. 2012. Parsing TCT with a Coarse-to-fine Approach. In *Proc. of CLP-2012*.

Mark Steedman. 1996. *Surface Structure and Interpretation*. MIT Press, Cambridge, MA.

Mark Steedman. 2000. *The Syntactic Process*. MIT Press, Cambridge, MA.

Xiangli Wang, TerumasaEhara and Yuan Li. 2012. Parsing Simplified Chinese and Traditional Chinese with Sentence Structure Grammar. In *Proc. of CLP-2012*.

Meishan Zhang, WanxiangChe and Ting Liu. 2012. Multiple TreeBanks Integration for Chinese Phrase Structure. In *Proc. of CLP-2012*.

Qiang Zhou. 2004. Chinese Treebank Annotation Scheme. *Journal of Chinese Information*, 18(4), p1-8.

Qiang Zhou, Yuemei Li. 2009. Evaluation report of CIPS-ParsEval-2009.In Proc. of First Workshop on Chinese Syntactic Parsing Evaluation, Beijing China, Nov. 2009.pIII—XIII.

Qiang Zhou, Jingbo Zhu. 2010. Chinese Syntactic Parsing Evaluation. *Proc. of CIPS-SIGHAN Joint Conference on Chinese Language Processing* (CLP-2010), Beijing, August 2010, pp 286-295.

Qiang Zhou. 2011. Automatically transform the TCT data into a CCG bank: designation specification Ver 3.0. Technical Report CSLT-20110512, Center for speech and language technology, Research Institute of Information Technology, Tsinghua University.

Table 4 Ranked results in the Open Track of the PSG parsing task

ID	Sys_ID	Models	SC_F1	ULC_P	ULC_R	ULC_F1	NoCross_P	LC_P	LC_R	LC_F1	Tot4_LC_P	Tot4_LC_R	Tot4_LC_F1	Rank
5	CPBag	Multiple	93.97%	90.30%	90.24%	90.27%	90.30%	82.19%	82.14%	82.16%	81.34%	81.26%	81.30%	1
5	Cbag	Multiple	93.29%	90.35%	90.29%	90.32%	90.35%	82.08%	82.03%	82.05%	81.20%	81.12%	81.16%	2
5	Bbag	Multiple	93.06%	89.57%	89.51%	89.54%	89.57%	81.12%	81.07%	81.10%	80.23%	80.11%	80.17%	3
6		Single	92.50%	87.44%	87.43%	87.44%	87.44%	78.01%	78.00%	78.01%	76.81%	76.66%	76.74%	1
4		Single	92.73%	87.11%	87.13%	87.12%	87.11%	63.95%	63.96%	63.95%	70.10%	68.08%	69.08%	2
8*		Single	59.00%	38.57%	23.07%	28.87%	38.72%	29.21%	17.48%	21.87%	27.75%	18.76%	22.39%	3

Table 5 Ranked results in the Close Track of the PSG parsing task

ID	Models	SC_F1	ULC_P	ULC_R	ULC_F1	NoCross_P	LC_P	LC_R	LC_F1	Tot4_LC_P	Tot4_LC_R	Tot4_LC_F1	Rank
6	Single	92.29%	87.02%	87.04%	87.03%	87.02%	77.29%	77.32%	77.30%	76.35%	76.20%	76.27%	1
7	Single	89.01%	72.74%	72.86%	72.80%	72.74%	60.45%	60.55%	60.50%	58.26%	58.15%	58.20%	2

Table 6 Evaluation results of the different classes in the Open Track (unlabeled constituents)

	Class 1			Class 2			Class 3			Class 4			Class 5			Class 6		
ID	P	R	F1	P	R	F1	P	R	F1	P	R	F1	P	R	F1	P	R	F1
4	87.20%	90.21%	88.68%	82.27%	82.64%	82.45%	91.55%	5.31%	10.04%	81.54%	100.00%	89.83%	84.69%	53.27%	65.40%	92.68%	4408.00%	181.55%
5-b	89.63%	90.41%	90.01%	87.02%	87.52%	87.27%	84.56%	72.96%	78.33%	89.19%	62.26%	73.33%	91.22%	91.55%	91.39%	100.00%	96.00%	97.96%
5-c	90.53%	91.50%	91.02%	87.19%	87.14%	87.16%	84.51%	72.22%	77.89%	94.12%	60.38%	73.56%	91.90%	92.01%	91.96%	100.00%	96.00%	97.96%
5-cp	90.51%	91.54%	91.02%	87.04%	86.82%	86.93%	84.47%	71.57%	77.49%	91.43%	60.38%	72.73%	91.79%	91.93%	91.86%	100.00%	96.00%	97.96%
6	87.35%	87.30%	87.33%	85.51%	87.52%	86.50%	80.24%	76.31%	78.22%	75.00%	67.92%	71.29%	90.15%	90.83%	90.49%	100.00%	96.00%	97.96%

Table 7 Evaluation results of the different classes in the Open Track (labeled constituents)

	Class 1			Class 2			Class 3			Class 4			Class 5			Class 6		
ID	P	R	F1	P	R	F1	P	R	F1	P	R	F1	P	R	F1	P	R	F1
4	74.42%	76.98%	75.68%	25.68%	25.79%	25.74%	39.44%	2.29%	4.32%	46.15%	56.60%	50.85%	75.54%	47.51%	58.34%	0.42%	20.00%	0.82%
5-b	83.77%	84.50%	84.13%	51.04%	51.33%	51.18%	68.47%	59.07%	63.42%	67.57%	47.17%	55.56%	84.57%	84.87%	84.72%	100.00%	96.00%	97.96%
5-c	84.79%	85.70%	85.24%	51.30%	51.27%	51.28%	68.74%	58.74%	63.35%	76.47%	49.06%	59.77%	85.50%	85.61%	85.55%	100.00%	96.00%	97.96%

5-cp	84.93%	85.89%	85.41%	51.40%	51.27%	51.33%	68.76%	58.25%	63.07%	77.14%	50.94%	61.36%	85.48%	85.61%	85.55%	100.00%	96.00%	97.96%
6	80.97%	80.92%	80.94%	48.17%	49.30%	48.73%	58.76%	55.88%	57.29%	41.67%	37.74%	39.60%	82.66%	83.29%	82.98%	100.00%	96.00%	97.96%

Table 8 Evaluation results of the different classes in the Closed Track (Unlabeled constituents)

	Class 1			Class 2			Class 3			Class 4			Class 5			Class 6		
ID	P	R	F1	P	R	F1	P	R	F1	P	R	F1	P	R	F1	P	R	F1
6	87.26%	87.17%	87.21%	84.69%	83.78%	84.23%	77.92%	76.96%	77.44%	76.56%	92.45%	83.76%	89.23%	90.12%	89.67%	100.00%	96.00%	97.96%
7	71.42%	71.31%	71.36%	80.81%	76.87%	78.79%	52.64%	52.94%	52.79%	46.85%	98.11%	63.41%	80.22%	81.54%	80.88%	100.00%	100.00%	100.00%

Table 9 Evaluation results of the different classes in the Closed Track (labeled constituents)

	Class 1			Class 2			Class 3			Class 4			Class 5			Class 6		
ID	P	R	F1	P	R	F1	P	R	F1	P	R	F1	P	R	F1	P	R	F1
6	80.76%	80.68%	80.72%	47.28%	46.77%	47.02%	55.25%	54.58%	54.91%	39.06%	47.17%	42.74%	80.91%	81.71%	81.31%	100.00%	96.00%	97.96%
7	62.93%	62.83%	62.88%	34.44%	32.76%	33.58%	28.68%	28.84%	28.76%	10.81%	22.64%	14.63%	68.91%	70.04%	69.47%	96.00%	96.00%	96.00%

Multiple TreeBanks Integration for Chinese Phrase Structure Grammar Parsing Using Bagging

Meishan Zhang Wanxiang Che Ting Liu
School of Computer Science and Technology
Harbin Institute of Technology, Harbin, China
{mszhang, car, tliu}@ir.hit.edu.cn

Abstract

We describe our method of traditional Phrase Structure Grammar (PSG) parsing in CIPS-Bakeoff2012 Task3. First, bagging is proposed to enhance the baseline performance of PSG parsing. Then we suggest exploiting another TreeBank (CTB7.0) to improve the performance further. Experimental results on the development data set demonstrate that bagging can boost the baseline F1 score from 81.33% to 84.41%. After exploiting the data of CTB7.0, the F1 score reaches 85.03%. Our final results on the official test data set show that the baseline closed system using bagging gets the F1 score of 80.17%. It outperforms the best closed system by nearly 4% which uses a single model. After exploiting the CTB7.0 data, the F1 score reaches 81.16%, demonstrating further increases of about 1%.

1 Introduction

Over the past decade, Phrase Structure Grammar (PSG) parsing has been investigated by many researchers. Most methods of PSG parsing exploited some manly annotated corpus and proposed a single statistical model (Petrov and Klein, 2007; Zhang and Clark, 2009) based on the corpus. For Chinese, Tsinghua Chinese Treebank (TCT) (Qiang, 2004) and Penn Chinese TreeBank (CTB) (Xue et al., 2005) are two most popular manly annotated corpus.

In this paper, we are especially interested in parser combination. Many past works have suggest a number of methods for parser combination. These methods concern on combing different parsers which are trained on the same corpus. Sagae and Lavie (2006) proposed a constituent reparsing method for multiple parsers combination. Zhang et al. (2009) proposed a linear model-based general framework to combine several lexicalized parsers (Collins, 1999; Zhang and Clark, 2009) and un-lexicalized parsers (Petrov et al., 2006; Petrov and Klein, 2007).

Out method is different from the past works in that we combine different parsers which exploit the same method but the models of which are trained on different corpus. We adopt Berkeley parser[1] (Petrov et al., 2006; Petrov and Klein, 2007) to train our sub-models. It is an un-lexicalized probabilistic context free grammar (PCFG) parser. At the beginning, we train a number of submodels by sampling TCT corpus repeatedly, and meanwhile train a number of submodels by sampling CTB corpus repeatedly. Then we combine these submodels by reparsing the parsing results of them using the CKY-parsing algorithm (Song et al., 2008).

To enable using CKY-parsing algorithm for combining, we must handle the following two issues:

1. Binarization should be applied to the parsing results of submodels.

2. The grammars of TCT corpus are very different that of CTB corpus. We should transform CTB grammars into TCT grammars before final combination.

If these two issues have been done already, we can apply CKY reparsing algorithm and get the final parsing result.

The rest of the paper is organized as follows. Section 2 introduces the overall system architecture. And then we introduce our method in detail. In section 3 we present the binarization algorithm used in the system. Section 4 describes the CKY reparsing algorithm. Section 5 describes our baseline method and multiple TreeBank bagging

[1] http://code.google.com/p/berkeleyparser

method systematically. Section 6 shows the experimental results and finally in section 7 we conclude our method and give our future works.

2 System Architecture

During the training phase, we sample the training corpus of TCT and CTB repeatedly, exploiting these sampled corpus to train a number of submodels. In the test phase, first we parse a sentence using these submodels, and then binarize the parsing results, extracting the binarized grammars together with their weights, and finally exploit CKY reparsing algorithm to get our final parsing results according to the weighted grammars . For the CTB results, we should add an extra transformation process to map the CTB grammars to TCT grammars. The transformation model are trained by mapping gold TCT results and Figure 1 shows the architecture of the training and testing process.

3 Binarization

The binarization process aims at a better combination using CKY reparsing. We must ensure that the binarization process is reversible.

For the unary grammar, we simply merge the label of leaf node into its parent node. We add a special mark during the merging so that we can reverse the merging conveniently.

For the grammars whose arity are more than two, we don't use a simple left most binarization or right most binarization algorithm. As these simple binarization can make the mapping between different TreeBanks very complex. Our goal is to get a better understanding binarization results which the grammars extracted from the different TreeBanks can be more easily forming one-to-one mapping. The most popular binary grammars extracted from the TreeBank are exploited for binarization. By this method, the grammars of binarization can be mostly understood.

We describe our binarization algorithm to handle the high-arity grammars. To prepare for binarization, we need collect binarization grammar and their weights. We denote the collection results by $G_{\text{bin}} = \{(A \rightarrow BC, \text{freq})\}$. This process is done simply extracting all the binary grammars from the original TreeBank and assigning the corresponding weight by their appearance frequency. The pseudo-code of the binarization is shown in Algorithm 1. We can get the binarization tree of a PS structure by applying Algorithm 1 on each non-terminal node from up to bottom.

The TCT training corpus has been already binarized that it contains unary and binary grammars, thus we can get the binarization results for the output of TCT submodels by simply merging unary grammars. The CTB corpus contains grammars of variety number of arity. We need first merge the unary grammars and then apply algorithm 1 to get the binarization results.

4 CKY Parsing

In this section, we describe the CKY parsing algorithm which aims for bagging system. The form of rules used CKY parsing are defined by a tuple $(A \rightarrow BC, \text{s}, \text{m}, \text{e})$. It denotes a binary tree structure, $A \rightarrow BC$, the start position is s, middle position is m which is also the end of tree labeled by B, and the end position e. The rules and their weights are basic input grammar for CKY parsing, and we denote it by $G_{\text{cky}} = \{((A \rightarrow BC, s, m, e), \text{w})\}$. The pseudo-code of the CKY parsing is shown in Algorithm 2. The algorithm is very similar to the binarization algorithm.

5 Methods

5.1 Baseline Bagging System

The training process of the baseline bagging system:

1. Sample k new training corpus from the overall TCT corpus. Assuming the size of overall TCT corpus is n, we repeatedly sample the overall TCT corpus for k times. Each time we get a new training corpus whose size is $64.3\% \times n$.

2. Train k submodels using the sampled k new train corpus.

The decoding process of the baseline bagging system:

1. Parse the input sentence by the k submodels and get k PS results of the sentence.

2. Binarize the k PS results.

3. Generate the grammar G_{cky}. We extract all rules $(A \rightarrow BC, s, m, e)$ from the k PS results. The weight of each rule equals their frequency.

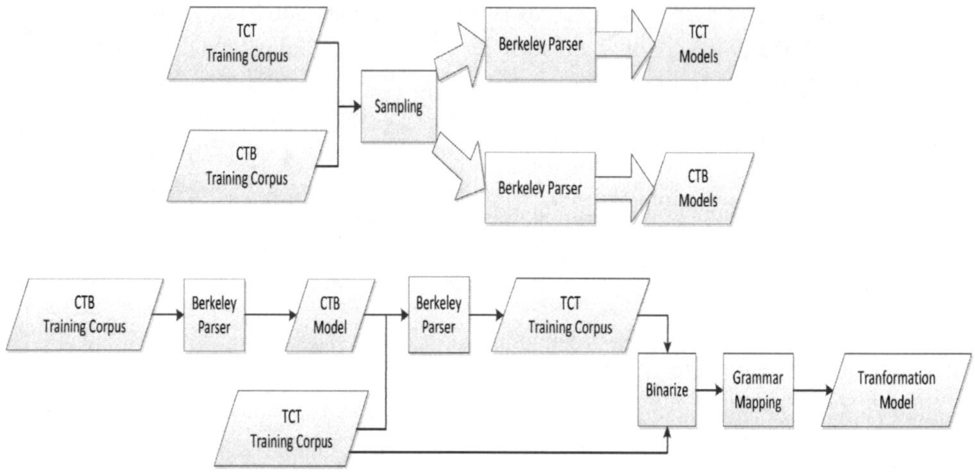

(a) Train

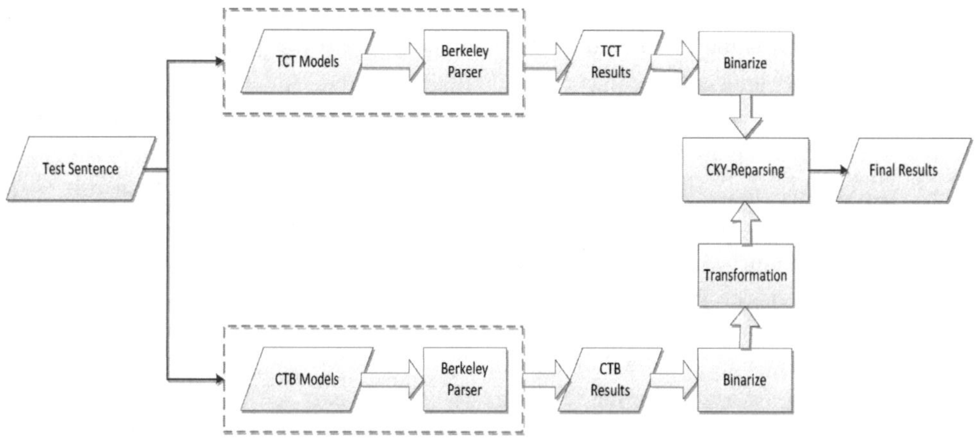

(b) Test

Figure 1: System architecture.

Algorithm 1 Binarization Algorithm. L denotes the set of non-terminal labels, and label(tr) denote the root label of tree tr.

Input: $\mathrm{G_{bin}}$, Tree : $\mathrm{tr}_0 \rightarrow \mathrm{tr}_1 \cdots \mathrm{tr}_n$
Initialization:
 for all $i \in \{1 \cdots n\}$, for all $A \in L$
  if $\mathrm{label}(\mathrm{tr}_i) = A$, $\pi(i, i, A) = 1$
  else $\pi(i, i, A) = 0$
Compute:
 for all $d \in \{1 \cdots n-1\}$
  for all $i \in \{1 \cdots n-j\}$
   set $j = i + l$
   for all $A \in L$
    $\pi(i, j, A) = \max_{A \rightarrow BC \in \mathrm{G_{bin}}, i<s<j} \pi(i, s, B) + \pi(s+1, j, C) + \mathrm{G_{bin}}(A \rightarrow BC)$
    $\delta(i, j, A) = \arg\max_{A \rightarrow BC \in \mathrm{G_{bin}}, i<s<j} \pi(i, s, B) + \pi(s+1, j, C) + \mathrm{G_{bin}}(A \rightarrow BC)$
Create a new tree tr:
 From $\delta(1, n, \mathrm{label}(\mathrm{tr}_0))$, generate middle nodes recursively.
 Add a special mark to the label of all middle nodes, which are used to restore.
Return: Binarized tree tr

Algorithm 2 CKY Parsing Algorithm. T denote the set of POS tags.

Input: G_{cky}, leaves : $\text{tr}_1 \cdots \text{tr}_n$
Initialization:
for all $i \in \{1 \cdots n\}$, for all $t \in T$
if $\text{label}(\text{tr}_i) = t$, $\pi(i, i, A) = 1$
else $\pi(i, i, A) = 0$
Compute:
for all $d \in \{1 \cdots n - 1\}$
for all $i \in \{1 \cdots n - j\}$
set $j = i + l$
for all $A \in L$
$\pi(i, j, A) = \max_{(A \to BC, i, s, j) \in \text{G}_{\text{cky}}} \pi(i, s, B) + \pi(s + 1, j, C) + \text{G}_{\text{bin}}(A \to BC, i, s, j)$
$\delta(i, j, A) = \arg\max_{(A \to BC, i, s, j) \in \text{G}_{\text{cky}}} \pi(i, s, B) + \pi(s + 1, j, C) + \text{G}_{\text{bin}}(A \to BC, i, s, j)$
Create a new tree tr:
From $\delta(1, n, \text{root})$, generate middle nodes recursively.
Return the tree tr

4. Generate the leaves : $\text{tr}_1 \cdots \text{tr}_n$. Each leaf tr_i are composed by a word w_i and its POS tag t_i, forming $t_i \to w_i$. As each word can have k results, thus we can use voting to assign the word's best POS tag t_i.

5. Reparse the sentence using CKY parsing algorithm with G_{cky} and leaves : $\text{tr}_1 \cdots \text{tr}_n$.

5.2 Bagging System Exploiting CTB Corpus

The training process of the baseline bagging system:

1. Sample k new training corpus from the overall TCT corpus and sample k new training corpus from the overall CTB corpus. We will get $2k$ new training corpus in this step.

2. Train $2k$ submodels using the sampled $2k$ new train corpus, where k submodels are the TCT stype parsers and the other k submodels are the CTB style parsers.

3. Train a transformation model from CTB style to TCT style $\text{Map}_{\text{CTB}\to\text{TCT}}$. It can be finished by the following steps.

   (a) Train a model using all CTB Corpus,

   (b) Parse the entire TCT training corpus,

   (c) Binarize the gold TCT style PS structure,

   (d) Binarize the predicted CTB style PS structure,

   (e) Compare the gold TCT results and the predicted results and get a final transformation model. For a TCT grammar $(A_{\text{tct}} \to B_{\text{tct}}C_{\text{tct}}, s_{\text{tct}}, m_{\text{tct}}, e_{\text{tct}})$ and a CTB grammar $(A_{\text{ctb}} \to B_{\text{ctb}}C_{\text{ctb}}, s_{\text{ctb}}, m_{\text{ctb}}, e_{\text{ctb}})$, if $(s_{\text{tct}}, m_{\text{tct}}, e_{\text{tct}}) = (s_{\text{ctb}}, m_{\text{ctb}}, e_{\text{ctb}})$, we would add a mapping rule $(A_{\text{tct}} \to B_{\text{tct}}C_{\text{tct}}, A_{\text{ctb}} \to B_{\text{ctb}}C_{\text{ctb}}, s_{\text{tct}}, m_{\text{tct}}, e_{\text{tct}})$ to $\text{Map}_{\text{CTB}\to\text{TCT}}$, and if $(s_{\text{tct}}, e_{\text{tct}}) = (s_{\text{ctb}}, e_{\text{ctb}})$, we would add a mapping rule $(A_{\text{tct}} \to B_{\text{tct}}C_{\text{tct}}, A_{\text{ctb}} \to B_{\text{ctb}}C_{\text{ctb}}, s_{\text{tct}}, e_{\text{tct}})$ to $\text{Map}_{\text{CTB}\to\text{TCT}}$.

The decoding process of the baseline bagging system:

1. Parse the input sentence by the k TCT submodels and get k PS results of TCT style.

2. Binarize the k PS results.

3. Generate the grammar G_{cky}. We extract all rules $(A \to BC, s, m, e)$ from the k PS results. The weight of each rule equals their frequency.

4. Generate the leaves : $\text{tr}_1 \cdots \text{tr}_n$. Each leaf tr_i are composed by a word w_i and its POS tag t_i, forming $t_i \to w_i$. As each word can have k results, thus we can use voting to assign the word's best POS tag t_i.

5. Parse the input sentence by the k CTB submodels and get k PS results of CTB style.

6. Adjust the grammar G_{cky} by k PS results of CTB style. First we extract all grammars from the k PS results. For each grammar $(A_{\text{ctb}} \to B_{\text{ctb}}C_{\text{ctb}}, s_{\text{ctb}}, m_{\text{ctb}}, e_{\text{ctb}})$, we find

its mapping rule from $\text{Map}_{\text{CTB}\rightarrow\text{TCT}}$. The mapping rule result can be either $(A_{\text{tct}} \rightarrow B_{\text{tct}}C_{\text{tct}}, A_{\text{ctb}} \rightarrow B_{\text{ctb}}C_{\text{ctb}}, s_{\text{tct}}, m_{\text{tct}}, e_{\text{tct}})$ or $(A_{\text{tct}} \rightarrow B_{\text{tct}}C_{\text{tct}}, A_{\text{ctb}} \rightarrow B_{\text{ctb}}C_{\text{ctb}}, s_{\text{tct}}, e_{\text{tct}})$. Then we traverse all grammars in G_{cky}, if the grammar matches with $(A_{\text{tct}} \rightarrow B_{\text{tct}}C_{\text{tct}}, s_{\text{tct}}, m_{\text{tct}}, e_{\text{tct}})$ or partially matches with $(A_{\text{tct}} \rightarrow B_{\text{tct}}C_{\text{tct}}, s_{\text{tct}}, e_{\text{tct}})$, then its weight will be increased by value α. The value α should be adjusted according to development set.

7. Reparse the sentence using CKY parsing algorithm with G_{cky} and leaves : $\text{tr}_1 \cdots \text{tr}_n$.

6 Experiments

6.1 Data Set

The task organizers have offered 17,758 annotated sentences for train our model. They are chosen from TCT corpus. Before they share us for train, the trees which have more than two leaves have been processed to ensure all the grammars in the train sentences containing only unaries and binaries. We use the training section of CTB7.0 to to train the models of CTB. The training sections are selected by the documents of LDC2010T07. The total number of CTB training is 46,572. To adjust some parameters in our model, we split a development data set from the entire training corpus. After get the value of these parameters, we retrain our system using all the corpus. Table 1 shows the statistics of the data set.

Corpus	Section	# sent.
Parameter Adjusting	Train	15802
	Devel	1756
CTB7.0	Train	46572
Final Test	Train	17558
	Test	1000

Table 1: Statistics of Data Set.

6.2 Parameter Adjusting

First we look at how bagging numbers k influence the the baseline bagging system. In this work, we set the bagging num $k = 15$. Figure 2 displays the result. As is shown in Figure 2, the performance increments gradually when the bagging number becomes larger. The performance is better than a single model since the bagging number is 3.

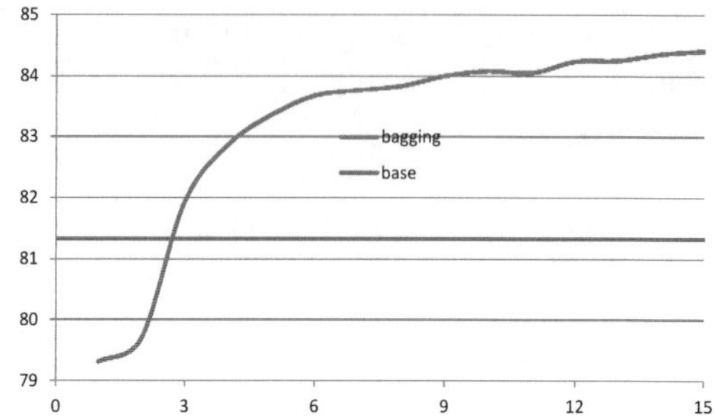

Figure 2: Bagging results. The baseline denotes the model which doesn't exploit sampling and bagging.

Second we adjust the parameter α by development also. The α should be less than 1 by intuition. We gradually increase the value of α from 0.5 to 1.0. Figure 3 display the results on development set. According to the results, we set $\alpha = 0.9$

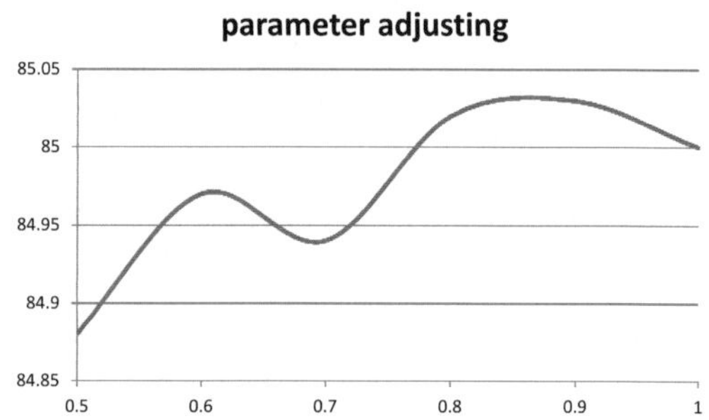

Figure 3: Parameter adjusting result.

6.3 Final Results

First, to get a better understanding of our system, we show the results on the development data set. **Berkeley** denotes the result of Berkeley parser which doesn't use bagging. **Bbag** denotes our baseline bagging system which uses only TCT corpus. **Cbag** denotes our final system which uses both TCT corpus and CTB corpus. Table 2 displays the results.

System	P	R	F1
Cbag	**85.04**	**85.03**	**85.03**
Bbag	84.4	84.42	84.41
Berkeley	81.31	81.35	81.33

Table 2: Final results on the development set.

Table 3 displays our final result on test data which the task organizers offered. **BestClosedSingle** denotes the best closed system of the task.

From the results in both Table 2 and Table 3, we can find that bagging is a very simple and effective method to combine multiple TreeBanks.

System	P	R	F1
Cbag	**81.20**	**81.12**	**81.16**
Bbag	80.23	80.11	80.17
BestClosedSingle	76.35	76.20	76.27

Table 3: Final results on the development set.

7 Conclusions and Future Work

In this paper, we propose to exploit bagging to enhance the performance PSG parsing. The method is very simple and effective. The bagging is implemented upon a CKY reparsing algorithm. We introduce CKY reparsing algorithm in detail and introduce the preprocess binarization algorithm. By bagging, we can achieve increases nearly 3% in F1 score. Further, we exploit bagging to integrate CTB corpus to enhance PSG parsing. And finally, we have achieved further increases nearly 1% after using CTB7.0.

In the future, we will investigate the transformation methods to better integrate multiple TreeBanks. We are very interested in statistical models to finish this transformation.

Acknowledgments

This work was supported by National Natural Science Foundation of China (NSFC) via grant 61133012, the National 863 Major Projects via grant 2011AA01A207, and the National 863 Leading Technology Research Project via grant 2012AA011102.

References

Michael Collins. 1999. *Head-Driven Statistical Models for Natural Language Parsing*. Ph.D. thesis, Pennsylvania University.

Slav Petrov and Dan Klein. 2007. Improved inference for unlexicalized parsing. In *Human Language Technologies 2007: The Conference of the North American Chapter of the Association for Computational Linguistics; Proceedings of the Main Conference*, pages 404–411, Rochester, New York, April. Association for Computational Linguistics.

Slav Petrov, Leon Barrett, Romain Thibaux, and Dan Klein. 2006. Learning accurate, compact, and interpretable tree annotation. In *Proceedings of the 21st International Conference on Computational Linguistics and 44th Annual Meeting of the Association for Computational Linguistics*, pages 433–440, Sydney, Australia, July. Association for Computational Linguistics.

Zhou Qiang. 2004. Annotation scheme for chinese treebank. *Journal of Chinese Information Processing*, 18(4):1–8.

Kenji Sagae and Alon Lavie. 2006. Parser combination by reparsing. In *Proceedings of the Human Language Technology Conference of the NAACL, Companion Volume: Short Papers*, pages 129–132, New York City, USA, June. Association for Computational Linguistics.

Xinying Song, Shilin Ding, and Chin-Yew Lin. 2008. Better binarization for the CKY parsing. In *Proceedings of the 2008 Conference on Empirical Methods in Natural Language Processing*, pages 167–176, Honolulu, Hawaii, October. Association for Computational Linguistics.

Nianwen Xue, Fei Xia, Fu-Dong Chiou, and Martha Palmer. 2005. The penn chinese treebank: Phrase structure annotation of a large corpus. *Natural Language Engineering*, 11(2):207–238.

Yue Zhang and Stephen Clark. 2009. Transition-based parsing of the chinese treebank using a global discriminative model. In *Proceedings of the 11th International Conference on Parsing Technologies (IWPT'09)*, pages 162–171, Paris, France, October. Association for Computational Linguistics.

Hui Zhang, Min Zhang, Chew Lim Tan, and Haizhou Li. 2009. K-best combination of syntactic parsers. In *Proceedings of the 2009 Conference on Empirical Methods in Natural Language Processing*, pages 1552–1560, Singapore, August. Association for Computational Linguistics.

Parsing TCT with Split Conjunction Categories

Li Dongchen
Key Laboratory of Machine Perception and Intelligence,
Speech and Hearing Research Center
Peking University, China
lidc@cis.pku.edu.cn

Wu Xihong
Key Laboratory of Machine Perception and Intelligence,
Speech and Hearing Research Center
Peking University, China
wxh@cis.pku.edu.cn

Abstract

We demonstrate that an unlexicalized PCFG with refined conjunction categories can parse much more accurately than previously shown, by making use of simple, linguistically motivated state splits, which break down false independence assumptions latent in a vanilla treebank grammar and reflect the Chinese idiosyncratic grammatical property. Indeed, its performance is the best result in the 3nd Chinese Parsing Evaluation of single model. This result has showed that refine the function words to represent Chinese subcat frame is a good method. An unlexicalized PCFG is much more compact, easier to replicate, and easier to interpret than more complex lexical models, and the parsing algorithms are simpler, more widely understood, of lower asymptotic complexity, and easier to optimize.

1 Introduction

In recent years, most research on parsing has focused on English and parsing on English has reported good performance (Charniak 2000, Collins 1999, Petrov 2006, 2008). However, parsing accuracy on Chinese is generally significantly inferior.

According to the first and second Chinese parsing evaluations (CIPS-ParsEval-2009(Qiang Zhou, 2009) and CIPS-SIGHAN-ParsEval-2010((Qiang Zhou, 2010)), the evaluation results in the Chinese clause and sentence levels show that the complex sentence parsing is still a big challenge for the Chinese language.

Other work has also investigated aspects of automatic grammar refinement, for example, Chiang and Bikel (2002) learn annotations such as head rules in a constrained declarative language for tree-adjoining grammars.

Probabilistic context-free grammars (PCFGs) underlie most high-performance parsers in one way or another (Collins, 1999; Charniak, 2000; Charniak and Johnson, 2005). However, as demonstrated in Charniak (1996) and Klein and Manning (2003), a PCFG which simply takes the empirical rules and probabilities off of a treebank does not perform well.

In this paper, we investigate the learning of a grammar consistent with a treebank at the level of evaluation symbols (such as NP, VP, etc.)

Klein and Manning (2003) addressed this question from a linguistic perspective, starting with a Markov grammar and manually splitting symbols in response to observed linguistic trends in the data. For example, the symbol NP might be split into the subsymbol NP^S in subject position and the subsymbol NP^VP in object position.

Matsuzaki et al. (2005), Prescher (2005), Petrov (2006) induce splits in a fully automatic fashion.

Klein (2003) parses with a well-engineered grammar (as supplied for English). It is fast, accurate, requires much less memory, and in many real-world uses, lexical preferences are unavailable or inaccurate across domains or genres and the unlexicalized parser will perform just as well as a lexicalized parser. However, the factored parser will sometimes provide greater accuracy on English through knowledge of lexical dependencies. Moreover, it is considerably better than the PCFG parser alone for most other languages (with less rigid word order), including German, Chinese, and Arabic.

Automatically split-merge approach is 4% higher than manual unlexicalized parsing in English. However, this may not be the case in Chinese due to the idiosyncratic property and specialized annotation style in Chinese Penn Treebank. With carefully engineered split from linguistic perspective and automatically split approach, we achieve a relatively accuracy interpretable parser.

Incorporating language-dependent idiosyncratic property improved performance on many languages. As for Chinese parsing, there is still a long way to go.

High-performance parsers on English have employed linguistically-motivated features. (Collins 1998) and (Charniak 2000) make use of lexicalized nonterminals, which allows lexical items' idiosyncratic parsing preferences to be modeled, but the preferences between head words and modifiers are language-dependent. Furthermore, model in (Collins 1998) include distance measure, subcat frame features and wh-movement, which are all tightly interrelated to particular language. (Charniak 1997) uses a scheme of clustering the head words like that in (Pereira, Tishby 1993).

There have been some attempts to adapt parsers developed for English to Chinese.

Adapting lexicalized parsers to other languages is not a trivial task as it requires at least the specification of head rules, and has had limited success. (Bikel, 2000) has transplanted lexicalized parsing to Chinese and the results on English and Chinese are far from equal. Adapting unlexicalized parsers appears to be equally difficult: (Levy and Manning, 2003) adapt the unlexicalized parser of (Klein and Manning, 2003) to Chinese. Automatically splitting grammars like the one of Matsuzaki it al. (2005) and Petrov et al. (2006) require a Treebank not additionally hand tailored to English. (Petro, 2007) exhibited a very accurate category split-and-merge approach without any language dependent modifications. This automatically inducing latent structure generalizes well across language boundaries and results in state of the art performance for Chinese.

All above are probabilistic methods on the utility of PCFGs, but the same situation is in other grammar systems. SPATTER parser based on decision-tree learning techniques in Magerman (1995) highly involves special characters of words. 30 binary questions represent 30 different binary partitions of the word vocabulary, and these questions are defined such that it is possible to identify each word by asking all 30 questions. Bikel (2000) adapts stochastic TAG model on English (Chiang, 2000) to Chinese and report Label Precision below 75%.

2 Linguistic Character of Chinese

Chinese is language with less morphology and more mixed headedness than English. As Levy and Manning (2003) showed, Chinese has a rather different set of salient ambiguities from the perspective of statistical parsing

Although basic linguistic discipline is quite the same between English and Chinese, There are salient differences which distinguish the two languages for purposes of statistical parsing. Chinese makes less use of morphology than English; whereas English is largely left-headed and right-branching, Chinese is more mixed.

Furthermore, the best-performing lexicalized PCFGs have increasingly made use of subcategorization. Charniak (2000) shows the value his parser gains from parent annotation of nodes. Collins (1999) uses a range of linguistically motivated and carefully hand-engineered subcategorizations to break down wrong context-freedom assumptions of the naive Penn treebank covering PCFG. Subcategorization is proven to be important whereas subcategorization is tightly relevant to function word, especially in Chinese.

3 Lexicalized Approach Is Incompetent

Although morphology variation is not explicit in Chinese, some function words around verbs distinguish their head verbal word tense. A straightforward way of incorporating this distinction is substitute Part-Of-Speech tag of function word to the word itself, similar to Hindle and Rooth's demonstration from PP attachment.

However, several results have brought into question how large a role lexicalization plays in such parsers. Johnson (1998) showed that the performance of an unlexicalized PCFG over the Penn Treebank could be improved enormously simply by annotating each node by its parent category. Klein and Manning (2003) exploited the capacity of an unlexicalized PCFG and affirmed the value of linguistic analysis for feature discovery. An unlexicalized PCFG is easier to interpret reason about, and improve than the more complex lexicalized models. The grammar representation is much more compact, and has much smaller grammar constants. We take this as a reflection of the fundamental sparseness of the lexical dependency information available in the Penn Treebank. As a speech person would say, one million words of training data just isn't enough. Even for topics central to the treebank's Wall Street Journal text, such as stocks, many very plausible dependencies occur only once, for example stocks stabilized, while many others occur not at all, for example stocks skyrocketed.2(2This observation motivates various class- or similarity based approaches to combating sparseness, and this remains a promising avenue of work, but success in this area has proven somewhat elusive, and, at any rate, current lexicalized PCFGs do simply use exact word matches if available, and interpolate with syntactic category-based estimates when they are not.) This is equally true for function word.

We do not want to argue that lexical selection is not a worthwhile component of a state-of the-art parser, though perhaps its usage method should be carefully tuned.

In this paper, we describe simple, linguistically motivated annotations which do much to close the gap between Chinese and English parsing models.

4 Tag Splitting Approach is Appropriate Here

The idea that part-of-speech tags are not fine-grained enough to abstract away from specific-word behavior is a cornerstone of lexicalization. Klein (2003) claimed the English Penn tag set conflates various grammatical distinctions that are commonly made in traditional and generative grammar, and brought performance improvement by part-of-tag splitting.

Just as the case in English Treebank, The Chinese Treebank tag set is sometimes too coarse to capture syntactic structure distinction. The Chinese Penn tag set conflates various grammatical distinctions that are commonly made in traditional and generative grammar. Thus a parser could hope to refine some tag to get useful information.

Some tags are too coarse to capture traditional grammatical distinctions. For example, coordinating conjunctions and subordinating conjunctions are collapsed to the unique tag "c". Furthermore, coordinating conjunctions ("和", "与", "而", "并且", "既", "不单是", "乃至于", "不论") all get the tag "c" in Tsinghua Chinese Treebank, However, there are exclusively noun-modifying conjunctions ("及", "兼"), exclusively verb-modifying conjunctions ("并且"), predominantly noun-modifying and subordinately verb-modifying ones ("不止", "甚至"), predominantly verb-modifying and subordinately IP-modifying ones ("也"), and so on.

Many of these distinctions are captured by parent-annotation (noun-modifying conjunctions occur under NP, verb-modifying conjunctions occur under VP and IP-modifying conjunctions occurs under CP), some are captured by grand-parent-annotation (verb-modifying CS occur with grandparent VP and parent ADVP, IP-modifying CS occur with grandparent CP and parent ADVP). But some are not (both subordinating conjunctions and complementizers appear under SBAR). What is more, the grammatical relation tag has something to do with particular function word tag, and its mapping is complicated. Thus we hope to get value from subcategorized tags for specific lexemes.

5 Hierarchical Category Refinement of Function Words

Function word is a mine full of linguistic discriminative treasure, whereas the way how its power should be exploited does matters. We presented a flexible approach which refines the function words in a hierarchy fashion where the hierarchy layers provide different granularity of specificity. We expect to compare the utility of different granularity in the hierarchy and select the most effective layer.

As in Zhou (2004), every Chinese sentence in Tsinghua Chinese Treebank is annotated with a complete parse tree, where each non-terminal constituent is assigned with two tags. One is the syntactic constituent tag, which describes its external functional relation with other constituents in the parse tree. The other is the grammatical relation tag, which describes the internal structural relation of its sub-components. These two tag sets consist of 16 and 27 tags respectively. They form an integrated annotation for the syntactic constituent in a parse tree through top-down and bottom-up descriptions.

In all function words, conjunction stand out to be essential helpful in predicting the syntactic structure and syntactic label. The refinement of conjunction words category is beneficial both to labeling the syntactic constituent tag and to labeling the grammatical relation tag.

The most obvious distinction among conjunctions is

First we split off conjunctions with the Distinguishment whether they are structural conjunctions or logical conjunctions. We refer structural conjunctions to the conjunctions which conjunct two nominal phrases. If a structural conjunction is deleted from a sentence, the sentence will be illegal in accordance to Chinese grammar. On the other hand, logical conjunctions refer to the conjunctions which conjunctions two verbal phrases.

In structural conjunctions, there are two major subcategories. The first one is coordination conjunctions which can be deeply divided into attachment conjunctions and selection conjunctions. Attachment conjunctions may represent correspondence, range or enlargement, while selection conjunctions represent the "or" relation, whether before the former option or the latter option.

Logical conjunctions are the ones representing logic coordination, transition, preference, progression, condition, cause and effect or purpose. Note that almost all the logical conjunctions can be divided by whether they are modifying the former clause or the latter clause. For example, the conjunctions representing cause and effect contains "because" and "so", where "because" should be modifying the cause, and "so" should be modifying the effect. The condition conjunctions are relatively complicated and divided separately.

6 Experimental Setup

We ran experiments on TCT. The training and test data set splits are described in Table below.

Treebank	Train Dataset	Develop Dataset	Test Dataset
TCT(Qiang Zhou, 2004)	16000 sentences	800 sentences	758 sentences

Table 1. Experiment DataSet Setup

Tsinghua Chinese Treebank is a 1,000,000 words Chinese treebank covering a balanced collection of journalistic, literary, academic, and other documents.

For our model, input trees were annotated or transformed to refine the conjunction word categories. Given a set of transformed trees, we viewed the local trees as grammar rewrite rules in the standard way, and used smoothed maximum-likelihood estimates for rule probabilities.

To parse the grammar, we used an array-based Java implementation of a generalized CKY scheme and automatically split and merge approach in Petrov (2006).

7 Final Results

We took the final model and used it to parse the specified test set in the 3nd Chinese Parsing Evaluation which contains 1000 sentences, and achieved the best precision, recall and F-measure. Because out model employed no lexical information, it is time and space efficient.

Table 1 Final results

SC_F1	ULC_P	ULC_R	ULC_F1
92.50%	87.44%	87.43%	87.44%

Table 2. Experiment Results of SC and ULC

NoCross_P	LC_P	LC_R	LC_F1
87.44%	78.01%	78.00%	78.01%

Table 2. Experiment Results of SC and ULC

Tot4_LC_P	Tot4_LC_R	Tot4_LC_F1
76.81%	76.66%	76.74%

Table 2. Experiment Results of SC and ULC

Where LR = label recall, LP = label precision, F1 = F-measure, EX = exact match, AC = average crossing, NC = no crossing, 2C = 2 or less crossing.

8 Conclusion

The advantages of unlexicalized grammars with refined function word categories are clear enough – easy to devise, easy to estimate, easy to parse with, and time- and space-efficient.
Here, we have shown that, surprisingly, simply refining the conjunction categories in a compact unlexicalized PCFG can parse accurately.

Acknowledgements
This research is supported in part by the National Basic Research Program of China (No.2013CB329304) and the Key Program of National Social Science Foundation of China (No. 12&ZD119).

References

Zhou Qiang. Annotation Scheme for Chinese Treebank. Journal of Chinese Information Processing. (2004)

Petrov, Klein, 2006. Learning Accurate, Compact, and Interpretable Tree Annotation , in ACL' 06.

N. Xue, F.-D. Chiou, and M. Palmer. Building a large scale annotated Chinese corpus. In COLING '02, 2002.

Qiang Zhou. Chinese Treebank Annotation Scheme. Journal of Chinese Information, 18(4), p1-8. (2004)

Qiang Zhou, Yuemei Li. Evaluation report of CIPS-ParsEval-2009. In Proc. of First Workshop on Chinese Syntactic Parsing Evaluation, Beijing China, Nov. 2009. pIII—XIII. (2009)

Qiang Zhou, Jingbo Zhu. Chinese Syntactic Parsing Evaluation. Proc. of CIPS-SIGHAN Joint Conference on Chinese Language Processing (CLP-2010), Beijing, August 2010, pp 286-295. (2010)

E. Charniak and M. Johnson. 2005. Coarse-to-fine n-best parsing and maxent discriminative reranking. In ACL'05, p. 173–180.

E. Charniak. 2000. A maximum–entropy–inspired parser. In NAACL '00, p. 132–139.

D. Chiang and D. Bikel. 2002. Recovering latent information in treebanks. In Computational Linguistics.

M. Collins. 1999. Head-Driven Statistical Models for Natural Language Parsing. Ph.D. thesis, U. of Pennsylvania.

M. Johnson. 1998. PCFG models of linguistic tree representations. Computational Linguistics, 24:613–632.

D. Klein and C. Manning. 2003. Accurate unlexicalized parsing. ACL '03, p. 423–430.

T. Matsuzaki, Y. Miyao, and J. Tsujii. 2005. Probabilistic CFG with latent annotations. In ACL '05, p. 75–82.

D. Prescher. 2005. Inducing head-driven PCFGs with latent heads: Refining a tree-bank grammar for parsing. In ECML'05.

S. Sekine and M. J. Collins. 1997. EVALB bracket scoring program. http://nlp.cs.nyu.edu/evalb/.

E. Charniak, S. Goldwater, and M. Johnson. 1998. Edge-based best-first chart parsing. 6th Wkshop on Very Large Corpora.

E. Charniak,M. Johnson, et al. 2006. Multi-level coarse-to-fine PCFG Parsing. In HLT-NAACL '06.

Z. Chi. 1999. Statistical properties of probabilistic context-free grammars. In Computational Linguistics.

M. Collins. 1999. Head-Driven Statistical Models for Natural Language Parsing. Ph.D. thesis, U. of Pennsylvania.

D. Gildea. 2001. Corpus variation and parser performance.EMNLP '01, pages 167–202.

R. Levy and C. Manning. 2003. Is it harder to parse Chinese, or the Chinese treebank? In ACL '03, pages 439–446.

M. Marcus, B. Santorini, and M. Marcinkiewicz. 1993. Building a large annotated corpus of English: The Penn Treebank. In Computational Linguistics.

W. Skut, B.Krenn, T. Brants, and H. Uszkoreit. 1997. An annotation scheme for free word order languages. In Conference on Applied Natural Language Processing.

H. Sun and D. Jurafsky. 2004. Shallow semantic parsing of Chinese. In HLT-NAACL '04, pages 249–256.

K. Vijay-Shanker and A. Joshi. 1985. Some computational properties of Tree Adjoining Grammars. In ACL '85.

N. Xue, F.-D. Chiou, and M. Palmer. 2002. Building a large scale annotated Chinese corpus. In COLING '02.

Parsing Simplified Chinese and Traditional Chinese with Sentence Structure Grammar

Xiangli Wang
Japan Patent Information Organization,
Tokyo, Japan
xiangli_wang@japio.or.jp

Terumasa Ehara
Yamanashi Eiwa College,
Yamanashi, Japan
eharate@{yamanashi-eiwa, y-eiwa}.ac.jp

Yuan Li
The University of Tokyo,
Tokyo, Japan
liyuan@is.s.u-tokyo.ac.jp

Abstract

We present a challenge to parse simplified Chinese and traditional Chinese with a same rule-based Chinese grammatical resource--- Chinese Sentence Structure Grammar: CSSG, which was developed based on a new grammar formalism idea: Sentence Structure Grammar: SSG. We participate in the simplified Chinese parsing task and the traditional Chinese parsing task of CLP 2012 with a same rule-based chart parser implemented the CSSG. The experiments show that the CSSG that was developed for covering simplified Chinese constructions can also analyze most traditional Chinese constructions.

1 Introduction

Chinese divides into simplified Chinese that is used in the mainland of China and Singapore, and traditional Chinese that is used in Taiwan and Hang Kong. Some treebank resources like Penn Chinese Treebank: CTB, Peking University Treebank: PKU, and Tsinghua Chinese Treebank: TCT had been built for training simplified Chinese parser (Yu, et al. 2010) while Sinica Treebank was developed for parsing traditional Chinese (Chen et al., 1999). Limit to our knowledge, there are still not grammatical resources that analyze both simplified Chinese and traditional Chinese.

Recently, a rule-based Chinese grammatical resource --- Chinese Sentence Structure Grammar: CSSG had been developed based on the idea of Sentence Structure Grammar: SSG (Wang and Miyazaki, 2007; Wang et al., 2011, Wang et al., 2012). The CSSG was developed to cover most constructions that are listed in well-discussed simplified Chinese grammatical literatures (Zhu, 1982; Liu et al., 1996; Fan, 1998; Xue and Xia, 2000), and many phenomena that are not discussed in above literatures but very typical and used frequently by Chinese native speakers.

We assume that a rule-based grammatical resource should analyze both simplified Chinese and traditional Chinese if there are no obvious differences between their grammatical constructions. Aiming at verifying this assumptions, we participate in the simplified Chinese parsing task (task 3) and the traditional Chinese parsing task (task 4) of CLP 2012 with the same rule-based parser that was implemented the grammatical resource CSSG.

CSSG includes two parts of resources: the grammatical rules and a simplified Chinese morphological dictionary. We transfer the simplified Chinese characters of the dictionary to traditional Chinese characters for obtaining a traditional Chinese morphological dictionary. We parse the test data of task 3 and task 4 with the same CSSG rules but different morphological dictionaries (simplified or traditional Chinese characters). We convert CSSG parsing trees to TCT-style trees and Sinica-style trees for participating in the evaluations of the two tasks. The experiments show that the CSSG rules can parse both simplified Chinese and traditional Chinese, but the performance of the latter is lower than the former. We noticed that a few traditional Chinese constructions are different from simplified Chinese.

This paper is organized as bellow: in section 2, we introduce what is CSSG; in section 3, we compare CSSG with TCT and Sinica Treebank; in section 4, we analyze the experimental results of the two tasks; in the last section, we conclude our work.

2 Chinese Sentence Structure Grammar

Chinese Sentence Structure Grammar: CSSG is a rule-based Chinese grammatical resource that was developed based on the idea of Sentence Structure Grammar: SSG.

SSG is a new idea to formalize grammatical rules. Sentence Structure Grammar has 3 main ideas (Wang et al., 2011; Wang et al., 2012):

1) Treat the construction of a sentence as a whole, which consists of a predicate (or more) and its semantic-related constituents.
2) Classify predicate verbs according to their semantic properties.
3) Indicate the semantic relations between predicate and its semantic-related constituents directly on parsing tree.

Predicate	Ex.	Sematic roles
Vad	飞/fly	Agent, Direction
Vaod	扔/throw	Agent, Object, Direction
Vaol	放/put	Agent, Object, Location

Table 1: examples of the predicate classification of CSSG

SSG is a kind of context-free grammar, but it differs from Phrase Structure Grammar: PSG: 1) the latter describes a sentence with some context-free phrase rules, but the former treats a sentence as a whole sentential construction, which consists of a predicate (or more) and its semantically-related constituents; 2) the former classify predicate verbs according to their semantic properties. For instance, as shown in figure 1, "停/park" and "飞/fly" have different semantic properties. "停/park" is a kind of verb that needs an agent, an object and a location. In contrast, "飞/fly" is a kind of verb that needs an agent and a direction. As shown in table 1, predicate verbs can be classified according to their semantic properties; 3) the latter does only syntactic analysis while the former does syntactic analysis and semantic analysis simultaneously. The semantic role set of SSG should be designed based on the idea of the deep cases in Case Grammar, which a linguistic theory proposed by Fillmore (1968).

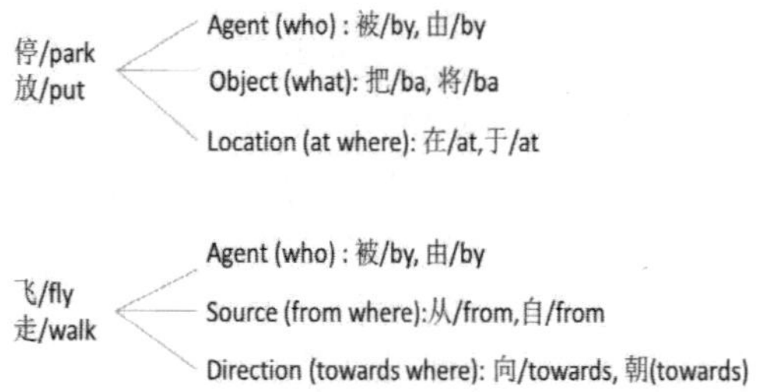

Figure 1: the semantic properties of verbs like "停/park" and "飞/fly"

For instance, a) is a passive construction. b) is the PSG rule set while c) is the SSG rule set to analyze a). Figure 2 and figure 3 show the SSG parsing tree and the PSG parsing tree of a). As shown in figure 2, the SSG parsing tree provide not only syntactic information like "np" and "sp" but sematic roles, like "Agent", "Object" and "Location", which indicate the semantic relations between the predicate and its semantic-related constituents. Syntactic parsing and sematic parsing can be done simultaneously with the formal grammatical framework SSG.

a. 车/car 被/by 约翰/John 停/park 在/at 停车场/car-park
The car is parked at the car-park by John

b. Rule1:s→ np vp
Rule2: vp→ pp vp
Rule3: vp→ v pp
Rule4: pp→p np
Rule5: np→ n
Rule6: sp→ sq

c. Rule1: s → Object bei Agent Vaol at Location
Rule2: Object→ np
Rule3: Agent→ np
Rule4: Location→ sp
Rule5: np→ n
Rule6: sp→ sq

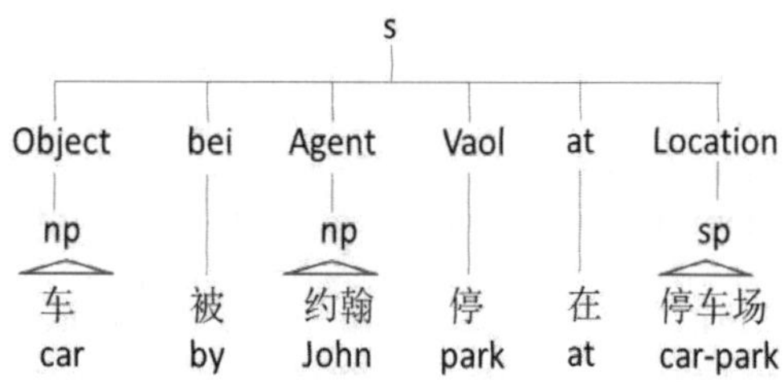

Figure 2: the SSG parsing tree of (a)

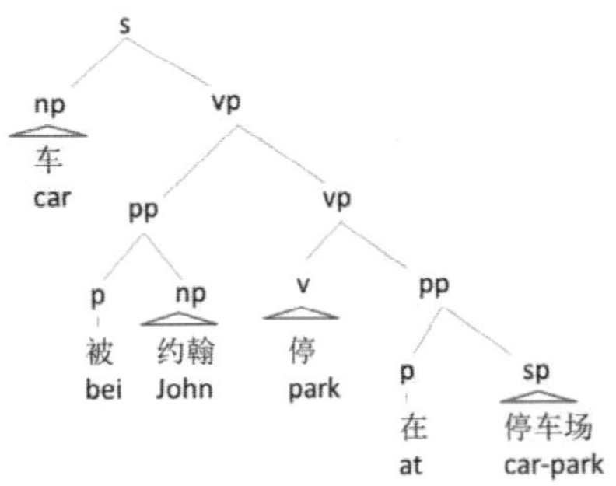

Figure 3: the PSG parsing tree of (a)

In CSSG, predicates are classified into 52 types according to their sematic properties. Table 1 shows some examples of the predicate classification. For instance, the type of verbs like "买/buy" or "拿/take" have same semantic property. They correspond to the same predicate-argument structure that is shown as figure 4. In CSSG, such semantic relations between a predicate and its arguments are showed on parsing rules directly. For instance, figure 5 shows the CSSG parsing tree of d): "买/buy" is the predicate, "他/he" is the agent case, "书店/bookshop" is the source case, "书/book" is the object case and "家/home" is the goal case. "把/ba" and "回/back" are treated as case-markers.

d. 他/he 从/from 书店/bookshop 把/ba 书/book 买/buy 回/back 家/home
He buys a book at the bookshop and takes it back home.

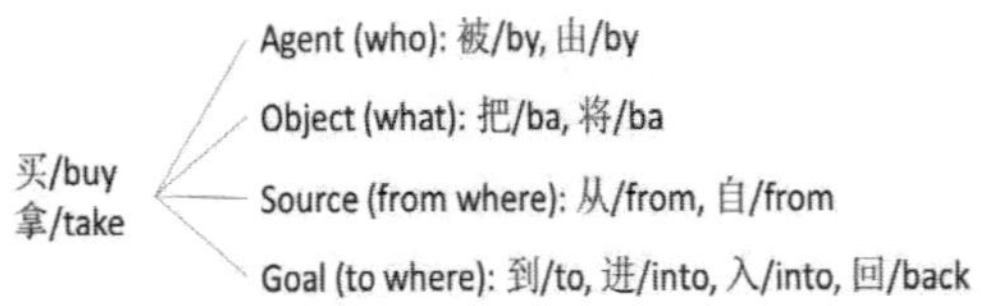

Figure 4: the semantic properties of the verbs like "买/buy" or "拿/take"

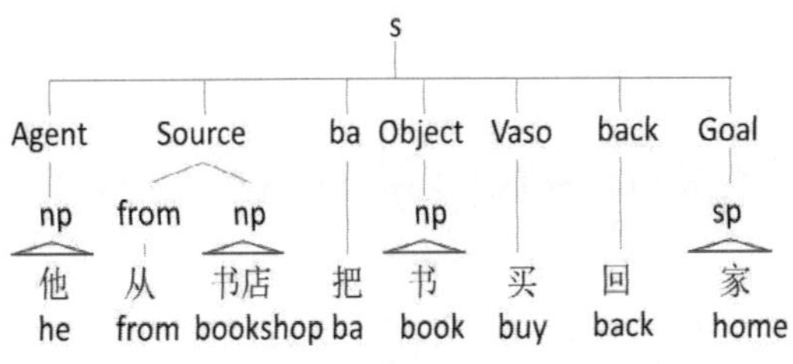

Figure 5: the CSSG parsing tree of (d)

CSSG includes two parts of resources: 8,511 grammatical rules and a morphological dictionary that contains 45,086 morphological entries.

The CSSG rules cover most constructions of simplified Chinese. Besides most constructions are listed in well-discussed simplified Chinese grammatical literatures (Zhu, 1982; Fan, 1998; Liu et al., 1996; Xue and Xia, 2000), the CSSG rules also cover many phenomena that were not discussed in above literatures but very typical and used frequently. For instance, e) is a ba-construction, f) is a bei-construction, g) is a topic construction, h) is not only a topic construction but a ba-construction and i) is not only a ba-construction but also a bei-construction. We observed many phenomena and found that there is a common feature in these different constructions, it is that one noun phrase "苹果 皮/skin of apples" is split into two parts, which have possessive relation each other but appear different syntactic positions in a sentence. Such constructions are called as "***apple-skin constructions***" in CSSG, and the possessive relation between the two split parts is indicated on the parsing tree. The CSSG rules analyze e), f), g), h) and i) as shown in figure 6, 7, 8, 9 and 10. "Object_of0" and " Ojbect_of1" show the possessive relation between "苹果/apple" and "皮/skin". Apple-skin constructions are used frequently by Chinese native speakers. We can make many sentences with them.

e. 约翰/John 把/ba 苹果/apple 削/peal 了/le 皮/skin
John pealed the apple's skin

f. 苹果/apple 被/by 约翰/him 削/peal 了/le 皮/skin
The skin of apples was pealed by John

g. 苹果/apple 约翰/John 削/peal 了/le 皮/skin
The apple, John pealed its skin

h. 苹果/apple 约翰/John 把/ba 皮/skin 削/peal 了/le
The apple, John pealed its skin

i. 苹果/apple 被/by 约翰/John 把/ba 皮/skin 削/peal 了/le
The skin of apples was pealed by John

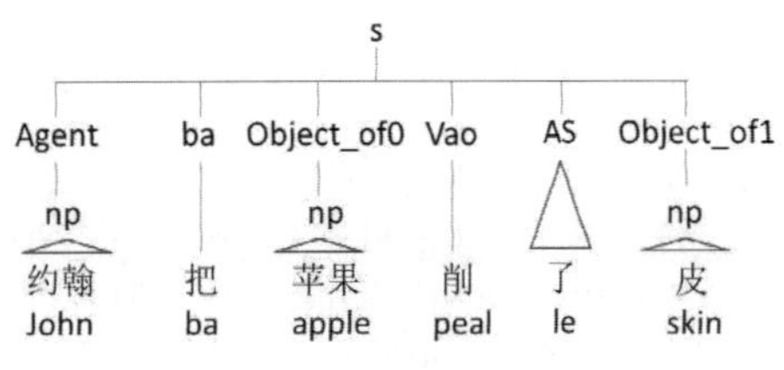

Figure 6: the CSSG parsing tree of (e)

The morphological dictionary of the CSSG includes two kinds of information: the morphology and its POS tag. Table 2 shows a small morphological dictionary for parsing a). The CSSG dictionary contains 45,086 simplified Chinese morphology entries. Table 3 shows the details of the dictionary. The word segmentation criteria and POS tag set of the CSSG were designed originally.

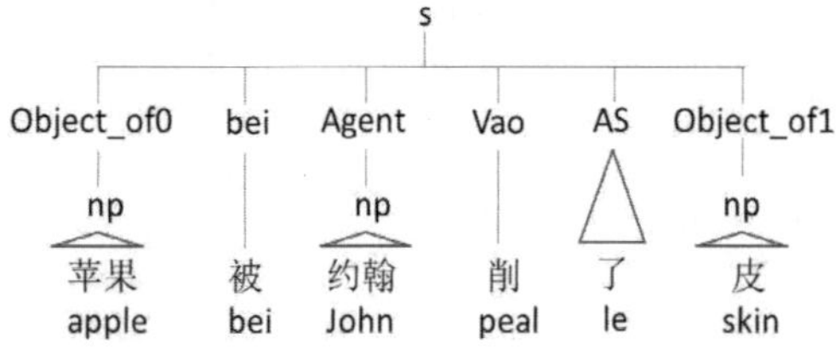

Figure 7: the CSSG parsing tree of (f)

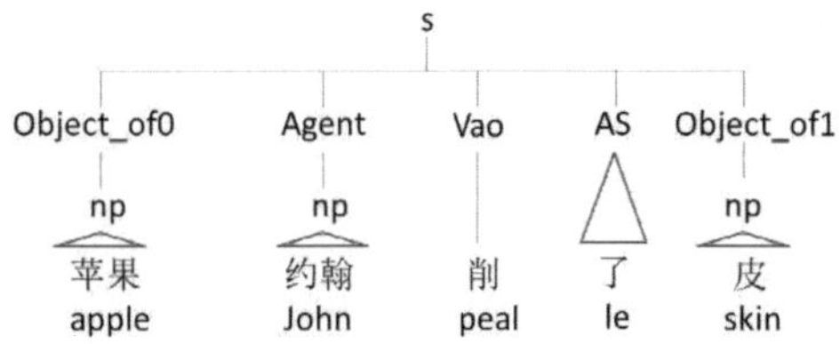

Figure 8: the CSSG parsing tree of (g)

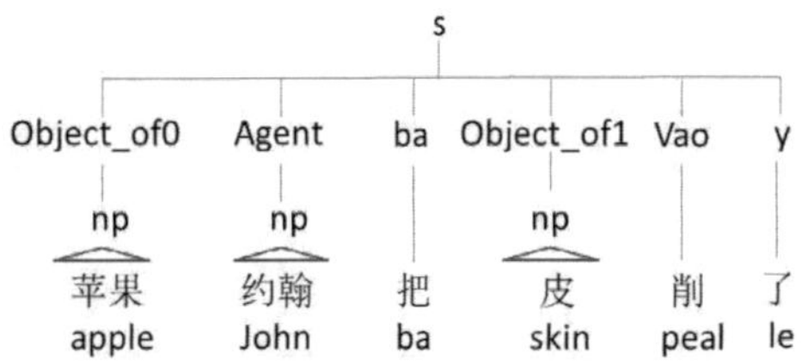

Figure 9: the CSSG parsing tree of (h)

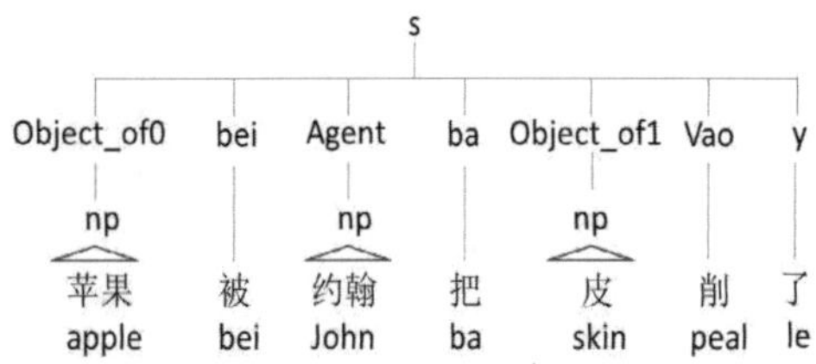

Figure 10: the CSSG parsing tree of (i)

Comparing with the existing Chinese treebanks, the design of the POS tag set of CSSG has some distinctive features. The major differences are: 1) verbs are classified according to their sematic properties; 2) some functional words are treated as a part of verbs in the existing treebanks are treated as Case-markers; 3) the localizers are divided into locative localizers and temporal localizers.

For instance, "买回/buy-back" is treated as one word in either TCT or CTB or Sinica Treebank, but in CSSG, as shown in figure 5, "买回/buy-back" is split into two words: "买/buy" and "回/back". "买/buy" is a predicate verb while "回/back" is a case-maker that marks a goal case.

Word	POS tag
车/car	n
约翰/John	n
停/park	Vaol
在/at	at
停车场/car-park	sq
被/by	bei

Table 2: a small dictionary for parsing (a)

part-of-speech	amount
verbs	6,878
nouns	26,191
adverbs	1,992
nominal verbs	5,028
temporal words	865
locative words	151
noun-modifier	2,439
measure words	446
pronouns	49
modal verbs	23
case markers	45
locative localizer	15
temporal localizer	17
others	947
total	45,086

Table 3: the details of the CSSG dictionary

j. 桌子/table 后/behind
Behind the table

k. 回/go-back 家/home 后/after
After going back home

Figure 11: the CSSG parsing trees of (j) and (k)

In every existing Chinese treebank, the words like "前" and "后" are treated as localizers. However, either "前" or "后" contains two notions: a locative notion and a temporal notion. For instance, "后/behind" in j) shows a location while "后/after" in k) indicates a period of time. In CSSG, such words are divided into two kinds of POSs: locative localizers and temporal localizers. A locative localizer leads a locative phrase while a temporal localizer leads a temporal phrase (as shown in figure 11).

3 Comparison between TCT, Sinica Treebank and CSSG

3.1 Tsinghua Chinese Treebank and CSSG

Tsinghua Chinese Treebank: TCT (Zhou, 2004) is used as the training data for the simplified Chinese parsing task. TCT and CSSG are very different grammatical resources.

	CSSG	TCT
Formalism	SSG	PSG
Form	Grammatical rules	Treebank
Word segmentation criteria	Original	Original
POS tag set	Original	Original
Phrase tag set	Original	Original
Semantic role set	Original	none

Table 4: the differences between CSSG and TCT

Their main differences are: 1) they were developed based on different formal grammatical framework. As shown in figure 2 and 3, the former is based on Context-free Phrase Structure Grammar: PSG while the latter is based on another kind of Context-free grammar formalism idea---Sentence Structure Grammar: SSG. Since PSG parses sentences in syntactic level but SSG analyze sentences more deeply, CSSG provides both syntactic information and semantic roles while TCT shows only syntactic information. Figure 2 is a CSSG parsing tree of a) that represents both phrase information and sematic role information. Figure 3 is a TCT parsing tree that shows only syntactic information; 2) CSSG is a rule-based grammatical resource while TCT is a Treebank. The designers and developers of the treebanks are usually different people. The designers draw up the annotation scheme first, then the developers annotate parsing trees according to the annotation scheme and their own intuition; in contrast, the designer and the developer of CSSG is the same person who designed and developed the CSSG rules introspectively to cover most simplified Chinese constructions; 3) both of them define the word segmentation criteria and POS tag set originally. For instance, as shown in figure 12 and figure 13, TCT treats "来自/come-from" as one verb while CSSG treats "来自/come-from" as two words: "来/come" is a predicate verb and "自/from" is treated as a case-marker that mark a source case for describing semantic roles precisely; 4) they design the phrase tag set originally. As shown in figure 12 and 13, verb phrases appear in TCT while there are no verb phrases in CSSG; their definitions of prepositional phrase are different; as shown in figure 11: CSSG and 14: TCT, both j) and k) are treated as locative phrases in TCT while j) is treated as a locative phrase and k) is treated as a temporal phrase in CSSG. Table 4 shows the differences between TCT and CSSG briefly.

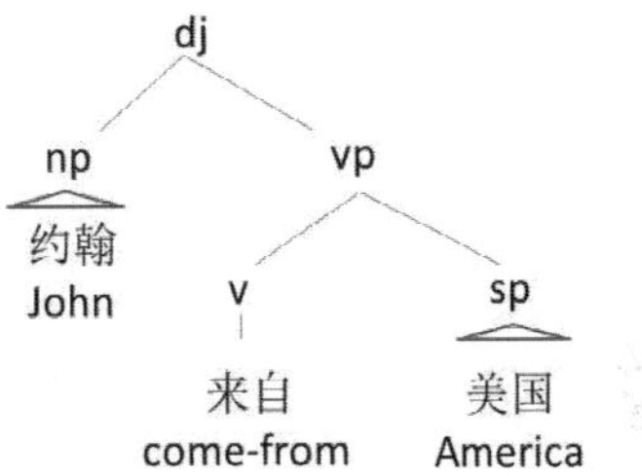

Figure 12: the TCT parsing tree of (l)

l. 约翰/John 来/come 自/from 美国/America
John comes from America

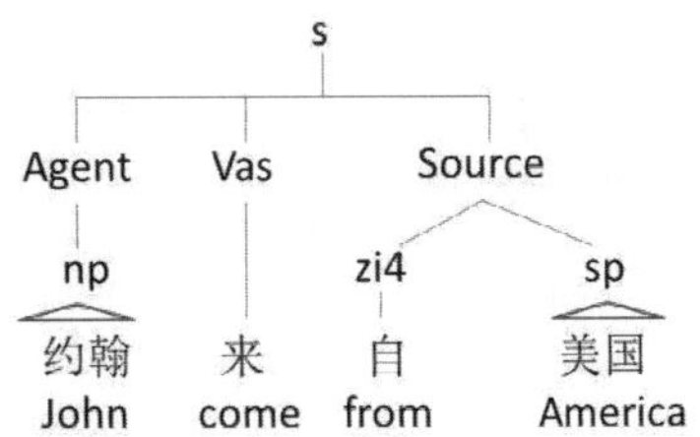

Figure 13: the CSSG parsing tree of (l)

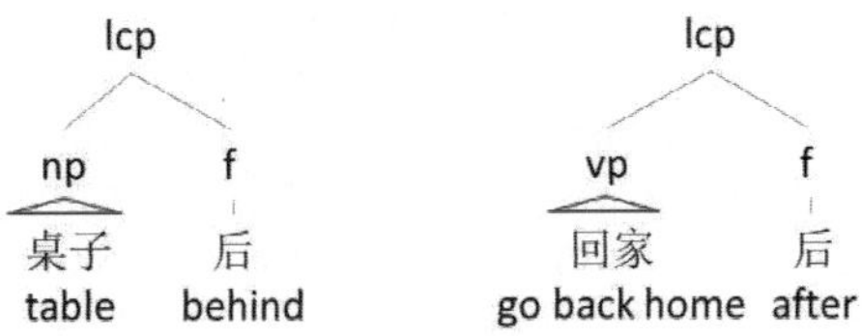

Figure 14: the TCT parsing trees of (j) and (k)

3.2 Sinica Treebank and CSSG

Sinica Treebank (Chen et al., 1999) is used as the training data for the traditional Chinese parsing task. CSSG are quite different from Sinica Treebank.

m. 那個/that 人/person 把/ba 老鼠/rat 帶/take 回/ back-to 茅屋/cottage
That man takes the rat back to the cottage

n. 約翰/John 從/from 房間/room 拿/take 出/out 一本/a 書/book
John takes a book out of the room

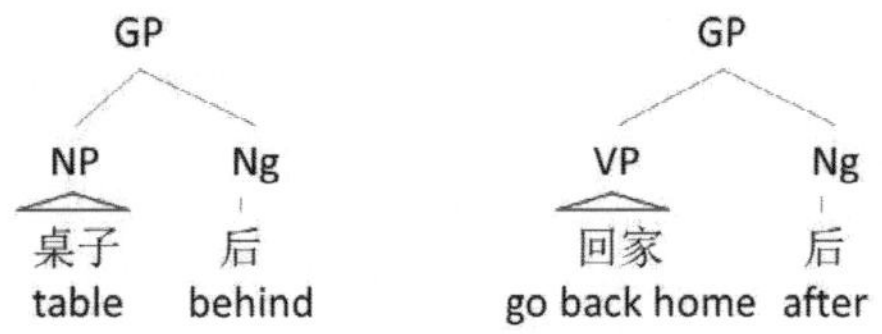

Figure 15: the TCT parsing trees of (j) and (k)

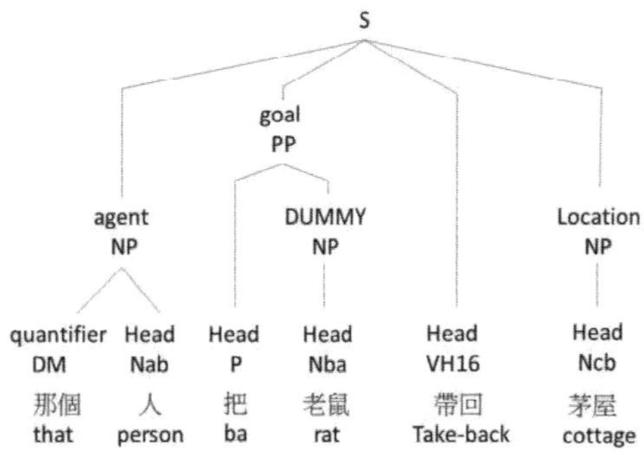

Figure 16: the Sinica parsing tree of (m)

They differ from each other in 6 respects: 1) Sinica Treebank consists of traditional Chinese parsing trees while CSSG is developed for covering simplified Chinese constructions; 2) the former is a rule-based grammatical resource while the latter is a Treebank; 3) both Sinica Treebank and CSSG represent syntactic and semantic information simultaneously, but their formal grammatical framework are different. Sinica Treebank is based on Information-based Case Grammar: ICG, which is a kind of unification-based formalism, and describe syntactic and semantic information in lexical entries (Chen and Huang, 1990); in contrast, CSSG is based on Sentence Structure Grammar: SSG, which is a kind of context-free grammar formalism that indicate both syntactic and semantic constraints in grammatical rules directly; 4) they define the word segmentation criteria and POS tag set originally. For instance, as figure 16 and 17 shown, "那個/that" is treated as one word in Sinica Treebank, but treated as two words in CSSG. "帶回/take-back" is one word in Sinica Treebank while it is split into a verb "帶/take" and a case-marker "回/back" that marks a goal case "茅屋/cottage" in CSSG; 5) they define the phrase tag set originally. For instance, the word "后" can lead not only a locative constituent like j) but a temporal constituent such as k). In Sinica Treebank, Both j) and k) are analyzed as a locative phrase (shown in figure 15); in contrast, the locative constituent is treated as a locative phrase while the temporal constituent is treat a temporal phrase in CSSG (shown in figure 10); 6) they define semantic role set originally. Their designs of the semantic role sets are very different. Figure 16 shows the Sinica-tree while figure 17 represents the CSSG tree of m). "老鼠/rat" is treated as a goal case and "茅屋/cottage" is analyzed as a location case in Sinica Treebank while "老鼠/rat" is regarded as an object case and "茅屋/cottage" is analyzed as a goal case in CSSG. As shown in figure 18 and 19, the source case "從/from 房間/room" in CSSG is treated as a location case in Sinica Treebank. Table 5 shows the differences between these two resources briefly.

	CSSG	Sinica Treebank
Character	Simplified	Traditional
Formalism	SSG	ICG
Form	Grammatical rules	Treebank
Word segmentation criteria	Original	Original
POS tag set	Original	Original
Phrase tag set	Original	Original
Semantic role set	Original	Original

Table 5: the differences between CSSG and Sinica Treebank

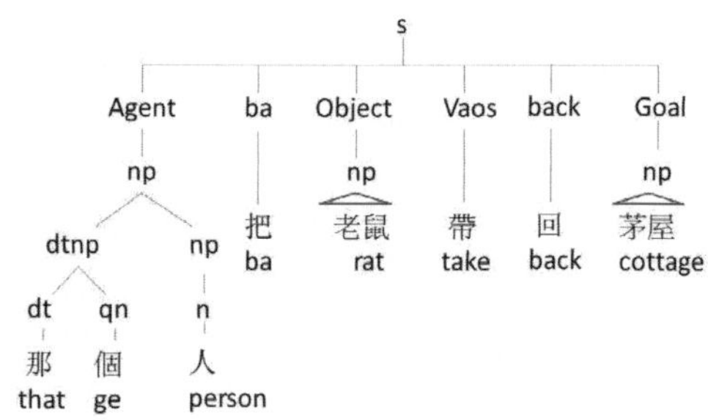

Figure 17: the CSSG parsing tree of (m)

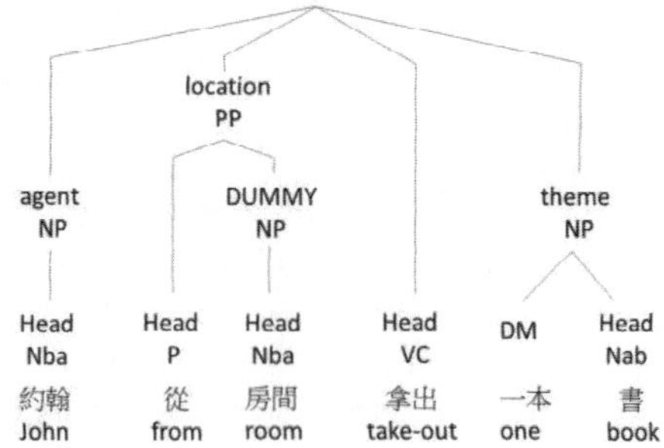

Figure 18: the Sinica parsing tree of (n)

Figure 19: the CSSG parsing tree of (n)

4 Experimental Results

4.1 Experimental Setting

There are two parsing tasks in CLP2012: the simplified Chinese parsing task (task 3) and the traditional Chinese parsing task (task 4). Task 3 includes two subtasks: CCG parsing task and PSG parsing task while Task 4 includes two sub-tasks: sentence parsing task and semantic role labeling task. For each sub-task, there are two tracks: the closed track and the open track. Our tasks are all in the open tracks. We participate in the open tracks of the PSG parsing sub-task of task 3 and both the two sub-tasks of task 4.

CSSG includes the grammatical rules and a simplified Chinese morphological dictionary. For participating in both simplified Chinese parsing task and traditional Chinese parsing task, we transfer the simplified Chinese characters of the dictionary of CSSG to traditional Chinese characters to obtain a traditional Chinese morphological dictionary.

For instance, the simplified Chinese sentence a) can be transferred into a traditional Chinese sentence o). As shown in figure 2 and 20, a) and o) have the same construction. We can parse o) also with CSSG if there was a traditional Chinese morphological dictionary shown in table 6. We can transfer the small dictionary shown in table 1 to traditional Chinese characters to obtain the dictionary shown in table 6.

Word	POS tag
車/car	n
約翰/John	n
停/park	Vaol
在/at	at
停車場/car-park	sq
被/by	bei

Table 6: some samples of traditional CSSG dictionary

o. 車/car 被/by 約翰/John 停/park 在/at 停車場/car-park
The car is parked at the car-park by John

We parse simplified Chinese test data from task 3 with the parser implemented the grammatical rules and the simplified morphological dictionary while we parse the traditional Chinese test data from task 4 with the parser implemented the same grammatical rules and the traditional morphological dictionary. Since the scale of the dictionaries is not large enough, there are some unknown words for CSSG in both test data of task 3 and task 4. We add the unknown words to CSSG dictionaries before parsing.

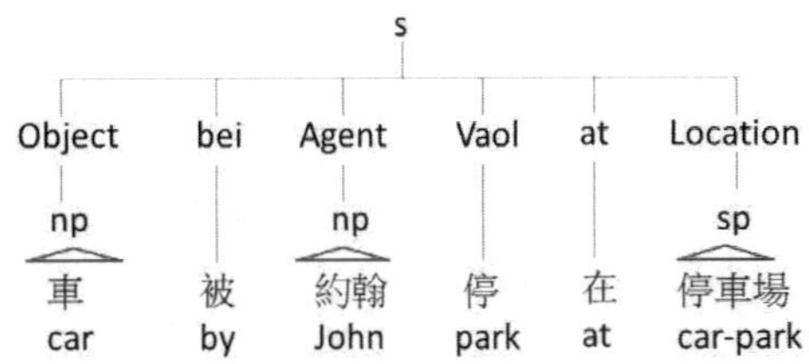

Figure 20: the CSSG parsing tree of (o)

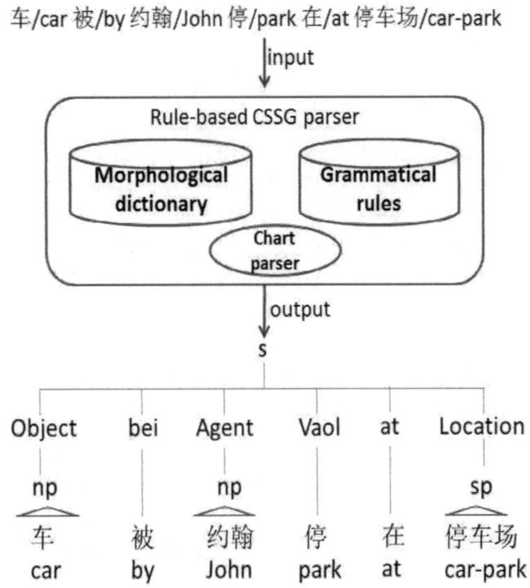

Figure 21: the input and output of (a) of the CSSG parser

As figure 21 shown: 1) the CSSG parser consists of three parts: the grammatical rules, a morphological dictionary and a chart parsing engine; 2) the input is a word-segmented sentence and the output is a CSSG parsing tree; 3) since there is not yet a postager based on CSSG, we have to parse all possible POS tag lists of a sentence with the CSSG parser.

After parsing the test data, we convert the CSSG parsing trees and make them are as similar as possible to TCT trees and Sinica-Treebank trees.

4.2 Evaluation Results

Table 7, 8 and 9 summarize the evaluation results of the simplified Chinese parse task 1: PSG parsing evaluation.

Table 7 shows the performance of the POS tag conversion from CSSG to TCT. Table 8 shows the results of the constituent boundary recognition. Table 9 represents the evaluation results of the parsing (both phrase boundaries and phrase labels recognition).

type	P	R	F1
nouns	74.4%	87.9%	80.6%
verbs	94.1%	94.1%	94.1%
others	62.7%	56.9%	59.7%
overall	71.3%	71.3%	71.3%

Table 7: the result for POS tag recognition

correct	gold	system	P	R	F1
85	92	158	53.8%	92.4%	68.0%

Table 8: the result for phrase boundary recognition

correct	gold	system	P	R	F1
85	92	158	42.4%	72.8%	53.6%

Table 9: the result for both phrase boundary and label recognition

Table 10 and 11 summarize the evaluation results of the two subtasks of the traditional Chinese parsing task. Table 10 presents the results of the parsing sub-task while table 11 shows the results of the semantic labeling sub-task.

Micro-averaging			Macro-averaging		
P	R	F1	P	R	F1
47.7%	40.1%	43.6%	53.6%	42.0%	47.1%

Table 10: the results of the parsing task

Micro-averaging			Macro-averaging		
P	R	F1	P	R	F1
20.4%	22.6%	21.4%	23.3%	24.2%	23.7%

Table 11: the results for the semantic labeling task

4.3 Discussion

As we anticipated, the evaluation results are lower than the real performance of the CSSG parser. There are three reasons should be considered: 1) because of the large differences between the design of CSSG and the two gold data: Sinica Treebank and CSSG, it is impossible to convert some CSSG trees to TCT trees or Sinica-Treebank trees. For instance, k) is treated as a temporal phrase in CSSG, so it does not correspond to any phrase in TCT or Sinica Treebank; 2) there is much inaccuracy in tree-conversion works. As shown in table 7 and 8, the system phrase counts is 158, that is much more than the gold phrase counts 92 so that the recall scores (92.4% and 72.8%) are much higher than the precision scores (68.0% and 53.6%). We checked the evaluation data and found that we converted noun phrases of CSSG like p) to TCT format like q), which might be counted as two noun phrases; 3) As shown in figure 16, 17, 18 and 19, the design of the semantic role set of CSSG are very different from Sinica Treebank, so we can only convert a small number of sematic roles correctly.

p. (np (nnp (n 葡萄牙) (n 政府)))

q. (np (np (n 葡萄牙) (n 政府)))

As discussed above, the evaluation results do not reflect the real performance of the CSSG parser because of the large differences between CSSG and the two gold data. We expect that more neutral evaluation metrics would be drawn up for the open parsing task.

The experiments show that the evaluation results of the traditional Chinese parsing task are lower than the simplified Chinese parsing task. One of the possible reasons is that there are some differences between the constructions of simplified Chinese and traditional Chinese. We noticed that a few traditional Chinese constructions differ from simplified Chinese. For example, in traditional Chinese sentence r), "食/food" is the direct object that appears at the left side of the indirect object "企鵝寶貝/penguin-baby". We had ever asked some Chinese native speakers whether they think the construction like r) is grammatical. Only one speaker who comes from Hang Kong thinks r) is a grammatical sentence while other speakers who come from the mainland of China think such constructions are ungrammatical. Therefore simplified Chinese sentence s) is an ungrammatical sentence. For Simplified Chinese native speakers, a function word "给/to" should be used to lead an indirect object, like t) and u), or the indirect object appears at the left side of the direct object, such as v). The CSSG rules cover the constructions of t), u) and v) but not cover the constructions of r) and s).

r. 工作人員/worker 每天/every-day 仍會/yet 餵/ feed 食/food 企鵝寶貝/penguin-baby
The worker feeds foods to penguin babies everyday

s. *工作人员/worker 每天/every-day 仍会/yet 喂/ feed 食/food 企鹅宝贝/penguin-baby
The worker feeds foods to penguin babies everyday

t. 工作人员/worker 每天/every-day 仍会/yet 喂/ feed 食/food 给/to 企鹅宝贝/penguin-baby
The worker feeds foods to penguin babies everyday

u. 工作人员/worker 每天/every-day 仍会/yet 给/to 企鹅宝贝/penguin-baby 喂/ feed 食/food
The worker feeds foods to penguin babies everyday

v. 工作人员/worker 每天/every-day 仍会/yet 喂/ feed 企鹅宝贝/penguin-baby 食/food
The worker feeds foods to penguin babies everyday

5 Conclusion and Future work

In this paper, we introduced a broad-coverage rule-based Chinese grammatical resource CSSG, which was developed based on a new grammar formalism idea: Sentence Structure Grammar; we compared briefly CSSG with a simplified Chinese Treebank TCT and a traditional Chinese resource Sinica Treebank; we also introduced our participation of CIPS-SIGHAN-2012 parsing task. We use a same rule-based chart parser implemented CSSG to participate in both simplified Chinese parsing task and traditional Chinese parsing task. The experiment shows that the rule-based grammatical resource CSSG that was developed for covering simplified Chinese constructions can also parse traditional Chinese sentences with a lower performance.

Since the CSSG provide rich information, it is possible to improve the precision and the recall of the evaluation task by optimizing the tree-conversion programs.

We prepare to open this resource to researchers who have an interest in it in the resent future.

References

Chen Feng-Yi, Pi-Fang Tsai, Keh-Jiann Chen, Chu-Ren Hunag. 1999. *The Construction of Sinica Treebank*. Computational Linguistics and Chinese Language Processing, vol. 4, No. 2. pp.87-104.

Chen Keh-jiann and Chu-Ren Huang. 1990. *Information-based Case Grammar*. Proceedings of the 13th Conference on Computational Linguistics, Volume 2, pages 54-59.

Fan Xiao. 1998. *The types of Chinese Sentences (In Chinese)*. Shanxi Shuhai Press.

Fillmore, Charles J. (1968). *The Case for Case*. In Bach and Harms (Ed.): Universals in Linguistic Theory. New York: Holt, Rinehart, and Winston, 1-88.

Liu Yuehua, Wenyu Pan and Wei Gu. 2001. *Practical Modern Chinese Grammar (In Chinese)*. Beijing: Commercial Press.

Wang Xiangli, Masahiro Miyazaki. *Chinese Syntactic Analysis Using Sentence Structure Grammar (In Japanese)*. Journal of Natural Language Processing. vol.14, No.2. April 2007.

Wang Xiangli, Takuya Matsuzaki, Yusuke Miyao, Kun Yu, Yuan Li and Junichi Tsujii. 2011. *Comparison between formal grammatical frameworks for Treebanking (In Japanese)*. Proceeding of Japan Natural Language Processing. 2011.

Wang Xiangli, Yusuke Miyao and Yuan Li. 2012. *Chinese Grammatical resources based on Sentence Structure Grammar and its application on patent field (In Japanese)*. Proceeding of Japan Natural Language Processing. 2012.

Xue Nianwen and Fei Xia. 2000. *The bracketing Guidelines for the Penn Chinese Treebank Project*. Technical Report IRCS 00-08, University of Pennsylvania.

Yu Kun, Yusuke Miyao, Takuya Matsuzaki, Xiangli Wang, Yaozhong Zhang, Kiyotaka Uchimoto, Junichi Tsujii. *Comparison of Chinese Treebanks for Corpus-oriented HPSG Grammar Development.* Journal of Natural Language Processing (Special Issue on Empirical Methods for Asian Language Processing). April 2010.

Zhu Dexi. 1982. *Lecture Notes on Grammar (In Chinese)*. Beijing: Commercial Press.

Zhou Qiang. 2004. *Annotation Scheme for Chinese Treebank (in Chinese)*. Journal of Chinese Information Processing, 18(4): 1-8.

A Simplified Chinese Parser with Factored Model

Qiuping Huang
Natural Language Processing & Portuguese-Chinese Machine Translation
Department of Computer and Information Science
University of Macau
michellehuang718@gmail.com

Liangye He
Natural Language Processing & Portuguese-Chinese Machine Translation
Department of Computer and Information Science
University of Macau
wutianshui0515@gmail.com

Derek F.Wong
Natural Language Processing & Portuguese-Chinese Machine Translation
Department of Computer and Information Science
University of Macau
derekfw@umac.mo

Lidia S.Chao
Natural Language Processing & Portuguese-Chinese Machine Translation
Department of Computer and Information Science
University of Macau
lidiasc@umac.mo

Abstract

This paper presents our work for participation in the 2012 CIPS-ParsEval shared task of Simplified Chinese parsing. We adopt a factored model to parse the Simplified Chinese. The factored model is one kind of combined structure between PCFG structure and dependency structure. It mainly uses an extremely effective A* parsing algorithm which enables to get a more optimal solution. Throughout this paper, we use TCT Treebank as experimental data. TCT mainly consists of binary trees, with a few single-branch trees. The final experiment result demonstrates that the head propagation table improves the parsing performance. Finally, we describe the implementation of the system we used as well as analyze our experiment result SC_F1 from 43% up to 63% and the LC_F1 is about 92% we have achieved.

1 Introduction

Parsing is an important and fundamental task in natural language processing. In recent years, Chinese parsing has received a great deal of attention, and lots of researchers have presented many of Chinese parsing models (Collins, 1999; Klein and Manning, 2003; Charniak and Johnson, 2005; Petrov, 2006). Nevertheless, the factored model is presented as a novel parsing model, which provides conceptually concise, straightforward opportunities for separately improving the component models (Klein and Manning, 2002).

With the efforts of many researchers, natural language processing makes a remarkable improvement and the syntactic analysis results can be directly used for machine translation, automatic question and answering and information extraction. However, most researches on parsing concentrating on English, and its parsing system has achieved quite a good performance. Thus the Chinese parsing is still a huge challenge in Chinese information processing.

Parsing is the thesis that analyzes the word's grammatical function in the sentence, and it also is a data driven process, its performance is determined by the amount of data in a Treebank on which a parser is trained (Song and Kit, 2009). Although much more multilingual parsing models have been presented, the data for English is still much more than any other languages that have been available so far. For this reason, most researches on parsing focus on English. If we directly apply any existing parser trained on an English Treebank for Chinese sentences, we cannot get a good parsing. However, the

Vertical Order	Horizontal Markov Order			
	$h = 0$	$h = 1$	$h = 2$	$h = \infty$
$v = 1$	$p(H\|L)$	$p(H\|L, M_k)$	$p(H\|L, M_k M_{k+1})$	$p(H\|L, M_1, M_2 \ldots M_x)$
$v = 2$	$p(H\|L, P)$	$p(H\|L, P, M_k)$	$p(H\|L, P, M_k M_{k+1})$	$p(H\|L, P, M_1, M_2 \ldots M_x)$
$v = 3$	$p(H\|L, P, G)$	$p(H\|L, P, G, M_k)$	$p(H\|L, P, G, M_k M_{k+1})$	$p(H\|L, P, G, M_1, M_2 \ldots M_x)$

Table 1: Markovization and corresponding statistical model

methodology of parsing can be highly applicable. Even for those corpora with different annotation format, there still has a well-performed parser to fit the specific structure for the data. In this work, we adopt an existing powerful parser, Stanford parser (Klein and Manning, 2003), which has shown its effectiveness in English. We make the necessary modifications for parsing Chinese and apply it to the shared task.

In this evaluation, we use TCT Treebank as the developing and experimental data. The Treebank uses an annotation scheme with double-tagging (Zhou, 2004). Under this scheme, every sentence is annotated with a complete parse tree, where each non-terminal constituent is assigned with two tags, the syntactic constituent tag and the grammatical relation tag, which also is a new annotation scheme that differs from with head constituents in previous TCT version. In order to fit to this annotation of TCT, we use the unlexicalized model to do the PCFG parsing and use CKY-based decoder in the Stanford parser. Finally we mainly use TregEx (Levy, 2006), which is a useful tool to visualize and query syntactic structures, to generate a head propagation table applying to the factored model in order to improve the performance.

In the next section, we will present the details of our approach. The experiment results and analysis are presented in section 3. The last section is the conclusion and further work.

2 Parsing Model

2.1 Stanford Factored Model

The Stanford parser, precisely, the highly optimized factored model (Klein and Manning, 2003) has been employed to perform our experiment. The factored model is the combination of unlexicalized PCFG model and dependency model. To our knowledge, the unlexicalized model did not encode word information and the dependency model can be viewed as postprocessing in the Stanford factored model. The factored model can be seen as $P(T, D) = p(T)p(D)$, Where T means the plain phrase-structure tree and D is dependency tree. In this view, the factored model is built by two sub-models.

The Stanford unlexicalized PCFG model makes horizontal and vertical grammar markovizations to solve two deficiencies of raw grammar: coarse category symbols and the unknown testing rules. Coarse category symbols make too strong independent assumptions; while unknown testing rules often get underestimated probabilities. Assumed that h stands for horizontal markovization order, v stands for vertical markovization order, and every grammar rules are in this type:

$$L \rightarrow M_1 \ldots M_i H M_{i+1} \ldots M_x$$

In this rule, L is the left-hand-side, H is the head word in the right-hand-side, M_x stands for the modifiers. P indicates parent nodes and G indicates grandparent nodes (Klein and Manning, 2003). Table 1 gives the unlexicalized parsing models corresponding to different horizontal and vertical orders.

The dependency models $p(D)$ is a pair $< h, a >$ of a head and argument, which are words in a sentence. A dependency structure D over a sentence is a set of dependencies (arrows) which form a planar, acyclic graph rooted at the special symbol *ROOT*, and in which each word in sentence appears as an argument exactly once (Klein and Manning, 2004). The arrow connects a head with a dependent, and the head $< h, a >$ of a constituent is generated by the head propagation table. The CKY algorithm is used in dependency parsing.

Actually, the factored model reaches to the efficient by factoring the two sub-models and simplified both. There is a brief top-level procedure described in (Klein and Manning, 2002).

1. Extract the PCFG sub-model and set up the PCFG parser.
2. Use the PCFG parser to find outside scores $\alpha_{PCFG}(e)$ for each edge.
3. Extract the dependency sub-model and set up the dependency parser.
4. Use the dependency parser to find outside scores $\alpha_{DEP}(e)$ for each edge.

Parent Node	Child Node	Frequency
ap	*a*	19
	ap	13
	pp	8
	d	7
	dD	7
	vp	5
	aD	3

Table 2: The classification and frequency of *ap* node

Parent	Direction	Priority List
np	right	*n, np,vN,nP, mp, v, vp, rN, nR, m, sp, t, rNP, dj*
vp	left	*vp, v, n, tp, sp, vM, a, ap, p, pp, t*
ap	left	*a, ap, aD, d, dD,vp*
bp	left	*b, u*
dj	left	*vp, dj, np, n,b*
dlc	right	*dlc, l, np*
dp	right	*uJDI, dN,d*
fj	left	*fj-RT, fj*
mp	left	*qN, mp, m, tp, mbar-XX*
pp	left	*np,sp, n, tp, rN, pp, v, a, f*
sp	right	*f, n, nS, s, sp, np*
tp	right	*qT, nT, f, tp, n,np, m*
yj	right	*yj-RT*
jq	left	*jq, zj-XX*

Table 3: The head propagation table used in Simplified Chinese parsing

5. Combine PCFG and dependency sub-models into the lexicalized model.
6. Form the combined outside estimate $a(e) = \alpha_{PCFG}(e) + \alpha_{DEP}(e)$.
7. Use the lexicalized A* parser, with $a(e)$ as an A* estimate of $\alpha(e)$.

2.2 Head Propagation Table

It is worth mentioning that the headword information does not reflect on the parsed syntax tree for a given sentence in the corpus. In the case of dependency model, Stanford model mainly uses constituency structure to extract dependency grammar. On this hand, the headword information plays an important role. The parser needs to pick out the head child in the internal rules with the head propagation table. Besides, the Stanford factored model also is the combination of unlexicalized PCFG models and lexicalized models, it has to encode the lexicalized information in each non-terminal node. Likewise, the lexicalized parser uses the head propagation table as well. However, the newest TCT corpus does not contain the head word information. To this end, we define a specific head propagation table using the TregEx tool after classifying the grammar rules and counting the frequency of some related tags. Which differs from the work of (Magerman, 1995) and (Collins, 1999) that the rules of head finding are defined based on linguistic knowledge. There are three steps to generate the head propagation table. Firstly, we extract all the grammar rules from the TCT corpus, and then classify the rules according to their parent nodes. Secondly, we calculate the frequency of each sort of child node that have the same parent node, then select the higher frequency child nodes as the candidate head word. For example, under the *ap* (adjective phrase) node, we get some relatively high frequency child nodes by counting showed in the table 2. Thirdly, we search the matched sub-trees that the candidate head is the real head in the TCT Treebank by using the TregEx specified pattern (Levy, 2006). Finally, through the distribution of the amount of the matched tree fragment, we generate the head propagation table and every child node is assigned with a priority score and direction. The generation of direction (left or right) is the combination of linguistic knowledge and experiment results. Table 3 gives the head propagation table used in our Simplified Chinese parsing. In the Stanford parser, there is an existed class of *LeftHeadFiner* which defaults the leftmost one is the head word. Similarly, we create a class of *RightHeadFinder* which defaults the rightmost one is the head word. In our task, we have used leftmost, rightmost, and the generated head propagation table to do three group experiments respectively. The experiment proved that after the head propagation table imported which indeed improves the result exceeding the other two experiments based on the same settings on the parser.

3 Experiment and Analysis

3.1 Data Set

In this work, all of news and academic articles annotated in the TCT version 1.0 (Zhou, 2004) are selected as the basic training data for the evaluation. 1,000 sentences extracted from the TCT-2010 version can be used as the basic test data. The Treebank uses a double-tagging annotation scheme. For example: *(zj-XX (fj-LS (dj (nP* 江泽民) (*v* 指出)) (*dj-RT* (*wP* ，) (*dj* (*vp* (*v* 搞好) (*np* (*n* 物价) (*n* 工作))) (*vp* (*dD* 极) (*vp* (*v* 为) (*a* 重要)))))) (*wE* 。)). In this sentence, *zj, dj, np*, etc. are the syntactic tags and *LS, RT* are grammatical relation tags. These two tag sets consist of 16 and 31 different tags respectively, which is a new annotation scheme with double-tagging that differing from with head constituents in previous version of TCT corpus. In addition, we have 10 different scale official released training data sets from TCT, but the latter data set has included the former data set. It is a cumulative manner. For example, the set 1 (means D_1) has 1,755 sentences , yet the set 2 has 3,512 sentences in all which includes all sentences of set 1. The any other data sets are generated according to the same idea. There are 17,558 sentences and about 480,000 Chinese words in the biggest official released training data set. In the corpus, every sentence contains 5 words at least and some sentences are more than 100 words. The more syntactic relation exists in the long sentence, the more difficulties exist in these complex sentences when parsing. In order to evaluate the effectiveness on the different scales of the training data for parser performance, we extract 90% data to training and 10% data for testing from 10 training data sets mentioned before, so there are 10 different training data sets and testing data sets. It is worth noting that the testing sets are also cumulative.

Furthermore, in order to use the Stanford parser, we need to transform format of the corpus that parentheses are added to delimiter the boundaries of sentences. Simultaneously, we create a Simplified Chinese package to do the parsing. This package mainly contains head finding rules, and some tuning of parser option for the TCT corpus.

3.2 Results and Analysis

The evaluation metrics used in 2012 CIPSParsEval shared task are shown in following:

$$Precision = \frac{\#\ of\ correct\ constituents\ in\ proposed\ parse}{\#\ of\ constituents\ in\ proposed\ parse}$$

$$Recall = \frac{\#\ of\ correct\ constituents\ in\ proposed\ parse}{\#\ of\ constituents\ in\ standard\ parse}$$

$$F1 = \frac{2 \times Precision \times Recall}{Precision + Recall}$$

There are two evaluation results in this shared task. One is the syntactic category (SC), the other is labeled constituent (LC).

As we mentioned before, we use cumulative manners to train 10 different training models. Table 4 gives the results which use the raw Treebank based on the default Chinese training setting on Stanford parser. This is an original model in our experiment. Table 5 shows the best results among three group experiments by importing three classes respectively. The first is the leftmost which always selects the leftmost as the headword (=1 in Table 5). The second is the rightmost which always selects the rightmost as the headword (=2 in Table 5) and the third is the head propagation table (=3 in Table 5). From the result, we can see that after the Simplified Chinese package and the head propagation table imported, we got the best PARSEVAL LC_F1 is about 92% and SC_F1 is close to 63% corresponding to $v = 2, h = \infty$. The table 6 shows the results of 10 different scales of the training data set in our adapted model by importing the head propagation table. We can see that with the more training data in a certain range, the model is more robust from 3 to 9 different scale data sets. However, tenth set declines slightly. There may be some reasons for the result. One, there are some unknown words appearing in the tenth set and cannot be recognized. Two, much more long sentences with more syntactic relation can not be parsed well in this data set. Three, the training data reaches an extreme point in the ninth set, with the more data, the more ambiguities when selecting the grammar rules.

Data	LC_F1	SC_F1
D_1	85.12	38.42
$D_2 \supseteq D_1$	84.15	38.74
$D_3 \supseteq D_2$	86.52	41.03
$D_4 \supseteq D_3$	87.66	41.14
$D_5 \supseteq D_4$	88.61	41.39
$D_6 \supseteq D_5$	89.02	41.84
$D_7 \supseteq D_6$	89.51	42.50
$D_8 \supseteq D_7$	89.79	42.54
$D_9 \supseteq D_8$	90.20	42.81
$D_{10} \supseteq D_9$	90.04	42.26

Table 4: The parsing results based on the original model trained on different scales of training data

Experiment	LC_F	SC_F
1	91.79	59.80
2	91.80	60.00
3	91.88	62.81

Table 5: The best results among three groups of experiment on the adapted model

Data	LC_F	SC_F
D_1	90.49	61.26
$D_2 \supseteq D_1$	89.05	61.09
$D_3 \supseteq D_2$	89.56	60.37
$D_4 \supseteq D_3$	91.13	61.60
$D_5 \supseteq D_4$	90.98	61.71
$D_6 \supseteq D_5$	91.18	62.13
$D_7 \supseteq D_6$	91.47	62.60
$D_8 \supseteq D_7$	91.68	62.78
$D_9 \supseteq D_8$	91.88	62.81
$D_{10} \supseteq D_9$	91.88	62.69

Table 6: The parsing results of the adapted model trained on different scales of training data

4 Conclusion and Future Work

We participate in the parsing subtask in CIPS-Parseval 2012. We use the factored model of Stanford parser to tackle the parsing. The framework of factored model is conceptually simple and can be easily extended in some ways that other parser models have been. Besides, we mainly use the TregEx searching Treebank tool and counting manner to generate the head propagation table, though it makes sense to the parsing result, we still hope to find a better way to extend its feasibility and not just used for Simplified Chinese. Whether we can create the head table automatically based on machine learning. Perhaps this is a thought-provoking question in future research. However, there are some improvements we can make. At first, we can further study the double-tagging annotation scheme in TCT Treebank in order to do the tag splitting as done on English Treebank (Klein and Manning, 2003). Because the tag splitting is another important feature of Stanford parser. In addition, the head constituent recognition is the key problem, we hope a breakthrough in this problem.

Acknowledgments

This work was partially supported by the Research Committee of University of Macau under grant UL019B/09-Y3/EEE/LYP01/FST, and also supported by Science and Technology Development Fund of Macau under grant 057/2009/A2.

References

Collins, M. (1999). Head-driven statistical models for natural language parsing. *Computational linguistics*, 29(4): 589-637.

Charniak, E. and Johnson, M. (2005). Coarse-to-fine n-best parsing and MaxEnt discriminative reranking. *Proceedings of the 43rd Annual Meeting on Association for Computational Linguistics*, 173–180.

Huang, L. (2008). Forest reranking: Discriminative parsing with non-local features. *Proceedings of ACL-08: HLT*, 586–594.

Klein, D. and Manning, C. D. (2002). Fast exact inference with a factored model for natural language parsing. *Advances in neural information processing systems*, *15*(2003), 3–10.

Klein, D. and Manning, C. D. (2003). Accurate unlexicalized parsing. *Proceedings of the 41st Annual Meeting on Association for Computational Linguistics-Volume 1*, 423–430.

Klein, D. and Manning, C. D. (2003). Factored A* Search for Models over Sequences and Trees. *Proceedings of the International Joint Conference on Artificial Intelligence*, *18*, 1246–1251.

Klein, D. and Manning, C. D. (2004). Corpus-based induction of syntactic structure: Models of dependency and constituency. *Proceedings of the 42nd Annual Meeting on Association for Computational Linguistics*, 478.

Levy, R. and Andrew, G. (2006). Tregex and Tsurgeon: tools for querying and manipulating tree data structures. *Proceedings of the fifth international conference on Language Resources and Evaluation*, 2231–2234.

Magerman, D. M. (1995). Statistical decision-tree models for parsing. *Proceedings of the 33rd annual meeting on Association for Computational Linguistics*, 276–283.

Petrov, S., Barrett, L., Thibaux, R. and Klein, D. (2006). Learning accurate, compact, and interpretable tree annotation. *Proceedings of the 21st International Conference on Computational Linguistics and the 44th annual meeting of the Association for Computational Linguistics*, 433–440.

Song, Y. and Kit, C. (2009). PCFG parsing with CRF tagging for head recognition. *Proceedings of CIPS-ParsEval*, 133–137.

Zhou Q. 2004. Annotation Scheme for Chinese treebank. *Journal of Chinese Information Processing,* 18(4):1-8.

Parsing TCT with a Coarse-to-fine Approach

Li Dongchen
Key Laboratory of Machine Perception and Intelligence,
Speech and Hearing Research Center
Peking University, China
lidc@cis.pku.edu.cn

Wu Xihong
Key Laboratory of Machine Perception and Intelligence,
Speech and Hearing Research Center
Peking University, China
wxh@cis.pku.edu.cn

Abstract

A key observation is that concept compound constituent labels are detrimental to parsing performance. We use a PCFG parsing algorithm that uses a multilevel coarse-to-fine scheme. Our approach requires a sequence of nested partitions or equivalence classes of the PCFG nonterminals, where the nonterminals of each PCFG are clusters of nonterminals of the finer PCFG. We use the results of parsing at a coarser level to prune the next finer level. The coarse-to-fine method use hierarchical projections for incremental pruning. We present experiments which show that parsing with hierarchical state-splitting is fast and accurate on Tsinghua Chinese Treebank. In addition, we propose a multiple-model method that adds concept compound labels to the output of the simple PCFG model and gains higher bracketing recall from the simple model. This scheme can be implemented by training two models on different labeling styles.

1 Introduction

The peculiarity of the annotation of this released edition of TCT is that the tree structure is very compact, where there are no unary productions except root nodes and leaf nodes.

A major observation is that parser on treebank with concept compound constituent labels performs worse than without concept compound constituent. The average crossing is 4% lower in presence of concept compound constituent labels.

Since all phrases have a clausal and phrasal constituent label, while only a fraction have concept compound constituent label. We can regard a phrase label with both clausal and phrasal constituent label and concept compound constituent label as a subsymbol of the clausal and phrasal constituent label merely.

The coarse categories in these grammars can be regarded as clusters or equivalence classes of the fine nonterminal categories. We require that the partition of the nonterminals defined by the equivalence classes at finer level be a refinement of the partition defined at coarser level. This means that each nonterminal category at finer level is mapped to a unique nonterminal category at coarser level (although in general the mapping is many to one, i.e., each nonterminal category at coarser level corresponds to several nonterminal categories at finer level). We use the correspondence between categories at different levels to prune possible constituents. A constituent is considered at finer level only if the corresponding constituent at coarser level has a probability exceeding some threshold. Parsing with hierarchical grammar leads to considerable efficiency improvements.

Treebank parsing comprises two problems: learning, in which we must select a model given a treebank, and inference, in which we must select a parse for a sentence given the learned model. Previous work has shown that high-quality unlexicalized PCFGs can be learned from a treebank, either by manual annotation (Klein and Manning, 2003) or automatic state splitting (Matsuzaki et al., 2005; Petrov et al., 2006). In particular, we demonstrated in Petrov et al. (2006) that a hierarchically split PCFG could exceed the accuracy of lexicalized PCFGs (Collins, 1999; Charniak and Johnson, 2005).

We adopted here a multilevel coarse-to-fine PCFG parsing algorithm as in Charniak (2006) and Petrov (2007). The multilevel coarse-to-fine PCFG parsing algorithm reduces the complexity of the search involved in finding the best parse and attempts to constrain the fine parsing space to the coarse parsing space. It defines a sequence of increasingly more complex PCFGs. Charniak (2006) has demonstrated that coarse PCFG identified the locations of correct constituents of the parse tree (the "gold constituents") with high recall.

2 Experiment Observation

We have parsed with three different annotation setups. First, we train our model our model with only phrasal labels, and evaluate the precision and recall on only the phrasal labels. Second, we train our model with full labels, and evaluate the precision and recall on only the phrasal labels. Third, we train the model with full labels, and evaluate the precision and recall on full labels.

Take a concrete example, we show two parsing output with different annotations as below:

The input sentence is:

"之后 ， 北京 一轻 总公司 根据 市政府 的 决定 ， 在 市 国有 资产 管理局 的 具体 指导 下 ， 经过 3 个 月 的 紧张 工作 ， 完成 了 公司 国有 资产 的 清查 、 重估 工作 。"

Parsing output with only phrasal constituent labels:

"((zj (dj (t 之后) (dj (wP ，) (dj (np (np (nS 北京) (n 一轻)) (n 总公司)) (vp (pp (p 根据) (np (np (n 市政府) (uJDE 的)) (n 决定))) (vp (wP ，) (vp (pp (p 在) (sp (np (np (np (n 市) (np (b 国有) (n 资产))) (n 管理局)) (uJDE 的)) (np (a 具体) (vN 指导))) (f 下))) (vp (wP ，) (vp (pp (p 经过) (np (np (tp (mp (m 3) (qN 个)) (qT 月)) (uJDE 的)) (np (a 紧张) (n 工作)))) (vp (wP ，) (vp (vp (v 完成) (uA 了)) (np (np (np (n 公司) (np (b 国有) (n 资产))) (uJDE 的)) (np (np (n 清查) (np (wD 、) (n 重估))) (n 工作))))))))))))) (wE 。)))"

Parsing output with full labels:

"((zj_XX (fj (f 之后) (fj_RT (wP ，) (fj_LG (dj (np (nS 北京) (np (n 一轻) (n 总公司))) (vp (pp (p 根据) (np (np (n 市政府) (uJDE 的)) (n 决定))) (vp_RT (wP ，) (vp (pp (p 在) (sp (np (np (np (n 市) (np (np (b 国有) (n 资产)) (n 管理局))) (uJDE 的)) (np (a 具体) (vN 指导))) (f 下))) (vp_RT (wP ，) (vp (v 经过) (np (np (tp (mp (m 3) (qN 个)) (qT 月)) (uJDE 的)) (np (a 紧张) (n 工作))))))))) (vp_RT (wP ，) (vp (vp (v 完成) (uA 了)) (np (np (np (n 公司) (np (b 国有) (n 资产))) (uJDE 的)) (np (np_LH (vN 清查) (np_RT (wD 、) (vN 重估))) (n 工作)))))))) (wE 。)))"

The gold parse tree is as follows:

"((zj (dj (f 之后) (dj (wP ，) (dj (np (np (nS 北京) (n 一轻)) (n 总公司)) (vp (pp (p 根据) (np (np (n 市政府) (uJDE 的)) (n 决定))) (vp (wP ，) (vp (pp (p 在) (sp (np (np (np (n 市) (np (b 国有) (np (n 资产) (n 管理局)))) (uJDE 的)) (vp (aD 具体) (v 指导))) (f 下))) (vp (wP ，) (vp (pp (p 经过) (np (np (tp (mp (m 3) (qN 个)) (qT 月)) (uJDE 的)) (np (a 紧张) (n 工作)))) (vp (wP ，) (vp (vp (v 完成) (uA 了)) (np (np (np (n 公司) (np (b 国有) (n 资产))) (uJDE 的)) (np (np (vN 清查) (np (wD 、) (vN 重估))) (n 工作))))))))))))) (wE 。)))"

In the former parsing result, not only the phrasal constituent tags are labels more accurately, its syntactic structures are segmented more reasonably.

The parsing performances metrics convinced that the concept compound is detrimental to the parser performance even we only evaluate the phrasal constituent labels' precision and recall.

Furthermore, we compare the metrics of exact match, average crossing, no crossing and 2 or less crossing, which show that the higher accuracy gained by stripping the concept compound labels lies in both its more accurate bracketing and tagging ability.

3 Previous Researches

Coarse-to-fine search is an idea that has appeared several times in the literature of computational linguistics and related areas. Maxwell and Kaplan (1993) extracted CFG automatically from a more detailed unification grammar and used it to identify the possible locations of constituents in the more detailed parses of the sentence. They use their covering CFG to prune the search of their unification grammar parser in essentially the same manner as we do here, and demonstrate significant performance improvements by using their coarse-to-fine approach.

Geman and Kochanek (2001) laid out the basic theory of coarse-to-fine approximations and dynamic programming in a stochastic framework. They describes the multilevel dynamic programming algorithm needed for coarse-to-fine analysis (which they apply to decoding rather than parsing), and show how to perform exact coarse-to-fine computation, rather than the heuristic search we perform here.

Goodman (1997)'s parser is a two-stage coarse to fine parser. The second stage is a standard tree-bank parser while the first stage is a regular-expression approximation of the grammar. Again, the second stage is constrained by the parses found in the first stage. Neither stage is smoothed.

The parser of Charniak (2000) is also a two-stage coarse to fine model, where the first stage is a smoothed Markov grammar (it uses up to three previous constituents as context), and the second stage is a lexicalized Markov grammar with extra annotations about parents and grandparents. The second stage explores all of the constituents not pruned out after the first stage. Related approaches are used in Hall (2004) and Charniak and Johnson (2005).

Klein and Manning (2003a) describe efficient A* for the most likely parse, where pruning is accomplished by using Equation 1 and a true upper bound on the outside probability. While their maximum is a looser estimate of the outside probability, it is an admissible heuristic and together with an A* search is guaranteed to find the best parse first. One question is if the guarantee is worth the extra search required by the looser estimate of the true outside probability.

Tsuruoka and Tsujii (2004) explore the framework developed in Klein and Manning (2003a), and seek ways to minimize the time required by the heap manipulations necessary in this scheme. They describe an iterative deepening algorithm that does not require a heap. They also speed computation by precomputing more accurate upper bounds on the outside probabilities of various kinds of constituents. They are able to reduce by half the number of constituents required to find the best parse (compared to CKY).

McDonald et al. (2005) have implemented a dependency parser with good accuracy (it is almost as good at dependency parsing as Charniak (2000)) and very impressive speed (it is about ten times faster than Collins (1997) and four times faster than Charniak (2000)). It achieves its speed in part because dependency parsing has a much lower grammar constant than does standard PCFG parsing — after all, there are no phrasal constituents to consider. The current paper can be thought of as a way to take the sting out of the grammar constant for PCFGs by parsing first with very few phrasal constituents and adding them only after most constituents have been pruned away.

4 Hierarchically Split PCFGs

We use a novel coarse-to-fine processing scheme for hierarchically split PCFGs. Our method considers the splitting history of the final grammar, projecting it onto its increasingly refined prior stages. For any projection of a grammar, we use techniques for infinite tree distributions (Corazza and Satta, 2006) and iterated fix point equations. We then parse with each refinement, in sequence, much along the lines of Charniak et al. (2006).

We consider PCFG grammars in a hierarchy fashion in Petrov et al. (2006). From the starting point of the raw treebank grammar, we iteratively refine the grammar in stages. The refined grammar is estimated using a variant of the forward-backward algorithm (Matsuzaki et al., 2005). After a splitting stage, many splits are rolled back based on (an approximation to) their likelihood gain. This procedure gives an ontogeny of grammars from the raw grammar to the final grammar. Empirically, the gains on the English Penn treebank level off after 6 rounds.

5 Coarse-to-Fine Search

When working with large grammars, it is standard to prune the search space in some way. In the case of lexicalized grammars, the unpruned chart often will not even fit in memory for long sentences. Several proven techniques exist. Collins (1999) combines a punctuation rule which eliminates many spans entirely, and then uses span-synchronous beams to prune in a bottom-up fashion. Charniak et al. (1998) introduces best-first parsing, in which a figure-of merit prioritizes agenda processing. Most relevant to our work is Charniak and Johnson (2005) which uses a pre-parse phase to rapidly parse with a very coarse, unlexicalized treebank grammar. Any item with sufficiently low posterior probability in the pre-parse triggers the pruning of its lexical variants in a subsequent full parse.

Charniak et al. (2006) introduces multi-level coarse-to-fine parsing, which extends the basic pre-parsing idea by adding more rounds of pruning. In their work, the extra pruning was with grammars even coarser than the raw treebank grammar, such as a grammar in which all nonterminals are collapsed. We propose a novel multi-stage coarse-to-fine method which is particularly natural for our hierarchically split grammar, but which is, in principle, applicable to any grammar.

Petrov et al. (2007) construct a sequence of increasingly refined grammars, reparsing with each refinement. They derive sequences of refinements and automatically tune the pruning thresholds on held-out data. Their hierarchical coarse-to-fine parsing take the projection that collapses split symbols in finer round to their earlier identities in coarser round. The final state-split grammars G come, by their construction process, with an ontogeny of grammars where each grammar is a (partial) splitting of the preceding one.

6 Experimental Setup

We ran experiments on TCT. The training and test data set splits are described in Table below.

Treebank	Train Dataset	Develop Dataset	Test Dataset
TCT(Qiang Zhou, 2004)	16000 sentences	800 sentences	758 sentences

Table 1. Experiment DataSet Setup

Tsinghua Chinese Treebank is a 1,000,000 words Chinese treebank covering a balanced collection of journalistic, literary, academic, and other documents.

7 Final Results

We took the final model and used it to parse the specified test set in the 3nd Chinese Parsing Evaluation which contains 1000 sentences, and achieved the best precision, recall and F-measure. We use the evaluation method released by CLP 2012.

SC_F1	ULC_P	ULC_R	ULC_F1
92.29%	87.02%	87.04%	87.03%

Table 2. Experiment Results of SC and ULC

NoCross_P	LC_P	LC_R	LC_F1
87.02%	77.29%	77.32%	77.30%

Table 3. Experiment Results of LC

LC_P	LC_R	LC_F1
76.35%	76.20%	76.27%

Table 4. Experiment Results of Tot4

Where LR = label recall, LP = label precision, F1 = F-measure, EX = exact match, AC = average crossing, NC = no crossing, 2C = 2 or less crossing.

8 Another Relabeling Method

A major observation is that concept compound constituent labels are detrimental to parsing performance. Since clausal and phrasal constituent labels are obligatory, while concept compound constituent labels are optional, we can strip concept compound constituent labels and parse with only clausal and phrasal constituent labels. Experiments show that parsing performance without concept compound constituents labels, especially the bracketing precision is significantly superior to the one with concept compound constituents labels.

Therefore, parsing directly with full labels (both clausal and phrasal constituent labels and concept compound labels) is unwise. In this paper, we get the concept compound label by the parser with full label, but get the extra performance gain by the parser with only clausal and phrasal constituent labels.

9 Integration of Both Parser

Clausal and phrasal constituent labels distinguish constituent phrasal categories, and full label (phrasal constituent label together with compound constituent label) moves forward to distinguish constituent structures.

A parser trained on the trees with only phrasal constituent labels have higher bracketing accuracy and phrasal constituent labels tagging accuracy. While another step can label the decoded tree with concept compound tags, either by incorporating the concept compound labels from the output of a parser trained on full label, or by relabeling the concept compound labels with a maximum entropy model.

In order to get strength from the both the parser output with and without concept compound labels, we train parser on both trees with only phrasal constituents label and full label, then add the concept compound labels from the later parser to the phrasal constituent labels from the former parser.

The simple PCFG identified the locations of correct constituents of the parse tree (the "gold constituents") with high precision and recall. Then we label the concept compound labels in corresponds to the complex PCFG.

10 Conclusion

We employ a novel parsing algorithm based upon the coarse-to-fine processing model. It takes the unpruned constituents and specifying them in the next level of granularity.

The coarse-to-fine scheme allows fast, accurate parsing. For training, one needs only a raw context-free treebank, and for decoding one needs only a final grammar, along with coarsening maps.

In addition, we propose a delicate integration method based upon two independently trained parsing models with different tree annotation style. The final output gains the higher bracketing label precision and recall from simpler tree annotation style, and adding the concept compound labels form the more complex tree annotation model.

Acknowledgements

This research is supported in part by the National Basic Research Program of China (No.2013CB329304) and the Key Program of National Social Science Foundation of China (No. 12&ZD119).

References

E. Charniak and M. Johnson. 2005. Coarse-to-Fine N-Best Parsing and MaxEnt Discriminative Reranking. In ACL'05.

E. Charniak, S. Goldwater, and M. Johnson. 1998. Edge-based best-first chart parsing. 6th Wkshop on Very Large Corpora.

E. Charniak,M. Johnson, et al. 2006. Multi-level coarse-to-fine PCFG Parsing. In HLT-NAACL '06.

Petrov, S., and Klein, D. 2007. Improved inference for unlexicalized parsing. In HLT-NAACL '07.

Petrov, S.; Barrett, L.; Thibaux, R.; and Klein, D. 2006. Learning accurate, compact, and interpretable tree annotation. In ACL '06.

M. Collins. 1999. Head-Driven Statistical Models for Natural Language Parsing. Ph.D. thesis, U. of Pennsylvania.

A. Corazza and G. Satta. 2006. Cross-entropy and estimation of probabilistic context-free grammars. In HLT-NAACL '06.

M. Dreyer and J. Eisner. 2006. Better informed training of latent syntactic features. In EMNLP '06, pages 317–326.

J. Finkel, C. Manning, and A. Ng. 2006. Solving the problem of cascading errors: approximate Bayesian inference for lingusitic annotation pipelines. In EMNLP '06.

J. Goodman. 1996. Parsing algorithms and metrics. ACL '96.

D. Klein and C. Manning. 2003. Accurate unlexicalized parsing. In ACL '03, pages 423–430.

T. Matsuzaki, Y. Miyao, and J. Tsujii. 2005. Probabilistic CFG with latent annotations. In ACL '05, pages 75–82.

D. McClosky, E. Charniak, and M. Johnson. 2006. Reranking and self-training for parser adaptation. In COLING-ACL'06.

M. Mohri and B. Roark. 2006. Probabilistic context-free grammar induction based on structural zeros. In HLT-NAACL '06.

S. Petrov, L. Barrett, R. Thibaux, and D. Klein. 2006. Learning accurate, compact, and interpretable tree annotation. In COLING-ACL '06, pages 443–440.

H. Sun and D. Jurafsky. 2004. Shallow semantic parsing of Chinese. In HLT-NAACL '04, pages 249–256.

Dan Klein and Chris Manning. 2003a. A* parsing: Fast exact viterbi parse selection. In Proceedings of HLT-NAACL'03.

N. Xue, F.-D. Chiou, and M. Palmer. Building a large scale annotated Chinese corpus. In COLING '02, 2002.

Qiang Zhou. Chinese Treebank Annotation Scheme. Journal of Chinese Information, 18(4), p1-8. (2004)

Qiang Zhou, Yuemei Li. Evaluation report of CIPS-ParsEval-2009. In Proc. of First Workshop on Chinese Syntactic Parsing Evaluation, Beijing China, Nov. 2009. pIII—XIII. (2009)

Qiang Zhou, Jingbo Zhu. Chinese Syntactic Parsing Evaluation. Proc. of CIPS-SIGHAN Joint Conference on Chinese Language Processing (CLP-2010), Beijing, August 2010, pp 286-295. (2010)

Traditional Chinese Parsing Evaluation at SIGHAN Bake-offs 2012

Yuen-Hsien Tseng[1], Lung-Hao Lee[1] and Liang-Chih Yu[2]
[1]Information Technology Center, National Taiwan Normal University, Taipei, Taiwan.
[2]Department of Information Management, Yuan Ze University, Chung-Li, Taiwan
{samtseng,lhlee}@ntnu.edu.tw, lcyu@saturn.yzu.edu.tw

Abstract

This paper presents the overview of traditional Chinese parsing task at SIGHAN Bake-offs 2012. On behalf of task organizers, we describe all aspects of the task for traditional Chinese parsing, i.e., task description, data preparation, performance metrics, and evaluation results. We summarize the performance results of all participant teams in this evaluation, in the hope to encourage more future studies on traditional Chinese parsing

1 Introduction

The Association of Computational Linguistics (ACL) is the international scientific ad professional society for people working on problems involving natural language and computation. There are about 20 Special Interest Groups (SIG) within ACL. Among these SIGs, SIGHAN provides an umbrella for researchers in industry and academia working in various aspects of Chinese language processing. Bake-offs are important events in SIGHAN, which provides Chinese evaluation platforms for developing and implementing various approaches to solve specific Chinese language issues.

Chinese parsing has been a resurged research area in recent years thanks to the commercial needs in mobile applications, and there is a pressing need for a common evaluation platform where different approaches can be fairly compared. Relevant events include the CoNLL-X (the 10th Conference on Computational Natural Language Learning, 2006) shared task, which evaluates multilingual dependency parsing techniques. This shared task provides the community with a benchmark for evaluating their parsers across different languages. The Chinese data is derived from the Sinica Treebank (Huang et al, 2000; Chen et al., 1999; Chen et al. 2003), which is regarded as the first data set designing for traditional Chinese parsing evaluation. The CoNLL 2007 shared task was the second year event devoted to dependency parsing. The task consists of two separate tasks: a multi-lingual track and a domain adaption track. The designed ideas of the shared task are motivated by the expectation that a parser should be trainable for any language, possibly by adjusting some parameters. The traditional Chinese data set can be used in this multilingual parsing evaluation.

At SIGHAN Bake-offs 2012, we organize the *Traditional Chinese Parsing* task that provides an evaluation platform for developing and implementing traditional Chinese parsers. The hope is that through such evaluation campaigns, more advanced Chinese syntactic parsing techniques will emerge, more effective Chinese language processing resources will be built, and the state-of-the-art techniques will be further advanced as a result.

On behalf of the task co-organizers, we give an overview of *Traditional Chinese Parsing* task at SIGHAN Bake-offs 2012, which is held within the second CIPS-SIGHAN joint conference on Chinese Language Processing (CLP 2012). The rest of this article is organized as follows. Section 2 describes the details of designed tasks, consisting of two sub-tasks, i.e. sentence parsing and semantic role labeling. Section 3 introduces the preparation procedure of data sets. Section 4 proposes the evaluation metrics for both sub-tasks. Section 5 presents the results of participants' approaches for performance comparison. Finally, we conclude this paper with the findings and future research direction in the Section 6.

2 Task Description

For the *Traditional Chinese Parsing* task (Task 4) of Bake-offs 2012, we designed two sub-tasks: 1) Task 4-1: *Sentence parsing* for evaluating the ability of automatic parsers on complete sentences in real texts. 2) Task 4-2: *Semantic role labeling* for evaluating the ability of automatic parsers on labeling semantic roles.

Each sub-task is separated as closed and open track. In the *Closed Track*, the participants can only use the training data provided by the organizers. In the *Open Track*, the participants can use any data sources in addition to the training data provided by the organizers. Submitted runs in these two tracks will be evaluated separately.

In addition, single systems and combined systems will also be evaluated separately in both tracks. *Single Systems* are parsers that use a single parsing model to accomplish the parsing task. *Combined Systems*, in comparison, are allowed to combine multiple models to hopefully improve performance. For example, collaborative decoding methods will be regarded as a combination method.

We further describe the details and give the examples of both sub-tasks as follows:

2.1 Sentence parsing

The goal of this sub-task is designed to evaluate the ability of automatic parsers on complete sentence parsing in real texts. Complete Chinese sentences with gold standard word segmentation are given as input, in which the word count of each sentence should be greater than 7. The designed parser should assign a POS tag to each word and recognize the syntactic structure of the given sentence as the output result.

The evaluation data sets are derived based on Sinica Treebank. The goal of Sinica Treebank is to provide a syntactic and structure-tagged corpus for improving the performance of automatic parsers by learning the syntactic knowledge. The complete set of part-of-speech tags is defined in the technical report #93-5 (CKIP, 1993). The structural information is defined as the phrase labels for representing syntactic knowledge. The complete set of phrase labels is defined in the construction process (Chen et al, 1999). We give the following example for more information:

- Input: 他 刊登 一則 廣告 在 報紙 上
- Output: **S**(agent:**NP**(Nh:他)| Head:VC: 刊登|theme:**NP**(DM:一則| Na:廣告)| location:**PP**(P:在|**GP**(**NP**(Na:報紙)|Ng:上)))

In this sub-task, we only focus on evaluating the ability of automatic parsers on syntactic structure recognition. That is, the **boundary** and **phrase label** of **a syntactic constituent** should be completely identical with the gold standard, which is regarded as a correctly recognized case. The semantic roles and part-of-speech tags in the output format will be ignored in this sub-task.

2.2 Semantic role labeling

In addition to syntactic information, the Sinica Treebank also contains sematic roles of each constituent. Hence, we design this sub-task for evaluating the ability of automatic parsers on labeling semantic roles. In this sub-task, the given input sentences are the same as the sentence-parsing sub-task. The parser should assign a semantic role of each top-level constituent. There are 74 abstract semantic roles including thematic roles, e.g. "agent" and "theme", the second roles of "location", "time" and "manner", and roles for nominal modifiers. The complete set of semantic roles is described in the related study (You & Chen, 2004). We also give the example shown as the follows:

- Input: 母親 帶 他們 到 溪 邊 去 釣魚
- Output: S(**agent**:NP(Na:母親)|**Head**:VC: 帶|**theme**:NP(Nh: 他們)|**location**:PP(P: 到 |NP(Na: 溪 |Ncd: 邊))|**complement**:VP(D: 去|VA:釣魚))

In this sub-task, we only evaluate the performance of automatic parsers on semantic role labeling. If the **boundary** and **semantic role** of **a syntactic constituent** is completely identical with the gold standard, that is a correct recognition. In the same way, we also ignore the phrase labels and part-of-speech tags in the output format for this sub-task.

3 Data Preparation

The data sets are divided into three distinct ones: 1) Training set: the sentences in this set are prepared for training the designed parsers. 2) Test set: there are 1000 newly developed sentences that are used for formal testing. 3) Validation set: the sentences are adopted for dry run. Table 1 shows the statistics of prepared sets, where #Word and #Sent denote the numbers of words and sentences, respectively. The details are described as follows.

Data Set	#Word	#Sent	Avg. Length
Training	391,505	65,243	6
Test	8,565	1,000	8.57
Validation	341	37	9.2

Table 1: Descriptive statistics of the data sets.

- Training Set

The training set is derived from Sinica Treebank according to sentence lengths and complexities. The original part-of-speech tags in the Treebank are simplified. Only the semantic roles of each top-level constituent are kept, the others are removed. Take the original sentence "S(theme:NP(Head:Nba:西遊記)|Head:V_11:是|range:NP(property:Ncb:我國|property:V‧的(head:VH11:著名|Head:DE:的)|Head:Nac:小說))" for example, this parsed sentence will be transformed as "S(theme:NP(Nb:西遊記) | Head:V_11:是 | range:NP(Nc:我國 | V‧的(VH:著名|DE:的)|Na:小說))" for training purpose.

- Test Set

One thousand newly developed sentences were selected from United Daily News Agency news corpus for both sub-tasks to cover different sentence lengths and complexities. Two annotators from the construction team of Sinica Treebank were asked to label the gold standard of the test set. For example, a selected sentence is "聯合國 大會 今天 並 未 調整 會員國 出資 比例". Its manually annotated gold standard is "S(agent:NP(Nc:聯合國|Na:大會)|time:Nd:今天|evaluation:D:並|negation:D:未|Head:VC:調整|goal:NP(S(NP(Na:會員國)|VC:出資)|Na:比例))"

- Validation Set

We also prepare additional 37 newly developed sentences as the validation set for dry run. The main purpose of dry run is for output format validation. The participants can submit several runs resulted from different models or parameter settings. During the dry run, each submitted run was evaluated to check whether the output format could be accepted in our developed evaluation tool. The evaluation reports will be returned to the participants to informat the paticipants whether their output formats are correct and how good are their current performance. With the dry run feedback, the participants can fine-tune their implemented systems to further enhance the performance.

4 Performance Metrics

For the sentence-parsing sub-task, we adopt the Precision (P), Recall (R) and F1 score as metrics for performance evaluation. The computation formulas are listed as follows:

- P= # of correctly recognized constituents / # of all constituents in the parsing output
- R= # of correctly recognized constituents / # of all constituents in the gold standard
- F1= (2*P*R) / (P + R)

The criterion for judging correctness is that the *boundary* and *phrase label* of a syntactic constituent should be completely identical with the gold standard. Only six phase labels (S, VP, NP, GP, PP, and XP) will be evaluated in the test set. The other labels such as "N‧的", "V‧地", and "得‧V" will be ignored.

For example, given an input sentence: "他 刊登 一則 廣告 在 報紙 上" and its parsing output of a proposed system: "S(agent:NP(Nh:他) | Head:VC:刊登| theme:NP(DM:一則| Na:廣告) | location:PP(P:在|NP(Na:報紙|Nc:上)))", the recognized constituents are: S(他刊登一則廣告在報紙上), NP(他), NP(一則廣告), PP(在報紙上), and NP(報紙上). The gold standard of this input sentence is: S(他刊登一則廣告在報紙上), NP(他), NP(一則廣告), PP(在報紙上), GP(報紙上), and NP(報紙). The evaluated tool will yield the following performance metrics:

- P = 0.8 (=4/5) Notes: #{S(他刊登一則廣告在報紙上), NP(他), NP(一則廣告), PP(在報紙上)} / #{S(他刊登一則廣告在報紙上), NP(他), NP(一則廣告), PP(在報紙上), NP(報紙上)}.
- R=0.6667 (=4/6) Notes: #{S(他刊登一則廣告在報紙上), NP(他), NP(一則廣告), PP(在報紙上)} / #{S(他刊登一則廣告在報紙上), NP(他), NP(一則廣告), PP(在報紙上), GP(報紙上), NP(報紙)}.
- F1=0.7273 (=2*0.8*0.6667/(0.8+0.6667))

For semantic role labeling sub-task, we adopt the same metrics. Similar computations are formulated as follows:

- P = # of correctly recognized roles / # of all roles in the recognized data
- R = # of correctly recognized roles / # of all roles in the gold standard data
- F1 = 2*P*R / (P + R)

The criterion for judging correctness is that the *boundary* and *semantic role* of a syntactic constituent should be completely identical with the gold standard. For example, given an input sentence: "母親 帶 他們 到 溪 邊 去 釣魚" and its possible parsing output: "S(agent:NP(Na:母親) | Head:VC: 帶 |agent:NP(Nh: 他們)|location:PP(P: 到|Na:溪邊)|deontics:D:去|Head:VA:釣魚)", the recognized semantic roles are: agent(母親), Head(帶), agent(他們), location(到溪邊), deontics(去), and Head(釣魚). The gold standard of this input sentence is: agent (母親), Head(帶), theme(他們), location(到溪邊), and complement(去釣魚). The evaluated tool will yield the following performance metrics:

- P =0.5 (=3/6) Notes: #{agent(母親), Head(帶), location(到溪邊)} / #{agent(母親), Head(帶), agent(他們), location(到溪邊), deontics(去), Head(釣魚)}.
- R =0.6 (=3/5) Notes: #{agent(母親), Head(帶), location(到溪邊)} / #{agent (母親), Head(帶), theme(他們), location(到溪邊), complement(去釣魚)}.
- F1=0.5455 (= (2*0.5*0.6) / (0.5+0.6))

In addition, we use micro-averaging and macro-averaging to measure the overall performance for both sub-tasks in the test set. Equation (1)~(6) show the formulations for measuring the performance, where P_{micro}, R_{micro} and $F1_{micro}$ denote micro-averaging precision, recall, and F1 score, respectively; P_{macro}, R_{macro} and $F1_{macro}$ stand for macro-averaging precision, recall, and F1 score, individually.

$$P_{micro} = \frac{\sum_{i=1}^{|S|} TP_i}{\sum_{i=1}^{|S|} TP_i + FP_i} \qquad (1)$$

$$R_{micro} = \frac{\sum_{i=1}^{|S|} TP_i}{\sum_{i=1}^{|S|} TP_i + FN_i} \qquad (2)$$

$$F1_{micro} = \frac{2 * P_{micro} * R_{micro}}{P_{micro} + R_{micro}} \qquad (3)$$

$$P_{macro} = \frac{1}{|S|} \sum_{i=1}^{|S|} \frac{TP_i}{TP_i + FP_i} \qquad (4)$$

$$R_{macro} = \frac{1}{|S|} \sum_{i=1}^{|S|} \frac{TP_i}{TP_i + FN_i} \qquad (5)$$

$$F1_{macro} = \frac{2 * P_{macro} * R_{macro}}{P_{macro} + R_{macro}} \qquad (6)$$

In the above equations, |S| denotes the number of sentence in the test set; TP is the number of constituents in the gold standard that are correctly recognized in the system output; FN is the number of constituents in the gold standard that are not correctly recognized in the system output; FP is the number of recognized constituents in the system output that are not in the gold standard.

5 Evaluation Results

Table 2 shows the participant teams and their submission statistics. The task 4 of Bakeoffs 2012 attracted 8 research teams. There are 4 teams that come from Taiwan, i.e. CYUT, NCU, NCYU, and NTUT & NCTU. The other 3 teams originate from China, i.e. UM, NEU and PKU. The remaining one is JAPIO from Japan.

Among 8 registered teams, 6 teams submitted their testing results. For formal testing, each participant can submit several runs that use different models or parameter settings. All submitted runs adopt a single parsing model, i.e. *Single System*, to accomplish the evaluated task. In Task 4-1, we received 8 submitted results, including 7 from closed track systems and 1 from an open track system. In Task 4-2, we received 4 submissions, including 3 from closed track systems and 1 from an open track system.

5.1 Analysis of sentence parsing

We evaluated the sentence parsing performance of both tracks separately. Table 3 and Table 4 show the evaluated results in closed track and open track, respectively. For closed track, we implement the baseline system using the Stanford parser (Klein and Manning, 2003; Levy and Manning, 2003) with default parameters for performance comparison. We only adopt the training set to learn the Chinese parsing model. In formal testing phase, there were 75 sentences that cannot be parsed using the re-train Stanford parser. Experimental results indicate that the baseline system achieves micro-averaging and macro-averaging F1 at 0.5822 and 0.5757, respectively.

Parts of the submitted runs perform better than the baseline results. Systems come from NEU-Run1 and NEU-Run2 achieve the best performance, i.e. 0.7078 for micro-averaging F1 and 0.7211 for macro-averaging F1. These two runs have the same syntactic structure, but different semantic role labels. However, only the phrase labels and their boundaries were evaluated in sub-task 1, so the performance is the same. Note that the NCTU&NTUT-Run1 was submitted a few days after the formal test deadline. However, we also evaluated their results for more information.

Only one team took part in the open track. The performance measures of this submission are micro-averaging F1 score: 0.4355 and macro-averaging F1 score: 0.4287. For performance comparison, we invited the Chinese Knowledge Information Processing Group (CKIP) in the Institute of information Science, Academia Sinica, to modify their designed Chinese parser (Yang et al. 2005; 2008; Hsieh et al. 2007) for this evaluation. The CKIP parser achieves the best micro-averaging and macro-averaging F1 scores at 0.7287 and 0.7448, respectively.

ID	Participants	Task 4-1		Task 4-2	
		Open	Closed	Open	Closed
1	Chaoyang University of Technology (CYUT)		1		
2	National Central University (NCU)		1		1
3	National Chiayi University (NCYU)		2		
4	National Chiao Tung University & National Taipei University of Technology (NCTU&NTUT)		1		
5	University of Macau (UM)		1		
6	Northeastern University (NEU)		2		2
7	Peking University (PKU)				
8	Japan Patent Information Organization (JAPIO)	1		1	
Total		1	8	1	3

Table 2: Result submission statistics of all participants in Task 4.

Submitted Runs	Micro-averaging			Macro-averaging		
	Precision	Recall	F1	Precision	Recall	F1
CYUT-Run1	0.6695	0.5781	0.6204	0.6944	0.5999	0.6437
NCU-Run1	0.6215	0.4764	0.5394	0.6317	0.4913	0.5527
NCYU-Run1	0.4116	0.4475	0.4288	0.4354	0.4663	0.4503
NCYU-Run2	0.4167	0.5104	0.4588	0.4352	0.5316	0.4786
*NCTU&NTUT-Run1	0.7215	0.387	0.5038	0.7343	0.4147	0.5301
UM-Run1	0.7165	0.6595	0.6868	0.7229	0.6718	0.6964
NEU-Run1	0.7293	0.6875	0.7078	0.7429	0.7005	0.7211
NEU-Run2	0.7293	0.6875	0.7078	0.7429	0.7005	0.7211
Stanford Parser (Baseline)	0.6208	0.5481	0.5822	0.5885	0.5634	0.5757

Table 3: Sentence parsing evaluation results of Task 4-1 (Closed Track), ordered with participant ID.

Submitted Runs	Micro-averaging			Macro-averaging		
	Precision	Recall	F1	Precision	Recall	F1
JAPIO-Run1	0.4767	0.4008	0.4355	0.5355	0.4195	0.4705
*CKIP Parser (Baseline)	0.7534	0.7057	0.7287	0.7693	0.7218	0.7448

Table 4: Sentence parsing evaluation results of Task 4-1 (Open Track), ordered with participant ID.

5.2 Analysis of semantic role labeling

Table 5 and Table 6 show the evaluation results of semantic role labeling in the closed and open tracks of Task 4-2, respectively. For closed track, we apply the well-known sequential model Conditional Random Field (CRF) as the baseline system for performance comparison. It scores at 0.4297 for micro-averaging F1 score and 0.4287 for macro-averaging F1 score. NEU's Run1 and

Run2 perform better slightly than the baseline when micro-averaging F1 is considered, which are 0.4343 and 0.4394, respectively. However, the baseline system achieves the best macro-averaging F1.

For open track, the only one submission achieves 0.2139 and 0.2374 of micro-averaging and macro-averaging F1 scores, respectively. The CKIP team was also asked to participate in this open track as the baseline system. The modified CKIP parser achieves the best results on labeling sematic roles of each top-level constituent. It accomplishes 0.6034 of micro-averaging F1 score and 0.6249 of macro-averaging F1 score.

Submitted Runs	Micro-averaging			Macro-averaging		
	Precision	**Recall**	**F1**	**Precision**	**Recall**	**F1**
NCU-Run1	0.3755	0.3429	0.3585	0.3506	0.3538	0.3522
NEU-Run1	0.4358	0.4328	0.4343	0.4192	0.416	0.4176
NEU-Run2	0.4409	0.4379	0.4394	0.4239	0.4209	0.4224
CRF (Baseline)	0.4382	0.4216	0.4297	0.4347	0.4229	0.4287

Table 5: Semantic role labeling results of Task 4-2 (Closed Track), ordered with participant ID.

Submitted Runs	Micro-averaging			Macro-averaging		
	Precision	**Recall**	**F1**	**Precision**	**Recall**	**F1**
JAPIO-Run1	0.2036	0.2255	0.2139	0.2333	0.2417	0.2374
*CKIP Parser (Baseline)	0.6019	0.6049	0.6034	0.6252	0.6247	0.6249

Table 6: Semantic role labeling results of Task 4-2 (Open Track), ordered with participant ID.

6 Conclusions

This paper describes the overview of traditional Chinese parsing evaluation at SIGHAN Bake-offs 2012. We describe the task designing ideas, data preparation details, evaluation metrics, and the results of performance evaluation.

For sentence parsing, the promising parsers achieve about 0.7 of F1 regardless which kind of training data is used to train the parsers. For the sub-task of semantic role labeling, the best system achieves about 0.6 of F1 score.

This Bake-off motivates us to build more Chinese language resources (e.g., modified Treebank and over 1000 new labeled sentences) for reuse in the future to possibly improve the state-of-the-art techniques for Chinese language processing. It also encourages researchers to bravely propose various ideas and implementations for possible break-through. No matter how well their implementations would perform, they contribute to the community by enriching the experience that some ideas or approaches are promising (or impractical), as verified in this bake-off. Their reports in this proceeding will reveal the details of these various approaches and contribute to our knowledge and experience about Chinese language processing.

After this bake-off evaluation, the resources and tools built for this evaluation will be released on the Web for the convenience of future studies.

Acknowledgements

Research fellow Keh-Jiann Chen, the leader of Chinese Knowledge Information Processing Group (CKIP) in Institute of information Science, Academia Sinica, is appreciated for supporting Sinica Treebank. We would like to thank Su-Chu Lin and Shih-Min Li for their hard work to prepare the test set for the evaluation. We would like to thank Kuei-Ching Lee for implementing the baseline systems for performance comparison. We thank Wei-Cheng He for developing the evaluation tools. Finally, we thank all the participants for taking part in the evaluation.

This research was partially supported by the "Aim for the Top University Project" of National Taiwan Normal University, sponsored by the Ministry of Education, Taiwan.

References

Chinese Knowledge Information Processing Group 1993. Categorical Analysis of Chinese. ACLCLP Technical Report # 93-05, Academia Sinica.

Chu-Ren Huang, Keh-Jiann Chen, Feng-Yi Chen, Keh-Jiann Chen, Zhao-Ming Gao, and Kuang-Yu

Chen. 2000. Sinica Treebank: Design Criteria, Annotation Guidelines, and On-line Interface. In *Proceedings of the 2nd Chinese Language Processing Workshop*, 29-37.

Dan Klein, and Christopher D. Manning. 2003. Accurate Unlexicalized Parsing. In *Proceedings of the 41st Annual Meeting of the Association for Computational Linguistics*. 423-430.

Duen-Chi Yang, Yu-Ming Hsieh, and Keh-Jiann Chen. 2005. Linguistically-Motivated Grammar Extraction, Generalization and Adaptation. In *Proceedings of the 2nd International Joint Conference on Natural Language Processing,* 177-187.

Duen-Chi Yang, Yu-Ming Hsieh, and Keh-Jiann Chen. 2008. Resolving Ambiguities of Chinese Conjunctive Structures by Divide-and-Conquer Approaches. In *Proceedings of the 3rd International Joint Conference on Natural Language Processing,* 715-720.

Feng-Yi Chen, Pi-Fang Tsai, Keh-Jiann Chen, and Chu-Ren Huang. 1999. The Construction of Sinica Treebank. *International Journal of Computational Linguistics and Chinese Language Processing,* 4(2): 87-104. (in Chinese)

Jia-Ming You and Keh-Jiann Chen. 2004. Automatic Semantic Role Assignment for a Tree Structure. In *Proceedings of the 3rd SIGHAN Workshop on Chinese Language Processing,* 1-8.

Keh-Jiann Chen, Chu-Ren Huang, Feng-Yi Chen, Chi-Ching Luo, Ming-Chung Chang, Chao-Jan Chen, and Zhao-Ming Gao. 2003. Sinica Treebank: Design Criteria, Representational Issues and Implementation. In *Anne Abeille (Ed.) Treebanks Building and Using Parsed Corpora*, Dordrecht:Kluwer, 231-248.

Roger Levy and Christopher D. Manning. 2003. Is it Harder to Parse Chinese, or the Chinese Treebank? In *Proceedings of the 41st Annual Meeting of the Association for Computational Linguistics*. 439-446.

Yu-Ming Hsieh, Duen-Chi Yang, and Keh-Jiann Chen. 2007. Improve Parsing Performance by Self-Learning. *International Journal of Computational Linguistics and Chinese Language Processing,* 12(2):195-216.

NEU Systems in SIGHAN Bakeoff 2012

Ji Ma, Longfei Bai, Ao Zhang, Zhuo Liu and Jingbo Zhu

Natural Language Processing Laboratory,
Northeastern University, Shenyang, Liaoning, China.
majineu@outlook.com
{longfeibai|liuzhuo|zhangao}@ics.neu.edu.cn
zhujingbo@mail.neu.edu.cn

Abstract

This paper describes the methods used for the parsing the Sinica Treebank for the bakeoff task of SigHan 2012. Based on the statistics of the training data and the experimental results, we show that the major difficulties in parsing the Sinica Treebank comes from both the data sparse problem caused by the fine-grained annotation and the tagging ambiguity.

1 Introduction

Parsing has been a major interest of research in the NLP community. For the last two decades, statistical approaches to parsing achieved great success and parsing performance has been significantly improved. One of the most important factors for developing accurate and robust statistical parsers for one language is the availability of large scale annotated Treebank in that language. The availability of the Sinica Treebank provides such an opportunity for developing statistical parsers for traditional Chinese.

In this paper, we analyze the difficulties in parsing the Sinica Treebank. By comparing the statistics between the Sinica Treebank and CTB we found that the fine-grained annotation schema adopted by the Sinica Treebank lead to more severe data sparse problem. By inspecting the parsing results, we also found that a great portion of parsing errors is caused by tagging errors. In particular, word classes such as Ng and Ncd are quite similar in their meaning. However, the two tags yield quite different syntactic structures.

2 Parsing Models

The probabilistic context free grammar is the basis for a great portion of parsing approaches developed in the last two decades. However, the vanilla probabilistic context free grammar achieves poor performance. This is due to its strong independence assumptions which lead to decisions made by the PCFG model extremely local thus lacks of discriminative power. In terms of weakening the independence assumption of the PCFG model, the approaches adopted by modern state-of-the-art parsers can be roughly divided into two categories.

Head driven methods or lexicalized methods (Collins, 1999; Charniak 2000) augment the PCFG model with bi-lexical dependencies, subcategorization frames and other information such direction and surface distances. With those information, the lexicalized parsers can make more informed decisions and parsing performance significantly improved over the vanilla PCFG model. However, the head driven methods may not suitable for the current task for two reasons. (1) to acquire the bi-lexical dependencies, a set of manually collected head finding rules are needed. To our knowledge, there is not such set of rules for the Sinica Treebank. (2) some of the information utilized by the head-driven model are specially designed for the Penn Treebank annotation scheme and when shifted to other annotation schemes, parsing performance dramatically decreases (Guldea, 2001).

Rather than using the bi-lexical dependencies, unlexicalized methods (Klein and Manning 2003; Matsuzaki et al., 2005; Petrov et al., 2006) augment the non-terminals of the PCFG model with latent annotations, PCFGLA hereafter. Those latent annotations are aimed to capture different behavioral preferences of the same non-terminal or production rule in different local context. For example, verb phrases are further split into several subcategories that capture the behavioral preference of infinitive VPs, passive VPs and intransitive VPs. With those latent annotations, parsing performance is greatly improved. Among the unlexicalized methods listed above, the one proposed by Petrov et al., (2006) can learn the latent annotations in a fully automatic manner.

Compare with the lexicalized methods, their approach does not rely on any head finding rules or corpus specific heuristics. Moreover, their approach consistently outperforms the lexicalized methods across corpus and languages (Petrov and Klein, 2007).

Thus, we choose the PCFG-LA proposed by Petrov et al., (2006) to be our model for the traditional Chinese parsing task.

2.1 A Brief Review of PCFG-LA

In this subsection we briefly review the method of Petrov et al., (2006). Petrov et al., (2006) learns a sequence of PCFG-LA models (G_0, G_1, ... ,G_6) in an iterative manner. The initial grammar G_0 is the one directly read off the Treebank with right binarization. In the *i-th* iteration, their method performs the following three sub-procedures:

Split: Each non-terminal are split into two new symbols. For example, suppose T is the parse tree of sentence S in the training corpus. F is a non-terminal in T and F generates span (r, t). L and R are also non-terminals in T. L and R generates span (r, s) span (s, t), respectively. After splitting, F is split into F1 and F2, L is split into L1 and L2, R is split into R1 and R2. The parameters are estimated using a variant of the EM algorithm. Specifically, the inside-outside probabilities can be computed as:

$$P_{in}(F_x, r, t) = \sum_{m,n} \beta(F_x \rightarrow L_m R_n) * P_{in}(L_m, r, s) * P_{in}(R_n, s, t) \quad (1)$$

$$P_{out}(L_m, r, s) = \sum_{x,n} \beta(F_x \rightarrow L_m R_n) * P_{out}(F_x, r, t) * P_{in}(R_n, s, t) \quad (2)$$

$$P_{out}(R_n, s, t) = \sum_{m,x} \beta(F_x \rightarrow L_m R_n) * P_{out}(F_x, r, t) * P_{in}(L_m, r, s) \quad (3)$$

Where β denotes the rule probabilities and the indexes m, n and x are all ranging from 1 to 2. In the E step, the partial count of the rule $P_x \rightarrow L_m R_n$ in T can be computed as

$$C(F_x, r, s, t \rightarrow L_m R_n) \propto P_{out}(F_x, r, t) * P_{in}(L_m, r, s) * P_{in}(R_n, s, t) \quad (4)$$

In the M step, the partial counts are used to re-estimate rule probabilities:

$$\beta(F_x \rightarrow L_m R_n) = \frac{C(F_x \rightarrow L_m R_n)}{\sum_{m,n} C(F_x \rightarrow L_m R_n)} \quad (5)$$

Merge: To control the grammar size, and also to prevent overfitting, in the merging stage, only the most important splits are reserved and all the others are merged back to the annotation before splitting. The importance of split each non-terminal is measured according to the loss of likelihood after merging it. Large loss denotes more important split therefore should be reserved. Petrov et al., (2006) adopted an efficient way to approximate the likelihood loss after merging each pair of new annotation.

Suppose T is the parse tree of sentence S in the training corpus. F is a non-terminal in T and F generates span (r, t). Suppose that in the i-th iteration, F is split into several new symbols F1, F2,.., Fk. The likelihood of the training data, the sentence-tree pair (S, T), can be computed using the inside-outside probability as

$$LL(S, T) = \sum_x P_{in}(F_x, r, t) * P_{out}(F_x, r, t) \quad (6)$$

Consider that we are going to merge F1 and F2 into F0, then the inside and outside probability are computed as:

$$P_{in}(F_0, r, t) = p_1 * P_{in}(F_1, r, t) + p_2 * P_{in}(F_2, r, t) \quad (7)$$

$$P_{out}(F_0, r, t) = P_{out}(F_1, r, t) + P_{out}(F_2, r, t) \quad (8)$$

Here p_1 and p_2 are relative weights of F1 and F2. Combining the new inside and outside probability, the likelihood after merging F1 and F2 is:

$$LL'(S, T) = P_{in}(F_0, r, t) * P_{out}(F_0, r, t) + \sum_{x=2}^{k} P_{in}(F_x, r, t) * P_{out}(F_x, r, t) \quad (9)$$

The likelihood is approximated as:

$$\Delta = \frac{LL'(S,T)}{LL(S,T)} \quad (10)$$

Smoothing: Smoothing is another way of preventing overfitting. In Petrov et al., (2006), the probability of a production rule $P(F_x \rightarrow L_m R_n)$ is smoothed by interpolate it with the average value of probabilities over x.

$$P'(F_x \rightarrow L_m R_n) = (1 - \alpha) * P(F_x \rightarrow L_m R_n) + \alpha * \sum_x P(F_x \rightarrow L_m R_n) \quad (11)$$

3 Experiments

3.1 Setup

We divided the original Sinica Treebank data provided by the organizer into training and development set. To construct a representative dev--elopment set, we select every 10th sentence of the original data to add to the development set and use the rest of the sentences as the training set. The statistics of the training set and the development set are shown in table 1. "#word type" and "#tag type" denotes the number of different word forms and POS tags. "#non-terminals" denotes the number of non-terminal labels.

	Training set	development set
#sentence	55606	6179
#words	333996	37058
#word type	40593	11534
#tag type	101	68
#non-terminals	78	52
average length	6.01	6.00

Table1. Statistics of the training and development set

Though out this paper, we use the Berkeley parser[1] with the default settings to train all the parsing models. Parsing performance is evaluated using the evalb[2] program.

3.2 Experimental Results

The initial models are trained using our training data without any treatments. The parsing performances are listed in table 2.

From table 2, we can see that the best parsing performance in terms of F1 score is 78.16, and the best tagging accuracy is 91.60. These numbers are far below that achieved on the Penn Chinese Treebank (5.1) even the average length of the sentences in CTB is longer than the Sinica Treebank and we assume that the Sinica Treebank suffers more from data sparse problem. Interestingly, from table 2 we can see that the best parsing and tagging performance are both achieved at the 4-th split-merge round and after that parsing performance started to drop. This further confirms our assumption since for the WSJ Penn Treebank and the Penn Chinese Treebank, the best performance is achieved around the 6-th split-merge round.

#Split	Recall	Prec	F1	POS
1	71.67	74.63	73.12	90.78
2	75.61	77.04	76.32	91.28
3	77.56	77.96	77.76	91.60
4	78.28	78.04	78.16	91.58
5	77.50	76.89	77.19	91.00
6	76.88	76.15	76.51	90.05

Table 2. Parsing performance on the development set. #Split is the number of split-merge round

One should note that we do not argue the parsing performance of the Sinica Treebank and CTB are directly comparable. However, we do believe that the difference between the statistics of the two Treebanks helps to identify some difficulties in parsing the Sinica Treebank.

By comparing the statistics between the training set in this work and the training set of CTB, we found that the CTB contains more words, totally 536806 words, while less different word forms, 36922 word forms. Moreover, CTB only contains 42 different POS tags which is less than a half of the POS tags of the Sinica Treebank. These numbers demonstrate that parameters are more sufficiently estimated on CTB than on the Sinica Treebank.

By inspecting the detail tree structures and labels in the Sinica Treebank, we found that the Sinica Treebank annotation is more fine-grained compare with that of CTB. For POS tags, all words are divided into 8 basic categories including nouns, verbs, prepositions... Each category contains several sub-classes. For nouns, person names are annotated as Nb and organizations are annotated as Nc while in CTB, these two types of nouns are all tagged as NR. Moreover, some of the sub-classes are further distinguished with suffix such as VC[+NEG]. Non-terminals are annotated in a similar manner. In Sinica Treebank, all non-terminals belong to one of the 7 basic classes including noun phrase, verb phrase, preposition phrase... Each of the class contains several sub-classes which might be further distinguished by some suffixes.

The Sinica Treebank annotation does make its labels carry more information. However, the data sparse problem caused by the fine grained annotation prevents the Berkeley parser from learning a high performance model. To examine the effect of decreasing the number of label types on parsing performance, we carried on another two experiments. In the first experiment, we removed all suffixes from the POS tags and non-terminal labels of Sinica Treebank. For example, removing suffix from V_11 yields V and removing suffix from VC[+NEG] yields VC. After removing suffixes, the number of different POS tags decreased to 55. For the second experiments, in addition to remove all suffixes, we also maps all non-terminal labels to one of the seven phrase labels including NP, VP, GP, PP, XP, DM and S. These labels are used to measure parsing performance by the official backoff task evaluation metrics. The mapping procedure is conducted according to the first letter of the non-terminal label of the Sinica Treebank. That is, non-terminal labels with the first letter 'N' are all mapped to NP and labels with first letter 'V' are all mapped to VP ...

[1] http://code.google.com/p/berkeleyparser/
[2] http://nlp.cs.nyu.edu/evalb/

Models	Prec	Recall	F1	POS
RAW	78.41	78.19	78.30	91.58
RMS	78.65	78.66	78.66	91.59
RMSM	75.77	75.62	75.69	89.97

Table 3. Parsing performance with different label set

Parsing performances are shown in table 3. "RAW" denotes the performance achieved on Sinica Treebank without any treatment. "RMS" denotes parsing performance achieved when label suffixes are removed. "RMSM" denotes parsing performance when both label suffixes are removed and non-terminals are mapped. For these settings, the best parsing performances in terms of F1 score are all achieved on the 4-th split-merge round and we omit the performance achieved on other rounds.

From table 3, we can see that on the one hand, 'RMS' improves parsing performance about 0.35 F1 points. This demonstrates that removing suffix to reduce the number of POS tag and non-terminal labels does to some degree helpful. On the other hand, aggressively maps non-terminal labels to only seven basic phrase labels hurts parsing performance dramatically.

Here, one may argue that these performances are not directly comparable since the gold development set for each setting are not annotated with the same label set. That is, scores for "RAW" setting is calculated against the development set without any treatment while scores for "RMS" setting is calculated against the development set which non-terminal labels' suffix are removed. For "RMSM", the gold development set only contains seven basic phrase labels. To handle this issue, we also mapped the parsing results of "RAW" and "RMS" to the seven basic phrase labels and the performance are listed in table 4. We see that "RMS_B" still yields the best performance.

Models	Prec	Recall	F1	POS
RAW_B	79.26	79.00	79.13	91.58
RMS_B	79.47	79.48	79.48	91.59
RMSM	75.77	75.62	75.69	89.97

Table 4. Parsing performance where non-terminal labels of the guess trees of "RAW" and "RMS" are mapped to seven basic phrase labels

The last issue we examine is tagging accuracy on parsing performance. To see this, we use the model trained with "RMS" setting to parse the development set where sentences are assigned with gold standard POS tags. The result is that parsing precision, recall and F1 boosted to 84.95, 84.44 and 84.69, respectively. These results illus trate that improving tagging accuracy can significantly boosting parsing performance on the Sinica Treebank. By inspecting the parsing errors which also evolve at least one tagging error, we found that one of the major sources of parsing errors is caused by Ncd-Ng ambiguity. Both the two POS tags denote position information such as 外/'outside', 中/'in'. For example 校外/'outside the school', 庭院中/'in the yard'. However, the two tags show quite different syntactic behavior. Ng always coupled with NP or VP and they together forms a GP while Ncd always comes after a NP or a sequence of nouns to form another NP as shown in Figure1.

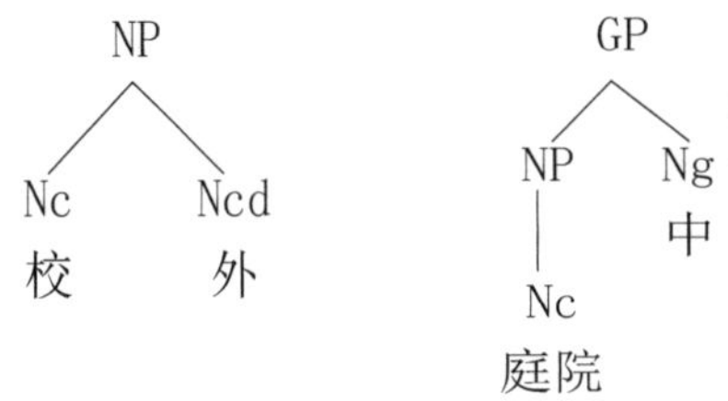

Figure1. Different syntactic structures between Ncd and Ng

Another major source of errors comes from noun-verb ambiguity which is also one of the most difficulty issues for tagging and parsing simplified Chinese. Such tagging error would results in a NP incorrectly analyzed as a VP and vice versa.

4 Conclusion

In this paper we analyze the difficulties in parsing the Sinica Treebank. We also examined the effect of tagging errors on parsing performance. We show that the fine-grained annotation schema of the Sinica Treebank is one major factor that prevents high parsing performance. In particular, the annotation schema leads to severe data sparse problem which makes the model parameters cannot be sufficiently estimated.

References

E. Charniak and M. Johnson. 2005. Coarse-to-fine n-best parsing and maxent discriminative reranking. In *ACL'05*, p. 173–180.

M. Candito, B. Crabbé and D. Seddah. On statistical parsing of French with supervised and semi-supervised strategies. 2009. In *EACL' 09*, p. 49-57

M. Collins. 1999. Head-Driven Statistical Models for Natural Language Parsing. Ph.D. thesis, U. of Pennsylva

D. Guldea. 2001. Corpus variation and parser performance. In *EMNLP '2001*, p. 167-202

D. Klein and C. Manning. 2003. Accurate unlexicalized parsing. *ACL '03*, p. 423–430.

T. Matsuzaki, Y. Miyao, and J. Tsujii. 2005. Probabilistic CFG with latent annotations. In *ACL '05*, p. 75–82.

P. Slav and D. Klein. 2007. Improved Inference for Unlexicalized Parsing. In *NAACL' 2007*, p. 404-411

P. Slav, B. Leon, T. Romain and D. Klein. 2006. Learning Accurate, Compact, and Interpretable Tree Annotation. *In COLING' 2006,* p. 433-440

Adapting Multilingual Parsing Models to Sinica Treebank

Liangye He, Derek F. Wong, Lidia S. Chao

Natural Language Processing & Portuguese-Chinese Machine Translation Lab
University of Macau
Macau SAR, China
wutianshui0515@gmail.com
{derekfw,lidiasc}@umac.mo

Abstract

This paper presents our work for participation in the 2012 CIPS-SIGHAN shared task of Traditional Chinese Parsing. We have adopted two multilingual parsing models – a factored model (Stanford Parser) and an unlexicalized model (Berkeley Parser) for parsing the Sinica Treebank. This paper also proposes a new Chinese unknown word model and integrates it into the Berkeley Parser. Our experiment gives the first result of adapting existing multilingual parsing models to the Sinica Treebank and shows that the parsing accuracy can be improved by our suggested approach.

1 Introduction

Work in syntactic parsing has developed substantial advanced Probabilistic Context-Free Grammar (PCFG) models (Collins, 2003; Klein and Manning, 2002; Charniak and Johnson, 2005; Petrov et al., 2006). The syntactic structures of English sentences can be well analyzed by utilizing these models. The highest traditional PARSEVAL F1 accuracy evaluation reported on English Parsing have already reached 92.4% (Fossum and Knight, 2009), which is very acceptable.

However, parsing Chinese still a tough task. Chinese varies from English in many linguistic aspects. That makes a big difference between the Chinese syntactic trees' structures and the English ones. For example, the Chinese syntactic tree is constructed flatter than the English one (Levy and Manning, 2003).

In this paper, we present our solution for the 2012 CIPS-SIGHAN shared task of Traditional Chinese parsing. We exploit two existing powerful parsing models – the factored model (Stanford Parser) and the unlexicalized model (Berkeley Parser), which have already shown their effectiveness in English, and adapt it to our task with necessary modification. First, in order to make use of Stanford Parser, we try to build a head propagation table of Traditional Chinese for the adaptation of the specific Traditional Chinese Corpus – Sinica Treebank (Chen et al., 2000). Second, we propose a new Chinese unknown word model to estimate the word emission probability, to improve the Traditional Chinese parsing performance for the Berkeley Parser.

2 Related Work

There have been several efforts to achieve high quality parsing results for Chinese by using varied parsing models (Bikel and Chiang, 2000; Levy and Manning, 2003; Petrov and Klein, 2007). Table 1 gives their respective performance.

We can see that the Berkeley Parser (Petrov and Klein, 2007) attained the state-of-the-art performance, around 83% PARSEVAL F1 measure on Penn Chinese Treebank (CTB) (Xue, 2002).

However, different corpus has different design criteria and annotation schema. As to our best knowledge, there is still no attempt to employ the existing parsing models to adapt to this Traditional Chinese Corpus. More work should be carried out to investigate what performances the

Work	Experimental Treebank	F1 Performance
Bikel and Chiang (2000)	CTB	76.7%
Levy and Manning (2003)	CTB	78.8%
Petrov and Klein (2007)	CTB	80.7%

Table 1: Previous Work on Parsing Chinese

mentioned existing sophisticated can get when utilized in different corpora.

2.1 The Sinica Treebank

In the 2012 CIPS-SIGHAN shared task of Traditional Chinese Parsing, the released training and testing datasets is extracted from the Sinica Treebank v3.0. The Sinica Treebank has some Traditional Chinese specific linguistic information annotated and is based on the Head-Driven Principle; each non-preterminal is made up of a Head and its modifiers. The phrasal type and the relations with other constituents are specified by the Head. For example, the traditional tree view of sentence *嘉珍和我住在同一條巷子* is shown in Figure 1:

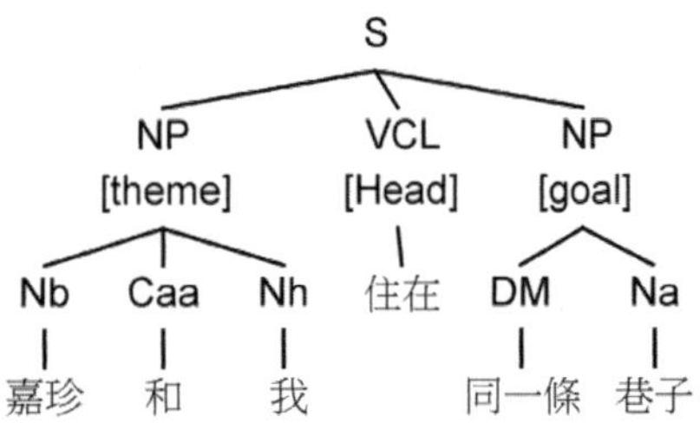

Figure 1: Part of the Sinica Treebank, each phrasal tag (in this case, *S*) is composed into Head and dependencies

3 Multilingual Parsing Models

In our experiments we will employ two multilingual statistical parsers – the Stanford Parser and the Berkeley Parser. We will describe the Stanford package and our modification in order to make this package adapt to the Sinica Treebank in Subsection 3.1. The Berkeley parser will be referred to in Section 3.2. In that Section we will also propose a new Chinese unknown word model.

3.1 The Stanford Parser

3.1.1 A Factored Model

A factored parser, which combine a high optimized unlexicalized parsing model (syntactic model) (Klein and Manning, 2003) and a dependency parser (semantic model) can be trained by the Stanford parser. The unlexicalized model produces a high optimized probabilistic context-free grammar, which adds some linguistically motivated annotation to both phrasal and Part-of-Speech tags to do disambiguation. In the lexical dependencies part, the information of direction, distance and valence between a constituent and its modifiers will be encoded into the dependency model. The probability of a tree is then calculated through the product of the probabilities that the syntactic model and the semantic model assign to that tree. Now the software package provides reinforcement for English, Chinese, Arabic, French and German.

3.1.2 Head Propagation Table for Sinica Treebank

In the newest version of Stanford parser, many languages are supported. In addition to using the default Chinese package[1], we have created the Sinica-specific extensions for Stanford parser. This package mainly contains a head propagation table, morphological features and some tuning of parser options for the Sinica Treebank.

In order to realize the rule binarization[2] for unlexicalized model and prepare the word-to-word affiliation for dependency model, the parser still needs to pick out the head child in the internal rule. Sinica Treebank indicates head information by adding some semantic label[3] to the phrasal tag, so we can build a head propagation table by traversing all the trees in the corpus.

[1] In the newest Stanford package, the default setting in Chinese Parsing is designed for CTB 5.0.
[2] See (Klein and Manning, 2003) for the explanation.
[3] We extract the head child which is tagged Head for the top phrasal tag

Parent	Direction	Priority List
S	left	*VP, VA, VA[+NEG], VA[+ASP], VA[+NEG,+ASP], VAC, VAC[+ASP], VB, VB[+ASP], VB[+DE], VB[+NEG], VC,VC[+ASP], VC[+NEG], VC[+DE], VC[+SPV], VC[+DE,+ASP], VCL,VD, VD[+NEG], VE, VE[+DE], VE[+NEG], VF, VG, VG[+DE], VG[+NEG], VH, VH[+D],VHC, VH[+ASP], VH[+NEG], VL, VK, VK[+ASP], VK[+DE], VK[+NEG], VI, VI[+ASP], VJ, VJ[+DE], VJ[+SPV], VJ[+NEG], V_11, V_12, V_2, V, S, NP, Na, Nb, Nc, Ndb, Ndc, Neqa, Neu, Ng, Nh, Nv, P,GP, DM, D, Dfa, A, Caa, Caa[P1], Caa[P2], Cab, Cbb*
VP	left	*VP, VA, VA[+NEG,+ASP], VA[+NEG], VA[+ASP], VAC, VAC[+SPV], VB, VB[+ASP], VB[+NEG], VC, VC[+NEG], VC[+DE], VC[+SPV], VCL, VCL[+NEG], VCL[+SPV], VD, VE, VE[+DE], VE[+NEG],VF, VG, VG[+NEG], VH, VH[+ASP], VH[+DE], VH[+NEG], VHC, VHC[+ASP], VHC[+SPV], VI, VJ, VJ[+DE], VJ[+NEG], VK, VK[+ASP], VK[+DE], VK[+NEG], VL, V_11, V_12, V_2, V, S, NP, Na, Nc, Ng, P, DM, D, Di, Dfa, Caa, Caa[P1], Caa[P2], Cab, Cbb,*
NP	left	*NP, N, Na, Nb, Nc, Ncd, Nd, Nda, Ndb, Ndc, Nde, Ndf, Nep, Neqa, Neqb, Neu, Nf, Nh, N・的, Nv, PP, P, GP, DE, DM, Caa, Caa[P1], Caa[P2], Cab*
GP	left	*VE, Ncd, Nes, Ng,P, GP, Caa, Caa[P1], Caa[P2]*
DM	left	*Neu, Nf, DM*

Table 2: The Head rules used for Sinica Treebank in the Stanford Parser

Table 2 gives our version of Traditional Chinese head propagation table. [4]

3.2 The Berkeley Parser

3.2.1 An Improved Unlexicalized Model

The Berkeley parser (Petrov et al. 2006; Petrov and Klein, 2007) enhanced the unlexicalized model which is adopted in the Stanford parser. In the grammar training phase, Berkeley parser use an automatic approach to realize the tree annotation which is analyzed and testified manually in Stanford's unlexicalized model; that is, iteratively rectify a raw X-bar grammar by repeatedly splitting and merging non-terminal symbols, with a reasonable smoothing. At first, the baseline X-bar grammar is obtained directly from the raw datasets by a binarization procedure. In each iteration, for splitting, the symbol could be split into subsymbols. This leads to a better parameter estimates for the probabilistic model. However, splitting will cause the overfitting problem. To solve this, the model will step into the merging and smoothing procedure. More details about the strategies of splitting, merging and smoothing, see (Petrov et al., 2006).

3.2.2 The Chinese Unknown Word Model

In parsing phase, if the unknown words belong to the categories of digit or date, the Berkeley Parser has some inbuilt ability to handle them. For words excluded these classes, the parser ignores character-level information and decide these words word categories only on the rare-word part-of-speech tag statistics. Let t denote the tag, and w denote the word. The model for estimation of the unknown word probability somehow can be written in this format:

$$P(w|t) \qquad (1)$$

In our work, we employ a more effective method, which is similar to but more detailed than the work of Huang et al. (2007), to compute the word emission probability to build up our

[4] We only show part of the head table which contains the main phrasal tags.

Model	PARSEVAL F1	POS Accuracy
Stanford-BA	45.20%	72.72%
Stanford-MOD	47.32%	72.92%
Berkeley-BA	49.60%	65.79%
Berkeley-MOD	50.42%	74.02%

Table 3: Experimental Results

new Chinese unknown word model. The geometric average[5] of the emission probability of the characters in the word is applied. We use c_k to denote k-th character in the word. Since some of the characters in w_i may not have appeared in any word tagged as t_i in that context in the training data, only characters that are mentioned in the context are included in the estimate of the geometric average then $P(c_k|t_i)$ is achieved:

$$P(w_i|t_i) = \sqrt[\Sigma\theta]{\prod_{c_k \epsilon w_i, P(c_k|t_{i_k}) \neq 0} P(c_k|t_{i_k})^{\theta_k}} \quad (2)$$

Where:

$$n = |\{c_k \in w_i | P(c_k|t_{i_k}) \neq 0\}|$$

$$\theta_k = \exp(-dis(c_k))$$

In (2), we use θ_k to assign a weight to the emission probability of each character c_k. We will determine the head character and use an exponential function to represent the distance between the head character and other characters. In our experiment, we will use the first character and the last character as the head character respectively and try out which position in a Chinese word is most important.

4 Experiment

4.1 Experimental Setup

In our experiment, we divide the Sinica Treebank in 3 parts following the traditional supervised parsing experimental protocol: training (first 80%), development (second 10%) and test (remaining 10%). We systematically report the result with treebank transformed. Namely, we preprocess the treebank in order to turn each tree into the same format[6] as in Penn Treebank since mentioned constituency parsers only accept this format.

4.2 Evaluation Metrics

We use the standard labeled bracketed PARSEVAL metric (Black et al., 1991) for constituency evaluation, all the phrasal tags will be taken into account.[7] Besides, we also report the POS accuracy.

4.3 Experimental Results

For better description, we name the basic version of Stanford parser as *Stanford-BA* and the modified version with the Traditional Chinese head propagation table as *Stanford-MOD*. While *Berkeley-BA* and *Berkeley-MOD* represent for the basic Berkeley parser and the intensive one respectively. Table 3 gives their performance on parsing Traditional Chinese.

Coming to a comparing among these two parsers, Berkeley parser has better overall performance. The basic version of Berkeley parser, *Berkeley-BA*, beat *Stanford-BA* in 4.4%, scored 45.20% and 49.60% F1 respectively. For each model, our modification for adaptation also makes an improvement. After deploying the specific head propagation table, we got 2.12% and 0.2% improvement in constituent accuracy and POS accuracy respectively. While the *Berkeley-MOD* benefits from the new Chinese Unknown word model, the constituent F1 and POS accuracy reach to 50.42% and 74.02% respectively[8].

5 Conclusion and Future Work

In this paper, we reported our participation in the CIPS-SIGHAN-2012 Traditional Chinese Parsing Task. We employed two statistical parsing models designed in multilingual style and apply them to parse the Traditional Chinese. Each baseline results were given. We also make this

[5] As Huang et al. (2007) suggested, the geometric average is better than arithmetic average, but we do not testify it in this paper due to tight schedule.

[6] All the Semantic Role Labels are eliminated.

[7] While the official evaluation only takes S, VP, NP, GP, PP, XP, and DM into account.

[8] We use Berkeley-MOD for CIPS-SIGHAN 2012 Bake-offs.

parser adapt to the Sinica Treebank. At first, For the Stanford Parser, we generated a head propagation table for Sinica Treebank. Besides, we also design a new Chinese unknown word model and integrate it into the Berkeley Parser. The result shows improvement over the base model.

However, after adapting those parsers to Traditional Chinese, we still find that probabilistic parsing was not efficient enough to provide accurate parsing result for Sinica Treebank compared to the work done in CTB. We still need to go deeper into the research of the corpus characteristics and the existing multilingual parsing models and make better adaptation.

Acknowledgments
This work was partially supported by the Research Committee of University of Macau under grant UL019B/09-Y3/EEE/LYP01/FST, and also supported by Science and Technology Development Fund of Macau under grant 057/2009/A2.

References

Bikel D. M. and Chiang D. 2000. Two Statistical Parsing Models Applied to the Chinese Treebank . *Second Chinese Language Processing Workshop*. 1–6.

Black E., Abney S., Flickenger S., Gdaniec C., Grishman C., Harrison P., Hindle D., Ingria R., Jelinek F., Klavans J. L., Liberman M. Y., Marcus M. P., Roukos S., Santorini B. and Strzalkowski T. 1991. A procedure for quantitatively comparing the syntactic coverage of English grammars. Proceedings of *the Workshop on Speech and Natural Language*. 306–311.

Charniak E. and Johnson M. 2005. Coarse-to-Fine n-Best Parsing and MaxEnt Discriminative Reranking. *Proceedings of the 43rd Annual Meeting of the Association for Computational Linguistics (ACL'05)*. 173–180.

Collins M. 2003. Head-driven statistical models for natural language parsing. *Computational Linguistics*. 29:589–637.

Fossum V. and Knight K. 2009. Combining Constituent Parsers. Proceedings of *Human Language Technologies: The 2009 Annual Conference of the North American Chapter of the Association for Computational Linguistics, Companion Volume: Short Papers*. 253–256.

Huang C. R., Chen F. Y., Chen K.J., Gao Z. M., and Chen K. Y. 2000. Sinica Treebank: Design Criteria, Annotation Guidelines, and On-line Interface. *Second Chinese Language Processing Workshop*. 29–37.

Huang Z., Harper M., and Wang W. 2007. Mandarin Part-of-Speech Tagging and Discriminative Reranking. Proceedings of *the 2007 Joint Conference on Empirical Methods in Natural Language Processing and Computational Natural Language Learning (EMNLP-CoNLL)*. 1093–1102.

Klein D. and Manning C. D. 2002. Fast exact inference with a factored model for natural language parsing. *Advances in Neural Information Processing Systems*. 15:3–10.

Klein D. and Manning C. D. 2003. Accurate Unlexicalized Parsing. Proceedings of *the 41st Annual Meeting of the Association for Computational Linguistics*. 423–430.

Levy R. and Manning C. D. 2003. Is it Harder to Parse Chinese, or the Chinese Treebank? Proceedings of *the 41st Annual Meeting of the Association for Computational Linguistics*. 439–446.

Petrov S., Barrett L., Thibaux R., and Klein D. 2006. Learning Accurate, Compact, and Interpretable Tree Annotation. Proceedings of *the 21st International Conference on Computational Linguistics and 44th Annual Meeting of the Association for Computational Linguistics*. 433–440.

Petrov S and Klein D. 2007. Improved Inference for Unlexicalized Parsing. *Human Language Technologies 2007: The Conference of the North American Chapter of the Association for Computational Linguistics; Proceedings of the Main Conference*. 404–411.

Xue N., Chiou F. D., and Palmer M. 2002. Building a large-scale annotated Chinese corpus. Proceedings of *the 19th International Conference on Computational linguistics-Volume 1*. 1–8.

Improving PCFG Chinese Parsing with Context-Dependent Probability Re-estimation

Yu-Ming Hsieh[1,2] **Ming-Hong Bai**[1,2] **Jason S. Chang**[2] **Keh-Jiann Chen**[1]
[1] Institute of Information Science, Academia Sinica, Taiwan
[2] Department of Computer Science, National Tsing-Hua University, Taiwan
morris@iis.sinica.edu.tw, mhbai@sinica.edu.tw,
jason.jschang@gmail.com, kchen@iis.sinica.edu.tw

Abstract

Selecting the best structure from several ambiguous structures produced by a syntactic parser is a challenging issue. The quality of the solution depends on the precision of the structure evaluation methods. In this paper, we propose a general model (context-dependent probability re-estimation model, CDM) to enhance the structure probabilities estimation. Compared with using rule probabilities only, the CDM has the advantage of an effective, flexible, and broader range of contexture-feature selection. We conduct experiments on the CDM parsing model by using Sinica Chinese Treebank. The results show that our proposed model significantly outperforms the baseline parser and the open source Berkeley statistical parser. More importantly, we demonstrate that the basic framework of the parsing model does not need to be changed, and the proposed re-estimation functions will adjust the probability estimation for every particular structure, and obtaining the better parsing results.

1 Introduction

Structure evaluation method is an important task in selecting the best structure from several ambiguous structures produced by a syntactic parser, particularly for Chinese. Since Chinese is an analytic language, words can play different grammatical functions without inflection. To implement a structure evaluation model, treebank is a necessary resource, since it provides useful statistical distributions regarding grammar rules, words, and part-of-speeches. Learning grammar rules and probabilities from treebanks is an effective way to improve parsing performance (Johnson, 1998). Unfortunately, sizes of treebanks are generally small; certain strategies of rule generalization and specialization have to be devised to improve the coverage and precision of the extracted grammar rules. However no matter how the grammar rules are refined, syntactic ambiguities are unavoidable. The ambiguous structures should be ranked according to their structural evaluation scores, which may be an accumulated score of rule probabilities and feature-based scores. In general, the evaluation functions are derived from very limited and biased resources, such as treebanks. Therefore we need to find a way to improve the evaluation functions under the constraint of very limited resources.

Suppose that the parsing environment is a model of probabilistic context-free grammar (PCFG). Several researchers are attaching many useful features to the grammar rules to improve the precision of the grammar rules (Johnson, 1998; Sun and Jurafsky, 2003; Klein and Manning, 2003; Hsieh et al., 2005). In this paper, we follow grammar representation in Hsieh et al. (2005), and propose a context-dependent probability re-estimation model (CDM) to enhance the performance of the original PCFG model. CDM combines rule probabilities and machine learning techniques in structure evaluation. Similar to other machine learning methods (Ratnaparkhi, 1999; Charniak, 2000; Wang et al., 2006), the CDM has the flexibility to adjust the features, and to obtain better re-estimated structure probabilities.

The remainder of this paper is organized as follows. Section 2 provides background on PCFG parsing with grammar rule representation. Section 3 describes the proposed CDM and our selected features. The experimental evaluation and results are in Section 4. The last section contains some concluding remarks.

2 Background

2.1 The baseline model, PCFG

PCFG-based parsing, a probabilistic context-free grammar parsing model that trains rule probabilities from treebank, is frequently used for parsing syntactic structures. Its parsing process is formulated as follows:

Given a sentence (S), a combination of words (W) and parts-of-speech (POS) sequences,

$$S = (W, POS) = (<w_1,...,w_m>, <t_1,...,t_m>),$$

a PCFG parser tries to find possible tree structures (T) of S. The parser then selects the best tree (T_{best}) according to the evaluation score of all possible trees:

$$T_{best} = \underset{T}{\operatorname{argmax}}\, Score(T,S)$$

Under the PCFG model, we divide a tree structure T into a set of sub-trees; that is, a set of grammar rules applied in T. If there are n context free grammar rules in a tree T, then:

$$Score(T,S) = \prod_{i=1 \in T}^{n} P(RHS_i \mid LHS_i)$$

Where LHS denotes the left-hand side of the grammar rule (e.g., non-terminal); RHS denotes the right-hand side of the grammar rule. To satisfy the probabilistic constraint, the following restriction is placed on the PCFG model:

$$\sum_{RHS \in R} P(RHS \mid LHS) = 1$$

We adopt logarithmic parsing probabilities in decoding; therefore, the cumulative product of probabilities $Score(T,S)$ can be replaced by accumulation of logarithmic probabilities in formula 1.

$$Score(T,S) = \sum_{i=1 \in T}^{n} \log(P(RHS_i \mid LHS_i)) = \sum_{i=1 \in T}^{n} RP_i \quad (1)$$

where RP_i represents the logarithmic probabilities of the i-th grammar rule in the tree T.

2.2 F-PCFG - the feature-extended PCFG

We adopt a linguistically-motivated grammar generalization method (Hsieh et al., 2005) to obtain a binarized grammar, called F-PCFG, from original CFG rules extracted from treebank. The binarized F-PCFG grammars are produced by grammar generalization and grammar specialization processes. The grammar binarization process may produce generalized grammars with better coverage. However, such grammars may degrade the representational precision. Therefore, a grammar specialization process is needed to improve precision of the generalized grammars under the constraint of without much sacrificing grammar coverage.

A method of embedding useful features in phrasal categories is adopted. In the following we use an example shown in Figure 1 to illustrate the grammar generalization and specialization processes. See Hsieh et al. (2005) for details. In this tree structure, Nh is pronoun; VF is active Verb with VP object; VC is Active transitive verb; Na is Noun. For detail explanation of POS, please refer to CKIP (1993).

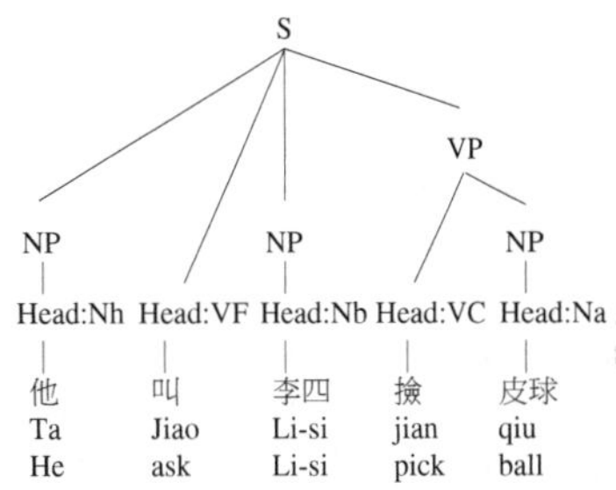

Figure 1. An example of a labeled syntactic tree structure in Treebank

Figure 2 shows the transformed tree representation by right-association binarization and feature embedding. We see that terminal nodes (i.e., $S_{\text{-NP-Head:VF}}$, $NP_{\text{-Head:Nh}}$) and intermediate nodes (i.e., $S'_{\text{-Head:VF-1}}$, $S'_{\text{-NP-0}}$, etc.). Both type of nodes attached the features of the left-most constituent of the RHS, phrasal category of parent-node, and existence of the phrasal head.

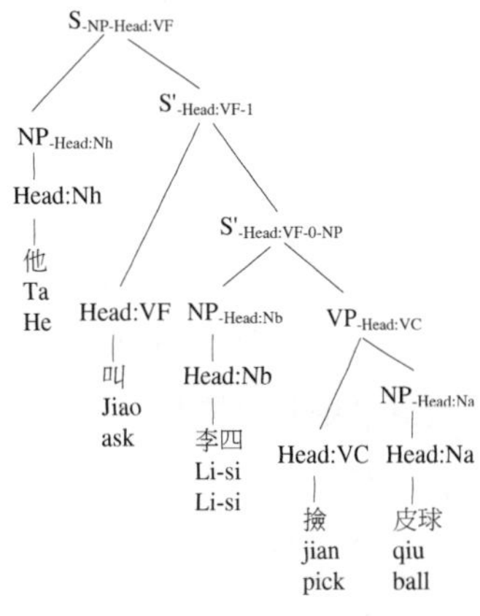

Figure 2. A transformed tree structure from original tree structure

We then use transformed binary trees to extract CFG and use maximum likelihood estimation to derive the rule probabilities from transformed Sinica Treebank (http://TreeBank.sinica.edu.tw).

3 Context-Dependent Probability Re-estimation Model

Many works try to improve rule probability estimation by using context-dependent probabilities in PCFG model, and show that rules with dependent context features perform better than PCFG alone (Ratnaparkhi, 1999; Charniak, 2000; Wang et al., 2006; Li et al., 2010). Charniak (2000) presented a maximum-entropy-inspired model to estimate probabilities in Markov grammar. The model uses a standard bottom-up best-first probabilistic chart parser to generate possible candidate parses in the first pass, and then evaluates the candidates with the proposed probabilistic model in the second pass. Therefore Charniak's method (2000) generates possible candidate parses first and then evaluates these candidates without early pruning. We adopt the maximum entropy method for structure evaluation, and integrate it into present PCFG model, called as CDM.

CDM integrates the original rule probabilities of PCFG and contextual probabilities as in the Formula 2:

$$Score(T,S) = \sum_{i=1 \in T}^{n} \lambda \times RP_i + (1-\lambda) \times CDP_i \, , \qquad (2)$$

where CDP_i represents the logarithmic probabilityestimated according to the *i-th* rule and related lexical, grammatical and contextual features. We calculated CDP_i by using the maximum-entropy toolkit (Zhang, 2004). The advantage of using the maximum entropy model is that it hasthe flexibility to adjust features. To set a proper ratio for the probabilities estimated by the joint RP_i and CDP_i, we use the parameter λ in Formula 2. We use Collins' (1999) smoothing method during the estimation of the probabilities.

3.1 Feature Design

Feature selection is the most important step of any classifier and directly influences the parsing performance. Johnson (1998) observed that adding linguistic features (such as a parent node's category) improves accuracy of grammar rules; and Collins (1999) assessed the importance of head word and word bigram information in phrases. Sun and Jurafsky (2003) posited that the number of syllables in a word plays an important role in Chinese syntax. Hence, we try to include useful features for parsing Chinese. Suppose we need to calculate CDP_i based on the related features, while the *i-th* rule is applied for covering a span of words [L…R]. The used context and contextual features are as follows:

- **Lexical features** include word (*W*), parts-of-speech (*C*) and word sense (*V*) features. Our word sense feature uses the E-HowNet (will be discussed in Section 4) sense definition.
- **Grammar features**, which provide relevant information used in applying grammar rules, include features of the phrasal category of the LHS (*LHS Category*), the constituents of the right-hand-side of rule (*RHS*), and the attached features of the LHS (*LHS Feature*) in our F-PCFG.
- **Context features** include span words and immediately neighboring lexical units.

Table 1 shows the details of the feature templates. After feature selection phase, we train a CDM model by the maximum entropy method and apply it to re-estimate structure evaluation score in every parsing stage.

Feature template and description
The word *L, R* information. (LW_0, LC_0, LV_0, RW_0, RC_0, RV_0)
The LHS, RHS and features of each grammar rule. (*LHS Category, RHS, LHS Feature*)
The previous and next lexical unit of the word L,R (LW_{-1}, LC_{-1}, LW_1, LC_1, RW_{-1}, RC_{-1}, RW_1, RC_1)
The word bigram information of the RHS, including word, parts-of-speech and word sense combination. ($RhsW_1$&$RhsW_2$, $RhsC_1$&$RhsC_2$, $RhsV_1$&$RhsV_2$)
The combination of *L* or *R* with the previous lexical unit, or with the next lexical unit. (LW_{-1}&LW_0, LC_{-1}&LC_0, LW_0&LW_1, LC_0&LC_1, RW_0&RW_1, RC_0&RC_1, RW_{-1}&RW_0, RC_{-1}&RC_0)
The combination of *L* and *R*'s immediate neighboring lexical units (LW_0&RW_0, LC_0&RC_0, LW_{-1}&RW_1, LC_{-1}&RC_1)

Table 1. Feature templates for context-dependent estimation of partial tree structure while covering a span of words [L…R]

For instance, Figure 3 shows a partial parsing stage. We estimate the structure evaluation score $P(S'_{-Head:VF+0+NP} \mid$ features as shown in Table 1) for the non-terminal $S'_{-Head:VF+0+NP}$ which covers a span of words [李四 Li-si … 皮球 ball] by the maximal entropy model. Some examples of contextual features are "LW_0=李四, RW_0=皮球, LW_{-1}=叫, LW_1=撿, RW_{-1}=撿, RW_1=X, LW_{-1}&LW_0=叫&李四, LW_0&LW_1=李四&撿, RW_{-1}&RW_0=撿&皮球, RW_0&RW_1=皮球&X, $RhsW_1$=李四, $RhsW_2$=撿, $RhsC_1$=Nb, $RhsC_2$=VC, RHS=$NP_{-Head:Nb}$_$VP_{-Head:VC}$, …", *etc.* Afterwards, we integrate and calculate the evaluation score by Formula 2.

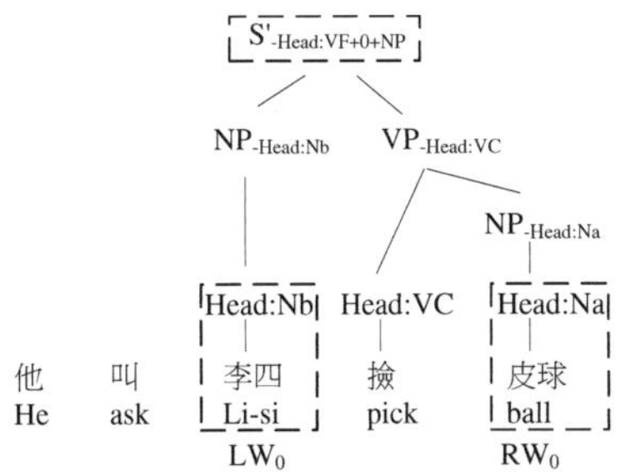

Figure 3. A partial tree of a parsing stage covered from "李四 Li-si" to "皮球 ball".

4 Experiments and Results

In this section, we describe the experiment design, and then evaluate the proposed models based on Sinica Treebank. We also analyze the results, and compare them with the results derived by the open source Berkeley statistical parser on the same test set.

4.1 Experimental Settings

Treebank: We employ Sinica Treebank as our experimental corpus. It contains 61,087 syntactic tree structures and 361,834 words. The syntactic theory of Sinica Treebank is based on the Head-Driven Principle (Huang et al., 2000); that is, a sentence or phrase is composed of a phrasal head and its arguments or adjuncts. We divide the treebank into four parts: the training data (55,888 sentences), the development set (1,068 sentences), the test data T06 (867 sentences), and the test data T07 (689 sentences). The test datasets (T06, T07) were used in CoNLL06 and CoNLL07 dependent parsing evaluation individually. The main difference between Sinica Treebank data and CoNLL data is that the CoNLL is in dependency format.

Word Sense: With regard to semantic features, we use the head senses of words expressed in E-HowNet (http://ehownet.iis.sinica.edu.tw/) as words' sense types. For example, the E-HowNet definition of 車輛 (Na), is {LandVehicle|車:quantity={mass|眾}}, and its head sense is "LandVehicle|車". For detailed description about E-HowNet, readers may refer to Huang et al. (2008).

Estimate Parsing Performance: To evaluate a model, we compare the parsing results with the gold standard. Black et al. (1991) proposed a structural evaluation system is called PARSEVAL. In all the experiments, we used the bracketed *f*-score (BF) as the parsing performance metric.

$$\text{Bracketed F-score (BF)} = \frac{\text{BP} * \text{BR} * 2}{\text{BP} + \text{BR}}$$

$$\text{Bracketed Precision (BP)} = \frac{\text{\# bracket correct consitituents in parser's parse of testing data}}{\text{\# bracket constituents in parser's of testing data}}$$

$$\text{Bracketed Recall (BR)} = \frac{\text{\# bracket correct consitituents in parser's parse of testing data}}{\text{\# bracket constituents in treebank's of testing data}}$$

For training *CDP* in CDM model, we extract relevant features from each parse tree in training data, in accordance with features setting in Table 1. Zhang (2004) provides a maximum entropy toolkit (MaxEnt) to help us training. We use option "-i 30 –gis –c 0" in MaxEnt training parameter. The training scale is 407 outcomes, 2438366 parameters and 1593985 predicates.

4.2 Results

Figure 4 shows the parsing performances on the developing data for different values of the parameter λ in Formula 2. The appropriate setting (λ=0.6) is learned and adopted for the future experiments.

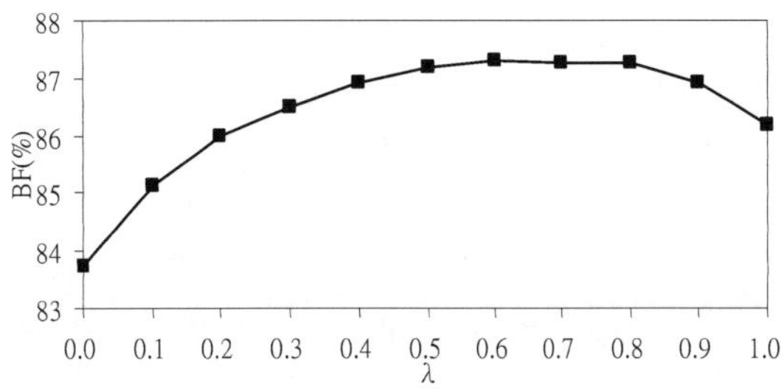

Figure 4. BF scores for different values of λ on the development data set

The results in Table 2 show that the integrated a general PCFG model with a CDM can improve the parsing performance. Implementing the integrated CDM on the T06 and T07 test datasets indicted improved the parsing performance by 1.45% and 1.53% respectively. The purpose in this research is to incorporate the rich contextual features to assist the constituent parsing. Results in Table 2 prove our method to be useful. As shown in the bracketed *f*-scores, about 20% of the errors are reduced. For instance, the ambiguous structures like "((Nh Nc) Nc)" and "(Nh (Nc Nc))" can be better resolved by our CDM model, since it can provide rich contextual features as additional information to help the parser making more precise evaluation scores in resolving ambiguous structures.

BF-Score (%)	T06	T07
PCFG	87.40	81.93
F-PCFG	88.56	83.96
CDM	90.01 (+1.45)	85.49 (+1.53)

Table 2. The bracketed *f*-score of the integrated CDM.

4.3 Comparison with the Berkeley Chinese parser

Berkeley parser[1] (Petrov et al., 2006) is used for comparison in our experiments because it appears to be the best PCFG parser for non-English languages. The parser has POS tagging and parsing functions; meanwhile, it takes word segmented data as input and outputs Penn Treebank style tree structures. We need to use pre-specified gold standard POS tags in our experiment, we transform our test data to "Berkeley CoNLL format" with word and POS. In addition, we need to transform our training data from Sinica Treebank style to Penn Treebank style (see Table 3) for Berkeley parser training model.

Tree style	Example
Sinica Treebank	S(NP(Head:Nh:他們)|Head:VC:散播 |NP(Head:Na:熱情))
Penn Treebank	((S (NP (Head:Nh (Nh 他們))) (Head:VC (VC 散播)) (NP (Head:Na (Na 熱情)))))

Table 3. Comparison of the Sinica and Penn Treebank styles

After re-training the Berkeley's parser with parameters, "*-treebank CHINESE –SMcycles 6 -useGoldPOS*", a new model is obtained. We parse the test dataset based on the gold standard word segmentation and POS tags. Then, we transform to Sinica Treebank style from the parsing results and evaluate by the same parsing performance metric. In our experiment, Berkeley's parser has best performance in using training model with 2th split-merge iterations. The bracketed *f*-score results of T06 and T07 test datasets are 88.58% and 83.56% respectively. The results of Berkeley's parser are closed to F-PCFG model in Table 2. Either Berkely's parser or F-PCFG represents the ceiling results of a general method, and they both outperform the naïve PCFG model.

[1] The version is "2009 1.1" and download from http://code.google.com/p/berkeleyparser/

4.4 Experiments for Task4 of CLP2012

Task 4 of CLP2012 includes two sub-tasks: sentence parsing and semantic role labeling task. For each sub-task, the testing data are complete Chinese sentence with gold standard word segmentation. Therefore, a pipeline process is needed to solve the POS tagging, syntactic parsing and semantic role assignment in our experiment. We adopt the context-rule tagger proposed by Tsai and Chen (2004) for the POS tagging. For syntactic parsing, we use the CDM parser with same training data in Section 4.1. For semantic role labeling, we follow You and Chen's (2004) method to assignment semantic role automatically. The detail parsing results of our systems on the test set can be found on the official evaluation report. Our system obtains acceptable results on both sentence parsing and semantic role labeling tasks.

F1-Score	Micro-Averaging	Macro-Averaging
Task 4-1	0.7287	0.7448
Task 4-2	0.6034	0.6249

Table 4. Official scores of sentence parsing (task4-1) and semantic role labeling (task4-2).

Table 4 shows the F1-score results are reported by the official organizer of the 2012 CIPS-SIGHAN bakeoff task. The result of the first sub-task (Task4-1) is about 0.7448. The POS tagging accuracy directly influences the sentential structure. Therefore, F1-score will be improved with better POS tagging accuracy. On the other hand, the result of the semantic role labeling (Task 4-2) is about 0.6249. Semantic role labeling is processed after sentence parsing. Our labeling system is based on different decision features, such as head-argument/modifier pairs, special cases, sentence structures, etc. These statistical information are extracted from training data (see Section 4.1), and we use a backoff approach to decide the best semantic role. In future work, we will try using lexical semantic and context information to improve accuracy of semantic role labeling.

5 Conclusion

In this paper, we propose effective models to improve the performance of Chinese parsing. The models employ a broad range of features to integrate general statistical parsing and machine learning techniques to re-estimate structure score in module and incremental way. Our evaluations show that by adding CDM models, the parser outperforms the baseline PCFG model and an open source statistical parser.

We also consider a number of future research directions. In addition to the current treebank and lexical semantic information, more knowledge could be obtained from massive amounts of unlabeled data to make CDM more precise through auto-parsing and self-learning process. Our ultimate goal is to generate unlimited amounts of training data by parsing web corpus. As a result, we expect that the overall performance of our parser will be improved continually by the never ending self-learning process.

References

Adwait Ratnaparkhi. 1999. Learning to Parse Natural Language with Maximum Entropy Models. *Machine Language*, 34(1-3):151-175.

Chu-Ren Huang, Keh-Jiann Chen, Feng-Yi Chen, Keh-Jiann Chen, Zhao-Ming Gao and Kuang-Yu Chen. 2000. Sinica Treebank: Design Criteria, Annotation Guidelines, and On-line Interface. In *Proceedings of 2nd Chinese Language Processing Workshop*, pages 29-37.

CKIP. 1993. *Chinese Electronic Dictionary*. Technical Report, No. 93-05, Academia Sinica, Taiwan.

Dan Klein and Christopher Manning. 2003. Accurate Unlexicalized Parsing. In *Proceedings of the ACL 2003*, pages 423-430.

E. Black, S. Abney, D. Flickinger, C. Gdaniec, R. Grishman, P. Harrison, D. Hindle, R. Ingria, F. Jelinek, J. Klavans, M. Liberman, M. Marcus, S. Roukos, B. Santorini, and T. Strzalkowski. 1991. A procedure for quantitatively comparing the syntactic coverage of English grammars. In *Proceedings of the DARPA Speech and Natural Language Workshop*, pages 306-311.

Eugene Charniak. 2000. A Maximum Entropy Inspired Parser. In *Proceedings of NAACL 2000*, pages 132-139.

Honglin Sun and Daniel Jurafsky. 2003. The effect of rhythm on structural disambiguation in Chinese. In *Proceedings of SIGHAN Workshop*.

Jia-Ming You, Keh-Jiann Chen. 2004. Automatic Semantic Role Assignment for a Tree Structure. In *Proceedings of SIGHAN Workshop*.

Junhji Li, Guodong Zhou, and Hwee Tou Ng. 2010. Joint Syntactic and Semantic Parsing of Chinese. In *Proceedings of ACL 2010*, pages 1108-1117.

Le Zhang. 2004. *Maximum Entropy Modeling Toolkit for Python and C++*. Reference Manual.

Mark Johnson. 1998. PCFG Models of Linguistics Tree Representations. *Computational Linguistics*, 24(4):613-632.

Mengqiu Wang, Kenji Sagae, and Teruko Mitamura. 2006. A Fast, Accurate Deterministic Parser for Chinese. In *Proceedings of COLING-ACL 2006*, pages 425-432.

Michael Collins. 1999. *Head-Driven Statistical Models for Natural Language Parsing*. Ph.D. thesis, University of Pennsylvania.

Shu-Ling Huang, You-Shan Chung, and Keh-Jiann Chen. 2008. E-HowNet: the Expansion of HowNet. In *Proceedings of the First National HowNet Workshop*.

Slav Petrov, Leon Barrett, Romain Thibaux and Dan Klein. 2006. Learning Accurate, Compact, and Interpretable Tree Annotation. In *Proceesings of COLING/ACL 2006*.

Yu-Fang Tsai and Keh-Jiann Chen. 2004. Reliable and Cost-Effective Pos-Tagging. *International Journal of Computational Linguistics and Chinese Language Processing*, 9(1):83-96.

Yu-Ming Hsieh, Duen-Chi Yang, and Keh-Jiann Chen. 2005. Linguistically-Motivated Grammar Extraction, Generalization and Adaptation. In *Proceedings of IJCNLP 2005*, pages 177-187.

Sentence Parsing with Double Sequential Labeling in Traditional Chinese Parsing Task

Shih-Hung Wu, Hsien-You Hsieh
Chaoyang University of Technology
Wufeng, Taichung, Taiwan, ROC.
shwu@cyut.edu.tw,
s10127602@gm.cyut.edu.tw

Liang-Pu Chen
Institute for Information Industry
Taipei, Taiwan, ROC.
eit@iii.org.tw

Abstract

In this paper, we propose a new sequential labeling scheme, double sequential labeling, that we apply it on Chinese parsing. The parser is built with conditional random field (CRF) sequential labeling models. One focuses on the beginning of a phrase and the phrase type, while the other focuses on the end of a phrase. Our system, CYUT, attended 2012 the second CIPS-SGHAN conference Bake-off Task4, traditional Chinese parsing task, and got promising result on the sentence parsing task.

1 Introduction

Parsing is to identify the syntactical role of each word in a sentence, which is the starting point of natural language understanding. Thus, parser is an important technology in many natural language processing (NLP) applications. Theoretically, given a correct grammar, a parser can parse any valid sentence. However, in real world each writer might have a different grammar in mind; it is hard to parse all the sentences in a corpus without a commonly accepted grammar. PARSEVAL measures help to evaluate the parsing results from different systems in English (Harrison et al., 1991).

Parsing Chinese is even harder since it lacks of morphological markers on different part-of-speech (POS) tags, not to mention the different standards of word segmentation and POS tags. In 2012 CIPS-SGHAN Joint Conference on Chinese Language Processing, a traditional Chinese parsing task was proposed. The task was similar to the previous simplified Chinese parsing task (Zhou and Zhu, 2010), but it was with different evaluation set and standard. In this task, systems should recognize the phrase labels (S, VP, NP, GP, PP, XP, and DM), corresponding to Clause, Verb Phrase, Noun Phrase, Geographic Phrase, Preposition Phrase, Conjunction Phrase, and Determiner Measure phrase, all of which were defined in the User Manual of Sinica Treebank v3.0[1]. The goal of the task is to evaluate the ability of automatic parsers on complete sentences in real texts. The task organizers provide segmented corpus and standard parse tree. Thus, the task attenders can bypass the problem of word segmentation and the POS tag set problem, and focus on identifying the phrase boundary and type. The test set is 1,000 segmented sentences. Each sentence has more than 7 words, for example:

他 刊登 一則 廣告 在 報紙 上.

(He published an advertisement on newspaper in)

The system should recognize the syntactic structure in the given sentences, such as:

S(agent:NP(Nh:他) | Head:VC:刊登 | theme: NP (DM:一則 | Na: 廣告) | location: PP (P:在 | GP(NP(Na:報紙) | Ng:上))).

In additional to the sentence parsing task, there is a semantic role labeling task, which aims to find semantic role of a syntactic constituent. The participants can use either the training data provided by the organizers, which is called closed track, or the additional data, which is called open track.

In the following sections we will report how we use sequential labeling models on sentence chunking in the sentence parsing task in the closed track.

2 Methodology

Sequential labeling is a machine learning method that can train a tagger to tag a sequence of data.

[1] http://turing.iis.sinica.edu.tw/treesearch, page 6

The method is widely used in various NLP applications such as word segmentation, POS tagging, named entity recognition, and parsing. Applying the method to different tasks requires different adjustment; first at all is to define the tag set. On POS tagging task, the tag set is defined naturally, since each word will have a tag on it from the POS tag set. On other tasks, the tag set is more complex, usually including the beginning, the end, and outside of a sub-sequence. With an appropriate tag set, the tagging sequence can indicate the boundary and the type of a constituent correctly.

Our parsing approach is based on chunking (Abney, 1991) as in the previous Chinese parsing works (Wu et al. 2005, Zhou et al. 2010). Finkel et al. (2008) suggested CRF to train the model for parsing English. Since chunking only provides one level of parsing, not full parsing, several different approaches were proposed to achieve full parsing. Tsuruoka et al. (2009) proposed a bottom-up approach that the smallest phrases were constructed first, and merge into large phrases. Zhou et al. (2010) proposed another approach that maximal noun phrases were recognized first, and then decomposed into basic noun phrases later. Since one large NP often contains small NPs in Chinese, this approach can simplify many Chinese sentences. In this paper, we also define a double sequential labeling scheme to deal with the problem in a simpler way.

2.1 Sequential labeling

Many NLP applications can be achieved by sequential labeling. Input X is a data sequence to be labeled, and output Y is a corresponding label sequence. While each label Y is taken from a specific tag set. The model can be defined as:

$$p(Y \mid X) = \frac{1}{Z(X)} \exp(\sum_k \lambda_k f_k) \quad (1)$$

where $Z(X)$ is the normalization factor, f_k is a set of features, λ_k is the corresponding weight. Many machine learning methods have been used on training the sequential labeling model, such as Hidden Markov Model, Maxima Entropy (Berger, 1996), and CRF (Lafferty, 2001). These models can be trained by a corpus with correct labeling and used as a tagger to label new input. The performance is proportional to the size of training set and counter proportional to the size of tag set. Therefore, if large training set is not available, decreasing the tag set can be a way to promote the performance. In this task, we define two small tag sets for the closed task.

2.2 Double sequential labeling scheme

Sequential tagging can be used for labeling a series of words as a chunk by tagging them as the Beginning, or Intermediate of the chunk. The tagging scheme is call the B-I-O scheme. For the parsing task, we have to define two tags for each type of phrase, such as B-NP and I-NP for the noun phrase. The B-I-O scheme works well on labeling non-overlapping chunks. However, it cannot specify overlapping chunks, such as nested named entities, or long NP including short NPs.

In order to specify the overlapping chunks, we define a double sequential tagging scheme, which consists of two taggers, one is tagging the input sequence with I-B tags, and the other is tagging the input sequence with I-E tags, where E means the ending of some chunk. The first tagger can give the type and beginning position of each phrase in the sentence, while the second tagger can indicate the ending point of each phrase. Thus, many overlapping phrase can be specified clearly with this technology.

3 The Parsing Technology

The architecture of our system is shown in Figure 1. The system consists of three tagging modules and one post-processing module.

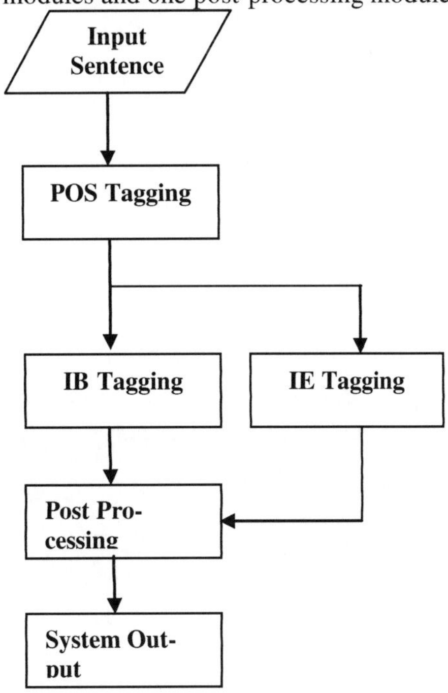

Figure 1. System architecture

The POS tagger will label each word in the input sentence with a POS tag. Then the sentence and the corresponding POS tags will be double labeled with beginning-or-intermediate-of-a-type and ending-or-not tag by the IB and IE taggers. A post-processing module will give the final boundary and the phrase type tag of the sentence. Each component will be described in the following subsections.

3.1 Part-of-Speech tagging

The POS tagging in our system is done by sequential labeling technology with CRF as in Lafferty (2001). We use the CRF++ toolkit[2] as our POS tagging tool. The model is trained from the official training set. We use the reduced POS tag set in our system. The tag set is the reduced POS tag set provided by CKIP. The complete set of POS tags is defined in CKIP[3]. Figure 2 shows the architecture of CRF tagger. For different applications, system developers have to update the tag set, feature set, preprocessing module and run the training process of the CRF model. Once the model is trained, it can be used to process input sentences with the same format.

The feature set for POS tagging is the word itself and the word preceding it and the word following it.

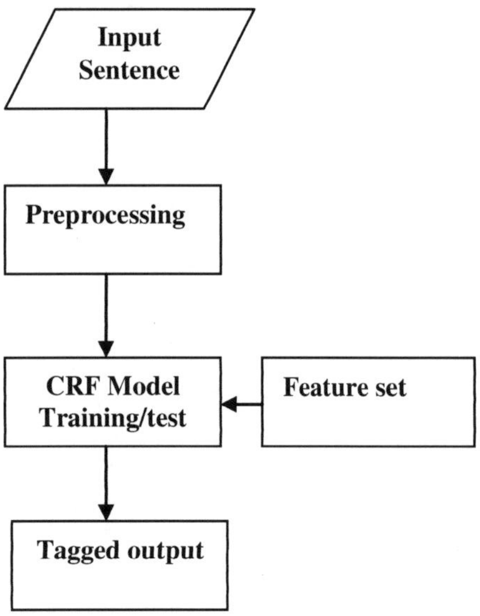

Figure 2. CRF tagger architecture

Preprocessing for POS tagging:

The training sentences have to be processed before they can be used as the input of CRF++ toolkit. Table 1 shows an example of the input format of training a CRF tagger. The original sentence in the training corpus is:
S(NP(Nh: 他 |DE: 的 |NP(NP(Na: 作品)|Caa: 與 |NP(Na:生活|Na:情形)))|PP(P:被)|VG:拍成|Di:了|NP(Na:電影)).

The first column shows the words in the sentence, the second column, which is for additional features, is not used in this case, and the third column is the POS tag. Since words in the DM phrases do not have POS tags in the training set, the tag DM itself is regarded as the POS tag for them.

Word	N/A	POS
他	NA	Nh
的	NA	DE
作品	NA	Na
與	NA	Caa
生活	NA	Na
情形	NA	Na
被	NA	P
拍成	NA	VG
了	NA	Di
電影	NA	Na

Table 1. A POS tagging training example

Table 2 shows the features used to train the POS tagger. In our system, due to the time limitation, the features are only the word itself, the word preceding it, and the word following it. Zhou et al. (2010) suggested that more features, such as more context words, prefix or suffix of the context words, might improve the accuracy of POS tagging.

Word Unigrams	W_{-1}, W_0,W_1

Table 2. Features used to train the POS tagger

3.2 Boundaries and types of constituents tagging

The POS tagging is not evaluated in this task, which is regarded as the feature preparation for parsing. The parsing result is based on both words and POS.

In our double sequential labeling scheme, every sentence will be labeled with two tags from

[2] http://crfpp.googlecode.com/svn/trunk/doc/
[3] http://ckipsvr.iis.sinica.edu.tw/cat.htm

two tag set. The first tag set is the IB set, which consists of B, the beginning word, and I, the intermediate word, of all the types of phrases in the task, ie., S, NP, VP, and PP. Note that DM and GP were processed separately. The second tag set is the IE set, which consists of only E, the ending word of any phrase or I, other words.

The training sentences also have to be processed before they can be used as the input of CRF++ toolkit. Table 3 shows an example of the input format of training the BIO CRF tagger. The first column shows the words in the sentence, the second column is the corresponding POS, and the third column is the IB tag.

Word	POS	IB tag
他	Nh	B-NP
的	DE	I-NP
作品	Na	B-NP
與	Caa	I-NP
生活	Na	B-NP
情形	Na	I-NP
被	P	B-PP
拍成	VG	I-S
了	Di	I-S
電影	Na	B-NP

Table 3. An IB tagging training example

Table 4 shows an example of the input format of training the EO CRF tagger. The first column shows the words in the sentence, the second column is the corresponding POS, and the third column is the IE tag.

Word	POS	IE tag
他	Nh	I
的	DE	I
作品	Na	E
與	Caa	I
生活	Na	I
情形	Na	E
被	P	E
拍成	VG	I
了	Di	I
電影	Na	E

Table 4. An IE tagging training example

Table 5 shows the features used to train the double sequential labeling tagger. In our system, also due to the time limitation, the features are the unigrams and bigrams of the word itself, the word preceding it, the word following it and the unigram, bigram, trigrams of the corresponding POSs of the context words. Zhou et al. (2010) suggested that the accuracy of tagging might be improved by more features, such as more context words, combination of POSs and words in the context.

Word Unigrams	W_{-1}、W_0、W_1
Word Bigrams	$W_{-1}W_0$、W_0W_1
POS Unigrams	P_{-1}、P_0、P_1
POS bigrams	$P_{-1}P_0$、P_0P_1
POS trigrams	$P_{-1}P_0P_1$

Table 5. Features used to train the double sequential labeling taggers

3.3 Post-processing to determine the boundaries and the types of constituents

After each word in the sentence is tagged with two tags, one from IB and one from IE, our system will determine the type and boundary of each phrase in the sentence. By integrating the information from both IB and IE labels, the boundary and type of phrases will be determined in the module.

Step 1: Combine the two labels to determine boundary. The B tags indicate the begging of a certain phrase. While the following I tags with the same phrase type indicate the intermediate of the same phrase. An I tag with different type or an E tag also indicates the end of a phrase. The type of the I tag which is different to the B tag will be stored for the next step.

Step 2: Put back the phrases with missing B tags during the step 1. The phrases contains I tag with different type will be labeled as a larger phrase with the type of the I tag.

Step 3: Add the GP phrase label according to the presentence of the Ng POS tag. Table 6 shows examples on how the post-processing works on GP. Phrases without ending tags will be tagged as ended at the last word.

Table 7 (at the end of the paper) shows a complete example.

<table>
<tr><td>S(agent:NP(Nh: 我)|time:D: 原本 |Head:VF: 打算 |goal:VP(PP(P:在|GP(NP(Na:自然|Na:科學類)|Ng:中))|VC:找|NP(Na:答案)))</td></tr>
<tr><td>PP(Head:P: 當 |DUMMY:GP(VP(VC: 教</td></tr>
</table>

|goal:NP(Nh:她)|NP(Na:水|Na:字))|Ng:時))
VP(concession:Cbb: 雖 |Head:VD: 帶 給 |theme:NP(Na: 人 們)|goal:NP(GP(NP(Na: 生活)|Ng: 上)|VP(Dfa: 很 |VH: 大)|DE: 的 |Nv: 方便))

Table 6. When there is a word labeled Ng, our system will treated that phrase as NG.

4 Experiment results

The training set size is 5.8 MB, about 65,000 parsed sentences. The test set size is 55.4 KB, which consists of 1,000 sentences. The closed test on our POS tagging system is 96.80%. Since the official test does not evaluate POS, we cannot report the POS accuracy in open test.

4.1 Official test result

The official-run result of our system in 2012 Sighan Traditional Chinese Sentence Parsing task is shown in Table 8, and the detail of each phrase type is shown in Table 9. The Precision, Recall, and F1 are all above the baseline. The official evaluation required that the boundary and phrase label of a syntactic constituent must be completely identical with the standard. The performance metrics are similar to the metrics of PARSEVAL as suggested in (Black et al., 1991): Precision, Recall, F1 measure are defined as follows:

Precision = # of correctly recognized constituents / # of all constituents in the automatic parse.

Recall = # of correctly recognized constituents / # of all constituents in the gold standard parse.

F1 = 2*P*R / (P + R).

	Micro-averaging		
	Precision	Recall	F1
CYUT-Run1	0.6695	0.5781	0.6204
Stanford Parser (Baseline)	0.6208	0.5481	0.5822

	Macro-Averaging		
	Precision	Recall	F1
CYUT-Run1	0.6944	0.5999	0.6437
Stanford Parser (Baseline)	0.5885	0.5634	0.5757

Table 8. Sentence parsing result of our system

(Type)	(#Truth)	(#Parser)	(%Ratio)
S	1233	938	76.07
VP	679	187	27.54
NP	2974	1737	58.41
GP	26	9	34.62
PP	96	24	25
XP	0	0	N/A

Table 9. Detailed result of our system

5 Error analysis on the official test result

In the official test, there were 87 sentences that our system gave correct full parsing. We find that most of the sentences contain large NP chunks. Since our system tend to chunk large NP, these sentences are best parsed by our system.

For example, sentence no.339:

{S(最好康贈品包括買筆電送液晶螢幕), NP(最好康贈品), VP(最好康), VP(買筆電送液晶螢幕), NP(筆電), VP(送液晶螢幕), NP(液晶螢幕)}

and sentence no.580:

{S(台中日光溫泉會館執行董事張榮福表示), NP(台中日光溫泉會館執行董事張榮福), NP(台中日光溫泉會館執行董事), NP(台中日光溫泉會館)}

In the formal run, there were 14 sentences that our system labeled wrong. We will analyze the causes and find a way to improve, especially on the missing S, GP error, and PP error sentences.

5.1 Error analysis on the missing S tag sentences

Our system will give an S tag if there is at least on word tagged B-S or I-S. Therefore, if there is no word tagged with S, our system will miss the S tag.

Consider sentence no. 97, the parsing result of our system is:

VP(VC:摩根富林明|NP(Nc:台灣|Na:增長|Na:基金|Na:經理人|Na:葉鴻儒)|VC:分析)

System result:

{VP(摩根富林明台灣增長基金經理人葉鴻儒分析), NP(台灣增長基金經理人葉鴻儒)}

Ground Truth:

{S(摩根富林明台灣增長基金經理人葉鴻儒分析), NP(摩根富林明台灣增長基金經理人葉鴻儒), NP(摩根富林明台灣增長基金經理人), NP(摩根富林明台灣增長基金)}

The precision, recall, and F1 are all 0. The main reason that our system failed to chunk the right NP is our system cannot tag the POS of the named entity 摩根富林明 as Nb. Also, since the NP is not complete and the last word of the sentence is a verb, our system failed to label the S. Named entity recognition is a crucial component of word segmentation, POS tagging, and parsing.

5.2 Error analysis on GP

Consider sentence no. 13, the parsing result of our system is:

S(GP(D: 然後 |NP(Nh: 我)|Ng: 後)|VC: 排 |NP(DM: 一個 |Na: 青年 |Na: 男子 |Na: 飛躍)|VP(Cbb:而|VC:起))

System result:

{S(然後我後排一個青年男子飛躍而起), GP(然後我後), NP(我), NP(一個青年男子飛躍), VP(而起)}

Ground Truth:

{S(然後我後排一個青年男子飛躍而起), NP(我後排一個青年男子), NP(我後排), VP(而起)}

The precision, recall, and F1 are 0.4, 0.5, and 0.4444 respectively. Our system reported an extra GP(然後我後). In this case, the error is caused by a wrong POS tagging error. The POS of '後' is not Ng. This case is hard to solve, since the CKIP online POS tagger also tag it as Ng. Our system will tag the phrase GP once the POS Ng appeared.

Consider sentence no. 43, the parsing result of our system is:

S(NP(Na: 司法院 |DM: 多年)|VP(GP(Ng: 來)|VL:持續|VP(VC:選派|NP(Na:法官)|PP(P:到 |NP(Nc:國外))|VC:進修|VC:學習)))

System result:

{S(司法院多年來持續選派法官到國外進修學習), NP(司法院多年), VP(來持續選派法官到國外進修學習), GP(來), VP(選派法官到國外進修學習), NP(法官), PP(到國外), NP(國外)}

Ground Truth:

{S(司法院多年來持續選派法官到國外進修學習), NP(司法院), GP(多年來), VP(選派法官到國外進修學習), NP(法官), VP(到國外進修學習), NP(國外), VP(進修學習)}

The precision, recall, and F1 are 0.5, 0.5, and 0.5. Our system found a wrong boundary of the GP(多年來). This is cause by another wrong boundary of VP.

Consider sentence no. 69, the parsing result of our system is:

VP(NP(S(NP(Na:總裁|Nb:莊秀石)|VE:預估 |VP(Dfa: 最 |VH: 快)|NP(Na: 一〇二年)|Ncd: 底)|VB:完工))

System result:

{VP(總裁莊秀石預估最快一〇二年底完工), NP(總裁莊秀石預估最快一〇二年底完工), S(總裁莊秀石預估最快一〇二年底), NP(總裁莊秀石), VP(最快), NP(一〇二年)}

Ground Truth:

{S(總裁莊秀石預估最快一〇二年底完工), NP(總裁莊秀石), VP(最快一〇二年底完工), VP(最快), GP(一〇二年底), NP(一〇二年)}

The precision, recall, and F1 are 0.5, 0.5, and 0.5. Our system missed the GP(一〇二年底). Because the POS of '底' is tagged wrongly as Ncd, should be Ng. This case is hard, the CKIP online system segmented and tagged it differently as 一〇二(Neu) 年底(Nd).

	#	%
Wrong boundary	11	42%
Wrong POS Ng	7	27%
Missing POS Ng	6	23%
Correct GP	9	35%

Table 10. Result analysis on the 26 GP in official test

5.3 Error analysis on PP

Consider sentence no. 53, the parsing result of our system is:

VP(NP(PP(P:如|NP(Na:簡易|Na:餐飲)|Neqa:部分|D:可|VC:分包|PP(P:給|NP(VH:專業|Na:餐飲|Na:業者))|VC:經營)))

System result:

{PP(如簡易餐飲部分可分包給專業餐飲業者經營), , PP(給專業餐飲業者) }

Ground Truth:

{PP(如簡易餐飲部分), PP(給專業餐飲業者)}

The precision, recall, and F1 are 0.5, 0.5, and 0.5. In this case, the error is caused by the missing ending tag of the first PP.

Consider sentence no. 237, the parsing result of our system is:

S(NP(NP(Na:周傑倫)|VA:前進|Nc:好萊塢 |Na:首作|Na:青蜂俠)|D:仍|PP(P:在|NP(VC:拍攝 |Na:階段)))

System result:

237 { PP(在拍攝階段) }

Ground Truth:

{no PP}

The precision, recall, and F1 are 0.6, 0.6, and 0.6. In this case, the ground truth does not include the PP(在拍攝階段). Because in this case, the POS of ‘在’ is not P, should be VCL. This case is hard to solve, since the CKIP online POS tagger also tag it as P.

Consider sentence no. 673, the parsing result of our system is:

S(S(Nd:目前|NP(DM:這波|Na:物價|Na:跌勢)|VH:主要)|V_11:是|NP(Cbb:因|Nc:全球|Na:金融|Na:危機)|VP(Cbb:而|VC:起))

System result:

{no PP}

Ground Truth:

{ PP(因全球金融危機) }

The precision, recall, and F1 are 0.4, 0.5, and 0.4444 respectively. In this case, our system missed the PP(因全球金融危機). Because the POS of ‘因’ is tagged as Cbb instead of P. This case is also hard to solve, since the CKIP online POS tagger also tag it as Cbb.

	#	%
Wrong boundary	24	25%
Wrong IB type	27	28%
Missing POS P	48	50%
Correct PP	24	25%

Table 11. Result analysis on the 96 PP in official test

5.4 Error analysis on NP and VP

We find that there are five types of error in the NP or VP chunking of our system result.

1. Error on the right boundary
2. Error on the left boundary
3. Missing the NP or VP type
4. A large phrase covered two or more small phrases with exactly substring.
5. Exchange on type labeling: NP into VP or VP into NP

Causes of the errors:

1. Error on the right boundary is caused by the error on IE tagging, one end tag is missing or labeled at a wrong word.
2. Error on the left boundary is caused by the error on IB tagging, one begin tag is labeled at a wrong word or an additional tag is tagged.
3. Missing type is caused by missing a begin tag of NP or VP.
4. In many sentences, there are two small NPs form a large NP. In this case, our system can only recognize the large NP only, thus the short NPs are missing.
5. The type of begin tag is wrong.

In the following examples, on the top is the output of our system, on the bottom is the ground truth.

NP error type examples:

Error type 1:

5 {S(富蘭克林華美投信日前舉辦迎接投資新時代), NP(富蘭克林華美), VP(日前舉辦迎接投資新時代), VP(迎接投資新時代), NP(投資新時代)}
{S(富蘭克林華美投信日前舉辦迎接投資新時代), NP(富蘭克林華美投信), VP(迎接投資新時代), NP(投資新時代)} 0.6 0.75 0.6667

Error type 2:

38 {NP(基隆市警察局外事課今年破獲一起人口販運集團案), S(基隆市警察局外事課今年破獲一起人口販運集團案), NP(基隆市警察局外事課今年破獲), NP(基隆市警察局外事課), NP(販運集團)}
{S(基隆市警察局外事課今年破獲一起人口販運集團案), NP(基隆市警察局外事課), NP(一起人口販運集團案), NP(人口販運集團案), NP(人口販運集團), NP(人口販運), NP(人口)} 0.4 0.2857 0.3333

Error type 3:

42 {S(詳情可上神乎科技官網瞭解), NP(詳情), NP(神乎科技官網)}
{S(詳情可上神乎科技官網瞭解), NP(詳情), NP(神乎科技官網), NP(神乎科技)} 1 0.75 0.8571

Error type 4:

1 {S(黨主席蔡英文元旦當天將到台東縣迎曙光), NP(黨主席蔡英文元旦當天), NP(黨主席蔡英文), PP(到台東縣), NP(台東縣), NP(曙光)}
{S(黨主席蔡英文元旦當天將到台東縣迎曙光), NP(黨主席蔡英文), NP(元旦當天), PP(到台東縣), NP(台東縣), NP(曙光)} 0.8333 0.8333 0.8333

Error type 5:

7 {S(不景氣時期舉債反易債留子孫), NP(不景氣時期舉債), NP(易債), NP(子孫)}
{S(不景氣時期舉債反易債留子孫), VP(不景氣時期舉債), NP(不景氣時期), S(債留子孫), NP(債), NP(子孫)} 0.5 0.3333 0.4

VP error type examples:

Error type 1:

31	{S(各球團需補助才請洋將實在說不過去), NP(各球團), VP(才請洋將), NP(洋將)}
	{S(各球團需補助才請洋將實在說不過去), NP(各球團), NP(補助), VP(才請洋將實在說不過去), NP(洋將), VP(實在說不過去)} 0.75 0.5 0.6

Error type 2:

82	{S(消防人員才能讓災損減到最低), NP(消防人員), VP(才能讓災損減到最低), NP(災損減到)}
	{S(消防人員才能讓災損減到最低), NP(消防人員), NP(災損), VP(減到最低), VP(最低)} 0.5 0.4 0.4444

Error type 3:

82	{S(消防人員才能讓災損減到最低), NP(消防人員), VP(才能讓災損減到最低), NP(災損減到)}
	{S(消防人員才能讓災損減到最低), NP(消防人員), NP(災損), VP(減到最低), VP(最低)} 0.5 0.4 0.4444

Error type 5:

7	{S(不景氣時期舉債反易債留子孫), NP(不景氣時期舉債), NP(易債), NP(子孫)}
	{S(不景氣時期舉債反易債留子孫), VP(不景氣時期舉債), NP(不景氣時期), S(債留子孫), NP(債), NP(子孫)} 0.5 0.3333 0.4

The error analysis on NP:

We manually analyze the error cases and show the percentage of each error type in the following tables. The percentage in table 12 is defined as: # of error cases / total # of NP in gold standard

Error type	#	%
1	265	8.92%
2	415	13.96%
3	673	22.63%
4	31	1.05%
5	59	1.99%
Correct	1730	58.41%

Table 12. Error distribution on NP

The error analysis on VP:

We manually analyze the error cases and show the percentage of each error type in the following table. The percentage in table 13 is defined as: # of error cases / total # of VP in gold standard

Error type	#	%
1	31	4.57%
2	154	22.69%
3	362	53.32%
4	0	0%
5	59	8.06%
Correct	187	27.54%

Table 13. Error distribution on VP

By observing the two tables, we find that missing the begin tag is the major cause of error. To overcome the shortage, IB tagging accuracy is the most important issue. Since the wrong type labeling error is not very heavy, our system should label more begin tag in the future.

6 Conclusion and Future work

This paper reports our approach to the traditional Chinese sentence parsing task in the 2012 CIPS-SIGHAN evaluation. We proposed a new labeling method, the double labeling scheme, on how to use linear chain CRF model on full parsing task. The experiment result shows that our approach is much better than the baseline result and has average performance on each phrase type.

According to the error analysis above, we can find that many error cases of our system were caused by wrong POS tags and wrong boundary of PP phrase. POS tagging accuracy can be improved by adding more effective features, as in the previous works, and enlarging the training set. The boundary of PP phrase determination can also be improved by a larger training set and rules. Our system works best on S, and worst on PP and VP. The main reason of missing VP and PP is the error of POS tagging. Therefore, a better POS tagger will improve the worst part significantly. Complicated NP is known to be the highest frequent phrase in Chinese and cannot be represented in linear chain CRF model. Our system still fails to recognize many NPs. The system performance on NP can be improved by defining better representation of tag set.

Due to the limitation of time and resource, our system is not tested under different experimental settings. In the future, we will test our system with more feature combination on both POS labeling and sentence parsing.

Acknowledgments

This study was conducted under the "III Innovative and Prospective Technologies Project" of the Institute for Information Industry which is subsidized by the Ministry of Economic Affairs, R.O.C.

References

Steven Abney. 1991. *Parsing by chunks*, Principle-Based Parsing, Kluwer Academic Publishers.

Adam L. Berger, Stephen A. Della Pietra, and Vincent J. Della Pietra. 1996. *A Maximum Entropy approach to Natural Language Processing*. Computational Linguistics, Vol. 22, No. 1., pp. 39-71.

E. Black; S. Abney; D. Flickenger; C. Gdaniec; R. Grishman; P. Harrison; D. Hindle; R. Ingria; F. Jelinek; J. Klavans; M. Liberman; M. Marcus; S. Roukos; B. Santorini; T. Strzalkowski. 1991. *A Procedure for Quantitatively Comparing the Syntactic Coverage of English Grammars*. In Speech and Natural Language workshop, Pacific Grove, California, USA, Feburay 1991.

Jenny Rose Finkel, Alex Kleeman, Christopher D. Manning. 2008. *Efficient, Feature-based, Conditional Random Field Parsing*, in Proceedings of ACL-08: HLT, pages 959–967, Columbus, Ohio, USA, June 2008.

Philip Harrison, Steven Abney, Ezra Black, Dan Flickinger, Ralph Grishman Claudia Gdaniec, Donald Hindle, Robert Ingria, Mitch Marcus, Beatrice Santorini, and Tomek Strzalkowski.1991. *Evaluating Syntax Performance of Parser/Grammars of English*. In Jeannette G. Neal and Sharon M. Walter, editors, Natural Language Processing Systems Evaluation Workshop, Technical Report RL-TR-91-362, pages 71-77.

John Lafferty, Andrew McCallum, and Fernando Pereira. *Conditional random fields: Probabilistic models for segmenting and labeling sequence data*. in Proceedings of 18th International Conference on Machine Learning, 2001.

Yoshimasa Tsuruoka, Jun'ichi Tsujii, Sophia Anaiakou. 2009. *Fast Full Parsing by Linear-Chain Conditional Random Fields*. In Proceedings of EACL'09, pages 790-798.

Shih-Hung Wu, Cheng-Wei Shih, Chia-Wei Wu, Tzong-Han Tsai, and Wen-Lian Hsu. 2005. *Applying Maximum Entropy to Robust Chinese Shallow Parsing*. in Proceedings of ROCLING 2005, pp 257-271.

Qiang Zhou; Jingbo Zhu. 2010. *Chinese Syntactic Parsing Evaluation*. in Proceedings of CIPS-SIGHAN Joint Conference on Chinese Language Processing, August 28-29, Beijing, China.

Qiaoli Zhou; Wenjing Lang; Yingying Wang; Yan Wang; Dongfeng Cai. 2010. *The SAU Report for the 1st CIPS-SIGHAN-ParsEval-2010*. in Proceedings of CIPS-SIGHAN Joint Conference on Chinese Language Processing, August 28-29, Beijing, China.

<table>
<tr><td>Words</td><td>他</td><td>的</td><td>作品</td><td>與</td><td>生活</td><td>情形</td><td>被</td><td>拍成</td><td>了</td><td>電影</td></tr>
<tr><td>POS</td><td>Nh</td><td>DE</td><td>Na</td><td>Caa</td><td>Na</td><td>Na</td><td>P</td><td>VG</td><td>Di</td><td>Na</td></tr>
<tr><td>BI</td><td>B-NP</td><td>I-NP</td><td>B-NP</td><td>I-NP</td><td>B-NP</td><td>I-NP</td><td>B-PP</td><td>I-S</td><td>I-S</td><td>B-NP</td></tr>
<tr><td>IE</td><td>I</td><td>I</td><td>E</td><td>I</td><td>I</td><td>E</td><td>E</td><td>I</td><td>I</td><td>E</td></tr>
<tr><td>Step 1</td><td colspan="10">NP(Nh:他|DE:的|NP(Na:作品)|Caa:與|NP(Na:生活|Na:情形)|PP(P:被)|VG:拍成|Di:了|NP(Na:電影)|@S</td></tr>
<tr><td>Step 2</td><td colspan="10">S(NP(Nh:他|DE:的|NP(Na:作品)|Caa:與|NP(Na:生活|Na:情形)|PP(P:被)|VG:拍成|Di:了|NP(Na:電影)|@</td></tr>
<tr><td>Step 3</td><td colspan="10">S(NP(Nh:他|DE:的|NP(Na:作品)|Caa:與|NP(Na:生活|Na:情形)|PP(P:被)|VG:拍成|Di:了|NP(Na:電影)))</td></tr>
</table>

Table 7. A complete example of the Post-processing steps

A Conditional Random Field-based Traditional Chinese Base-Phrase Parser for SIGHAN Bake-off 2012 Evaluation

Yih-Ru Wang
National Chaio Tung University
Hsinchu, Taiwan, ROC.
yrwang@mail.nctu.edu.tw

Yuan-Fu Liao
National Taipei University of Technology, Taipei, Taiwan, ROC
yfliao@ntut.edu.tw

Abstract

This paper describes our system for the subtask 1 of traditional Chinese Parsing of SIGHAN Bake-off 2012 evaluation. Since this research mainly focuses on speech recognition and synthesis applications, only base phrase chunking was implemented using three Conditional Random Field (CRF) modules, including word segmentation, POS tagging and base phrase chunking sub-systems. The official evaluation results show that the system achieved 0.5038 (0.7210/0.387) micro- and 0.5301 (0.7343/0.4147) macro-averaging F1 (precision/recall) rates on full sentence parsing task. However, if only the performance of base phrase chunking was considered, the F-measures may be around 0.70 and is somehow good enough for speech recognition and synthesis applications.

1 Introduction

For NLP researches, a semantic parser is used for mapping a natural-language sentence into a formal representation of its meaning. It usually first groups the elements in a sentence into words, phrases and clause and then tags each word, phrase and clause with a semantic label.

There are still many challenges in semantic parsing, but the intermediate results of the semantic parsing are already quite useful for speech recognition and text-to-speech applications. For example, word sequences information could be used to build the language model in automatic speech recognition (ASR), and the phrase and clause results can be used to further verify the recognition result. In text-to-speech system, boundary information of the words, phrases and clauses can be used to better predict the prosody of synthesis speech.

There are many tasks in the Chinese parser, such as word segmentation, POS tagging, base phrase chunking and full parsing. They are basically sequential learning problems. Thus in the past decade, many statistical methods, such as Support Vector Machine (SVM) (Vapnik, 1995), conditional random field (CRF) (Lafferty et al, 2011), Maximum entropy Markov models (MEMMs) (Berger, etc, 1996), etc. were proposed for handling this sequential learning task.

Among them, CRF-based approach has been shown to be especially effective and with very low computational complexity by past studies (Zhan and Huang, 2006). Thus, in this paper, the CRF-based method was adopted to implement our system.

Instead of full parsing, base phrase chunking that identifies non-recursively cores of various types of phrases is possibly just the precursor of full parsing. However, in our text-to-speech and speech recognition applications, the information of base phrase is somehow the most useful cues. Moreover, the complexity of base phrase chunking is much lower than full chunking. Therefore, only base phrase chunking was implemented in our system.

In this paper, a traditional Chinese base phrase chunking system developed for the Bakeoff-2012 evaluation was described in section 2. In section 3, the evaluation result of our system was discussed. Finally, the conclusion was given in section 4.

2 CRF-based Traditional Chinese Base-Phrase Chunking System

The block diagram of our system is shown in Fig. 1. There are five sub-systems including a text normalization, a word segmentation, a POS tagging, a compound word construction and a base-phrase chunking modules.

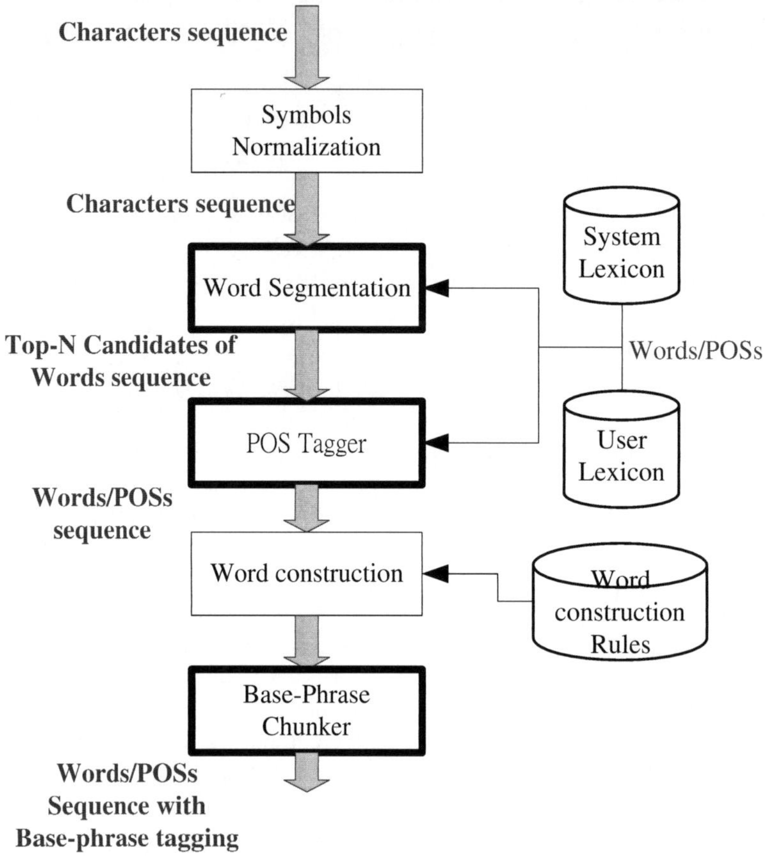

Fig. 1. The schematic diagram of the proposed system.

First of all, in Chinese, there are lots of canonical composition glyphs. The word construction sub-system canonical composition glyphs, or variant characters, were handled in a text-normalization sub-system. The other modules will be briefly described as follows:

2.1 Word Segmentation

The word segmentation sub-system is a CRF-based system. It follows the Zhan's work (Zhan and Huang, 2006). The 6 tags, named *B1*, *B2*, *B3*, *M*, *E* and *S*, were used to represent the activated function in CRF. The information using in feature template are

- C_n : Unicode current character (Unicode plain-0 only).
- B_n : radical of current character ("bushu", 部首)
- SB_n : if B_n==B_n-1
- WL_n : maximum length word in lexicon match to string including current character, the 87,000 lexicon from Sinica[1] was used as the system internal lexicon, and a user-defined lexicon was allowed to define more words, and in most cases they will be named entities.
- WT_n : tags of current characters in the maximum word length matched word in lexicon (indicate character position in word using *B1, B2, B3, M, E, S*).
- D/E_n : whether the current character is a digit.
- PM_n : whether the current character is a punctuation mark (PM).

The above features and the templates used in our system were commonly used in Chinese word segmentation task. It's worth to mention that the radical of Chinese character was a useful feature for same OOV words. The top-n sequences of word segmentation sub-system were sent to the next sub-system.

[1] http://www.aclclp.org.tw/use_ced_c.php

The sub-system was trained by using the Sinica corpus, version 4.0[2]. A lot of data was corrected in the database by using consistence check.

About more than 1% of data in Sinica Corpus was corrected. The word unigram and unigram of Sinica corpus were first generated, and we find all the word-pairs were also combined into a single word in the corpus besides the words with POS "*Nf*" and "*Neu*". There are about 10% of the word-pairs can also be segmented into single words. Some word segmentation inconsistency were checked and corrected, like

(1) /民意代表(Na)/ and /民意(Na) 代表(Na)/ both appeared in the corpus,

(2) The word /長途(A) 電話(Na)/ are segmented in all the cases in corpus, but the word /長途電話(Na)/ was included in the Sinica lexicon. In this case, the lexicon was modified,

(3) Most of the bound morphemes (prefixes, suffixes), named entities, compound words, idioms, abbreviations.

Some words, especially function words, were segmented into more than one segmentation and POS possibilities, like [就是(T), 就是 (SHI), 就是(Nc), 就(D) 是(SHI), 就是(D), 就是(Cbb)] and [真是(VG), 真是(D), 真(D) 是(SHI)], while these were not yet checked in our study.

The researchers have set a high standard for their significant works in developing the corpus, yet it is still impossible to ignore the words proposed by Andrew Rosenberg (2012): "*The corpus is an invaluable resource in Spoken and Natural Language Processing. Consistent data sets have allowed for empirical evaluation of competing algorithms. .... However, despite dubbing these annotations as "gold-standard", many corpora contain labeling errors and idiosyncrasies. The current view of the corpus as a static resource makes correction of errors and other modifications prohibitively difficult.*" Hence, we hope to see the dynamic Chinese linguistic resources as soon as possible and the users of corpus could then contribute their error corrections.

Then, 9/10 of the corpus (about 1 million words) was used for training and 1/10 (about 120K words) was used as evaluation data. The F-measure of the word segmentation sub-system is 97.37%. The difference of precision and recall rate was less than 0.1%.

[2] http://www.aclclp.org.tw/use_asbc_c.php

2.2 POS tagging

In our system, the top-N output sequences of the word segmentation were sent to the POS tagger. The possible POS types of each word should be the most effective feature for POS tagging. Since a lexicon was used in word segmentation sub-system, the possible POS's of each lexical word was also store in the lexicon. The information using in feature template are

- PM_n : Unicode of the first character of current word when it is PM, or "X" if it is not PM,
- WL_n : word length of current word.
- $LPOS_n$: all possible POSs of current words if the word is in the internal and external lexicons, or "X" if it is not in the lexicons, i.e., for word "一"(one) can be "Cbb_Di_D_Neu"
- FC_n : first character of current word if the word is not in lexicon, or "X" if it is in lexicon.
- LC_n : last character if the word is not in lexicon, or "X" if it is in lexicon.

There are 47 types of POS in the system those are used in Sinica corpus version 4.0 as well.

The sub-system was also trained by the same corpus used in word segmentation sub-system. The accuracy of the POS tagging sub-system is 94.16%. The recognition of 47 POS types was reasonable except noun type "*Nv*" due to its ambiguity.

In the basic system, the POS tagger will process the top-N sequences out from word segmentation. The log-likelihood of word segmentation and POS tagging were added and found the best output sequence.

The F-measure of word segmentation and recognition rate of POS tagger were usually used as the performance measures of a parsing system. In our study, we also check the effectiveness of our word segmentation and POS tagger sub-system in the speech recognition application. The above two sub-system was used in building the language model in ASR system. Sinica corpus, CIRB030[3] and Taiwan Panorama Magazine[4], contain 380 million words totally, were parsed to build the trigram language model for speech recognizer. 60K words were used in the recognition

[3] http://www.aclclp.org.tw/use_cir_c.php
[4] http://www.aclclp.org.tw/use_gh_c.php

lexicon. The performance of the Mandarin speech recognizer was evaluated in the TCC-300 speech database[5]. The out-of-vocabulary rate is 3.1% for 15479 words test data. Word error rate (WER) of the recognizer reduces to 13.4%. About 40% word error rate reduction was achieved comparing to the CRF-based word segmentation and POS tagger system we built from Bakeoff-2005 training database[6].

2.3 Compound word construction

The first compound word construction rule which was implemented in our system is the Determinative-Measure compound word. In Sinica Treebank[7], except the 47 POS types, one more POS tagger DM, Determinative-Measure compounds, was used. The following DM construction rules, which check the POS of word sequence, were used to construct the DM compound in the word sequence, recursively.

- Neu + Nf + Neu + !(Nf)
  $\Rightarrow$ DM+ !(Nf)

  where !(Nf) means that the POS of the next word is not Nf, for example :

  一(Neu) 米(Nf) 二(Neu)

- Neu+ Neqb $\Rightarrow$ Neu
- (Neu, Nes, Nep, Neqa, Neqb)+Nf

  $\Rightarrow$ DM
- DM+(Nf, Neqb) $\Rightarrow$ DM
- (Nep, Nes)+DM $\Rightarrow$ DM
- Neu+("大"(/da/, big),
  "小"(/xian/,small)) +Nf $\Rightarrow$ DM

In "*Chinese information processing issued by the Central Standards Bureau*"[8], there are lots of rules for constructing traditional Chinese compound words. In our system, some of them were implemented. Those rules are listed in follows,

- *半A半B,*
- *一A一B,*
- *如A如B,*
- *ADAB, D* is a character with POS *Di,*
- *AABB, AB* is a lexical word with POS *Vx,* where *A*, *B* are single character.

2.4 Base-phrase chunking

In the base-phrase chunking sub-system, the POS sequence was the most useful feature in base-phrase chunking. Beside the POS and simplified POS, some character information of the word were also used.

- POS_n : POS of current word.
- SP_n : simplified POS of current word.

  The types of POS was simplified from 47 to 13 categories, { *A, C, D, DE, FW, I, N, P, PM, SHI, T, V* }
- LW_n : word length of current word.
- $SW1_n$: set to 1 if word W_n is same as word W_{n-1}, 0 if otherwise.
- $SW2_n$: set to 1 if word W_n is same as word W_{n-2}, 0 if otherwise.
- FC_n : first character of current word.
- EC_n : last character of current word.

The templates used in the system were shown in Figure 2.

POS n-gram	POS_{n-2}, POS_{n-1}, POS_n, POS_{n+1}, POS_{n+2}, (POS_{n-2} POS_{n-1} POS_n), (POS_n POS_{n+1} POS_{n+2}), (POS_{n-1} POS_n POS_{n+1}), (POS_{n-2} POS_{n-1} POS_n POS_{n+1} POS_{n+2})
Simplified POS n-gram	SP_{n-2}, SP_{n-1}, SP_n, SP_{n+1}, SP_{n+2}, (SP_{n-2} SP_{n-1} $SPOS_n$), (SP_n SP_{n+1} SP_{n+2}), (SP_{n-1} SP_n SP_{n+1}), (SP_{n-2} SP_{n-1} SP_n SP_{n+1} SP_{n+2})
POS and word-length	(POS_n LC_n), (POS_{n-1} LC_{n-1}), (POS_{n+1} LC_{n+1})
POS and first/last character	(POS_n FC_n), (POS_{n-1} FC_{n-1}), (POS_{n+1} FC_{n+1}) (POS_n LC_n), (POS_{n-1} LC_{n-1}), (POS_{n+1} LC_{n+1})
Repeated word	(LW_n $SW1_n$), (LW_n $SW2_n$)

Fig. 2. List of CRF features for base phrase chunking sub-system.

In the knowledge bases for semantic parsing, the lexical senses, like information in Wordnet, …, etc, are important features for parsing (Mel'čuk, 1996; Shi and Mihalcea, 2005), however in our current system the lexical sense information is not considered yet. The activated

[5] http://www.aclclp.org.tw/use_mat_c.php#tcc300edu
[6] http://www.sighan.org/bakeoff2005/
[7] http://www.aclclp.org.tw/use_stb_c.php
[8] http://rocling.iis.sinica.edu.tw/CKIP/paper/wordsegment_standard.pdf

function of the BP chunking was set to 7 tags, {ADVP, GP, NP, PP, S, VP, XDE(X・DE)}.

Then, 9/10 of the Bakeoff-2012 Task-4 training corpus was used for training the base-phrase chunking module and 1/10 for was used as self-evaluation data. The result of the base-phrase chunking was shown in Table 1.

The Chinese parsing system as shown in Figure 1 was implemented by using the CRF++ package[9]. The base phrase tags, ADVP and XDE, were combined into XP as the Bakeoff-2012 result.

BP types	Precision	Recall	F-measure
ADVP	90.00%	72.00%	80.00
GP	91.06%	95.54%	93.25
NP	86.61%	87.73%	87.17
PP	88.61%	91.48%	90.03
S	66.43%	57.85%	61.84
VP	79.95%	75.91%	77.88
XDE	86.35%	88.69%	87.51
total	84.61%	84.20%	84.41

Table 1. The performance of base phrase chunking in training and self-evaluation database.

<NP>清晨(Nd) 五點(Nd)</NP> ，(PM) <NP>哈佛(Nb) 大學(Nc)</NP> 的(DE) 宗教(Na) 藝術史(Na) 教授(Na) 羅伯特・蘭登(Nb) 在(P) <GP>睡夢(Na) 中(Ng)</GP> 被(P) 一[Neu]陣[Nf](DM) <XP>急促(VH) 的(DE)</XP> 電話(Na) 鈴聲(Na) 吵醒(VC) 。(PM)

<NP>電話(Na) 裡(Ncd)</NP> 的(DE) 人(Na) 自稱(VG) 是(SHI) <NP>歐洲(Nc) 原子核(Na)</NP> 研究(VE) 組織(Na) 的(DE) 首領(Na) ，(PM) <VP>名叫(VG) 馬克西米利安・科勒(Nb)</VP> ，(PM) 他(Nh) 是(SHI) 在(P) <NP>互聯網(Na) 上(Ncd)</NP> 找到(VC) <XP>蘭登(Nb) 的(DE)</XP> 電話(Na) 號碼(Na) 的(T) 。(PM)

Fig. 3. Partial parsing result of "*Angels & Demons*", Dan Brown, 2000.

In the speech applications, the accuracy of BP phrase still needs to be improved. Using more training data will be the most effective way to improve the BP chunking.

[9] http://crfpp.googlecode.com/svn/trunk/doc/index.html

Since our system is also used as a front end of text-to-speech (TTS) system, usually the input is taken from books and released news. Fig. 3 shows partial parsing result. The context is from "*Angels & Demons*", Dan Brown, 2000. The performance is acceptable for TTS application.

3 Evaluation Results on Traditional Chinese Parsing Sub-task 1

The system use for Bakeoff-2012 Traditional Chinese Parsing sub-task 1 is modified from the basic parser described in last section.

In the Bakeoff-2012 Traditional Chinese Parsing sub-task 1, the input sentences were segmented with gold standard word sequences. Thus, the basic system was modified to generate the n-best word sequences in POS tagging and compound word construction stages for this evaluation. The n-best word sequences satisfied with the defined principles, minimum edit-distance and maximum log-likelihood, in the test data set were returned as pre-processing word sequences. Finally, the n-best word sequences with their corresponding POS tags can be sent into base-phrase chunking module for getting the base-phrase chunking results.

The official evaluation report of our system for Traditional Chinese Parsing sub-Task 1 is shown in Fig. 4.

Task : Subtask1
Track : Closed
System : Single
Run : Run1

[Part 1] Overall Performance
Micro-averaging Precision : 0.7215
Micro-averaging Recall : 0.387
Micro-averaging F1 : 0.5038
Macro-averaging Precision : 0.7343
Macro-averaging Recall : 0.4147
Macro-averaging F1 : 0.5301

[Part 2] Summary

(Type)	(#Truth)	(#Parser)	(%Ratio)
S	1233	877	71.13
VP	679	132	19.44
NP	2974	902	30.33
GP	26	15	57.69
PP	96	12	12.5
XP	0	0	N/A

Fig. 4. Official Bake-off 2012 test results of our base-phrase chunking system.

Basically, the evaluation results show that our system achieved 0.5038 (0.7210/0.387) micro- and 0.5301 (0.7343/0.4147) macro-averaging F1 (precision/recall) on full sentence parsing task.

However, it is believed that the main reason for low recall rate is only base phrases were tagged in our system. Therefore, if only the performance of base phrase chunking were considered, the F-measures may be around 0.70. The results are somehow good enough for speech recognition and synthesis applications.

Another possibility of performance degradation is that the number of (X·DE) phrases in the training corpus is above 13% of total base phrases (In fact, 的(/de/) should be one of the most frequently occurred words in traditional Chinese text). But, there is no (X·DE) phrase in the evaluation data. It may be the reason why the performance of base phrase chunking was degenerate from 0.84 to 0.70.

4 Conclusions

In this paper, a Tradition Chinese base phrase parser that considered only base phrase chunking was implemented. The official Bake-off 2012 evaluation results on full sentence parsing task show that our system achieved 0.5038 (0.7210/0.387) micro- and 0.5301 (0.7343/ 0.4147) macro-averaging F1 (precision/recall) rates. However, if only the performance of base phrase chunking was considered, the F-measures may be around 0.70. Therefore, the results are somehow good enough for speech recognition and synthesis applications. In the near future, word senses and semantic information in Wordnet database will be explored to improve the performance of our system.

Acknowledgments

This work was supported by the National Science Council, Taiwan, ROC, under the project with contract NSC 101-2221-E-009-149-MY2 and 101-2221-E-027-129.

References

Adam L. Berger, Stephen A. Della Pietra, and Vincent J. Della Pietra. 1996. *A maximum entropy approach to natural language processing*. Computational Linguistics, 22(1):39-71.

Andrew Rosenberg. 2012. *Rethinking The Corpus: Moving towards Dynamic Linguistic Resources,* In Proceedings of INTERSPEECH-2012, Portland, USA.

Hai Zhao, Chang-Ning Huang and Mu Li. 2006. *An Improved Chinese Word Segmentation System with Conditional Random Field*. In Proceedings of the Fifth SIGHAN Workshop on Chinese Language Processing : 108-117. Sidney, Australia.

Igor Mel'čuk. 1996. *Lexical Functions in Lexicography and Natural Language Processing,* chapter *Lexical Functions: A Tool for the Description of Lexical Relations in the Lexicon*, Benjamins Publishing Corp.

J. Lafferty, A. McCallum, and F. Pereira. 2001. *Conditional random fields: Probabilistic models for segmenting and labeling sequence data*. In Proceedings of In Intl. Conf. on Machine Learning : 282-289.

L. Shi and R. Mihalcea. 2005. *Putting pieces together: Combining FrameNet, VerbNet and WordNet for robust semantic parsing*. In Proceedings of Computational Linguistics and Intelligent Text Processing; Sixth International Conference : 100–111, Mexico City, Mexico.

V. Vapnik. 1995. *The Nature of Statistical Learning Theory*. Springer-Verlag, New York.

Wenliang Chen, Yujie Zhang, and Hitoshi Isahara. 2006. *An empirical study of Chinese chunking*. In Proceedings of the COLING/ACL 2006 Main Conference Poster Sessions : 97–104, Sydney, Australia, July. Association for Computational Linguistics.

Hierarchical Maximum Pattern Matching with Rule Induction Approach for Sentence Parsing

Yi-Syun Tan, Yuan-Cheng, Chu, Jui-Feng Yeh*
Department of Computer Science and Information Engineering,
National Chiayi University,
No.300 Syuefu Rd., Chiayi City 60004, Taiwan (R.O.C.).
Ralph@mail.ncyu.edu.tw

Abstract

Chinese parsing has been a highly active research area in recent years. This paper describes a hierarchical maximum pattern matching to integrate rule induction approach for sentence parsing on traditional Chinese parsing task. We have analyzed and extracted statistical POS (part-of-speech) tagging information from training corpus, then used the related information for labeling unknown words in test data. Finally, the rule induction regulation was applied to extract of the structure of short-term syntactic and then performed maximum pattern matching for long-term syntactic structure. On Sentence Parsing task, our system performs at 44% precision, 53% recall, and F1 is 48% in the formal testing evaluation. The proposed method can achieve the significant performance in traditional Chinese sentence parsing.

1 Introduction

Recently, natural language processing has become one of the most essential issues in computational linguistics especially in human centric computing. In Chinese text processing, it is important to distinguish words significance in syntactic analysis. In order to comprehend the word significance, sentence parsing becomes one of the important techniques in the natural language understanding. The aim of sentence parsing is assigning a Part of Speech (POS) tag to each word and recognizing the syntactic structure in a given sentence. Therefore, it will help us to understand the text by correct sentence parsing by give the structure information.

For Chinese knowledge, there was a research on Categorical analyzing (Chinese Knowledge Information Processing Group, 1993). and then developed balanced Chinese corpora (Chen et al., 1996). The Sinica Treebank has been developed and released for academic research since 2000 by Chinese Knowledge Information Processing (CKIP) group at Academia Sinica (Huang et al., 2000; Chen et al., 2003), it under the framework of the Information-based Case grammar (ICG), a lexical feature-based grammar formalism, each lexical item containing both syntactic and semantic information

In word segmentation, Hidden Markov Models were used to solve word segmentation problem (Lu, 2005). Asahara et al. (2003) combined Hidden Markov Model-based word segment and a Support Vector Machine-based chunker for Chinese word segmentation. In later research, Goh et al.(2005) used a dictionary-based approach, and then apply a machine-learning-based approach to solve the segmentation problem.

In sentence parsing, there were two kinds of general methods, one was the statistical-based and the other was the rule-based. In rule-based, it wanted Expert knowledge and needed human labeling, but human labeling would not only produce a lot of problems but spent a lot of time. In rule-based approaches, Tsai and Chen (2003) showed that used context-rule classifier for part-of-speech tagging and performed better than Markov bi-gram model. In statistical-based, recently commonly used machine learning algorithm to solve it. For example, Support Vector Machine (SVM), Hidden Markov Model (HMM), Maximum Entropy (ME) and Transformation-Based Learning Algorithm (TBL) be used widely. However, single machine learning algorithm had not enough, in order to had better performance that usually combined different machine learning algorithm , for instance (Lin et al., 2010) purposed a method that used maximum matching to upgrade accuracy of Hidden Markov Model (HMM) and conditional random fields (CRF). However, if only used statistical-based methods and machine learning algorithm was need for a lot of corpus to train models, and it lack for expert knowledge.

In semantic role labeling, (You and Chen, 2004.) showed that adopted dependency decision making and example-based approaches to automatic semantic roles labeling system for structured trees of Chinese sentences. It used statistical information and combined with grammar rules for role assignments (Gildea and Hockenmaier, 2003).

Unknown word extraction was an important issue in many Chinese text processing tasks. (Chen and Ma, 2002) showed that used statistical information and as much information as possible, such as morphology, syntax, semantics, and world knowledge in unknown word extraction. In 2003 research, (Ma and Chen, 2003) showed that proposed a bottom-up merging algorithm to solve a problem that superfluous character strings with strong statistical associations were extracted as well.

In Traditional Chinese Parsing Bakeoff, there are two sub-tasks: Sentence Parsing and Semantic Role Labeling. This paper focuses on Sentence Parsing task and proposes hierarchical maximum pattern matching with rule induction approach to recognize the syntactic structure. We present the bakeoff results evaluation and provide analysis on the system performance in the following sections.

In the opening section of the paper, we illustrated the research motivations and related works. The system framework is illustrated in the section 2 that is composed of rule induction regulation and maximum pattern matching. The evaluate data and results are both described in third part. Finally, some findings and future works is shown in conclusion illustrated in section 4.

2 System Overview

Figure 1 illustrates the block diagram of the proposed parsing system for traditional Chinese sentence. In preparation of starting the system, we created a dictionary by training data that the words with only one POS tagging, and also extracted the relation information according to their POS tagging. The POS tagging frequency is calculated in proceeding and cascading of each POS tagging, and used to predict the POS tagging of those token undefined in the dictionary.

2.1 Rule induction regulation

Our concern is to consider the syntactic structure of traditional Chinese sentence. Herein, a two steps method is proposed in this paper. The first step is the Part-Of-Speech tagging using the lexical dictionary. It also performs two steps for accuracy. First, the tokens with only one POS tagging are detected in dictionary, and then POS-to-POS relations are performed to modify by calculating the POS tagging of tokens those were not defined in dictionary. For instance, in Figure 2(1), after performed dictionary mapping, the words "實際(actual)" and "公佈(announcement)" were not found in the dictionary. That is to say, no corresponding with the POS tagging is matched here, so they were marked as 'Null'. However, we performed POS-to-POS relations modification, it could be found POS tagging by calculating POS relation information to obtain 'VH' and 'VE' for those token, as shown Figure 2(2).

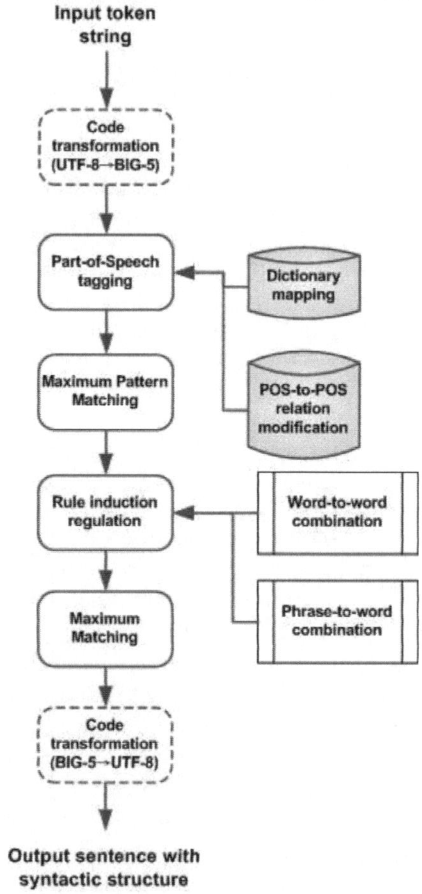

Figure 1. Flowchart of proposed system

(1) 觀看 (VC) 實際 (Null) 公佈 (Null) 數據 (Na)
observe actual announcement data
(Observe the actual announcement data.)

(2) 觀看 (VC) 實際 (VH) 公佈 (VE) 數據 (Na)
observe actual announcement data
(Observe the actual announcement data.)

(3) NP(Nc:大陸|Na:方面)
(The mainland side.)

(4) VP(NP(DM:多家|Nc:銀行)|VC:表達)
(The expression of a number of banks.)

Figure 2. Two examples for POS-to-POS relations modification

In rule induction regulation, we were able to observe the syntactic structure in training data, and instituted syntactic structure rules of word-to-word and phrase-to-word in following:

1. **NP-Phrase structure:** It is composed of combining by noun and noun, or noun-phrase and noun.
   Na Na → NP
   NP Na → NP

2. **VP-Phrase structure:** It is composed of combining by adverb and verb, or verb and noun-phrase.
   D VC → VP
   VC NP → VP

3. **PP-Phrase structure:** It is composed of combining by preposition and noun-phrase.
   P NP → PP

4. **GP-Phrase structure:** It is composed of combining by noun-phrase and 'Ng', or verb-phrase and 'Ng'.
   VP Ng → GP
   NP Ng → GP

According to the rule categories defined previous, it could further be used to process the short-term syntactic structure, as shown in Figure 2 (3) and Figure2 (4).

2.2 Maximum pattern matching

In order to obtain desired information, the statistics method is used to obtain the syntactic information from training data. In the proposed method, a statistics approach used to extract the chunks is called as maximum pattern matching. The data *m1* is obtained by keeping part of speech (POS) and parser label of each word obtained from training corpus, the semantic role labeling is ignored in this stage. Furthermore, lexical text without any parse label expect the most outside parse label named *m1*, and the parse label order according to NP-VP-S-PP-GP sequence. Then utilized training data to get an only lexical text that existed everyone lexical or parse label named *m2*, and separated parse label for brackets named *m3* (see the Figure 3).

We could get the lexical of query sentence by part-of-speech, and used the lexical sequence to search for m1. In case all lexical of query sentence was totally matching m1, and we determine the query that to be part of m2, and we add to boundary and parse label for query sentence that utilized information of *m2*.

If lexical sequence was not complete corresponding to *m1*, the query sentence integrated by rule-based, and result that integrated with parse label by rule-based used m3 information to integrated again (see the Figure 4). It is maximum pattern matching for that integrated with parse label, because we compared lexical sequence of query sentence with *m3* information, always search for the maximum length of query sentence, and reduced length slowly until length equal to one.

Training data example

S(theme:NP(N(Nb:嘉珍|Caa:和|Nh:我))
|Head:VCL:住在|goal:NP(DM:同一條|Na:巷子))

m1 format
S(NP(N(Nb|Caa|Nh))|VCL|NP(DM|Na))

m2 format
S Nb Caa Nh VCL DM Na

m3 format
S(NP|VCL|NP)
NP(N)
N(Nb|Caa|Nh)
NP(DM|Na)

Figure 3. An example about the relationship between lexical and parse label extracted from training data

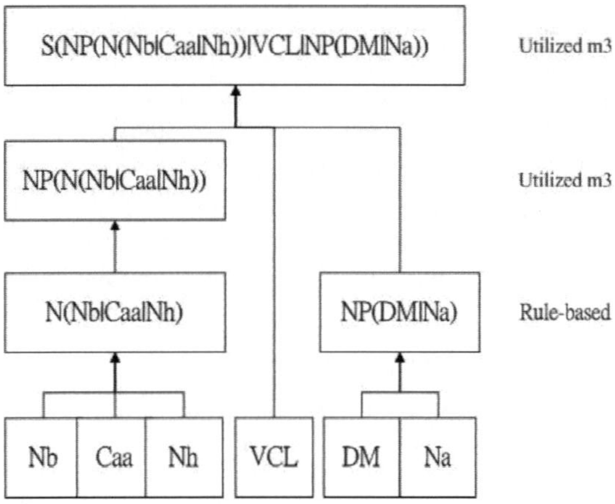

Figure 4. An example about the sentence added to boundary and parse label

3 Evaluation Results and Discussions

In training data, there are 65K token strings, we extract 39K token to create the dictionary. In testing evaluations, there are 1K token strings to be testing.

Table 1. Evaluation result

	Precision	Recall	F1
Closed	0.435	0.532	0.479

The evaluation of our system in sentence parsing sub-task is shown in table 1. Our system obtains 44% precision, 53% recall and 48% F1.

Table 2 shows the details parser ratio of each syntactic structure. For the result, it has highest ratio about 80% on sentence level parser. In test data, the token of each string are more than 6, it has more probability correspond to the syntactic structure of sentence level parser. For NP-Phrase parser, it has second rank. During we observe the training data, there are most NP-Phrase structures, and some noun of type can be NP-Phrase itself. So we focus on NP-Phrase when design the rule induction. VP-Phrase and PP-Phrase have lower ratio, some verb will combine noun to be NP-Phrase, and the rule we design on both VP-Phrase and PP-Phrase are not robustness to cause maximum pattern matching fail. GP-Phrase sample is rare in training data, it only a rule in our system.

Table 2. Evaluation result in details

Type	Truth	Parser	Ratio(%)
S	1233	987	80.5
VP	679	104	15.32
NP	2974	1449	48.72
GP	26	0	0
PP	96	16	16.67
XP	0	0	N/A

4 Conclusion

The evaluation results show that our system performs well in sentence level, but has lower performance in VP-Phrase and PP-Phrase, even for GP-Phrase, our system can't detect the syntactic structure.

By observing the evaluation result, we discover that have much errors in the POS tagging due to the out of vocabulary (OOV). For instance, proper noun such as personal names "張蘭(Zhang Lan)" and "寶來(Polaris)" that are not defined in the dictionary. During POS tagging step, it usually causes errors by using the POS-to-POS relation modification. The wrong POS labeling affects the performance in rule induction regulation step significantly and maximum pattern matching. In maximum pattern matching, the parse labeling is ordered according to NP-VP-S-PP-GP sequence. Maximum pattern matching was possible to correct the wrong structure and labeling of the parsing because it always searches for NP first.

In future works, we will focus on improving the POS tagging methods and enhance the unknown word tagging. For rule induction, there are more robustness rule we can design and achieve the improvement in the performance of maximum pattern matching

Reference

Chu-Ren Huang, Keh-Jiann Chen, Feng-Yi Chen, Keh-Jiann Chen, Zhao-Ming Gao, Kuang-Yu Chen . 2000. Sinica Treebank: Design Criteria, Annotation Guide-lines, and On-line Interface. In Proceedings of 2nd Chinese Language Processing Workshop (Held in conjunction with ACL-2000). 29-37.

Keh-Jiann Chen, Chu-Ren Huang, Feng-Yi Chen, Chi-Ching Luo, Ming-Chung Chang, Chao-Jan Chen, Zhao-Ming Gao. 2003. Sinica Treebank: Design Cri-teria, Representational Issues and Implementation. In Anne Abeille (Ed.) Treebanks Building and Using Parsed Corpora. Language and Speech series. Dor-drecht:Kluwer, 231-248.

Keh-Jiann Chen, Wei-Yun Ma. 2002. Unknown word extraction for Chinese documents. In Proceedings of COLING 2002, pages 169-175.

Wei-Yun Ma, Keh-Jiann Chen. 2003. A bottom-up merging algorithm for Chinese unknown word extraction. In Proceedings of the second SIGHAN workshop on Chinese language processing, Pages 31-38.

Chen Keh-Jiann, Chu-Ren Huang, Li-Ping Chang, Hui-Li Hsu. 1996. Sinica Corpus: Design Methodology for Balanced Corpra. Proceedings of the 11th Pacific Asia Conference on Language, Information, and Computation (PACLIC II), SeoulKorea, pp.167-176.

Chinese Knowledge Information Processing Group. 1993. Categorical Analysis of Chinese. ACLCLP Technical Report # 93-05, Academia Sinica.

Jia-Ming You, Keh-Jiann Chen. 2004. Automatic Semantic Role Assignment for a Tree Structure. Proceedings of SIGHAN workshop.

Qian-Xiang Lin, Chia-Hui Chang, Chen-Ling Chen. 2010. A Simple and Effective Closed Test for Chinese Word Segmentation Based on Sequence Labeling. International Journal of Computational Linguistics & Chinese Language Processing, Vol. 15, No. 3-4, September/December 2010.

Tsai Yu-Fang and Keh-Jiann Chen. 2003, Context-rule Model for POS Tagging. Proceedings of PACLIC 17, pp146-151.

Asahara, M., C.L. Goh, X.J. Wang, Y. Matsumoto. 2003. Combining Segmenter and Chunker for Chinese Word Segmentation. In Proceedings of Second SIGHAN Workshop on Chinese Language Processing, pp. 144–147.

Chooi-Ling Goh, Masayuki Asahara, Yuji Matsumoto. 2005. Chinese Word Segmentation by Classification of Characters. Computational Linguistics and Chinese Language Processing, 10(3), pp. 381-96.

Daniel Gildea and Julia Hockenmaier. 2003. Identifying Semantic Roles Using Combinatory Categorial Grammar. Conference on Empirical Methods in Natural Language Processing (EMNLP), Pages 57-64.

Lu, X. 2005. Towards a Hybrid Model for Chinese Word Segmentation. In Proceedings of Fourth SIGHAN Workshop on Chinese Language Processing, 189-192.

Author Index